Singing the New Song

THE MIDDLE AGES SERIES

Ruth Mazo Karras, Series Editor

Edward Peters, Founding Editor

A complete list of books in the series
is available from the publisher.

Singing the New Song

Literacy and Liturgy in Late Medieval England

Katherine Zieman

PENN

UNIVERSITY OF PENNSYLVANIA PRESS

Philadelphia

Published by
University of Pennsylvania Press
Philadelphia, Pennsylvania 19104-4112

Printed in the United States of America on acid-free paper

10 9 8 7 6 5 4 3 2 1

A Cataloging-in-Publication record is available from the Library of Congress
ISBN-13: 978-0-8122-4051-1
ISBN-10: 0-8122-4051-0

Contents

Illustrations

Preface

This study began—and in fact still begins—with Chaucer's "litel clergeon," the infantile hero of the *Prioress's Tale*. My initial interest was not so much in the tale itself but in the early educational practices it represented and their formalization in that distinctively medieval institution, the "song school." Presuming, as I did, that reading ability was regularly acquired by learning to sing, I had hoped to discover the implications of such a practice for a historical understanding of literacy. After I had surveyed the extant evidence and current scholarship, however, two things became apparent: first, that the "song school," as a determinate institution that remained a stable element of elementary education throughout the medieval period, was in part the creation of modern scholarship; and second, that this creation was inflected by attitudes toward and investments in the medieval liturgy that had not been fully examined. As the project continued, the "song school" became merely the starting point for a much more extensive study of medieval liturgical practice and its relationship to literacy. The present book represents only a partial result of this investigation.

Many scholars acknowledge innovations in literate practices in England in the fourteenth- and early fifteenth-century period covered by this study. Most of these innovations, however, have been related to the ascendancy of the vernacular, which is seen as competing with, and even subverting, Latin as the firmly installed language of privilege.[1] Such changes are frequently attributed to an aspiring laity, often characterized as "increasingly literate," though this literacy is most often associated with vernacular speculative and devotional writings. Liturgical practice—Latin textual practice governed by ecclesiastical institutions—rarely enters significantly into such discussions. The cultural function of the liturgy is generally considered one of conservative repetition, not innovation or creation. My study of patterns in educational benefaction connected with song, however, suggested a different picture: that liturgical practice was in fact central to fourteenth- and fifteenth-century developments in the field of literacy. In attending to the terms by which young boys would be initiated into some form of clerical status, patrons of liturgy and learning were able to dissect and stratify components of clerical literacy at an institutional level. Further research revealed that the institutional gestures of wealthy benefactors represented merely one instance of the centrality of liturgy to issues of learning and literacy. Whatever innovations emerged elsewhere, liturgy remained a site in which changing textual practices and religious values were integrated in a culture that still conceived of itself as a Christian textual community for whom the performance of sacred texts played a vital role.

Because my primary interest is literacy, for the purposes of this study I have treated liturgy—at least the central liturgical activities of reading and singing on which I focus—primarily as verbal practice. In so doing I by no means wish to deny the importance of the musical textuality of song;[2] I merely concede that song's relationship to other uses of the written word can be elucidated most easily by focusing on its verbal aspects. In like fashion, I have privileged the verbal aspects of the liturgy over other ritual and sacramental action, using the term "liturgy" to refer above all to the Liturgy of the Word and related verbal practices.[3] While isolating the verbal does limit the investigation, it has the virtue of focusing attention on the salient paradox of medieval Christian liturgy: that it participated simultaneously in the worlds of both orality and literacy. My examination of this hybrid textual practice and the institutions and social relations it engendered is meant to serve as a counterpoint to studies by M. T. Clanchy and Richard Firth Green that have clearly demonstrated that the late medieval period was a time of transition in terms of uses of writing in other spheres of social interaction.[4] Both have described how writing came to supplant oral forms of communication or how it objectified relations of power formerly transacted through ritual and ceremony. The presence and persistence of a ritual practice that from its inception was based on the written word does not contradict their findings, but it does complicate any binary distinctions between oral and written and between ritual and documentary culture that one might be tempted to extrapolate from them.

Though it involved both oral and written practices, medieval liturgy is more commonly associated with orality and ritual or traditional culture. As a performative practice centered on the voice, it elicits notions of embodied, communal knowledge that requires physical proximity to be enacted. Liturgy is thus the quintessential signifier of presence or, more specifically, of a recuperative presence that allowed the Word of God to be re-presented and thus heard as the voice of God. The common claim that punctuation used in manuscripts is descended from neumatic notation of music—a claim Leo Treitler has persuasively called into question[5]—suggests that liturgical song stands in the minds of many as a metonymy for an originary performativity and orality of all language, not merely sacred language. Historical accounts generated by this notion of language tend to be narratives of loss—the loss of the audible voice of God or, more generally, the loss of organic social relations structured by embodied, communal knowledge or tradition. Such accounts are proffered not only by scholars we might associate with older modes of criticism, like Eamon Duffy and Walter J. Ong, but also by those like Michel de Certeau, who are aligned with postmodern thought.[6] The conception of voice that liturgical song seems to exemplify is, in other words, aligned not merely with a "nostalgic" definition of traditional culture but also with a particular construction of modernity as a condition of permanent alienation—one that is fundamentally opposed to the presence of the voice and the hermeneutical enclosures of the liturgical.

These are, of course, relatively standard critiques of attitudes toward the premodern (though a more thorough critique would also have to account for the explanatory power of studies by Ong and de Certeau that continues to make them engaging and useful in spite of the rigid, teleological categorizations).[7] More intriguing, perhaps, than the potential for liturgical song to stand for a romanticized presence within conceptions of premodernity is the potential for it to signify the obverse. Especially in accounts of the later, autumnal centuries of the Middle Ages, liturgical performance is just as likely to stand for a sense of absence or lack of self-presence usually associated with writing as it is with the presence assigned to the voice. Closely related to Enlightenment notions of rationality and free speech, such views are often connected to the practice, more widely attested in the later Middle Ages, of singing Latin song without training in Latin grammar. Chaucer's "litel clergeon" is the most prominent example of this habit, though it was by no means universal and, I will argue, it was less widespread than has been assumed. For some, such uncomprehending performances merely exemplify the alterity of medieval textual practice, if not medieval culture as a whole. For others, it has broader political implications. Usually considered a lay activity, illiterate singing or singing without understanding represents the laity's active participation in their own disenfranchisement from latinate culture in general. Figured simultaneously as a site of presence and absence, liturgy appears "both everywhere and nowhere in the cultural history of premodern England."[8]

Both of these assessments rely on considering liturgy as ritual. More specifically, they rely on a particular conception of ritual, one that depends, as Catherine Bell has noted, on a binary division between thought and action.[9] Ritual simultaneously represents both the realm of embodied action instead of thought and the site in which action becomes thought. The images of liturgy as absence and liturgy as presence merely emphasize different aspects of this inner contradiction. Liturgy as disenfranchisement and its romanticizing converse—positions roughly assimilable to Protestant and Catholic historical narratives—are the Scylla and Charybdis of attitudes toward ritual between which this study attempts to chart a course. Such a project involves turning away from conceptions of *ritual* as a specific cultural mode or a defined set of practices toward a consideration of *ritualization* as "a way of acting that is designed and orchestrated to distinguish and privilege what is being done in comparison to other, usually more quotidian, activities."[10] As such, ritualization can be said to occur in any culture and is not rooted in a particular cultural or social organization. More significantly, modes of ritualization can change, and these changes can be significant. This acknowledgment is especially important to discussions of liturgy, since some scholars have taken its cyclical structure to be opposed to history itself.[11] Rather than label changes in practice as additions or accretions that merely reinforce the traditional character of late medieval religion or, conversely, as decadent departures from an authentic, originary state, I seek instead to examine the implications changes such as the rise of chantries have for the social relations that liturgy performs and the connections these relations bear to the reading and singing that is ritualized.

The activity with which I am most concerned is reading, which the Liturgy of the Word ritualizes as a clerical privilege and as an activity controlled by clerical institutions such as grammar. The changes I examine occur both at the level of practice—namely, how clergy and layfolk are expected to behave in relation to the performed Word—and at the institutional level—namely, what kind of institutions, corporations, or social groups generated liturgical services and determined their ostensible purpose—both of which deal with the critical question (much contested in late fourteenth-century England) of how sacred texts should mediate religious experience. The ultimate outcome of these changes was to destabilize the possible functions of ritualized reading and singing such that they could serve purposes beyond communal celebration of the Word and beyond performing the clerical stewardship of sacred texts. In the most extreme cases—for example, lay recitation of Hours (which, although it could be described as private and "devotional" rather than public and "liturgical," nonetheless remains a ritualized practice)—these changes affected the institutionally regulated circumstances that define ritual practice: who performs the action, at what times, and in what settings. As a result, practices that were figured as metonymic of clerical literacy as a whole could also be perceived autonomously, as practices separable from clerical authority. While this development changed perceptions of the verbal aspects of the liturgy, it also had implications for literate practice as a whole in that "reading and singing" were articulated as discrete activities, and in some cases discrete skills, unmoored from the institutional setting that defined and regulated their appropriate use. Chapter 1 charts this process of destabilizing or unmooring by looking at the transformation of the "song school" as an institutionally embedded entity to the various deracinated skills and activities that were originally derived from choral practice. Throughout the study, I place all such unmoored practices under the rubric so often used to describe them: "reading and singing."

This unmooring, to my mind, is not part of the general alienations or deracinations that characterize modernity. The institutional setting I designate as the "origin" of reading and singing—the choir and the choral institutions that housed them—was defined in terms of one among many idealized notions of community that existed in medieval culture. Though these communities exhibit some social dynamics characteristic of traditional culture, as I describe most extensively in Chapter 2, they do not exemplify *communitas* even in idealized depictions.[12] The practices of reading and singing become unmoored not because of any dissolution or loss of this institutional context but rather because the practice spread beyond its boundaries. In this respect, the deracination to which I refer is part of a larger transformation of the ways in which late medieval culture categorized, distributed, and regulated its intellectual resources, the necessity of doing this in some form being an aspect of any sociopolitical structure. The result is not a set of "free-floating" practices but rather of practices redefined and recontextualized in different settings. Over the longue durée, larger patterns of change emerge. Among the most important, also discussed in Chapter 2, is a shift in the definition of "literate" from primarily repertory-based knowledge—that is, familiarity and facility with culturally important texts—to primarily skill-based knowledge—ultimately, the capacity to decipher unfamiliar texts, though this transformation extends beyond the medieval period. The unmooring of reading and singing signals a critical moment in that shift—one that is the result not of rejecting liturgical performance but of increased liturgical and devotional activity.

Chapter 3 describes some of this increased activity in more detail—specifically, the socioeconomic and cultural implications of the rise of "private" or, as I call it, "contractual" liturgy. These changes, I claim, did more than determine who had access to and who "understood" the liturgy and its texts. They opened up speculation as to what constitutes understanding in the first place as well as what sociopolitical function understanding might play. As I claim in the latter part of this chapter, concerns about these changes find expression in the postpandemic fixation with unbeneficed mass priests, who appeared to represent the disruption of social and linguistic order. These issues had formerly been—and to a large extent continued to be—regulated by *grammatica*, the "master discourse" of medieval language and learning.[13] Chapter 4, however, examines ways of interacting with sacred texts and sacred language that fell outside the parameters of textual engagement determined by grammatical institutions. Though these "extragrammatical" practices could involve anything from pragmatic uses of documents to vernacular theology, I focus on the varied uses of Latin liturgical and devotional texts by those both with and without grammatical training. While I am sensitive to medieval definitions of literacy and do, in fact, discuss medieval terminology in detail in Chapter 2, I also define the extragrammatical practices of these chapters as "literacies." In such instances, I use the term "literacy" to acknowledge strategic but unofficial practice, defining literacy as any practice that allows the systematic manipulation of the symbolic capital associated with clerical letters. This definition, though broad, should not be confused with metaphoric uses of "literacy" to refer to any kind of discursive mastery whatsoever. Though literacy as I define it technically does not necessarily require interactions with *litteras*, let alone knowledge of grammar, it is connected to the social power of *litteras* that is performed in the ritualized reading of the liturgy. The unofficial or unspoken nature of these literacies also accounts for the fact that I follow Clanchy in relying heavily on anecdotal evidence,[14] though I have benefited greatly from the more systematic research of scholars such as Nicholas Orme, Jo Ann Moran Cruz, Roger Bowers, and Leona Gabel.

The final two chapters explore the impact of the various practices and attitudes I describe in the first four chapters on the production of Middle English literature, particularly on the works of William Langland and Geoffrey Chaucer. Though this study had its genesis in a literary text, I see vernacular making as one of many areas of cultural production inflected by the changes associated with reading and singing. Prior studies of liturgy and literature have tended to deal at the level of literary allusion or quotation, treating the liturgy primarily as a text or set of texts upon which writers drew. My examination, however, considers liturgy and devotion as textual practices. My focus on reading and singing, furthermore, attends to emergent rather than traditional or residual textual practices. Several passages that I examine in both writers' texts—the C 5 *apologia* of *Piers Plowman* and Chaucer's *Prioress's Tale* and *Second Nun's Tale* among them—show the affinities these poets saw between their own emergent literary practice and modes of reading and singing that were the subject of public debate. Both kinds of extragrammatical practice arose from the fragmentation of clerical literacy that grammar and liturgy once unified. While they had pretensions to forms of authority and to public signification, they also had unstable institutional positions—a proliferation of proper places from which one could speak and *personae* one could inhabit beyond those regulated by Church and Court. As a result of this instability, matters of the ethics, intentions, and social and spiritual value of verbal production were set in sharp relief. Above all both practices were marked with a kind of linguistic and textual self-consciousness I situate under the category of "voicing": concerns about the ways in which "public" language circulates, the relationship of speaker to utterance, or the various ways that individuals and groups might incorporate or assimilate themselves to preexisting texts and verbal performances.

Though the study was never intended to be comprehensive, the issues of liturgical and devotional practice treated here impinged upon more spheres of activity than could be examined in a single study. Some of the topics I chose to leave out deserve some explanation. I avoided extensive discussion of Lollardy in part because I think that it would be more productively examined in a study that reaches further into the fifteenth century so as to include a fuller range of material than could be accommodated in this study. More important, so many representations of Lollardy, from the Reformation on, have been put forth to celebrate their championing of biblical translation and lay access to scriptures as democratizing gestures. Though more recent work has shown both that many of these hermeneutical matters were not solely the preserve of Lollardy and that Lollard hermeneutics were not as democratizing as they might at first appear,[15] the focus of attention has remained on the conventicles and vernacular hermeneutics, which, while in no way inappropriate, has the potential in the context of this study to devolve into a dualistic approach pitting vernacular dissent against latinate privilege that I am trying to avoid. Given that the

Lollard position on the Eucharist was one that reconceived the terms of its ritualized signification rather than dismissed it and given that what scant evidence exists suggests that at least some Lollards may have heard or conducted services in Latin,[16] it is likely that Lollardy's relationship to ritual is more complex than has been recognized and deserves a full study in its own right.

Other important topics proved too vast to incorporate meaningfully into the study within the conceptual framework I had developed. Among these is the rise of vernacular drama. While the development of the Corpus Christi cycle is contemporary with and related to the unmooring of reading and singing, most extant evidence comes from later in the fifteenth century. The amount of recent scholarly work that considers definitions of drama, as well as the dynamics and politics of performativity,[17] makes this area one that, like Lollardy, could not be usefully subordinated to my focus on literacy and textual practice. The same is the case with the liturgical practices of women religious. The function of liturgy in the lives of women religious has been overlooked, as I have suggested elsewhere, in favor of topics more likely to demonstrate their intellectual achievements.[18] Women religious also served a critical role in the development of devotional practice as well as clerical attitudes toward such practices. Beyond a brief discussion of these matters in Chapter 4, they await a full exposition of their importance elsewhere.

The chronological scope of the study as I originally pursued it stretched from the late thirteenth century, when interest in choristers first becomes noticeable, to the middle of the fifteenth, by which time there is evidence that liturgy and learning were on divergent paths: forms of benefaction such as the chantry school, which did not require choral duties of its scholars, the specifically "musical" exploitation of boys' voices in the production of polyphony, the first signs that English was being taught as a subject rather than a medium of written language instruction, and the separation of the chapel staff and administrative staff in the foundation of Eton are just a few of the indicators.[19] As I began to relate this material to other modes of religious experience and ecclesiastical politics—trends in private devotion and pastoral teaching, the rise of the perpetual chantry, and the use of literacy tests in claims to benefit clergy—it became clear that this scope needed to be curtailed in some fashion. This study, therefore, deals with the period from the late thirteenth to the earliest years of the fifteenth century. This limitation is based, first, on my desire to connect the issues of this study to fourteenth-century vernacular writers, chiefly

Chaucer and Langland. Second, the first half of the fifteenth century offers complexities that require more sustained treatment, such as the promulgation of Arundel's Constitutions, along with other anti-Lollard initiates, and Henry V's founding of the monasteries of Syon and Sheen, which became major centers of textual production as well as "powerhouses of prayer."[20] This book, therefore, should be considered the first part of a larger project.

* * *

This book has been long in the making. More people have helped than I could ever possibly acknowledge. I have benefited greatly from helpful conversations with Henry Abelove, Katy Breen, Celia Chavez, Giles Constable, Bruce Holsinger, David Lurie, Marie Anne Polo de Beaulieu, Masha Raskolnikov, Michael Roberts, Martha Rust, Emily Steiner, Fiona Somerset, Zrinka Stahuljak, Robert Swanson, Jelena Trkulja, Steven Vanderputten, John Vincent, Heinrich von Staden, Katy Vulic, and Laura Weigert, who helped me with the articulation of ideas and readings or translations of particular texts. I am indebted to Michael Clanchy, Ralph Hanna, Jerry Singerman, and Nicholas Watson for the advice and encouragement they offered at critical points in the drafting of the manuscript as well as to the Institute for Advanced Study, whose Friends Membership provided me with the financial, scholarly, and moral support to complete the manuscript. Caroline Bynum, Marianne Constable, Jo Ann Moran Cruz, Indira Karamcheti, Kathryn Kerby-Fulton, Bob Longsworth, and Khachig Tololyan were all gracious enough to read parts of the manuscript at various stages, offering helpful criticism and comments. Special thanks go to Allan Isaac and especially to Elizabeth Schirmer, who both went far above and beyond the call as collegial sounding boards, interlocutors, and readers. Finally, this book would never have come to fruition were it not for the enduring assistance of Steven Justice and Anne Middleton, who did all of the above and much more. This book is dedicated to my parents, William and Mary Jo Zieman, who supported me throughout the process, and to the memory of Robert Brentano, a wonderful scholar and teacher who first taught me what documents were.

I

Ex ore infantium: Literacy and Elementary Educational Practices in Late Medieval England

"I kan but smal grammeere"

CHAUCER'S *PRIORESS'S TALE* of the unlettered boy who piously learns to sing the Marian antiphon, *Alma redemptoris mater*, has become a locus classicus for describing a medieval elementary educational institution generally referred to as the "song school." Few accounts of the history of education in medieval England fail to mention the "litel clergeon" or his school as illustrative of contemporary elementary educational practice.[1] Yet far more intriguing than the ubiquity of the *clergeon* in such accounts is the virtually obligatory quotation of the boy's nameless "felawe" who teaches him the song, specifically his famous response to the *clergeon*'s inquiry about the song's meaning: "I lerne song; I kan but smal grammeere."[2] Though it is true that the "felawe," having learned the antiphon under the appropriate institutional auspices, is a more fitting spokesperson for medieval practice than the tale's misbehaving protagonist, his qualifications are not what make his words so memorable. It is, rather, the content—the confession of grammatical ignorance itself—that has caught the attention of modern readers. This confession has been variously interpreted. For some, the passage makes clear the existence of at least two (in some cases, three) distinct subjects in the medieval curriculum.[3] More commonly, it is invoked to substantiate what is often assumed to be the standard elementary practice of learning Latin texts without grammatical understanding.[4] Yet while different points can be drawn from it, its persistent quotation suggests that the passage expresses something unusual enough to warrant verbal exemplification rather than mere description, something that even resists reduction to such description. The *clergeon*'s fellow gives voice to the fundamental alterity the idea of the song school has for modern scholars precisely where it appears to distinguish itself from the study of grammar.

This alterity has its source in song's connection to the liturgy—a set of practices that, due to their "ritual" and musical nature, seem dissonant with notions of education associated with grammar. In the most pragmatic terms, it is unclear what, if any, rudimentary value music might possess that would explain its inclusion in elementary pedagogy of letters. Indeed, song seems to offer melodic structures that can substitute for grammatical structures in aiding the assimilation and retention of texts; it could therefore be said to make grammatically disengaged performance possible. Its emphasis on performance itself, to which grammatical understanding can be subordinated, even appears to lend institutional sanction to such disengagement. This potential conflict with grammar, unarguably the dominant discourse of letters, helps account for the fact that modern scholars of early education and clerical training have not arrived at a consensus concerning either the function, the clientele, or even the precise subject matter of the "song school." The designation "elementary" represents but one strategy by which scholars have rationalized song's relationship to grammar. By implying that song serves as pre-grammatical learning within a standardized sequence of skills, "elementary" conveys the impression that the liturgical will eventually be subsumed in the grammatical, just as ignorance will be subsumed in understanding. Other configurations have been proposed, as I will detail in the next section, yet all need somehow to contend with the possibility, seemingly confirmed by the *clergeon*'s fellow (albeit with a paratactic vagueness that does little to clarify the logic of his ignorance), that ritualized expression be opposed to grammar as well as to the linguistic agency and "hermeneutical enfranchisement" we expect "education" to transmit.[5]

If the knowledge possessed by the *clergeon*'s fellow seems inconsistent with that imparted by "education," it might be that our definition of the concept is too narrow. Noting that past studies have focused exclusively on documented "schools," and above all on the grammar school, researchers like Nicholas Orme have broadened their interpretation of "education," taking into account both alternative topics of instruction— arms, courtesy, craft knowledge—and less formal modes of transmission, including those in the home and at court.[6] Such revisions are extremely beneficial in establishing that what we call "education" is merely one of many mechanisms by which cultural resources and social roles are reproduced. They also help guard against the presumptive values often placed on the cognitive, social, and even political abilities we imagine literacy to impart—abilities frequently associated or even equated with concepts of freedom and individualized agency that may not have been valued in the same way in medieval culture. Locating the place of song does indeed require a reconsideration of the importance of both the liturgy and the skills required to produce it in late medieval culture, yet its position was clearly distinct from that of courtesy or craft knowledge in that song was demonstrably a part of, rather than an alternative to, education in letters. It was, in other words, among the cultural resources conceptually designated as "intellectual." As advantageous as it might be to consider education in less narrowly conceived terms, investigating the functions of song as an intellectual resource—one that, as the fellow's comment implies, was both linked and contrasted to grammar—provides the opportunity to examine the very nature of these resources as well as the nature of the cultural authority granted to those who mastered them.

The continuous presence of technologies like literacy and discourses like grammar among these resources can (and are often meant to) give the impression of stability, yet intellectual resources can vary greatly in terms of their definitions—what forms of knowledge are determined to transcend the body to reside primarily in the mind—as well as their distribution. Though a great deal of social change has been ascribed to the hoarding or poaching of these resources, it is rarely a matter of access alone but rather one of redefinition and reallocation, arising as much from quotidian circulation as from expropriation or usurpation. The boundaries of intellectual resources, in fact, are never fixed. Some historical periods, however, show greater fluidity than others. The late fourteenth and early fifteenth centuries, in which this study is based, is, for England at least, one of those periods by all accounts. The rise of Lollardy and the Oxford translation debates, the uprising of 1381 and the cultivation of vernacular poetry, to say nothing of "vernacular theology," are just a few indicators of this mobility that have garnered scholarly attention.[7] These developments have been associated primarily with the ascendancy of English (simultaneous with the almost mythic decline of French) as a textualized language,[8] capable of accomplishing tasks formerly reserved for Latin. As I will argue in this study, however, the complex reconfigurations of intellectual resources that marked late medieval England, especially those encompassing textual knowledge and textual authority, equally involved the texts and practices of the Latin liturgy. Still more specifically, I will show how traces of the liturgical, signaled by the collocation "reading and singing," can be discerned in both Latin and vernacular textual practices that were among the most mobile and innovative of late medieval England.

To claim that the liturgy was a site of social change may seem counterintuitive, for the same attitudes toward ritual practice that have consigned the "song school" to a fate of irreducible alterity have situated the liturgy more generally as a site of traditional culture vested in conservatism, whether this conservatism is viewed as evidence of the vitality of an organic textual community or as disenfranchising capitulation to dominant authority.[9] Yet, as I will demonstrate more fully in Chapter 3, the socioeconomic circumstances of liturgical performance did change significantly in the late Middle Ages in matters concerning patronage, personnel, and training. With the evolution of what I term "contractual" liturgy, patrons were able to determine which services would be performed by which persons on whose behalf, thus affecting the very relations the liturgy performed. The fact that the socioeconomic and spiritual relations forged through the production of divine worship changed does not necessarily contradict the idea that the liturgy itself ritualized a perception of liturgical time as cyclical and recursive rather than linear and progressive.[10] But apart from, and in some ways prior to, the staging of any such perception, Christian liturgy also performed its participants' relationship to the Word and to its officially sanctioned uses. In this respect, it was a central practice by which intellectual resources were regulated. The activity surrounding the "song school" serves as an especially useful point of departure for examining the dynamic function of the liturgy in the textual and hermeneutical politics of fourteenth- and early fifteenth-century England that affected this regulation. Training in "reading and singing" was self-consciously regarded as a point of entry into the discourse of letters that allowed access to several contiguous resources of social identity: literate, clerical, and spiritual, among others. As I will show, the practices associated with this form of education were used to articulate the lower boundary of formal learning and thus of grammatical discourse more generally.

Positioned at sites of training and initiation, this type of instruction invited and, in fact, required the articulation and anatomization of the skills of the *litteratus*, making assumptions otherwise tacit available for manipulation. There is ample evidence to suggest that the practices and institutions involving the training and liturgical performance of young children that proliferated throughout fourteenth- and fifteenth-century England were an unusually active site of speculation concerning language and literacy. It is because of this activity and the sharp relief in which it places issues surrounding the definition, value, and appropriate uses of literacy that I use early educational and liturgical activity, like that represented in Chaucer's *Prioress's Tale,* as my starting point to consider the role of the liturgy more broadly as the source of emergent rather than residual textual practices that played a vital role in determining the social, political, and economic dynamics of Christian textual community in late medieval England.[11]

The history of scholarship on song and grammar schools also serves as an index of the ways in which perceptions of education, ritual practice, and the relationship between the two have changed since the medieval period. There is a certain irony in the fact that discussions of song education have so often focused on the oft-quoted Chaucerian passage that opposes it to grammar, as it would appear that the verbal repetition modern culture associates with ritual and has disavowed as mindless has insidiously reproduced itself in scholarship on institutions believed to impart critical thinking. In calling attention to this repetition, I by no means wish to suggest that modern scholars have been mindless in their research. I would suggest, however, that this ossification in historical accounts of song is fundamentally connected to a critical impasse scholars have encountered in attempting to reconcile textual and literate practices we now perceive as diametrically opposed. Within this opposition, grammar, as the more broadly enabling subject of study, has been presumed to be the most productive of social change. In what follows, however, I hope to show how this construction of grammar stems from perceptions of literacy that were not universal in late medieval culture. In order to recover alternative perceptions of literacy that consider the relationship between the grammatical and the liturgical in different terms, I will offer a history of the song school and song education that more fully develops the implications of their liturgical foundations. This history will in turn allow me to demonstrate how the liturgically derived skills of reading and singing, generally thought to be firmly ensconced in conservative institutions, were marked by a mobility that would lead to their unmooring from their institutional settings. Through this unmooring, reading and singing contributed to a diffusion and redistribution of literacy skills that would ultimately change the definition of literacy itself.

The History of the "Song School"

Though the term *scola cantus,* or "song school," does appear with regularity in medieval documents, its currency in medieval scholarship owes more

to the works of the antiquarian A. F. Leach, whose studies of medieval
schooling set the terms for all subsequent debate. Leach disagreed with
the prevailing nineteenth-century accounts of medieval education, which
frequently adduced Chaucer's *clergeon* as indicative of the deplorable standards of learning under the medieval church. For these post-Reformation
writers, the *clergeon* demonstrated Catholic England's lack of enlightenment in its preoccupation with the recitation of liturgy. Valuing mere
repetition of prescribed texts to the detriment of understanding the meaning of those texts, education in song schools not only exemplified but also
reproduced the enslavement of reason and inner conviction to the sovereign power of superstition and outward observance. Leach's revisionary
claims were not designed to question these values but rather to dispute
the accuracy of this depiction. He thus set out to prove that schools in
medieval England taught subjects beyond the liturgy—that they did
indeed offer instruction "fit to be called liberal education" in the curriculum of the grammar school.[12]

Leach sought to isolate the teaching of letters from the chanting of
psalms by pointing out that learning in grammar was institutionally separate from learning in song. Although the "twin schools of Grammar and
Song ... are found side by side in connexion with all the great churches,"
they were, according to Leach, "completely differentiated in function as
they were in teaching, and generally in their government."[13] Most secular
cathedrals, as we shall see, did have "song" and "grammar" schools, but
Leach's description of them as fully distinguished "twins" was motivated
primarily by his desire to show that the teaching of song accounted for
only a small part of medieval education.

The teaching of singing and music, so often rashly asserted to be the main work
of the pre-Reformation school, and the Song Schools which gave it, were always
subordinate and secondary to the teaching of grammar and the Grammar School.
... For the Song Schools were in essence special or professional schools for those
engaged in the actual performance of the services, and useful mainly for them,
whereas the Grammar Schools gave a general education, as much needed by the
statesman, the lawyer, the civil servant, and the clerk as by the priest or cleric. For
a Grammar School meant a school which taught the classics, especially the Latin
language and literature.[14]

It was instruction in grammar, not song, that was the primary activity of
medieval schooling and would be the primary focus of his attention, not
simply because of its relative importance but because only grammar could

be equated with "education" as he understood the term. Grammar schools offered instruction in letters—the "classics"—a mode of learning that has no direct practical application but is generally enabling. In Leach's view, grammar represented a form of knowledge that could be freely deployed precisely because it lacked institutional affiliations and thus transcended knowledge required by particular vocations. The study of ecclesiastical chant, by contrast, possessed both the institutional affiliation and vocational particularity constitutive of "training" rather than "education."

Because of this perceived disparity, Leach did not really consider song to be grammar's "twin" but rather an institution of specialized, technical training, which needed to be grouped with all other specialized institutions that were not "schools *simpliciter.*"

All schools, in the ordinary parlance, schools *simpliciter,* schools without an epithet, schools other than special schools, such as schools of law, of medicine, or later, of theology, or of song, or writing, or of arms, of dancing, or of needlework, were Grammar Schools, *scole gramaticales, ludi literarii.* These schools descend direct from Rome and indirectly from Alexandria.[15]

Whatever relation of equality might be understood by song's status as grammar's twin is dissolved as song is relegated to a heterogeneous group of academic disciplines, skills, crafts, and courtly customs. Leach's designation more importantly shows that grammar's distinctive claim to the term "school," and song's necessary consignment to the realm of supplementary, technical schooling, is based in lineage. Although much of the study was devoted to the cathedral grammar school, the Church was merely a temporary custodian of a curriculum that could be traced not to the institutions of Catholic Rome but rather to the culture of classical civilization, whose continuing prestige as an instrument of civilizing (and imperial) power is signaled by Leach's own invocation of latinate phrases. In tracing the presence of the grammar schools back to the earliest moments of British history, Leach was paradoxically able to use this classical heritage to secure a fundamentally British claim to liberal education by identifying a continuous strand of the humanistic tradition that long preceded the Erasmian and Italian imports of the sixteenth century.

But the song school could not be so easily dispensed with, for "song" is indeed an "epithet" that modifies *scola,* whereas "writing," "arms," "dancing," and "needlework" are not. And while law, medicine, and theology were at least disciplines, if not "schools," only the song school was so frequently situated in conjunction with the grammar school. Beyond mentions of song schools, medieval documents contain references to young boys singing as well as to requirements that aspiring grammar scholars be trained in reading and song. Leach accounted for this evidence by asserting that this "special" school was also an elementary school that provided knowledge less advanced than that taught in grammar schools. The song school, he claimed, involved curricula beyond music and even clientele beyond the choir; it was "a school in which not only singing but elementary subjects, reading, and the rudiments of grammar were taught, and which was mainly, though not wholly, attended by the choir-boys."[16]

In defining the form and function of the song school, Leach exhibits what Jo Ann Moran Cruz has called his "bias towards institutional history":[17] he assumed that learning cannot take place without a formalized educational apparatus (that is, without schools), so where learning takes place there must be a school. But whereas in the case of the grammar school this assumption allowed him to solidify his sense of the historical continuity of such an apparatus, in the case of the song school it served as a way to contain literate practices that did not fit in with his ideal of "education" and that looked too much like the grim view of rote learning presented by his opponents. To counter those who adduced Chaucer's *Prioress's Tale*, with its unlearned protagonist, as an example of poor education in late medieval England, he stated that he found it "lamentable" that "the whole of the schools of the Middle Ages, that is, from 450 to 1550, are judged and condemned by the standard of a small song-school described in a fifteenth century work of fiction."[18] The song school's subject matter was not merely affiliated too closely with ecclesiastical institutions to serve as liberal education, but it was also an inferior, or at least imperfect, form of knowledge. Pointing to the great intellectual achievements of the medieval university, he argued that such an institution "could not flourish if it was fed only by schools in which boys had learnt nothing more than to stumble through a few psalms."[19] Although the school represented in Chaucer's *Prioress's Tale* evidences neither psalms nor stumbling as such (to say nothing of the fact that it is never explicitly referred to as a "song school"), Leach assimilated it to the generalizations he drew from various documentary sources to describe an institution characterized by a restricted and minimally productive mastery, one that promoted rote repetition instead of the analytic and generative knowledge that constituted the study of grammar. Leach's song school was thus a negative institution: its subject matter helped define the proper province of schooling *simpliciter* by being both more specialized and less intellectually rigorous than grammar.

By placing various practices under the rubric of "song school," Leach created the impression of a definite, determinate institution, one that functioned within an established educational apparatus and even a systematically articulated sequence of skills. As such, however, it was to some degree contradictory: it was an institution that offered both elementary education—the entry-level rudiments of a general knowledge of letters—and specialized training—technical skills applicable only within the particular institution of liturgical singing.[20] Critical debates about the song school in modern scholarship have attempted to resolve this contradiction by setting the general and the vocational in hierarchical relationships that might make them cohere. Maintaining song's subordination to grammar and to general education, Nicholas Orme followed Leach in characterizing the song school as an elementary school and rationalized its curriculum in the context of literacy acquisition. The teaching of chant not only helped "to train the scholar for the clerical life" but also "taught good pronunciation."[21] John Lawson and Harold Silver, by contrast, put general knowledge in the service of specialized practice, claiming that the song school's primary function was "to teach boys to sing the choral parts of the liturgy in order to help out with the parish services," while noting that "to do this some reading would have to be taught as well."[22] Musicologist Roger Bowers rejects entirely the idea that song schools provided elementary education. Categorizing as "song schools" only the formal institutions that taught choristers at cathedrals and major choral foundations, he claims that they could not have provided general knowledge, "considering the highly specialised nature of the education of chorister-boys, such as their liturgical duties demanded." Nor could training in song have preceded education in grammar, since choristers would need some grammatical training to read liturgical texts.[23] More recently, Jo Ann Moran Cruz has resolved the dilemma by categorizing "reading schools" and "song schools" separately. Though she considers both "elementary," only the subject matter of the reading school was dedicated to training in literacy. Although the song school may have provided the rudiments of reading in order to help children perform the services, Moran Cruz emphasizes the possibility that this knowledge could be transmitted without recourse to the written page. Whether or not material taught in the song schools had vocational application, it was distinct from "literacy" or pre-grammatical linguistic knowledge.[24]

Evidence can be adduced to support each of these positions, yet each also leaves critical questions unanswered. The fact that song could be rationalized as part of grammatical training does not tell us why it might have been. The fact that song schools did teach choristers does not by itself shed light on the evidence that children without choral duties were also instructed in reading and singing. The possibility that reading was perceived as a distinct subject from song fails to explain why the two are so often found together. The key to answering such questions and determining the role of the song school, I would suggest, lies less in attempting to clarify a stable hierarchy of skills and subject matter than in recasting the categories and assumptions of analysis that are the legacy of Leach's liberal humanism. Perhaps the most important of these is the distinction between general and vocational that usually marks the latter as inferior or non-complex skill transmission that has general value only insofar as it is subsumed in unaffiliated knowledge that leads to conceptual and ethical refinement. Such a distinction rests on assumptions about the telos of letters and education that differ from those of a culture in which all education was arguably considered "vocational." Since the articulation and evaluation of skills defined as "literate," as well as the forms of knowledge dignified by the reflexivity implicit in the terms *ars* or *scientia*, vary in accordance with these assumptions and premises, questioning the distinction between general and vocational might also lead us to question the opposition between rote practice and the assimilation of repertoire, on the one hand, and generative or analytic modes of textual interaction on the other. The textual instantiation of the opposition between thought and action (hence the frequent epithet "mindless" to describe rote practice), this distinction is most prevalent in cultures that privilege writing and the production of new texts as the most functional component of literacy. Accommodating these kinds of changes—both those between medieval and modern culture and those within the medieval period—requires an approach to the history of the song school focused on textual practices in all of their variability rather than on the educational practices that seek to reproduce and validate them. Such an approach will then allow us to define the place of song and its relationship to letters as it was determined by the dynamics of textual communities and the literate practices that sustained them.

*   *   *

The *scola cantus* can be traced back to the *scola cantorum*, the choir of the papal court in Rome, which dates from the second half of the seventh century.[25] This "school" of singers consisted not of those who needed to learn how to sing but of specialists already trained in singing: *scola*, in this context, refers to a group of specialized practitioners and not solely to learners.[26] Nor was their task the assimilation of repertoire, for such a repertoire did not yet exist.[27] If James McKinnon's claims are correct, the *scola* was responsible for generating much of the material that later Carolingian reformers would refer to as "Gregorian chant." The founding of the *scola*, in fact, marks a critical moment in the history of Christian textual community: "a shift from what one might call 'lector chant' to 'schola chant,' that is, a shift from the solo chanting of psalms by a lector or cantor to the composition and maintenance of a large repertory of solo and choral chants by a group of expert musicians."[28] In this sense the creation of the *scola* (or, at the very least, of the repertoire) constitutes the beginning of "song" as a mode of scriptural performance distinct from the performative reading of the lector inherited from the Jewish tradition.[29]

With the adoption of the Roman style of chant, mostly as a result of the Carolingian reforms of the second half of the eighth century, the *scola*'s practice was transformed into knowledge that needed to be transmitted and therefore needed to be taught.[30] Singing thus became a mode of textual proficiency that was authoritative and exclusive; the *scola* with which it was associated was not considered secondary to a grammatical mode of textual proficiency such as that which Leach associated with "schools *simpliciter*." In fact, when Archbishop Leidrad describes the schools he established in Lyon at the end of the eighth century, he gives the opposite impression.

Nam habeo scolas cantorum, ex quibus plerique ita sunt eruditi, ut etiam alios erudire possint. Praeter haec vero habeo scolas lectorum, non solum qui officiorum lectionibus exerceantur, sed etiam qui in divinorum librorum meditatione spiritualis intelligentiae fructus consequantur.[31]

[For I have a school of singers, among which many are educated, that they might educate others. Beyond that, I have a school of readers, who not only read the lessons of the Office, but who also pursue the fruits of spiritual understanding though meditation on divine books.]

Leidrad speaks of two schools—of singers and of readers—yet both pertain to liturgical performance: the singing and reading of the Divine Office.

While the school of readers does incorporate a second mode of reading, Leidrad describes it as institutionally derived from the first; the pursuit of spiritual understanding is an innovative addition to the reading of lessons. Although this second mode of reading might be understood as part of the grammatical curriculum—as a species of grammatical *enarratio*—the mention of meditation as the means by which spiritual understanding is achieved suggests more strongly the more comprehensive practices of the monastic *lectio divina*.[32] Facility with grammar in the most basic sense of parsing and construing is, in fact, presumed—an implicit prerequisite to participation in the *scola* instead of a school in itself. Still less are these performative modes of textual engagement seen as temporally prior or inferior to elementary grammar instruction, as rote to analytic verbal skill.

Leidrad's understanding of the *scola* differs from Leach's in more than opinions about the relative value of subjects. Leidrad's *scole cantorum et lectorum* are predicated on a different conception of literacy and its social function. If Leach felt that education in letters provided knowledge that could be used in any chosen profession, Leidrad imagines it to form the core of a textual community in which all knowledge is vocational and its deployment is an obligation.[33] Within such a community, there is a functional differentiation of skill—or rather of textual practices, each defined and embodied by a *scola* of practitioners. Considered together, the *scole* circumscribe the totality of authorized textual practices that define the community as many members of a single body. Although Leidrad's boasting tone seems to exult in the diverse practices of his *scole*, he is not celebrating pure difference in any sense that precludes a hierarchy of skills or eliminates the degree of dignity ascribed to each practice. Rather, his boast represents the cultivation and, more important, the preemptive containment of the various alternative textual practices used within the dominant clerical community—reading, singing, glossing, troping—such that they remain subordinate to the ideal of a unified body.[34] This community is perceived as stable and, in some sense, already constituted because it is embodied by the choir—a more generally inclusive body that precedes and unifies the various *scole*.[35] Leach's *scola*, by contrast, seeks to create unity of textual practice rather than diversity, a unity maintained in the service of a self-consciously political unity (participation in the *res publica*). To that end, different skills, abstracted or disembodied from their particular practitioners, are articulated as sequential: the hierarchy of skills thus becomes a teleological progression of increasingly enabling, structurally unified competencies. The *scola*, in turn, is constituted by the unified skill—grammar—rather than by its personnel. If Leidrad's *scole* are contained by the textual community, Leach's community is formed by the *scola*.

Yet although Leidrad's description of his *scole* exhibits characteristics that are antithetical to Leach's conception of the *scola gramaticalis*, the educational project in which he was engaged was not the binary opposite of Leach's understanding of the function of letters. Leidrad was, after all, making his boast to Charlemagne, who did seek to standardize and regulate liturgical practice in the service of aligning and consolidating his political authority with that of Rome.[36] And it was in relation to this project that his oft-quoted *Admonitio generalis* of 789 devoted a chapter to schooling in which "song" (*cantus*) is included, along with "grammar," in a list of objectified competences that are to be made available at all cathedrals and monasteries.[37] Unlike the crypto-classical topics mentioned by Leach, however, the disciplines set forth in Charlemagne's legislation maintain their ecclesiastical affiliation and the religious authority with which the Carolingian kings sought to align themselves. Nor is there a clear structural hierarchy that either unifies and sequentializes these skills under the larger rubric of grammar or delimits "specialized" skills from the generally enabling or "liberal" skills.

It might, then, be best to consider Leidrad's *scole cantorum et lectorum* not so much as representing the "premodern" conceptualization of intellectual formation but rather as a particular moment in what Suzanne Reynolds has described as "a gradual shift in reading itself, broadly from the ruminative *lectio* of monastic meditation to the more public, structured reading processes of the classroom."[38] This shift involved a reconfiguration of all textual practice, one that would eventually produce modern perceptions of "education" and the "school" but which at this point reflect the gradual articulation and increasing objectification of dominant textual practice that attended the centralization and expansion of ecclesiastical institutions in the post-classical West and, more generally, the formation of Western Christendom as a textual community.

A central feature of this shift was the emergence of grammar as the "master discourse," as Rita Copeland has described it.[39] "*Grammatica,*" Martin Irvine has claimed, "was the chief discipline of Charlemagne's *renovatio* of textual culture, and the increased valorization of the written word in the Carolingian kingdoms parallels the increased authority of grammatical methodology."[40] Copeland's term "master discourse" refers specifically to the grammatical procedure of *enarratio*, which takes over much of the function and prestige once claimed by rhetoric as the central discourse of textual interpretation, yet it is possible to situate this shift within a broader redistribution or reordering of skill. This reorganization collated a variety of textual practices under the rubric of grammar and grafted them onto the rigid sequentiality of the grammatical curriculum that Irvine has characterized as a "lock-step program."[41] It is through this gradual redistribution that Leidrad's *scola lectorum* would eventually become the cathedral grammar school, as the liturgical reading of *lectiones* was appropriated to the grammatical component skill (*officium*) of *lectio*, knowledge of which enabled the reader "to vocalize, construe, and understand the text at hand."[42] This connection between the two traditions of *lectio* would ultimately be institutionalized in the administrative structure of English secular cathedrals as well, where the chancellor was responsible not simply for the maintenance of the grammar school but also for selecting the readers of lessons for the cathedral services.[43]

Irvine, in fact, considers the liturgy entirely within the context of *grammatica*, with the liturgical reading of lessons being a practice informed primarily by grammatical *lectio* and song being an extension of that practice.[44] Yet while it is true that the reading of lessons could be understood within the terms of grammatical culture as a performance that constituted the culture's texts as primary objects of understanding, the lector's reading originally derived from Jewish traditions of cantillation—a stylized form of reading that incorporated extralinguistic elements not entirely reducible to the rules of grammatical *lectio*. Further, if reading was nonetheless absorbed into the grammatical sequence, however imperfectly, song could not be. Although liturgy was consistently referred to as a form of *litteras*,[45] chant had no counterpart in the grammatical curriculum to which it could be fully assimilated. It was not so much the case that song somehow resisted appropriation: it would be more accurate to say that song was not elaborated within the curriculum of grammar, since the formal structures of "schola-chant" were still in the process of formation.[46] This formation, as we shall see, was more frequently imagined as a transformation of Jewish textual practice—as the singing of the "new song"—than as a practice of *translatio studii et imperii*.[47] Song was in no way inconsistent with *grammatica* and bore an important discursive relation to grammar, but it held no clear or stable position within the sequence of grammatical *officia* and remained separate from them. Its continued presence alongside grammar as a distinct, yet parallel, form of lettered knowledge that performed a distinct, and partially redundant, ideological function in relation to the pre-Christian past thus represented, even at the earliest pairing of the two, a more complex and less stable set of textual and ideological relations than a consideration of grammatical culture alone can fully account for.

The parallel between song and grammar was manifested above all in England, where, as Leach noted (with some exaggeration), grammar schools and song schools generally appeared "side by side in connexion with all the great churches." "Song school" (*scola cantus*), in fact, appears to be a term peculiar to England, though the terms "song" and "grammar" are consistently paired in continental sources.[48] The reasons for this distinctively English institutional nomenclature must remain a matter of speculation, but it is clear that the dissemination of liturgical practices was every bit as important as the cultivation of other forms of learning in the early English church. Even before Bede, in his *Historia ecclesiastica*, tells of how Sigbert established "a school in which boys should be instructed in letters,"[49] he mentions how James the Deacon, "most skilled in singing in church," took it upon himself to be "master of church song according the customs of Rome and Kent" for the faithful of York.[50] Though it was obviously important to teach grammar, singing was a distinctively Christian textual practice that served to affirm the community of the faithful within Britain and beyond. When the repertoire became standardized, McKinnon has suggested, it was likely that Charlemagne's Anglo-Saxon advisors had a hand in attributing the entire corpus (incorrectly) to Gregory the Great, allowing them to consolidate their missionary origins with those of the Roman Christian rite itself.[51]

The presence of song instruction in Anglo-Saxon England does not, however, lead to the conclusion that there was a "song school" that remained a continuous, determinate institution throughout the Middle Ages, or even that the institutional status it did achieve was universally perceived in the same manner throughout the medieval period. In fact, a closer examination of the terminology used in surviving documents suggests neither institutional permanence nor stability. Historians of education have tended to apply the label "song school" to evidence in which the term does not appear, on the reasoning that apparent continuity of practice warrants an identifying label even if none appears among the random evidentiary survivals. Restricting the inquiry to actual mentions of the term, however, yields some suggestive patterns. Although Leach placed the first song school at York in 627, Bede, his chief source, never uses the term, and it is unlikely that these early references describe "schola-chant" at all until Bede mentions John the Cantor, who is said to have taught "the series chants for the liturgical year as it was performed at St. Peter's in Rome" (c. 680).[52] Despite the presence of such instruction, the earliest surviving occurrences of *scola cantus* in English documents appear only at the beginning of the twelfth century, in documents from religious houses under canonical rule, which variously convey the right of collation to the song schools as an ancient prerogative.[53] Though these examples are likely chance survivals of a broader practice, none of these schools can be shown to have had a continuous existence beyond the early thirteenth century.

Over the course of the twelfth and thirteenth centuries, *scole cantus* are mentioned primarily in the customaries and statutes of the secular cathedrals, which also refer to older traditions. In these collections, the rule of the *scola cantus* is listed among the privileges pertaining to officials of the cathedral administration, either the precentor, as at Wells (c. 1140), York (before the mid-thirteenth century), and London (c. 1300), or his deputy, the succentor, as at Lichfield (early thirteenth century) and Salisbury (c. 1200).[54] While the 1214 statutes of Lincoln make no mention of a song school, a mid-thirteenth-century document, conferring the precentorship of the cathedral, similarly lists the song school among the dignities pertaining to the office.[55] The specification "song school" in these cases seems to pertain more decisively to an institutional prerogative rather than an educational function, curriculum, or skill. While Joseph Smits van Waesberghe noted the presence of young boys in the papal choir from the ninth century,[56] and while the cathedral statutes also refer to boys, there is no evidence through the thirteenth century to suggest that the *scola cantus* was specifically or even primarily intended for young boys. "The instruction and discipline of the boys" is, in fact, listed as a separate entry among the duties of the precentor;[57] it remains the precentor's duty even when "the rule of the song school" has been deputed to the succentor, as at Lichfield and Salisbury. None of these documents provides details of what the rule of the song school involves; their concern is rather to maintain the privileges accruing to the holder of the office rather than to institute any particular curriculum or assert the importance of certain skills.

Nicholas Orme refers to a "strange silence about the cathedral song school after 1300."[58] Roger Bowers similarly notes that in the numerous extant Chapter Acts of Salisbury, there are only two mentions of a "master of the song school," and these occur in the early fifteenth century.[59] Silence, of course, is not reliable evidence, but this silence is suggestively interrupted by mentions of song schools outside the cathedral community. These occur in disputes in dioceses such as Lincoln and York that maintained monopolies over education that took place within the limits of their cities. Schools (grammar or song) that were held without license from the precentor (or chancellor in the case of grammar schools) were considered "adulterine" (*adulterinas*), as in the following example from Archbishop Thoresby's register, dated 1367.

Quamplures … capellani, aquebajuli et multi alii hujusmodi scolas cantus, sive informationis puerorum in cantu in ecclesiis parochialibus, domibus et aliis locis infra dictam civitatem Ebor. teneant actualiter et excercent in prejudicium dicti Precentoris et ejus precentoriae non modicum et gravamen, ac in privilegiorum et libertatis ecclesiae nostrae cathedralis multiplicem lesionem.[60]

[Several chaplains, holy-water-carriers and many others actually hold and run schools of song or in the instruction of boys in song in parish churches, homes and other places within the city of York, to the prejudice of the said Precentor and his precentorship, and to the great harm of the privileges and liberties of our cathedral church.]

The adulterine practices are designated *scolas* to make clear that they infringe on the cathedral's ancient rights, whatever their form of instruction. Paradoxically, they are granted the institutional status of *scolas* only to point out that their teachers do not have the authority to make any such claim. As was the case in the cathedral customaries and statutes, discussion of the *scola* is concerned less with education than with privilege—in this case, with jurisdictional and economic privilege, a trait shared by many of the documents that mention the *scola cantus*. Virtually all extant fourteenth-century occurrences of the term *scola cantus*, in fact, have some important similarities: they are all associated with ancient institutions—not only the secular cathedrals of York and Lincoln but also the ancient collegiate church of St. Mary's, Warwick, the royal hospital of St. Leonard's, York, and the Benedictine monastery of Bury St. Edmunds—and they all arise out of some form of institutional dispute. At York, Lincoln, and Bury, the dispute involved the infringement of the monopoly over the *scola cantus*;[61] at St. Leonard's, the terms show up in a list of personnel produced in the context of a royal inquisition into the state of the hospital;[62] and in Warwick a rivalry between the grammar master and song master resulted in newly promulgated statutes defining the privileges of each office.[63] Despite numerous mentions of the teaching and performance of song throughout this period, the designation "song school" is virtually restricted to these moments of institutional definition.

The similarity of contexts in which the *scola cantus* appears is not matched by occurrences of the *scola grammaticalis*, nor can it be explained away by reference to the serendipitous survival of documents given the number of contexts in which "song" but not "song school" occurs. The implication of this pattern is that by the fourteenth century, the *scola cantus* was effectively a residual institution. This is not to suggest that song was not being taught, since the presence of adulterine schools signifies if anything that a greater number of pupils were studying song. Rather, it appears that the notion of the *scola cantus* was sustained not because it denoted an identifiable, structured practice within these ancient institutions but because its residual power could be mobilized as a defense against newer configurations of practice springing up within that institution's sphere of influence. These less formalized *scole* did not simply pose a threat to the prerogatives of the masters of the song school; they signaled changes in the institutional structures and even the ideology that had formerly produced and sustained the song school itself. The more frequent mention of song education that modern scholars have noted from at least the late fourteenth century thus represents something more complex than a "growth" in schooling, as it has been characterized. It reflects a rethinking of values and a redistribution of skills in response to developments beyond the immediate context of schooling. Chief among these were new uses of literacy and changes in the material and spiritual economies of prayer that marked the late thirteenth and fourteenth centuries. These developments destabilized the parallel relationship between song and grammar that the "twin schools" implied and, more important, placed the hitherto unquestioned affiliations of liturgy and learning under scrutiny.

Learning and Liturgy

Within a choral institution such as Leidrad's, there would be little doubt that the knowledge required for performance of the liturgy was constitutive of "letteredness" or that it was knowledge that clerics and religious were expected to possess. Yet by the thirteenth century in England, as Clanchy has shown,[64] uses of the written word had expanded beyond those used in the context of these institutions such that there was an increasing number of clerical vocations that did not require choral duties or liturgical skills. One might expect, under such circumstances, that education in grammar might develop an autonomous institutional status to cater specifically to the needs of various clerics and laymen whose literate pursuits required only training in grammar. To some extent, this was the case, since one is far more likely to encounter a town grammar master than a town song school master. The schools run by these men, however, did not achieve the stability or autonomy in England that scholars have documented, for example, in Italian civic schools.[65] Their authority and structure emanated predominantly from the person of the master (and sometimes indirectly from the person who appointed him) rather than from the institution itself.

Liturgy, by contrast, had the institutional stability that grammar lacked, which partly explains why the most influential institutional models for grammar education, such as Winchester and Eton colleges, were in essence choral foundations. Colleges of this sort were related in their institutional motivations to the academic colleges that had appeared in university towns. Academic study may have been the focus of attention, but it could not, by itself, serve as the organizing practice of a common life; that role was performed by the liturgical celebration that bound its members in prayer. Yet educational innovation alone cannot account for the various kinds of liturgical foundations and benefactions that became so prevalent in late medieval England. Liturgical practice was itself undergoing changes, especially in the structures of patronage, that lent independent momentum to choral foundations and other similar charitable endowments. Performance of the *opus Dei* had functioned, on the one hand, as obligatory homage required by God and, on the other hand, as a form of display that reflected upon its patrons and therefore served their interests. But these functions were complicated by growing institutional trends in private or "peculiar" liturgy, such as chantries and commissioned obits, annuals, or trentals, which allowed its patrons not simply to partake of the secular benefits of display or the generalized spiritual benefits of piously invested wealth but also to make specific claims on the spiritual benefits of the services they funded. New forms of liturgical benefaction, from the founding of collegiate churches and perpetual chantries to the funding of anniversaries and single antiphons, accounted for a much larger proportion of charitable expenditure than the funding of grammar education.

The motives of liturgical patrons were not reducible solely to self-interested desires for appropriatable spiritual benefits. The inclusion of provisions for grammar scholars, among other gestures that went beyond "the increase of divine worship," as it was formulaically put, suggests, rather, that for many, the *commercium sacrum* of peculiar liturgy was both a way to reap spiritual rewards and a way to make public gestures toward bettering the state of communities on earth.[66] A palette of such gestures emerged—a set of more or less conventional possibilities that could be combined and recombined in different institutional configurations. As the self-consciousness of such choices grew, the terms by which foundations were constituted came to be increasingly objectified. Where an early college might select its members by means of an elaborate "flow chart" of patrons—getting the "right kind of people" by designating the "right kind of people" to appoint them—founders of colleges increasingly got the "right kind of people" by setting (equally elaborate) lists of prerequisites.[67] Where matters of learning were concerned, many of these prerequisites designate specific qualities and skills that the founder valued or thought necessary and thus represent personal statements of value attached to some skills *over* others. The statutes of liturgical benefactors, in other words, articulated differing evaluations of clerical skills within a community that included both clerics and layfolk.[68]

Included in many of these institutions were provisions to feed, clothe, and educate boys, and yet all of these charitable gestures become increasingly located in and around diversely motivated desires to have boys *sing* and the attendant need to train them to perform. Consciously or unconsciously, patrons articulated their values through a consideration of these young pre-clerics by specifying what they should know, what they should learn, and how they should use their learning. Grammar was frequently invoked in these circumstances, but its relative value and function within this new liturgical economy could no longer be taken for granted; these needed to be specified in relation both to performance and to training in song. Within these discussions, the concept of the *scola cantus* became less and less relevant. The term had denoted part of the structure of ancient choral institutions that prepared their members (originally not confined to boys) to participate in the traditional rehearsal of the *opus Dei* as determined by the Church. The broader contexts in which the liturgy was performed and funded in the fourteenth century as well as its variable relationship to grammar make searching for "schools" less productive than examining the practices and attitudes surrounding the terms that by their prevalence signal new preoccupations: "choristers" (*choriste*)—the term for the boys whose duties and required knowledge needed to be specified, which I will treat in the next section—and "reading and singing" (*legere et cantare*)—the activity in which they engaged, which I will discuss afterward.

* * *

Newly founded liturgical institutions were not the first to make provisions for choristers but were following the model of the secular cathedrals. The traditions of the cathedrals themselves, however, were not stable and show evidence of changes that mirror the trends of new foundations. Boys had long formed a part of secular cathedral communities, where they may have sung or learned singing, but choral performance was only one of several possible occupations for them: boys were maintained in almonries as objects of charity, functioned as personal servants, helped serve at private masses, received education in grammar, and trained to become future priests. It is only from the mid-thirteenth century that the term "choristers" (*choriste*) begins to appear consistently in the records to refer to such boys as a group and that financial and custodial arrangements were made to provide for them as a body within the choral community.[69] Such arrangements first appear in 1258, when Richard Gravesend, Bishop of Lincoln, secured a stable income for the choristers.[70] In 1264, he made provisions for their lodging, appointed a warden for them, and fixed their numbers at twelve.[71] Similar provisions were made for the *pueri chori* of Exeter in 1276.[72] In 1322, Roger Martival, Bishop of Salisbury, appropriated the church of Preschute to the choristers (noting that the *pueri choriste* were having to beg food from the canons) and assigned them a master to teach them letters and morals (*litteris et moribus*), with whom they were to live together in a house that had been assigned to them.[73] It is not always clear that their duties changed as a result of such endowments (though prohibitions against their use as personal servants were usually included in their custodial provisions), but it is somewhat clearer that their identities were more closely associated with their presence in the choir, as part of the choral community. As endowed choristers they were more visible as a group and more recognizable as belonging to an institutionalized, ministering, and at least marginally clerical category.

Early secular colleges, founded in the late thirteenth century, sometimes made provisions for groups of boys but rarely called them *choriste*. The statutes of Glasney College, Penryn (fd. 1276), do not explicitly make provisions for boys in their statutory number but mention *pueri* incidentally in the instructions for performing divine service.[74] The College of St. Nicholas, Wallingford (refd. 1278), provided for four boys in its statutes, but they were called *cerophanii* ("taper-bearers"), denoting their liturgical yet non-choral function.[75] At St. Elizabeth's in Winchester (fd. 1301), boys were known as *clericuli* (Middle English *clergeon*), calling attention to their pre-clerical status.[76] A greater number of colleges, however, provide no evidence of boys in their statutes or extant records. By contrast, collegiate foundations from the mid-fourteenth century on were more likely to include groups of boys, and more likely to call those boys *choriste*.[77] And even at institutions that did not provide for choristers, they were sometimes added to the foundation later, or, in some cases, boys already present came to be called choristers in spite of their statutory designation. At Glasney College, two *choriste* were added to the foundation by Sir John Beaupre and his wife in 1355.[78] The taper-bearers of St. Nicholas are referred to as *choriste* in 1444.[79] Like the boys of the secular cathedrals, the *choriste* of secular colleges were recognized as part of the trappings of choral institutions.

Yet even if *choriste* became standard equipment of a well-endowed college, their purposes did not become equally standardized. The term *choriste* marked their inclusion in the choir, but the choir at such institutions was a locus of community both within and beyond the parameters of liturgical performance: to belong to the choir did not necessarily restrict one's activities to singing. In fact, it was precisely because of the range of functions that could be assigned to them that they became a locus of cultural preoccupations: in creating hierarchies of roles for choristers to fill, founders were articulating hierarchies of value in relation to education, skills, and the appropriate uses of either. For some, singing was, in fact, a first priority. In Stoke-by-Clare, Edmund Mortimer, Earl of March, founded a college in 1415 for a dean and six canons, eight vicars, four clerks, and five choristers, who were to sing and minister in the choir.[80] These boys were not explicitly required to have any knowledge or training upon admission, and a master was to be assigned to them to teach them in "reading, plainsong and descant, as well as in other good and seemly manners" (*lectura, plano cantu, et discantu, ac aliis bonis moribus et honestis*). Grammar instruction, frequently linked with instruction in "manners" (*moribus*),[81] is conspicuously missing from the list. Although terminology was not stable, *lectura* ("reading") was often distinguished from *litteratura*, the latter term referring decisively to grammar, the former being more difficult to pin down. Its inclusion before the specifically liturgical skills of plainchant and descant suggests a performative ability (i.e., the ability required of the *lector*), yet the framers of the statutes must also have considered *lectura* a form of rudimentary knowledge, for the older members of the choir are required to be fully instructed in plainchant and descant only, their knowledge of *lectura* being presumed.[82] The choristers' study may well have included elementary concepts involving letters, but the grammatical aspects of study are subordinated to a characterization of their learning as geared toward liturgical performance in general and toward the choral obligations of their institution in particular.

For other founders, choral service was not an end in itself. Reading and singing, rather, functioned as a form of payment or as part of a charitable exchange. Liturgical duties could be expected in return for one's livelihood, as stated in the revised statutes of Sibthorpe College (1342/3),[83] where provision is made for a "poor clerk of the parish, whose voice has not changed and who sings well" (*pauperem clericum de parochia predicta in puerili voce bene cantantem*), to be maintained by the college until his voice broke. Although one of the chantry's stipendiary clerks, who was to be "sufficiently instructed in reading and song" (*in lectura et cantu sufficienter instructum*), was directed to teach the children of the parish when his liturgical duties allowed,[84] no mention is made of educating the one poor clerk, even though he is required to sing and to serve the priests during services. More frequently, however, liturgical service was exchanged for education in letters, as at Clare Hall, Cambridge. Similar to arrangements at several other academic colleges, Clare Hall's statutes (1359) mention ten poor boys who, along with six chaplains, were "strictly obligated to say divine service."[85] In exchange, the boys were provided for from the common fund and given instruction in "song, grammar, and dialectic" (*cantu, grammatica, et dialectica*). The last of these subjects was, of course, clearly in excess of what liturgical duties might require. The boys were furthermore allowed to stay until the age of twenty—by which point their voices would have broken—and could thereafter be accepted as fellows of the college if they passed an examination. Thus, although the statutes generally suggest that the boys' primary institutional function is liturgical, their education is meant to serve ends beyond performative competence and is ultimately not subordinated to choral service. Indeed, for some choristers, the position was a charitable means to provide eventual access to university study, though they were expected to provide choral services in return.

Education in grammar was more clearly a first priority for some patrons, though benefactions for the study of grammar rarely appeared without some connection to liturgical performance that required prayers or services of either the master, the students, or both. Thus even when William Wykeham founded Winchester College in 1373 for the express purpose of preparing boys for university study and the priesthood by instructing them in grammar, he still structured his institution around the perpetual celebration of the *opus Dei* and required his seventy grammar scholars to participate in services on Sundays and feast days.[86] He further provided for an additional sixteen choristers to help the chapel staff celebrate on a regular basis, though their status in the college was distinctly inferior to that of grammar scholars.[87] Other founders required more participation in divine service but nonetheless specified that services should not interfere with grammar instruction. These patrons no doubt valued liturgical performance, but, unlike Mortimer and his fellow patrons of the Stoke-by-Clare college, they felt it to be distinct from and potentially in conflict with learning. For them, reading and singing functioned as both an institutional justification for devoting resources to young scholars and as a productive use of their time when not engaged in study.

Still others, while clearly interested in grammatical training, exploited the value of liturgy. Unlike grammar, the practices of liturgy produced benefits that could be appropriated to specific recipients. Most commonly patrons directed that masses and prayers be said for themselves or their kin, but liturgical labor could have benefits in this world as well. A chantry college, for example, founded in memory of Henry Burghersh, Bishop of Lincoln, was found to have extra funds in 1349. The Chapter of Lincoln therefore chose to add six boys to its original staff of five priests and to teach these boys grammar.[88] Grammar education receives priority, since the boys are to attend the city grammar school whenever it was in session, yet this charitable desire to educate was matched by a desire to have them sing and they were required to have knowledge of song and elementary grammar upon admission.[89] The boys were to say daily prayers for the bishop in the chantry chapel, but their chief choral duties involved "singing the psalms and reading" in the parish church of St. Mary Magdalene on feast days. Their singing and reading, then, were not performed for the benefit of their deceased patron's soul but to enhance the services of a local parish, though care is taken to first secure the parish's permission. Thus the very activities of singing and reading became gifts that a benefactor might appropriate and alienate as he or she saw fit. For the Chapter of Lincoln, they became a way of extending the network of charitable exchange by providing, but not imposing, a more decorous form of congregational celebration.

At least one founder exploited the pairing of liturgy and learning in more elaborate ways, based on his assumption that such liturgical enhancements might appeal to the boys who performed them as well as to the communities for which they were performed. In 1392, Robert Bredgar helped found a chantry consisting of a single chaplain and two scholars, who were to devote themselves to the study of "reading, song, grammar, and other liberal arts" (*lecturae, cantare, grammaticae, et aliarum scienciarum liberalium*) and were to be allowed to continue their studies at the university under the terms of the scholarship.[90] When they were not in school they were, like the boys of the Burghersh chantry, directed to celebrate divine service in the parish church, and they, too, were required to have knowledge of reading and singing upon admission.[91] But whereas the boys of the Burghersh chantry merely required permission of the parish, the boys of Bredgar College had to show in addition that they had acquired the ability to "read, sing, construe, and compose twenty-four verses" before they could help with divine service.[92] While reading, singing, and construing would ensure knowledgeable performance of liturgy, skill in composition marks a prerequisite in excess of liturgical necessity, a bar to be passed, for which the opportunity to help celebrate would serve as a reward. Liturgy thus could function not simply as a service to be exchanged for grammar instruction or as prerequisite knowledge for the study of grammar but as a coaxing incentive to, as much as a reason for, such learning.

The values attached to reading and singing are most visible at collegiate foundations, where statutes often survive that articulate the founders' interests, but the growing attention to choristers that these statutes and records exhibit was part of a larger trend that can also be seen at other institutions. In hospitals, for example, boys maintained as objects of charity sometimes assumed singing duties. At older foundations, such as St. Leonard's Hospital in York and St. Cross Hospital near Winchester, we hear of them partially by chance. They are not numbered among the staff in Walter Langton's set of statutes for St. Leonard's (1294), but an unspecified number of *pueri choriste* appear in his directions for divine service.[93] St. Cross Hospital also maintained seven boys, who "participated as choristers in all canonical hours and, when they had completed these, attended school within the hospital," but these boys are said to have been maintained by custom, as an informal accretion to the foundation, rather than by statutory regulation.[94] At other hospitals, boys either took on singing duties or became more closely related with the singing they were already performing, as at the Royal Hospital of St. Katherine by the Tower, where six "scholars" supported at the initiative of Queen Eleanor in 1273 had become six "choristers" by 1464.[95] Though informal accretions such as these cannot shed light on the motivations of individual benefactors, a more specifically suggestive case is that of the Lancastrian foundation of Newarke College, Leicester. In 1350, Henry, Earl of Derby, returned from the wars in France, having declined all the booty offered him by the king and accepted instead a thorn of the Holy Crown from the Sainte-Chapelle. He then refounded the hospital his father, the Earl of Lancaster, had established in Leicester in 1330/1 as a collegiate church, complete with a full chapel staff to celebrate divine service and the relic as a centerpiece of devotion. The hospital was maintained, but it became part of the larger collegiate institution, to which it was subordinated. For the founder, a choir articulated charitable and devotional desires in a different manner than the presence of impoverished laity. The extravagant gesture of creating a liturgical showcase for a prized relic itself shows an interest in the opportunities for display that the liturgy afforded, whether in the service of profound piety or Lancastrian regional power (most likely both). These opportunities could only be enhanced by the addition of six choristers, who were to "enter the church wearing black copes and surplices and to perform the same duties customarily assigned to the choristers of Salisbury."[96] By invoking the model of Salisbury Cathedral, Henry may well have been deferring to what was being promoted as the liturgical standard, but the specific emphasis on the choristers' ritual garb, even over the particulars of their duties, reveals an interest in the ceremony's visual impact that is in keeping with the complexity and elegance for which the Salisbury rite was known. Although other hospitals gained chapel staffs through less formal means and more diffuse motivations, they similarly show that the desire for full choral celebration was not limited to collegiate foundations and that choral service was increasingly considered a suitable occupation for the boys they supported.

The extravagant devotional display evident at Newarke College both mimicked and was mimicked by the display provided by lay and ecclesiastical magnates within their household chapels. The practice of maintaining private chapel staffs began with the papal *scola cantorum*, but the preeminent model of such an institution in England was the Chapel Royal, which can be traced back as far as 1279.[97] We first hear of "children of the chapel" in 1302, and children appear to have been recruited for service in the chapel from this point on.[98] Not surprisingly, ecclesiastical magnates maintained such chapels as well. The earliest ecclesiastical household chapel clearly including boys appears in 1335/6 in the household of Richard Bury, Bishop of Durham, and by the early fifteenth century they appear to have been a regular feature of episcopal households.[99] Chapels became an increasingly popular feature in lesser lay households as well, and by the mid-fifteenth century it was possible for a knight (though an exceedingly rich knight, Sir

Andrew Ogard) to maintain a staff of four priests and sixteen clerks and choristers.[100] Not all chapels maintained boys, but their presence added to the ceremony of the courtly ritual, signaling a full choir like those found in collegiate institutions rather than a mere chapel staff. Boys thus functioned not only as symbols of devotion but as symbols of status. The arrangements obviously benefited the boys as well, since they were provided for as members of the household. There is evidence, too, that they, and perhaps other boys in the household, received instruction in letters in varying degrees from the chapel staff. The Household Book of Queen Isabella for 1311–12, for example, lists among the expenses for the household chapel 4d. paid for "an alphabet for little Tommy to learn."[101] Accounts for the household of Thomas Arundel for 1381–84 show payments to a "magister puerorum."[102] Grammar masters appear sporadically in documents related to the Chapel Royal,[103] but more important, the choristers' position often entitled them to university study. In 1317 twelve children of the chapel were sent to study at King's Hall, Cambridge, a tradition that continued until the mid-fifteenth century.[104] In 1405, an exception was requested on behalf of a boy of the chapel that he might be accepted as a fellow in spite of the fact that he had not been fully educated in grammar,[105] which suggests that the household may on occasion have made up in influence what it did not provide in instruction.

Monasteries also participated in the fashion of maintaining boy singers. Although they had not taught young boys within their precincts since child oblation had been discouraged in the early twelfth century, it became a common practice toward the end of the thirteenth century—particularly at Benedictine houses—to maintain boys in almonries.[106] Frequently these boys received education in grammar at the expense of the almonry, as was the case at Norwich (by 1309); Ely (from 1314); Christchurch, Canterbury (from 1320); St. Albans (from 1339); and Worcester (from c. 1340).[107] These earlier fourteenth-century references show only that the almonry boys learned grammar and had little to do with the liturgical life of the monastery or cathedral apart from possibly serving at altars.[108] Toward the end of the century, however, the monasteries began to have boys participate in the daily Lady Mass.[109] Evidence of Lady Chapel choirs consisting of secular boys can be found at Westminster in 1384, Winchester in 1402, and Ely in 1407, to name just a few of the earlier examples.[110] All of these foundations included an instructor of choristers, though records are not always explicit about what the instructor taught. Regardless of the nature of their learning, their inclusion within a monastic liturgical setting represents the creation of a new institution of song derived from its association with charity, learning, devotion, and display.

Whatever claims might be made for a growing interest in education over the course of the fourteenth and early fifteenth centuries, the growing interest in choristers during this period is incontrovertible. This discussion, furthermore, has only dealt with formal institutional settings where these interests were most thoroughly documented. Evidence from bequests made to reading and singing boys provides a glimpse into the less formal area of requiem masses, obits, and votive antiphons that boys were often asked to perform. Though boys in these generally parochial settings were not always called "choristers," testators' mentions of them suggest that they, too, were situated at the convergence of questions about liturgy, charity, and learning that were pursued in similarly varied configurations and thus that contemplation of these matters was not restricted to patrons with the means to found chantries.[111]

In shifting the focus of investigation slightly away from the identification of schools or evidence of education to evidence of boys engaged in liturgical performance, I am not suggesting that a narrative of growth in schooling be replaced by a narrative of growth in liturgical endowment. Such an explanation would be equally unsatisfying, since liturgical performance did not require boys' voices. Though Orme, among others, once speculated that the fashion of including boy singers was motivated by the development of polyphonic settings of liturgical music, Bowers has since shown that boys were not commonly used to perform polyphony until the second half of the fifteenth century.[112] The presence of choristers may have signaled a heightened degree of ceremony even in the absence of polyphony, but they were only one of several options for enhanced celebration open to the patron with limited means. Unlike those other options, however, choristers seem to have allowed patrons to consider in institutional terms the nature and value of practices central to determining the function of the written word within their culture. Especially in their attention to lettered practices deemed to be either pre-grammatical or extragrammatical—that is, the practices of reading and singing that were not as clearly defined or situated as grammar—patrons developed a "grammar" of a different sort: a set of broader institutional gestures that involved objectifying and manipulating the apparatus of institutional forms internal to the choral community, such as the song school. By means of this "grammar," patrons articulated the relationship of liturgical performance to charity, devotion, display, and, of course, their own salvation. Boys, with their status as potential clerics, allowed patrons to consider the boundaries of clerical identity in light of these relationships, which in turn involved consideration of both the boundaries of clerical knowledge and the means by which it should be reproduced.

The "song school" founded by Thomas Langley, Bishop of Durham, provides a good index of the changes such manipulations had wrought.[113] In 1414, Langley founded a chantry for two priests to celebrate in the Lady Chapel he was having constructed in the monastic cathedral of Durham. The chantry chaplains, however, were required to do more than celebrate; they were to be "competently instructed, one in grammar, the other in song, that they might be able to run schools, one in grammar, the other in song, in the city of Durham, and to instruct and teach youths and other unlearned (*indoctos*) in such competencies (*scienciis*) sufficiently."[114] The song school master was further required to sing the Lady Mass each day with a sufficient number of his scholars. Both schoolmasters were allowed to take fees for their teaching from those who could afford them, but rather than set a specific rate for such teaching, Langley merely suggests that they take "the moderate fees that it is customary to be paid in other grammar or song schools" (*recipiendo stipendia moderata in aliis scolis gramatice vel cantus solvi consueta*). Langley thus created a "song school" and assumed the presence of other such institutions to have been so ordinary that there was a commonly agreed upon fee for the instruction they offered, and yet this usage of the term is virtually unique among extant contemporary sources.[115] The institution that he deems a song school is in fact a collection of multiple gestures: it combines a chantry college with a monastic Lady Chapel choir and invokes the educational terms of the secular cathedral's song and grammar schools, yet it relies on the fee-paying structures of the town grammar master.

Langley's song school is not the same institution that was under the rule of the precentor in secular cathedrals of the thirteenth century, though it is perhaps meant to look like it and to function within a tradition that Langley saw as stable and continuous. Under the guise of stability, the multiplicity of patrons' institutional gestures, each with their own implicit definitions and valuations of knowledge and ability, created a mobile field of articulation with the potential to define the terms of "education" and the textual practices it would promote. The late fourteenth and early fifteenth centuries did indeed see more schools and more evidence of instruction in literacy skills, yet these developments do not indicate the reduplication of preexisting practices and institutions as much as they point to an emerging dialogue about the status of lettered and textual knowledge. Understanding the nature of that dialogue and its effect on the reproduction and distribution of intellectual resources in late medieval England requires further exploration not solely of the personnel involved or the motivations of patrons but also of how the continued interanimation of liturgy and grammatical literacy was manifested in the skills themselves, as evinced in the persistent collocation of "reading" and "singing."

Sciencia legendi et cantandi

The frequent appearance of "reading" and "singing" in documents related to early education has led modern scholars to equate the two terms with pre-grammatical training in letters. The consistency with which they not only appear but appear together as paired activities has even led some to regard the two as synonyms denoting a capacity to translate letters into phonemes, a skill usually learned from basic Christian prayers rather than from "grammatical" texts as such.[116] Although more recent scholarship by Moran Cruz has sought to separate "reading" and "singing" as distinct pre-grammatical and extragrammatical skills, respectively,[117] their consistent collocation and the function of either within a curriculum for young children remains to be accounted for. Part of the difficulty in determining the meaning of these terms is the result of limiting the investigation solely to "educational" contexts—that is, where they appear to refer to elementary literacy acquisition. Reading and singing collocate in settings beyond early reading pedagogy (and even, as we shall see, beyond the liturgy). It is, in fact, the movement of the collocation from one setting to another that provides insight into the dynamics of Christian textual communities, both within and beyond the choir, that "reading and singing" come to embody.

   The origin of the collocation is, of course, the reading and singing of the liturgy, the primary activities cultivated in Leidrad's *scole cantorum et lectorum*. These activities, as we have seen, were performed by literate, adult clerics and religious; for them, learning to read and sing prepared them for divine service, not for the study of grammar. The development of two distinct *scole* stems from the evolution of the two kinds of chant discussed earlier—the lector-chant and the schola-chant. Whereas the former ("reading") involved knowledge of recitation tones, akin to Jewish traditions of cantillation, the latter involved the transmission of a repertoire of textualized melodies ("song") to which particular texts would be sung. In practice, however, the distinction between the two was not entirely a matter of form. Psalms, for example, which were performed on "psalm tones," were nonetheless considered to be "sung" in liturgical performance—indeed, the verb *psallere* and its derivatives often served as synonyms for *cantare*. In late medieval practice, the difference between "singing" and "reading" was ultimately one of performance dynamic: "singing" was a choral activity, ideally performed from memory; "reading," by contrast, featured the single *lector* reciting from the Book. Both the pairing of reading and singing and the distinction between the two served ideological, rather than pedagogical, purposes. They functioned as two complementary modes of Christian textual practice whereby communal singing from memory evinced the choral community's full internalization of its texts, while "reading" from the book performed these texts' scriptural origin.[118]

As stylized forms of scriptural performance, reading and singing were considered distinct, and distinctively liturgical, skills in choral settings. Statutes of choral institutions indicate that this definition of reading and singing persisted well into the fifteenth century. Many choral institutions required these skills of the adult members of their communities and indeed of anyone who regularly performed divine service, regardless of age or status, as at Sibthorpe College, where the two chantry chaplains (necessarily in priests' orders) were required to be "knowledgeable, able, and willing in reading and singing competently in church" (*scientes, valentes, et volentes in ecclesia ... cantare et legere competentur*).[119] Although knowledge of grammar was clearly desirable for those who performed the liturgy, "literate" or "lettered" status was not synonymous with, nor did it presume knowledge of, "reading and singing." Thus William Wykeham's statutes for New College, Oxford (1400), required the ten chaplains of the college, who celebrated divine service daily, to be possessed of "sufficient grammar," yet also required them to be "sufficiently instructed in reading and song" (*sufficientis literaturae ... et ... in lectura et cantu sufficienter instructi*), while the fellows, who had limited choral duties, were required only to be "fully instructed in grammar."[120] In 1352, John Grandisson similarly required the dean of the collegiate church in Crantock to admit to the position of vicar choral only those who were "sufficiently literate, and fully expert in song and reading" (*competenter literatos, et in cantu et lectura bene expertos*).[121] Full command of reading and singing in this context was even thought by some to be too advanced to be expected of young boys. The statutes of Fotheringhay College (fd. 1415), for instance, require chaplains, clerks, and choristers to be instructed in reading and singing only as their level and status in the choir necessitated.[122]

The desire to have choristers perform the liturgy gradually created a new context in which to define reading and singing. As dictated by the practical realities of employing young boys—some with "smal grammeere"—in liturgical performance, the reading and singing abilities expected of aspiring choristers were vastly simplified. Far from the distinguished knowledge of which Leidrad boasted, this form of "reading and singing" was equated with knowledge that could be expected of seven- and eight-year-old boys. This shift did not entail the simplification of the liturgy itself or even of the knowledge it required; rather, it involved fashioning a hierarchy of that knowledge, situating more "advanced" skills outside the parameters delineated by the collocation "reading and singing." At Ottery St. Mary (fd. 1339), for example, John Grandisson required all to have competence in reading and singing (*scientia legendi et cantandi*), but he required the older members of the choir to have additional knowledge of the Tonary and Invitatorium (books that provide the various melodic formulae needed to perform lessons and to modulate between psalms and antiphons),[123] knowledge that in choirs made up entirely of adults might be understood as part of "reading and singing." To the extent that these less inclusive forms of reading and singing prioritized performance itself, there was likely a great deal of latitude in determining what this kind of knowledge consisted of and how it should be transmitted, but no matter how they were defined in specific instances, "reading and singing" were articulated in many places as skills with particular relevance for the young, in other words, as "elementary."

With this recontextualization, "reading and singing" came to be combined or conflated with other practices designated as *primitiva*, or "first things," just as they came to be articulated as more generalized skills that might have value apart from the immediate needs of performance. Such value did not necessarily lie in any perceived relevance or applicability to future learning. Indeed, some rationalized song's elementary status by precisely the opposite logic. A statute from the Diocesan Council of Winchester in 1295 states the reasons for the importance of song in the early stages of learning.

Inducantur insuper parentes puerorum quod ipsos pueros postquam psalterium legere sciverint cantum addiscant ne postquam forte maiora didicerint ad hoc discendum redire cogantur, vel tanquam huius inscii ad divinum obsequium sint suo perpetuo minus apti.[124]

[Let boys' parents also be induced to let their boys, when they know how to read the psalter, learn song, lest perchance they might be forced to return to learn this after they have learned greater things, or inasmuch as they are ignorant of this, they might always be the less fit for divine service.]

Though it was considered knowledge that would be required of future priests, song was not felt to inform the study of *maiora* in any way that would make it pedagogically indispensable. Situating it among the first stages of learning, rather, serves to categorize it as a lesser form of knowledge, the assimilation of which would be tedious to those who had moved on to greater things further along in the sequence. Thus, at least in this case, song is among the *primitiva* of priestly knowledge in a way that divorces it from grammatical study.

If song was seen by some as irrelevant to grammatical study, the same could not be said of reading.[125] Liturgical reading, I have noted, had come to be associated with the grammatical skill of *lectio*, involving familiarity with letters, syllables, and their phonemic values. The place of *lectio* as the first *officium* in the study of grammar made it by definition a form of introductory learning. Its connection with the capacity to vocalize texts, furthermore, surely facilitated its conflation with the performance of ritual texts, which had itself served as an initiatory skill, both in the Jewish tradition and in the early medieval church where *lector* or *psalmista* was the first of the minor orders.[126] This ritualized reading was, to be sure, a far more stylized form of giving voice to the written word than that taught under the rubric of *lectio*. Implicit characterizations such as Grandisson's, however, which place some of the knowledge required for stylized performance (for example, knowledge of the Tonary) outside the parameters of "reading and singing," suggest that a simplified version of this ability—one much closer to the component skill of *lectio*—had come to be understood as appropriate for young boys. Elsewhere Grandisson similarly requires that boys applying for grammar scholarships at a local hospital "know the Psalter proficiently, in the manner that boys do" (*sciant psalterium competenti more puerorum*),[127] again suggesting a modification of liturgical practice to suit younger pupils. Yet if liturgical reading became more like *lectio*, grammatical *lectio* underwent important changes in the process as well. Though the isolation of "reading" may seem like a natural division, *lectio* was merely one part of the larger sequence of classical grammatical pedagogy, a pedagogy that was, furthermore, designed for native speakers of Latin. Although some of the skills of *lectio* were reducible to a set of rules for pronunciation, these rules presumed semantic recognition of the words being pronounced.[128] Separated from the rest of the grammatical curriculum meant to provide this recognition, "reading" would generally not be considered a meaningful skill. Only in a context in which ritualized, performative reading was at least imaginatively prioritized might knowledge related to *lectio* be figured as an autonomous skill.

It is easy to underestimate the significance of this articulation, in part because it gestures toward a perception of literacy that is closer to our own. Medieval literacy, as Clanchy and others have shown, was founded on experience with texts rather than on the capacity to assimilate them.[129] Although "reading" was indispensable in that it was the means by which texts were realized, this activity was subordinated to cumulative experience with and knowledge of those texts, as implied by the label *litteratus*, or "lettered." Since participation in the Christian community involved learning its constituent texts as much as learning how to read them, repertory knowledge was not fully distinguished from skill-based knowledge. With the isolation of "reading" as a discrete skill, one sees an indication that the abstract skill it signifies has discrete value as well. The emergence of the term *lectura* to describe this elementary skill also underscores such a modification insofar as it contrasts with other common grammatical terms associated with literacy acquisition: *lectio*, which names a specific action; *litteratura*, which denotes the object upon which the action is performed; and *litteratus*, which indicates the effect these objects have on the reading subject. *Lectura* shares with *litteratus* a participial derivation, yet unlike the passive past participle *litteratus*, *lectura* is formed from a future participle and evokes a potential or skill to be exploited. In at least one case an effort is made to objectify this potential as a form of knowledge independent of its actual use. The statutes of Winchester College consistently distinguish the prerequisite abilities demanded of the college's grammar scholars, who had minimal choral duties, from those of its choristers, who did not receive formal training in grammar. Whereas the latter were required to "know how to read and sing competently" (*scientes competenter legere et cantare*) for the explicitly stated reason "to minister, read, and sing in the chapel," the former were to be "competently instructed in reading, plainchant, and Donatus" (*in lectura, plano cantu, et antiquo Donato competenter instructi*).[130] The distinction drawn here between nominal areas of knowledge, *lectura* and *planus cantus*, and verbal areas of competence, *legere* and *cantare*, is unusual, but it does show an awareness of a second kind of reading (and singing) that is understood and valued differently from that needed by choristers to fulfill their immediate choral obligations.

The possibility that *lectura* represents a form of knowledge that was both assimilated to and articulated as a semi-autonomous part of the grammatical curriculum, however, does little to explain why song is so frequently included alongside reading. The existence of schools teaching reading and singing to pupils without evident choral duties, such as those in Barnack (1359), Kingston-on-Thames (1377), and Southwark (1365),[131] not to mention the "adulterine" schools in Lincoln and York, suggests that it was "reading and singing" rather than "reading" alone that had developed into autonomous forms of knowledge not directly related to the immediate needs of liturgical performance. As was the case at Winchester College, this kind of reading and singing was often linked to introductory knowledge of Latin inflectional endings ("*antiquus Donatus*"). An entry in the Canterbury Letter Book, dated 1324, contains a rejection of a prospective monk on the grounds that he did not yet possess "facility and skill in singing and reading" (*usum et artem cantandi et legendi*). When the grounds of his rejection are reiterated, it is stated appositively that he should learn "grammatical inflections and facility and skill in singing and reading" (*terminos grammaticales et usum et artem cantandi et legendi*) while he was still in his youth and had time and that he would be admitted upon attaining these competencies.[132] On the surface, examples like these seem to evoke an evolving sequence of skills prepatory to the study of grammar; insofar as they do, they represent a significant recontextualization of reading and singing, yet one that makes song's persistence all the more baffling.

The collocation of reading and singing becomes less mysterious if we acknowledge that it is also possible to overestimate the degree to which the activity of reading was conceptualized as an autonomous skill, abstracted from its particular objects. Though *lectura* conveys the sense of a potential to be fulfilled in the future, that potential has more to do with the ability to perform than the ability to decode per se. Proficiency in rendering texts, in other words, does not necessarily depend on the ability that is the sine qua non of modern literacy: the capacity to decode unfamiliar material instantaneously—to "sight read," in musical terms. Nor does it depend

on the ability to decode all manner of texts. "Reading," as transmitted at
this elementary stage, seems rather to have consisted almost exclusively
of reading the most basic ritualized Christian texts—prayers, creeds, the
Psalter—that would be regularly repeated by the faithful. Not only did
such a syllabus provide an introduction to the central texts of the faith,
it served to sacralize these texts and to perpetuate the idea that whatever
other pragmatic, mundane tasks writing might accomplish, its foremost
function was the preservation of sacred language. The obligatory connection of reading to a particular object is underscored by the fact that
the term "reading" rarely appears by itself in documents describing early
education during this period but rather in combinations that contextualize
it.[133] In the late thirteenth century, references tend to emphasize the text
that was most commonly used for early reading pedagogy: one does not
simply learn to "read"; one learns to "read the Psalter." In the fourteenth
century, the ritualized, performative context of elementary reading becomes increasingly marked by pairing it with "singing."

To claim that "singing" serves to contextualize "reading" is not to
claim that it is synonymous with "reading," nor that it is meaningless. The
emergence of the collocation signals a broadening of both the texts and
the textual practices this stage of learning conveyed. While the gradual
shift to "reading and singing" demonstrates the greater attention given
to the participation of boys in divine service (actual or anticipated), it is
also contemporary with the evolution of the primer—a more diverse (and
less decisively clerical) collection of texts that would eventually supersede
the Psalter as introductory reading material.[134] Central to the primer repertoire were votive offices—the Hours of the Virgin, the Hours of the
Cross—which, however much they had been adapted for private use, still
evoked the "singing and reading" of the choir's celebration of the *opus
Dei*. It is perhaps an index of the potential difference between the liturgical and the educational that the hybrid construction one occasionally
encounters in educational documents—"reading the Psalter and song"—is
the opposite of the locution used to described choral performance of the
Office—"singing the psalms (or *psallere*) and reading."[135] The seeming
interchangeability of "reading" and "singing" that allows this inversion,
however, arguably reinforces the idea that the two practices were distinct.
The overdetermined centrality of the Psalter as a quintessentially clergial
text enables it to sustain more than one textual practice: "reading," or
decoding, which exemplifies clerical literacy and the individual's initiating
acquisition thereof, and "singing," or internalization, which demonstrates

membership in the clerical community. As with the strictly liturgical modes of reading and singing I have discussed, the two are complementary yet distinct practices, defined as much by their dialogical relationship to each other as by their formal properties. This differentiation remains even in settings beyond the textual communities of choral institutions, where they served to affirm clerical identity. Books of Hours, for example, often mark the "sung" portions of the text with a smaller script, though there is little evidence that users of such books made practical variations in their private performances to signal the distinction.

"Reading" and "singing" were therefore distinct, but the ways in which they could be distinguished from one another were numerous, since the precise definition of each was not systematically articulated. The subject matter of "song" could range from the tonal complexities of hexa-chords to "rote" memorization of the most basic Christian hymns and antiphons; the subject matter of "reading" could similarly range from rec-ognition of the phonemic value of letters and syllables to the ability to decode certain psalter or primer texts to facility with the variety of lection tones used in the liturgy. Both could either presume grammatical knowl-edge or claim to prepare the aspiring scholar for entry into grammatical discourse. Both could be considered in terms of portable, generalized skills or primarily in terms of assimilated repertoire. The variety of definitions, I have suggested, was a product of the values patrons and practitioners placed on liturgy, learning, charity, and display. Each foundation, scholar-ship, and bequest required at least an implicit definition of "reading" and of "singing," of the relationship between the two, and of the relationship of both to grammar. The multiple articulations of skills and values served to create an area of speculation that remained all the more fluid as a result of the constant circulation between institutions and personnel. Wykeham, for example, may have attempted to distinguish between the knowledge of choristers and scholars with his differentiation between *lectura et planus cantus* and *legere et cantare* in his Winchester College statutes, yet such a configuration was but one of many to be found within a one-mile radius of the college. The choristers of Winchester College sometimes went on to become grammar scholars.[136] The boys of Wykeham's private chapel were lodged at the college on at least one occasion.[137] Also attending the college were fee-paying commoners, some of whom lodged at the nearby St. Elizabeth's, where *clericuli* read and sang, and functioned as ser-vants.[138] The college was also situated just outside the Close wall of Win-chester Cathedral, where a small number of boys participated in a Lady

Chapel choir,[139] perhaps the same boys whom Wykeham endowed to sing a Marian antiphon nightly in the cathedral.[140] They may have attended the town grammar school along with other boys of the cathedral's almonry, where they would have had contact with the twelve scholars of the grammar school who received their meals through the charity of St. Cross Hospital, which maintained its own choristers and its own school.[141] Almost all of these boys engaged in some form of reading and singing, though in each case the practices understood by those terms were prioritized, motivated, and possibly even defined in different ways.

"Collocation" is perhaps the best term to describe this seemingly obligatory conjunction of "reading" and "singing," along with the fluidity that resulted from the many ways of defining the terms dialogically. It may seem an ironic term to apply to changes in perceptions of literacy, since I have borrowed it from the conceptual vocabulary of oral-formulaic theory.[142] There it refers to a generative organizational strategy used in some oral traditions, whereby poets draw upon a stock of paired terms that form unconscious matrices capable of producing endless variation. My invocation of the term here is meant to distinguish usage of "reading and singing" from the "formulae" more familiar to documentary culture: those in which ossified phrases (*sciant presentes et futuri* or, I would argue, *scola cantus*) announce and potentially authorize their institutional contexts. The precise institutional location of reading and singing, by contrast, becomes increasingly less clear as the practices to which they originally referred gradually come unmoored from the *scole cantorum et lectorum* as well as from the textual communities and textual practices those institutions sustained. This unmooring was partly the result of changes in the social relations that liturgy shaped and mediated. It was also partly the result of changes in attitudes toward grammatical literacy, which was simultaneously perceived as fragmented by proliferating uses of the written word and as a more generalized skill that might be transported among these fragmented literacies. I will discuss both of these developments in later chapters; my point here is that the site of "reading and singing" was one of dialogic interaction between these two changing fields. That such a dialogue should occur is not coincidental, of course, since the grammatical and the liturgical governed two integrally related approaches to ritualizing textual practice, whether through the chanting of psalms or the chanting of paradigms. It is not simply words that collocate, then, but also the practices to which they refer and the discursive formations that give rise to them and through their interaction determine which textual practices are validated and for what reasons.

By focusing on the collocation "reading and singing," I also hope to draw attention away from the oddly ossified "smal grammeere" of the *clergeon*'s friend that has influenced the study of song and re-center it on the ambiguity—both ethical and intellectual—that marks the school where Christian children learn "to syngen and to rede," as well as the dialogue between the liturgical and the grammatical that produces this ambiguity. Though studies of medieval schooling have provided invaluable information and insight, they have been guided by humanist definitions and values that risk obscuring the dynamism of intellectual resources in late medieval England and, more specifically, the influence of liturgical performance on that dynamism. This influence extended beyond the setting of early schooling, affecting the circulation of texts and the social relations forged through that circulation in several spheres. Early education, indeed, is only one, if perhaps the most evident, context in which we see the unmooring of both liturgical practices and the skills employed in their performance from the choral institutions that engendered them. Before moving on to other contexts, though, it will be useful to examine choral institutions more closely in terms of the social relations found in conjunction with them as well as the role of choral celebration of the liturgy in articulating and maintaining these relations.

Singing the New Song:
Literacy, Clerical Identity, and the
Discourse of Choral Community

The Discourse of Choral Community

LEIDRAD'S DESCRIPTION OF his *scole cantorum et lectorum*, I have suggested, stems from a fundamentally different conception of the role of literacy in structuring social relations from that implied by the humanist models that have informed studies of medieval reading and education. It remains now to examine more fully the discourse that produced these earlier perceptions—what I refer to as the discourse of choral community—and to consider the effects of its resonances in late medieval England. "Choral community," as I have been using the term, refers most concretely to the textual communities found at institutions, both monastic and secular, in which liturgical performance was central to the constitution and reproduction of social bonds. These were the institutions that originally contextualized the practices of reading and singing. The discourse undergirding communities created within such institutions imagined the choir to be an ideal social body—an intellectual organic community of sorts, made up of those whose literacy was embodied rather than objectified and whose knowledge was both acquired and used in the context of that community. The social relations and interactions idealized within this discourse are those that might, in a different context, be labeled "traditional" or, more paradoxically, "oral"—in other words, they describe relations considered to be characteristic of cultures without writing.[1] Organized through practices characterized as "ritual," social bonds governed by the discourse of choral community might easily be considered in the same vein as other relations associated with ritual: as resistant to social change and ultimately doomed to be replaced by the objectified institutional structures that writing allows. My describing the song school as a "residual" institution by the fourteenth century might even be said to uphold such a narrative of supplantation. Yet as was the case with the emergence of "reading and singing" from the context of the song school, social change can often be traced to the continued invocation of liturgical practice rather than its replacement. In this chapter, I will demonstrate a similar relationship between the discourse of choral community and emerging definitions of literacy.

Scholars have perceived the history of literacy in terms of these more radical shifts because their research has generally focused on institutions of *writing*. The choir, by contrast, was a community organized around *reading*, which changes the terms of discussion considerably. Writing is generally portrayed as inconsistent with traditional relations because of its capacity to objectify—to store cultural resources in forms external to the body—which allows for different forms of social organization. Yet while the production of written objects surely allows the disembodiment of cultural resources, those objects would not be meaningful unless they could be reincorporated and the cultural capital inhering in them retrieved through reading—an activity less easily classifiable as external to the body. What becomes especially apparent when we turn our attention to institutions of reading is that "reading" and "literacy" are not themselves intrinsically objectified abilities, abstracted from particular uses and transportable to any context, as I have suggested. The degree and character of their objectification, furthermore, are no more preordained than the uses to which, as skills, they are put. To treat literacy as a fully constituted object that "spreads" or is simply "acquired" is to overlook the role of ideology in determining how and why we read.[2] By contrast, an examination of the processes and forms of reading's objectification, such as we see in connection with the discourse of choral community as well as with the unmooring of reading and singing, allows us to see socially and even politically significant distinctions in the variety of readerly processes modern culture has taught us to regard as unitary.

Choral communities also imagined reading as a unitary activity, but this activity performed different social functions. The communities themselves were articulated through the act of ritualized reading, through which they reproduced the cultural and intellectual resources of which they were stewards. This stewardship did constitute a "partial or total monopolizing of the society's symbolic resources" of the sort that Pierre Bourdieu associates with writing and the "primitive accumulation of cultural capital" it enables.[3] Yet within the discourse of choral community, the choir is imagined primarily from the inside, as an enclosed group committed to the preservation of cultural resources that might otherwise lose their integrity rather than as a group committed to the accumulation of these resources through direct expropriation. Knowledge was thus reproduced endogamously, by which I mean that membership in the group was a precondition of learning, in contradistinction to the humanistic model of cultural reproduction articulated by Leach, wherein learning is a precondition of membership. Within this discourse, literate practices were contained within the parameters of the community, such that inclusion within the group was a more meaningful boundary for self-identification than the possession of particular threshold skills. In accordance with this logic, the label *litteratus* functioned as a term of prestige that dignified certain readers in relation to other readers rather than one that distinguished readers from nonreaders. It signaled an awareness of literacy as a specific form of knowledge, but one that was neither as fully unified nor as fully objectified as that which would regularly be contrasted with illiteracy.

The focal point of the choral community, after all, was not so much literacy as textuality, which, as Brian Stock has pointed out, is distinguishable from writing, even if the notion of a stable verbal text is predicated on the concept of writing.[4] Since the community's foundational texts were primarily realized in performance, they required communal participation and were embedded in social and symbolic relations. Within the discourse of choral community, choral celebration of the liturgy was the primary means by which the social relations of the group were articulated. Seated in three rows according to their degree of dignity, participants ritualized their relations to each other as well as to God's Word in their performances. Reading and singing, the primary activities of the *opus Dei*, underscored the textual foundation of choral community, I have claimed, in two complementary aspects.[5] Reading, performed by a single person from the lectern, emphasized the presence of the Book and the choir's attentive and communal submission to God's Word as vocalized from that Book.[6] Singing, by contrast, was performed by the entire choir, either in unison or in various groupings, and often from memory. It both demonstrated the community's internalization of those texts and enacted the incorporation of the group's members through their sharing of texts. The psalms, above all, were indicative of choral singing and the desire for univocality and community singing expressed. St. Ambrose describes their unifying function: "a psalm joins those with differences, unites those at odds and reconciles those who have been offended, for who will not concede to him with whom one sings to God in one voice?"[7] A group exercise in subject formation within the textual community, the performance of the lyric "I" of the psalms was conducted as a dialogue between two alternating sides of the choir, each singing in unison. Thus while subjects were united to each other through monody, the spatial dynamics of antiphonal singing united the individual subject to the entire group by visually and acoustically articulating the perimeter of the choral body. Such an articulation of community is predicated on a notion of song as a fundamentally embodied practice.[8] Its conciliatory powers stem not from arbitration or appeals to reason but from submission to a greater synchrony that requires both the physical and the metaphysical presence of those concerned. The ideal of memorization so highly valued at late medieval choral institutions was in part meant to ensure that this unity would be achieved by the communal rendering of internalized texts unmediated by the physical presence of the written page, making each person's incorporation of the text a precondition of the incorporation of the group.

While the relations internal to choral communities continued to be ritualized through liturgical performance, evidence from the late Middle Ages suggests an increased awareness of liturgy's role in ritualizing relations in the broader Christian textual community as well. Choral performance maintained its function of sacralizing the Word as the textual foundation of the Christian community, yet in this larger context it also sacralized the distinctive, privileged textual practices of the clerical community. Liturgy consecrated the equation of the *litteratus* with the *clericus* in that it was the site in which the authority and responsibility to ventriloquize God's Word was exercised by the clergy categorically. Because the self-interests of choir members were to be surrendered to the unity of that group, the choir could stand for the clergy as a whole and for its generalized authority. Song's connection to the written word and to the clergy's stewardship of the Word was so central that song was, in fact, perceived as a communal form of reading. Despite the convention of singing from memory, the most common iconic representation of liturgical singing was one that stressed the presence of the Book as well as communal performance: several clerics, mouths open, gathered around a single book or roll. Although the clerics in such depictions often serve as representatives for the entire Christian community in their relationship to the written page, their communal performance signaled not only distinctively clerical practices but also the unity of those practices, particularly in relation to other, unauthorized interactions with the written word.

A traditional series of historiated initials found from the thirteenth century in "ferial" or "liturgical" psalters—those in which the *littere notabiliores* mark the chief divisions of the traditional *cursus* of psalms[9]—shows the metonymic potential of song to stand for the authorized reading of the clergy. Psalters depicting the "David cycle," as this series of illuminations is called, almost invariably include the image of singing described above in the initial of Psalm 97 (AV 98)—*Cantate Domino canticum novum* ("Sing to the Lord a new song").[10] This illustration establishes an iconographical series of identifications, linking choral psalmody to the "new song" and ultimately to Christian exegesis in general.[11] One fourteenth-century example makes these associations explicit. The initial "C" of Psalm 97 that appears in a psalter made for Stephen of Derby, prior of Christchurch, Dublin,[12] juxtaposes the clerical singers of the new song inside the initial with two marginal readers, each reading from private volumes (Fig. 1). These marginal readers are marked as Jews, both by the hooves of the figure in the upper left corner (symbolizing also the bestial irrationality of the unlearned) and by the "Judenhut" worn by both (here figuring also the inverse of the clerical tonsure).[13] Only the Christian clerics sing the "new song" referred to in the psalm; the Jews serve as a reminder of the "old song"—the reading of the Psalter before Christ. Choral singing thus becomes aligned not merely with clerical performance but with clerical hermeneutics as their "new song" comes to be associated with the allegorical reading of the scriptures.[14]

The marginal readers in the Derby Psalter are somewhat unusual, yet they merely render explicit the associations implied in other such psalters. The customarily illuminated initials of the David cycle that precede Psalm 97 (Pss. 1, 26, 38, 52, 68, and 80) usually involve "literal" or "historical" depictions of David himself. The initial immediately preceding Psalm 97, Psalm 80 (*Exultate Deo adiutori nostro*; "Rejoice in God our strength"), is particularly instructive in this regard. Illuminations of the initial "E" usually depict David playing a set of bells (Fig. 2)—an image that elsewhere represents the proportional relationships of musical intervals that characterize *musica mundana* (Fig. 3). David and with him the old song thus come to be associated with the rational but earthly music that will be transcended by the new song. There is therefore a broader tradition aligning choral psalmody with the enlightened knowledge of Christian hermeneutics at work that

Figure 1. Initial "C" of Psalm 97 (*Cantate Domino canticum novum*) in the "Derby Psalter," c. 1350–80, depicting Christian clerics communally singing the "new song" from a single page, along with marginal grotesques reading from private volumes. University of Oxford, Bodleian Library MS Rawlinson G. 185, f. 81v. Reproduced by permission of the Bodleian Library, University of Oxford.

generally took the "new song" to betoken a shift to the Christian choral community.[15] What the Derby Psalter suggests in its explicit juxtaposition of the "old song," however, is that the harmonious unity of the choral community and the integrity of the cultural resources they preserve depend on the exclusionary logic common to all understandings of literacy. "Literacy," Irvine has pointed out, "is always literacy of some*thing* and not simply a set of abstract linguistic rules."[16] It is worth adding to that formulation that the way in which any literacy constitutes its object, as well the way it delineates the actions that can be performed upon or with these objects, are determinations born of difference—that is, of relegating certain forms of writing

Figure 3. Miniature for Book 20 on the "differences of numbers, weights, and sounds," from *Livre des propriétés des choses*, depicting King David striking weighted bells, fifteenth century. London, British Library MS Cotton Aug. VI, f. 457r. Reproduced by permission of the British Library.

Figure 2. Initial for Psalm 80 (*Exultate Deo adiutori nostro*) depicting King David striking bells, part of the "David cycle" of psalter illustrations, c. 1410–15. University of Oxford, Bodleian Library MS Don. d.85, f. 50. Reproduced by permission of the Bodleian Library, University of Oxford.

and skills to the margins by designating them as unauthorized or merely nonauthoritative. The "objectification" of literacy that I am charting in this chapter is essentially the process of making these exclusions explicit. It was not a simple process—then, as now, the mastery of literacy depends on the reader's success in internalizing its implicit rules more than in explicating its procedures—but it was only through such a process that authorized practices might cohere as a resource of hegemony.

Such depictions of excluded readers were not responses to non-Christian textual practices as such. The representation of Jews long after they had been expelled from England, rather, signals yet another level of visual encoding in the image. Already situated as the defining opposition to orthodox practice, representations of the Jews (in some sense emptied out by their expulsion) stand as ready containers to which contemporary unauthorized practice might be relegated. Here, the visual features that distinguish the new song from the old—private readers versus choral singers, rising and falling lines of musical notation versus rows of illegible letters—have less to do with any late medieval conceptions of Jewish practice than with the practices of private devotion. The spatial depiction furthermore unavoidably suggests a simultaneity more reflective of the emerging practice of reading prayer books during Mass than of the temporal anteriority of the Jews' "old song."[17] The initial thus isolates private devotion and private reading as practices in conflict with the unity of the choir, and identifies these with the literal, ignorant reading associated with constructions of Jews. Such potentially threatening practices—particularly the devotional use of private prayer books—have generally been regarded as the preserve of the laity. Indeed, a great deal of religious conflict and innovation in the late medieval period has been described in terms of the clergy's response, in one form or another, to "an increasingly literate laity." Such an identification lends meaning to the way in which the initial elides Christian song with clerical singing, making clear that the privileged knowledge of the new song belongs primarily to the tonsured clerics of the choir who possess the specialized knowledge required for its performance. Song, then, would signify not simply Christian hermeneutics but the hermeneutical enfranchisement of the clergy—its particular claims on the cultural capital of the Christian community. But this interpretation, though useful, leaves much unexamined. Apart from the fact that there is more evidence of the clergy's encouragement of private devotion as a nonauthoritative practice than of their demonizing it, explanations that rely on the "increasingly literate laity" tend to take the skills that constitute that literacy for granted.

They do not allow us to examine the logic by which exclusive skills—in the Derby Psalter, for example, the literacy of musical notation—are isolated and represented to distinguish clerical performance as superior. Nor are they likely to lead to questions about the meanings attached to particular skills. It is worth considering, for example, why song remains the metonym of hermeneutical enfranchisement precisely when its relations to grammar, the source of that enfranchisement, are becoming increasingly unstable and when it is becoming increasingly common to consider song to be the most salient clerical practice that does *not* require full grammatical training or priest's orders. At stake in conflicts over literacy and clerical knowledge was not simply the possession of an object but rather the capacity to define the terms of authorized reading itself as well as the nature of the authority that *clerici* and *litterati* could wield.

Clerics were as avid manipulators of the terms *clericus* and *litteratus* as any layfolk. In their efforts either to extend or specify the authority the terms guaranteed, they also contributed to the breakdown of the equation of *clericus* and *litteratus* that choral celebration of the liturgy performed. Though I will discuss the dialectical relationship between clergy and laity in more detail in Chapter 3, my attention to the discourse of choral community is intended to place the focus on the internal drama of self-definition that beset the clergy during this period of reconfiguration and, in this manner, to serve as a complicating preface to the more frequently broached topic of clergy's struggles with the laity. The examination of a dispute over St. Cross Hospital that follows here provides just one example of the manipulations of which clerics were capable and thus calls attention to the complex social and political dynamics of these developments that the binary categorization of clergy/laity served (often ineffectively) to occlude. Whereas with this example I also consider how the label *litteratus* begins to be used as a general institutional category that defines a specific mode of authority, I follow with two other sites of contest that more clearly invoke the discourse of choral community as a reaction against the slippage exemplified at St. Cross. The two situations I consider here, one in the seemingly unrelated juridical realm of benefit of clergy, the other in the choral community of Salisbury, can be viewed as reassertions of the ideals valued in the discourse of choral community that sought to define membership in the clerical body and to unify the textual practices of which they were stewards. In both situations, membership in the community is established by isolating particular literate skills and identifying them as the lower threshold of legitimate knowledge. In this respect, ecclesiastical authorities were using strategies similar to those used by liturgical patrons in their limited and particularized authority as benefactors by establishing prerequisites. In both cases, too, the abilities they isolate as the basis of authorized textual practice are liturgical in origin, despite the fact that they define literacy in terms of diametrically opposed skills. Thus, although the two examples do not reveal a coherent ecclesiastical strategy to maintain the boundaries of clerical knowledge or literate practices, textual performance as ritualized in the liturgy continued to serve as a fundamental resource of clerical identity.

The Meanings of *Litteratus* and *Clericus*

The interchangeability of the labels *litteratus* and *clericus* was at the heart of the choral community, where the two terms functioned as mutually defining resources of identity.[18] The meaning of both, however, began to change during the late medieval period. Leona Gabel described an expansion in the thirteenth century of the category of persons who might be considered *clerici* from men in major orders only to anyone who had taken first tonsure.[19] M. T. Clanchy has similarly described a change in the meaning of *litteratus* in the fourteenth century from an honorific, denoting a person of erudition, to a term to describe "a person with a minimal ability to read, albeit in Latin."[20] Underneath these changes in meaning, however, can lie equally important changes in function that are not always reflected in meaning. When *litteratus* served as an honorific, for example, it did not really denote specific skills; its primary function was to register the symbolic capital commensurate with maximum ability rather than to specify what, precisely, those abilities were. A certain ambiguity of referent was, therefore, already built into the term, though this ambiguity did not by itself represent any emerging instability. These later shifts, however, affected the terms' discursive functions, altering when and how they were invoked. Though neither *clericus* nor *litteratus* has a more stable meaning in the fourteenth century, both come to signal generalizable, institutional categories that could be manipulated to serve specific interests.

One set of records is especially illuminating in the several definitions and functions of both terms it evidences. An ancillary document to William Wykeham's episcopal register, New College Archives MS 3691, contains the proceedings the bishop conducted in 1370 against four successive masters of St. Cross Hospital within his Winchester diocese.[21] This document has received notice in modern scholarship precisely because of its varied invocations of the term *litteratus*, though these usages have yet to be fully contextualized.[22] The analysis I provide here focuses on the objectification of institutional structures that was partly the result of the more general benefactoral tinkering with regard to the personnel, resources, and even the institutional identities of religious houses discussed in the previous chapter. This development led to an awareness on the part of those within and without the hospital's precincts of the malleability of such structures and how they could be manipulated to specific ends. Definitions of *clericus* and *litteratus* played a substantial role in these manipulations; in the process they, too, come to be objectified in ways that significantly register their changing functions.

*   *   *

St. Cross Hospital, founded just outside the town of Winchester circa 1136, had a long history of disputes, usually over control of its substantial endowment.[23] Immediate oversight of the hospital and its funds was deputed to the master or warden, a wealthy position that the Knights Hospitallers, the Bishop of Winchester, the pope, and the king all, at various points, claimed to have within their gift. In 1370, Wykeham had reason to believe that the last four masters, including the present master, Roger Cloune, had been misappropriating the hospital's funds and had ceased to feed the poor. He therefore demanded inventories from all four of them, as he claimed was his right under the papal mandate governing oversight of hospitals, *Quia continget*.[24] Though all four refused to supply them, Cloune's response was the most detailed and telling, as it suggests that he had a fundamentally different assessment not simply of the nature of the position he had accepted but of the institution itself. His refusal was based on his professed belief that St. Cross was not covered by the papal mandate because it was not really a hospital at all but rather "was and is founded principally to the honor of divine worship (*ad honorem cultus diuini*)." The House of St. Cross was, in other words, a choral institution, and the position he held was not a mastership but a sinecure benefice (*beneficium perpetuum et non curatum*)[25]—an income without responsibility either to a cure or to the poor.

The claim was more plausible than it might seem. Cloune, like the two masters before him, had gotten the position by exchanging his current benefice for it—a transaction that implied that the two positions were comparable.[26] Furthermore, St. Cross did indeed have, from the time of its foundation, a chapel staff of four priests who, along with thirteen clerks, were responsible for performing the *opus Dei* for the inhabitants of the hospital rather than administering a parish or undertaking a cure of souls. By 1370, it had become customary to maintain seven choristers, filling out the ranks of the choir. There were also religious houses similar to St. Cross that would have been exceptions to *Quia continget*, even though they maintained hospitals: the College and Hospital of St. Mary Newarke, Leicester, for example, was founded as a hospital in 1330, then reendowed as a collegiate church in 1355, staffed by canons with benefices,[27] and the Hospital of St. Leonard's, York, of ancient royal foundation, was considered a Royal Free Chapel, exempt from diocesan authority.[28] Like St. Cross, both were large institutions in which the care of the poor played an important role, but they also maintained full choral staffs. Unlike the chapel of St. Cross, however, their chapels were institutionally defining in that their status as hospitals was nominally subordinated to the Royal Free Chapel in the one case and to the collegiate church in the other. Cloune's argument, therefore, was not a matter of fabrication but of institutional subordination. It is, in fact, possible that his defense was as much a product of misapprehension as bad faith.

Since the defense had been made in institutional terms, it was Wykeham's prosecutorial burden to attack it in those terms. To this end, he shepherded virtually all available forms of proof in support of his contention that St. Cross was, both by statute and by custom, a hospital whose principal duty was the care of the poor. These proofs included not only the written testimony of documents and muniments but oral testimony as well. Thirty witnesses were presented with a series of articles drawn up by the prosecution, with which they could agree or disagree, elaborating as needed. The articles were written with special care regarding the chapel staff to show the master's financial responsibility for them without suggesting that they had any clearly defined institutional position. A paradoxical antithesis to the ideal of choral community, Cloune's self-interest was vested in the centrality of the choir, if only to absolve himself of any responsibility for the maintenance of the chapel staff. To restore institutional stability Wykeham had, conversely, to prove that the chapel staff was not the institutionally defining feature of the community.

The articles accomplish this task by manipulating the terms used to refer to chapel staff—a process that gives some insight into possible uses of both *clericus* and *litteratus*. In the final pronouncement on the case (unsurprisingly in Wykeham's favor) the judge subdelegate refers to the members of the chapel with general, neutral terms: "priests" (*presbyteri*), "secular clerks" (*clerici seculari*), and "poor clerks" (*pauperes clerici*) to refer to the choristers (f. 19v). In order to defend against Cloune's claim, however, the articles submitted to the witnesses required greater precision. They specify that the "priests" are "stipendiary priests," lest they be confused with canons or prebendaries, who would have their own sources of income, as might be the case at a collegiate church (f. 23v). Because such choral institutions often did support their clerks with stipends, the clerks of St. Cross are termed "poor secular clerks" (*pauperes clerici seculari*), to make clear that they were not "hired help" but were supported by the hospital's alms (f. 23v). The choristers presented a problem, however, since their presence might give the impression of a choir rather than a mere chapel staff, and the appellation "chorister" would only support such an impression. The judge subdelegate's "poor clerks" was an unusual label for choristers, though it was not an unusual way to refer to students supported by hospitals, a popular practice from the mid-thirteenth century.[29] Yet if "poor clerks" was chosen to give the desired institutional signals, it also caused problems, since it could easily lead one to confuse the boys with the "poor secular clerks" mentioned in the articles as well as with another group of boys the hospital supported: the thirteen "poorer scholars" (*paupiores scolares*) of the town grammar school, sent by the grammar master to take their meals at the hospital.[30] To make the distinctions clear, the seven boys who lived, celebrated divine service, and attended school within the hospital were distinguished by describing them as "seven poor literate boys (*pauperes pueri litterati*), who lived off the alms of the master ... and who were called 'choristers.'"[31] *Litteratus*, in this case, obviously does not denote mastery—their level of learning was probably similar to that of the "poorer scholars." It is not really a description of positive skills at all as much as it is a substitute term for *clericus* that assigns to them a particular institutional signification, for the phrase *pauperes pueri litterati* allows the term "choristers" to be subordinated syntactically, just as their choral function needed to be subordinated institutionally.

The designation *pueri litterati* is extremely unusual and by itself suggests little about the label *litteratus*. When considered as a substitute for *clericus*, however, particularly in combination with the numerous *clerici* who inhabited the hospital, it registers a more general fragmentation of the concept of the *clericus* and what it might stand for in terms of knowledge, vocation, occupation, and ecclesiastical status. The notion of a fragmented clergy is likely to conjure images of specialized scribal or notarial practices, yet the juggling of epithets in these articles evinces a perception, even within these more traditionally clergial roles, that the term *clericus* had simply become too broad and that there were not enough ways to make distinctions despite the institutional significance of such distinctions. This perception becomes still more apparent in the scribe's occasional difficulty in consistently maintaining the epithets in the articles.[32] Still more significantly, these matters arise specifically in relation to the minor clergy. Whereas Gabel noted an expansion in the concept of the *clericus* in the thirteenth century, in some discursive fields the term arguably becomes narrower in the fourteenth century: *clericus* becomes the label to distinguish those in holy orders without sacerdotal powers. This distinction had particular relevance in liturgical contexts, where the authority to celebrate Mass placed one's labor in a different category from those who could only read and sing or serve, but it is maintained throughout all the St. Cross proceedings, even in contexts unrelated to liturgy. More generally, then, the term *clericus*, largely through a lack of any consistent categorical mechanisms, came to label the diffuse area of ecclesiastical affiliation that did not include priestly ordination or sacramental authority—an area where the relations of knowledge, vocation, and status were increasingly vexed.

Because it marked ecclesiastical affiliation, *clericus* served as a general institutional category that could be modified by epithets. *Litteratus*, however, usually did not serve such a purpose. For it to appear, as it does here, as a general institutional category marks a change in its discursive function—a change that gains significance when viewed in conjunction with similarly categorical uses elsewhere in the St. Cross proceedings. The account of the official inspection of St. Cross's documents, registers, and muniments, for example, provides a list of participating witnesses that includes four men with ecclesiastical titles and two termed *viri litterati* (f. 52r). Here *litteratus* functions as a kind of credential, as if the symbolic capital the term signified had been appropriated to a particular mode of authority and competence, namely, the ability to verify the contents of written legal instruments. Of further interest, though, is the fact that it appears to distinguish the last two witnesses as laymen whose literacy qualified them to participate in this inquiry. While the other witnesses are certified by their ecclesiastical titles, of which literacy is presumed to be a part, literacy itself becomes a discrete credential for these non-clerical witnesses. The character of their knowledge in this case is less important than the character of their authority. At once particularized and disembodied, the authority of these *litterati* emanates from the skill itself and its appropriateness to the situation at hand, no matter who possesses it. One can be labeled *litteratus* because of what one knows rather than because one is the kind of person who knows things.

The criterion of appropriate skill, however, cannot be consistently applied to the other set of witnesses who are sometimes labeled *litteratus*. These were the thirty witnesses gathered to hear the articles. The names of these men are listed with their ages and titles, where appropriate, and, in some cases, the designations *litteratus* or *laicus*.[33] Neither label is used for the fifteen witnesses who had titled ecclesiastical positions. All of these are styled either *dominus* or *magister*, indicating that they were priests and that some were university graduates. Although a few of the others have lay titles ("citizen" or "lord"), they are all classified as either *litteratus* or *laicus*. That the label *litteratus* should be applied to any of the witnesses might give one pause, since their testimony was oral. It is, in fact, impossible to know what the criteria were for making these designations. There is no clear or uniform relationship between whatever reading ability we might imagine *litteratus* to signify and the nature of the witness's testimony. Some witnesses, it is true, base their testimony on their reading of documents. One witness, for example, claimed to know the terms of the original foundation because he had "often seen, inspected, read and understood the charter of the first foundation (*sepius vidit et inspexit, legit et intellexit cartam prime fundacionis*)" (f. 24r). Yet only five witnesses made this claim, and the five include all four jurors styled *magister* and one priest,[34] suggesting that the title *magister*, rather than *litteratus*, distinguished the authoritative reader. Many other witnesses, however, both priests and "literates," claimed to have "heard" of the contents of the documents or "heard" of their existence but point out that they had never "seen or inspected" the documents themselves.[35] Jurors termed *laicus* did not make this claim, but neither is it consistently recorded in the testimony of the remaining literate or priestly witnesses.

Because corroboration of the contents of written documents constituted legal proof in the testimony, the label *litteratus* here does seem to function as a credential, as in the other case. Yet while it gestures to the capacity for such corroboration, it refers neither to the fact nor even to the necessity of using that capacity. And while knowledge of documentary writing may have been appropriate to confirm some articles, it was not the only resource of authoritative testimony, which was intended to clarify the customary as well as the statutory constitution of St. Cross. Inspection of documents pertained to fewer than half of the nineteen articles, and no single witness mentions them in reference to more than six. The distribution of ages between "literate" and "lay" witnesses, furthermore, suggests that *laicus*, rather than indicating a lack of literacy, marked the witness as an authoritative custodian of living memory: whereas "literate" witnesses range in age from forty to seventy, the "lay" witnesses range from eighty to eighty-eight and claimed to remember the state of the house from over sixty years before. *Litteratus*, correspondingly, seems in part to signify that the younger witnesses are simply a different kind of resource and bore a different kind of authority.

Even if the logic of classification remains opaque, the fact of classification is significant enough, particularly when the terms *litteratus* and *laicus* are used for the purpose. Whatever the terms might mean, they also signify the notary's bureaucratic desire to maintain consistent, stable categories among multiple and hybrid forms of proof and authority. As was the case with the choristers, *litteratus* functions as a general, institutional category, though here the category has been abstracted from actual practice to a far greater degree. And whereas the choristers were deemed *litteratus* to distinguish them from other *clerici*, the witnesses are so labeled to separate them from nonreading layfolk. There is no indication that the term labels "minimal ability," but it does gesture toward a notion of uniformity on which the conception of "minimal ability" is predicated. It is the possibility of such a standard—one that is not dependent on a particular institutional function—that perhaps marks the most significant development in perceptions of literacy in the fourteenth century. The fragmentation of literate skills in the late medieval period surely owes much to the new and varied uses of writing and literate expertise introduced at that time. But variety and multiplicity of skills had been acknowledged, and celebrated, from the time of Leidrad's schools of readers and singers. With the imaginative construction of a uniform literacy, however, came a new mechanism to define institutional boundaries. As a result, the licit multiplicity of textual practice that once dignified the *litteratus* among his fellow readers slowly transformed into a sense of problematic fragmentation that made it difficult to distinguish the legitimate *clericus* from the pretender.

The uniformity imputed to the label *litteratus* did little to stabilize the confusing multiplicity of the *clerici*, at least in this context. The persisting interchangeability of the two terms, in fact, created even greater ambiguity in categorizing the minor clergy. Among the witnesses who gave oral testimony were five men who had served as *clerici* and one former chorister of the hospital. Of these, two of the *clerici* went on to become priests and are listed with their current titles. The others were clearly more difficult to classify. The ex-chorister and one of the ex-*clerici* are listed as *litterati*. One former clerk is labeled *clericus* in one list and *litteratus* in another. The last is ambiguously listed as "Robert Clerk, *litteratus*." While none seems to be serving in the hospital any longer, the current occupation of each is not made clear. It is possible that their labeling as *litterati* indicates that they were no longer considered clerks. Yet it is also possible that in the absence of a title that would identify a specific ecclesiastical position, *clericus* by itself was not considered a meaningful categorizing term—that it was coming to indicate more an occupation or ephemeral state than a vocation or permanent position. *Litteratus*, as used in the document as a whole, does seem capable of functioning as a meaningful title or credential, but insofar as it does, it is no longer the preserve solely of the clergy. And insofar as it denotes a skill abstracted from particular uses, it becomes increasingly difficult to specify what kind and what degree of knowledge might warrant such a credential.

Legit ut clericus: Reading in Benefit of Clergy Examinations

The dispute over St. Cross, and the terminological distinctions that arose in the course of that dispute, are unusual but not unique and were only made possible by the destabilization of the conceptual and ideological equation of *clericus* with *litteratus*. The categorization of non-clerical witnesses as literate, as well as the acceptance of those witnesses' authority in matters pertaining to documents, shows that the interchangeability of the two concepts was no longer fully symmetrical: while those in holy orders might be presumed to be literate, there is an acknowledgment that not all literates are necessarily clerics. This problem was compounded by the fact that many who considered themselves *clerici* were indistinguishable from literate layfolk, particularly if they were not currently following a clerical occupation.[36] Under such circumstances, it is not clear what, precisely, identified the *clericus* in minor orders as a member of the clergy.

The issues raised by the dispute provide a useful backdrop against which to consider the first articulation of a lower boundary of legitimate knowledge I will examine here: the adoption of reading tests as a means of authenticating the clerical status of prisoners who claimed benefit of clergy. These tests have been seen as a benchmark in the gradual shift in perceptions of literacy from maximum skill to minimal ability.[37] An official practice instituted throughout the realm with force of law, the reading tests articulated yet again the concept (if not the actual practice) of a uniform standard that would define an institutional boundary, distinguishing authoritative reading from all other modes of engaging the written word. A lower threshold of literacy was, in this case, situated in a legal context, one in which the stakes were dramatically high and, more generally, of substantial political import in defining how literacy might serve to structure relations between laity and clergy. Although the apparent function of such a divisive standard was to reinforce the identification of literacy with the clergy, some scholars have noted that in actual practice, it had the opposite effect of encouraging the laity to acquire literate skills in order to escape the death penalty by spuriously claiming benefit of clergy.[38] The number of literate laymen involved in the St. Cross dispute, as well as the difficulty of distinguishing them from their clerical or ex-clerical counterparts, would seem to substantiate the plausibility of such scheming.

Contemporary attitudes, furthermore, show an awareness of the laity's capacity to manipulate a standard of literacy to their own advantage. The tests were something of a scandal, known for their purported abuse by clever laymen who had learned the "neck verse" well enough to satisfy the ecclesiastical Ordinary that they could read.[39] Whether or not such abuses occurred in great numbers, the anecdotes and sarcastic comments manifest the widespread opinion that the reading tests created an opportunity for "authority" to be duped by those whom it was supposed to regulate. This sentiment, however, was merely a corollary to the underlying presumption that many of those who availed themselves of clerical privilege had no real claim to it. The presumption seems valid for those who never functioned in any remotely clerical capacity and did not gain their lettered knowledge under clerical auspices of any kind—a laborer who suddenly develops the capacity to "read" after two boys have coached him in jail, for example.[40] But for those whose experience with letters did involve the clergy in some fashion, like the St. Cross witness listed as "Robert Clerk, *litteratus*" or the ex-chorister who did not go on to a clerical career, such a presumption should not be automatic. Although it is difficult to determine how many could conceivably have classified themselves in this manner, the heavy contemporaneous emphasis on crafty and illegitimate knowledge of the neck verse appears selective in its attentions.

The extreme examples of fishmongers with two hours of death-row instruction are irresistibly sensational, but as the focus of analysis, they emphasize only individual strategies posited against presumptively unwitting or unconcerned ecclesiastical and secular authorities. Such is the case in Leona Gabel's study (which nonetheless remains definitive), in which the situation that enabled the fishmonger's manipulation seems the unforeseen result of disconnected developments: the dilution of the category *clericus* to include those in minor orders and the increasing literacy of the laity, combined with the increasing weight of the literacy test as proof of clergy, created a loophole that allowed the fishmonger to escape hanging.[41] Her detailed study of the Gaol Delivery Rolls did indeed show a consistent correlation between the emergence of the reading test as the primary evidence of clergy and the listing of unmistakably secular pursuits as the claimants' occupations, but turning from the loophole to the possible logic behind this emerging correlation might produce a different interpretation. In fact, to grant the interpretation that these claimants were criminous layfolk taking advantage of a loophole only prompts a more baffling question when considered from the perspective of ecclesiastical authority: why make literacy the definitive feature of clerical status precisely when it is increasingly becoming a less distinctive feature of the clerical life?

Part of the appeal of the reading test for the Church was the growing perception of its superiority over the other forms of proof. Literacy was coming to be perceived as a more stable feature of clerical identity than the visible signs of tonsure and habit. As an internalized capability, it was more continuous and authentic than tonsure—the symbol of the ritual of entry into holy orders—or clerical robes—a symbol (albeit less precise) of investiture—which up to this point had been the primary forms of proof.[42] The robes and tonsure that made up the *habitus clericalis*, in other words, came to be regarded as signs that were separable from the status they were meant to signify as well as from the ritual they were meant to commemorate—as trappings that did not truly denote clerical identity and could easily be donned illegitimately. Reading, by contrast, was a performance of clergy, a *habitus* of a different sort. It was also a more immediate and accessible demonstration than the authentication of ordination papers could provide. These values exemplify a particular understanding of literacy in which "faking it" would be difficult on epistemological grounds, but, more important, they bespeak a desire that "clergy" be just as stable and continuous as the proofs they demanded—that it be matter of being rather than of having. Viewed from this perspective, the growing reliance on the reading test can be seen as an almost reactionary gesture to restore a sense of permanent vocation to what was becoming for many a temporary occupation.

The examination to which claimants were subjected did not, after all, test reading ability as a fully objectified, abstract skill, transferable to any text or context, but rather consistently sought to verify the claimant's capacity to render that most clergial of clerical texts, the Psalter. The ideal of vocational literacy was grounded in the discourse of choral community, where the performance of the Psalter was at once an entry-level skill and a metonymic figure of clerical unity and hermeneutical enfranchisement. In the place of the communal recitation of psalms, benefit of clergy tests substituted a solo demonstration of the capacity for such performance as a precondition to a claimant's acceptance into the jurisdictional body of the clergy. In so doing, this highly attenuated form of psalmody was implicitly asserted as the sine qua non of clerical literacy.

Benefit of clergy examinations, however, were not liturgical perfor-mances. And they were surely not themselves performances of unity, as tests are by nature exclusionary. Thus although it appears that some of the values of choral community had been reasserted, it is critical to note that the prerequisite relation of group membership to skill acquisition had been reversed. Determining what abilities to isolate as legitimately clerical required the partial objectification of literacy in order to create a sense of a coherent institutional category defined by the possession of particular threshold skills. At the same time, however, the precise nature of those skills was not clearly articulated at an institutional level and remained far murkier than the nature of the skills designated by patrons of educational establishments. Most of the time it was the ecclesiastical Ordinary who himself had to determine what distinguished clerical reading—that is, authoritative reading—from other textual encounters, and he had then to isolate that skill in order to verify it in dubious cases. One unusually detailed entry from the Gaol Delivery Rolls shows this process.[43] In 1365, "John, son of Thomas Dennyson' Trotter senior," a prisoner accused of murder, insisted on his claim to clerical status. When given a psalter from which to read in order to prove his claim, the record states that "he could neither read nor syllabify in the book, except in certain places in which he had been instructed"; these passages he appeared to know "without the book through repetition."[44] Probing further, the secular judge gave him the psalter to read from again, but this time upside down. When John simply continued to read the verses he had learned, oblivious to the book's orientation, the ecclesiastical Ordinary refused to claim him as clergy and he remained under secular jurisdiction, having been declared "a layman and not literate, knowing nothing of letters (*laicus et non literatus nec aliqualiter sciuit literaturam*)."

It is unlikely that the examiners regularly resorted to the trick of turning the book upside down. Yet the example is instructive in that the tactic was calculated to isolate a particular skill within the claimant's performance: the ability to vocalize texts from the written page. Though this was surely not an activity that would tax the resources of the *bene litteratus*, it is not self-evidently a minimal or threshold skill. Indeed, it is not self-evidently a discrete skill at all except insofar as the Ordinary's discretion determined it to be one. In this respect, it is worth noticing how difficult it was for the judges to determine whether the claimant was gleaning the words from the page or from memory and, further, that the two strategies were articulated as contradictory—in short, that the claimant's rendering of the text resulted from either one or the other and that it mattered which one. The *bene litteratus*, trained in grammar and experienced in clerical texts, would (in the unlikely event that he did not know the psalm already) employ a number of inextricable strategies simultaneously in the complex matter of word recognition, including knowledge of letter forms, morphology, syntax, characteristic formulae, and intertextual reference, all of which can be said to require "memory" at some level. If these strategies were invisible or unremarkable to those who were charged with establishing a claimant's literacy, it is because by themselves they were not salient in the construction of clerical literacy invoked by the examinations. This construction, a legacy of the discourse of choral community, stressed performance from the Book above all other abilities, thereby articulating a skill that preceded other word recognition technologies as the ground of clerical knowledge: an isolatable connection to the written page and an unalloyed capacity to give it voice.

The unusual tactic used in this example is an extension of the formulaic expression regularly used to denote "minimal ability" in these tests: *legere aut silabicare*—"read or syllabify." The phrase more frequently shows up in the negative, to note that the claimant "could neither read nor syllabify" and therefore lacked the sine qua non of clerical literacy.[45] As a formulaic expression, its similarity to "reading and singing" should be obvious. Here, however, "reading" is contextualized by pairing it with "syllabifying," which affiliates the practice more decisively with the beginning stages of *lectio* in the grammatical curriculum. The emphasis nonetheless remains on *lectio* as inflected by the elementary educational/ liturgical practices that isolated performative ability from hermeneutical control, for the syllable is fundamentally a phonemic (rather than morphemic) unit—the smallest linguistic unit that can be sustained by the voice. "Reading or syllabifying" is not synonymous with "reading and singing," but it is clearly related and similarly situates skills manifested primarily in performance of sacred written texts as the lowest common denominator of clerical knowledge.

The reading tests thus legally instituted a particular form of performative ability as the definitive resource of clerical identity. Adapting the discourse of choral community to incorporate a larger and more diffuse group, they substituted common knowledge for communal practice. There were, then, broader ideological reasons to place performative practice at the entry level of clerical education, in addition to the more self-interested and pragmatic reasons promoted by liturgical benefactors. Yet the prestige of liturgical knowledge—the prestige that had sustained the song school—was much diminished in the process. Placing performative practice at the lowest level of learning by no means implied that clerical knowledge was reducible to reading or syllabifying but that clerical knowledge proceeded from the capacity and authority to vocalize sacred texts. For this reason, reading or syllabifying alone, even in these contexts, did not constitute the knowledge of the *litteratus*. While unsuccessful claimants like John, son of Thomas Dennyson' Trotter senior, are said (repeatedly, in his case) to be "not literate," successful claimants, at least from the reign of Richard II, do not warrant the title *litteratus* but are characterized by a statement about their clerical performance: "when the book had been handed over to him, he read like a cleric (*tradito ei libro . . . legit ut clericus*)."[46] Such abilities may have qualified the boys of St. Cross to be labeled *litterati*, but in a context such as this, where the nature of clerical identity and the prestige of clerical knowledge was at stake, it was not invoked to describe skills legally deemed minimal. The term *litteratus* and the honorific status the term maintained were rather applied only to those *clerici litterati* who stood in judgment upon the claimant.[47]

The formula *legit ut clericus* does nonetheless tacitly acknowledge non-clerical reading in however small a way, and it is the potential of such an acknowledgment that might help explain the correlation between the use of the reading test and the rise of claimants with stated non-clerical occupations. The case of John, son of Thomas Dennyson' Trotter senior is unusual for its detail but also because the claimant was denied benefit of clergy. Gabel states that the vast majority of these claimants of questionable status were successful in escaping lay jurisdiction.[48] If John, like the more successful bakers, barbers, and servants, was taking advantage of a loophole, as Gabel suggests, it cannot have been without clerical collusion. Indeed, if the purpose was to exclude either inauthentic clerics or inauthentic literacies, the conventional use not simply of the Psalter but of the same verse from the Psalter would be a preposterously obvious oversight. These inclusive gestures signal a desire to unify practice more than an effort to prevent spurious claims. To the extent that non-clerical reading is acknowledged, it is so that it can be reappropriated, if only by making it in the best interests of the claimant to situate his knowledge within the boundaries of the clerical. Producing a definitively clerical skill as a lowest common denominator of a set of increasingly diversified and fragmented literacies and practices allowed the clergy both to reassert the equivalence of literate competence with clerical identity and, conversely, to assert that all literate capabilities are fundamentally clerical in origin.

Psallite sapienter: Vicars Choral in the Choral Community

Though benefit of clergy examinations were a widespread phenomenon and reported abuses of the neck verse had achieved widespread infamy, the reading tests were only one of several boundaries of legitimate knowledge articulated in late medieval England. Among the other institutions that asserted such boundaries were the choral institutions themselves, where reactions against new uses of clerical knowledge resonated strongly with matters of liturgical practice constructed within the discourse of choral community. The terms of these assertions differed from those of the benefit of clergy exams. Particular choral institutions were not, after all, in a position to determine anyone's clerical status, though they were in a position to regulate clerical practices—textual and otherwise—within their own communities. In the process, they employed regulatory mechanisms similar to that of benefit of clergy examinations by asserting a boundary to define behavior appropriate to the clerical body, yet choral institutions were responding to a different set of anxieties. They perceived their communities to be unsettled less in terms of any diffusion of uses and users of literate skills than in terms of a breakdown of the relations of textual community precipitated by new forms of liturgical endowment. The larger stakes of these new forms will be discussed in greater detail in the next chapter, but the reactions to them in some choral institutions show how different aspects of the discourse of choral community were drawn upon to isolate components of clerical literacy as the boundary of legitimate knowledge.

In particular, choral institutions were invested not solely in the capacity to vocalize sacred texts but in the capacity for performance to serve as a resource of community. This understanding of community was closely linked to a specific conception of the nature and function of sacred language in mediating the presence of the divine. Although psalmody was clearly perceived as "musical"—witness the musical notation that distinguishes performance of the new song in the Derby Psalter—and informed performance would require knowledge of pitches, melodic formulae, and the musical structures of the Tonary,[49] references in the more quotidian records and collections of choral institutions—customaries, statutes, visitation records, and miscellanies—tend to focus more on matters of verbal articulation, and therefore matters of language, than on pitch. Complete elocution, synchronization, and uniformity are stressed to ensure that each syllable was correctly and communally uttered. The insistence on completeness in enunciation stems in part from grammatical epistemology, in which the text is constituted as an object of interpretation only by its vocalization. Yet the duty to perform the *opus Dei* also participated in the "conceptual economy" Richard Firth Green has associated with folklaw, which presumed that "all solemn agreements must partake of the corporeal ... and thus that any failure to honor them is a kind of tort, a breach of duty *in rem*." The rendering of sacred texts had a status analogous to oral contract, such that the words possessed "some of the qualities of a piece of property to be defended against the world."[50] These qualities come through clearly in stories about the "recording demon."[51] In the early thirteenth century, Jacques de Vitry related the story of a sack-carrying devil spied from the choir by celebrating monks. When asked about the contents of his sack, the demon replies, "These are the syllables and syncopated words and verses of the psalms which these very clerics in their matins stole from God; you can be sure I am keeping these diligently for their accusation."[52] By the fourteenth century, the demon had acquired a name—Titivillus—and his story, widely disseminated throughout Europe in the fourteenth and fifteenth centuries, culminated in the refrain,

Fragmina verborum Titivillus colligit horum
Quibus die mille vicibus se sarcinat ille.[53]

[Titivillus collects the fragments of those words, with
which he loads himself a thousand times a day.]

At stake in such stories was the integrity of the Word—both God's
and one's own—and the scandal of failing to maintain it generated a list of
opprobrious vernacular epithets to shame the offender: *forskyper*, *momelar*,
overleper, *overhupper*, and others.[54] The crime of the *overleper*, though, was
additionally one against the choral community in that "overlept" syllables
would invariably disturb the synchronization of the choir. Authoritative
directions for and critique of psalmody, in fact, most frequently sought to
ensure that one side of the choir was allowed to finish their verse before
the other side began the next and that singers maintained the medial inflectional pause within verses. Thomas Walsingham, while extolling the virtues
of Abbot Thomas (1349–96) in reforming the liturgy of St. Albans, reports
the abbot's direction that this pause be long enough that one could say
Ave Maria, gratia plena, dominus tecum before beginning the second half
of the verse.[55] This interpolation of putative *aves* underscores the abbot's
desire that the pauses signal not only unity but devotion. The medial pause
especially was stressed in reaction to the fear that choirs were, in fact, unified, but unified in their desire to rush through divine service as quickly
as possible, that the "work of God" was perceived as a burden to be per-
functorily dispatched in order to get on with more important matters. This
concern is echoed by William Langland in the C Version of *Piers Plowman*
when Liberum Arbitrium warns priests that they should "ouerhippe nat
for hastite" in the performance of services.[56] Priests, according to Liberum
Arbitrium, should say their masses "lelly" (C 17.117), with respect to God,
for whom the work is performed, and for its own sake—they should not
allow their loyalties to lie elsewhere.

Loyalty to the text was the basis of community. Unity within the
choir—and within the larger Christian community—was achieved by its
members granting sovereignty to the text and relinquishing all self-interest.
This sentiment was often expressed in terms of an intrasubjective unity
between intent and utterance. A fifteenth-century collection of musical
treatises contains (in addition to the Titivillus story) some verses that
relate the individual mind to the communal voice.

Psallite deuote, distincte metra tenete,
Vocibus estote concordes, vana cauete.
Nam vox frustatur si mens hinc inde vagatur;
Vox sepe quassatur si mens vana meditatur[57]

[Sing with devotion, keep clearly the meter,
Let your voices be harmonious, be wary of vanity,
For the voice fractures if the mind wanders here and there;
The voice is often shattered if the mind contemplates vain things.]

In moving from imperative to generalized precept, the writer of these verses exemplifies the unification he extols by shifting from the plural *vocibus estote concordes* (lit. "be in agreement with your voices") to the singular *vox*. The singer who lets his mind wander from the words or focuses instead on the beauty of his own voice threatens to disrupt the univocality of the group. The reading tests undertaken to claim benefit of clergy encouraged just such a rupture between speech act and intent through the cultivation of self-interest, but similar opportunities could be pursued by the unequivocally clerical within choral institutions in ways that directly impinged upon their performances of the *opus Dei*.

Benefactions of private liturgy superimposed contracts between mortal individuals onto the cleric's oral contract with God.[58] Within these more complicated relations the instrumental qualities of sacred language became potentially abstracted or even alienable from their performers, allowing priests, clerks, and choristers to turn their sacred knowledge into commodifiable craft knowledge, geared primarily toward the creation of a product. Walsingham, complaining about the mundane style of psalmody before Abbot Thomas's reforms, states that "formerly psalmody was sung without rests, without pauses, in the manner of smiths who strike heated iron, which seemed absurd to one [sc. Abbot Thomas] so ardently devoted to holy religion."[59] The monks Walsingham refers to are not, it is true, singing chantry masses, and yet such private masses were celebrated in the same locations (even at monasteries and nunneries) and sometimes at the same time as the *opus Dei* or High Mass.[60] Langland registers the transferability of these essentially different performative contexts: in the B Version, Anima admonishes those who "ouerhippe" in "Office and Houres"[61]—the part of the liturgy most closely associated with the discourse of choral community—whereas in the C Version priests are warned against hurried performance of the Mass—which could equally apply to the chantry priest, parish priest, or monk.

The Office, for that matter, was not entirely free of the potential for alienation and self-interest, particularly at secular cathedrals, where canons had long since deputed vicars to perform the *opus Dei* for them. The diminished prestige of reading and singing that had resulted from their articulation as lowest common denominator skills and as currency for aspiring choristers also helped create a clerical service class who exchanged their daily performance for a fixed stipend, freeing canons and other more dignified ecclesiasts from the burden of residency and choral duties. The position of "vicar choral" thus already represented the alienation of singing duties by absent canons. Those who sang for them, furthermore, were often younger clerks waiting to take priests' orders or priests waiting for benefices,[62] providing them with their own self-interested desires that, if fulfilled, might well result in their leaving the choir. In many cases, then, vicars choral and singing clerks elsewhere were as "alienated" from their liturgical labor as the chantry priests were.

The uncomfortable presence of alienated singers within the choir registered for some in the same manner as the menacing Jews/layfolk of the Derby Psalter. Another Psalm 97 initial from an English psalter dated to the first half of the fourteenth century represents this possibility (Fig. 4). The choir's new song in this case is figured by the letters "quare fremu//" visible on their communal page—the incipit of Psalm 2, *Quare fremuerunt*: "Why have the Gentiles raged, and the people devised vain things? The kings of the earth stood up, and the princes came together as one, against the Lord, and against his Christ."[63] Conventionally read as a messianic prophecy, the psalm was sung on both Good Friday and Easter, but a reference that isolates this psalm in particular in the context of the "new song" occurs in Acts 4:24-30, which tells of the body of believers who, upon hearing Peter and John tell of their arrest by the chief priests and Sadducees, spontaneously "lifted their voice to God, as with a single mind" (*unianimiter levaverunt vocem ad Deum*) and prayed the opening verses of Psalm 2 as a prophecy newly fulfilled, equating the Sadducees with the psalm's conspiratorial princes. The choral community in this instance, then, imagines itself as reprising this performance in which the early church acknowledges the threat of its prophesied persecution. As in the initial of the Derby Psalter, there is a marginal reader with a private volume and the bestial legs of a grotesque. This reader, however, is not figured as the hermeneutical Other but a tonsured cleric—one who seems to represent

Figure 4. Initial "C" of Psalm 97 (*Cantate Domino canticum novum*) in the "Elles-mere" Psalter, first half of the fourteenth century, with errant cleric-grotesque in the margin. San Marino, Huntington Library, MS EL 9 H 17, f. 129v. Reproduced by permission of the Huntington Library, San Marino, California.

the conflict between the unified choral *vox* and the *mens vagans*: while his clerical torso and head continue to sing with the choir, his grotesque bot-tom half pulls him in the opposite direction, as if wandering toward the vain imaginings of the people outside the choir.

This initial has a striking counterpart in a conflict recorded in one of the surviving Chapter Act Books of Salisbury Cathedral.[64] In 1388/9, Wil-liam Elys, vicar choral of Salisbury, appeared before the chapter to answer to various charges. Although he had been a vicar for six years, he had never presented himself for examination in the liturgical texts he was to have memorized, which he was supposed to have done after his first year. The record continues with his other crimes, alleging

quod idem Willelmus solitus fuit et est in villa post et ante prandium et multociens Sarisburiensi de nocte absque causa racionabile spaciatur et vagatur, et quod libente et frequenter contendit et insurgit contra vicarios in ecclesia et alibi verbis contumeliosis, et quod in nocte octauarum sancti Johanni Euangeliste nesciuit canere sine libro aliquod responsorium seruicij illius diei cum vicarij socijs suis in choris, et quod eadem nocte in matutinis contendebat cum socijs suis vicarius in choro et in ecclesia et ipsos horribiliter maledixit vnde turbabatur pax inter ipsos vicarios ac ira eodem generauitur in scandalum magnum ipsius ecclesie et perniciosum exemplum aliorum.

[that this same William was and is accustomed to be in town after and before supper and often walks about and wanders in Salisbury at night without reasonable cause; and that he freely and frequently contends and rises up against the vicars in the church and elsewhere with contumelious words; and that on the night of the Octave of St. John the Apostle (3 Jan.), he was unable to sing any of the responsories of the service of that day with his fellow vicars in the choir without the book; and that on the same night at matins he contended with his fellow vicars in the choir and in the church and horribly cursed them, whereby the peace among the vicars was disturbed and wrath provoked among them, to the great scandal of this church and setting a pernicious example to others.]

Although William's failure to memorize his services and submit himself to examination is the first item mentioned, it is clearly not what got him into trouble, for if the chapter wanted to be strict on this matter they would have dealt with him five years earlier. Nor was it that he did not know those particular responsories; as we shall see, he did not know any of his services very well. It was rather his picking a fight with his fellow vicars during service that seems to have been the final straw for the chapter—his substitutions of disruptive curses for the words he did not know.[65]

William's disruption of the services, however, was not his only crime against the community. His faulty singing is linked as if by a transparent logic to his suspicious perambulations in the town, another bodily manifestation of the *mens vagans*. With these accusations, William's actions are associated with another ideological construction prevalent in late fourteenth-century England: that of the vagrant whose unlicensed speech disrupts the general peace. This construction was already a complex amalgam, related to economic concerns surrounding laborers whose mobility threatened traditional manorial ties and further linked with the potential of seditious speech after 1381. These connections and their broader implications have been documented and discussed by others,[66] but what is important to note in this context is the affiliation of the vicar's suspicious mobility with his verbal labor. Invoking the image of the disruptive wanderer allows William's faulty singing to be perceived not merely as a result of his ineptitude or laziness but as symptomatic of a threat he posed to the choral community and, ultimately, to clerical identity.

Equating the vicar's behavior and his communal participation with his capacity to perform liturgical texts, conversely, allowed the chapter to regulate his behavior by scrutinizing his textual knowledge. Although the chapter surely could have merely censured his behavior, they chose instead to submit him to his formal examination. While William's clerical status was obviously not at issue, the chapter's strategy was similar to that used in benefit of clergy examinations in that a lower threshold of knowledge was determined as a standard by which to classify and regulate acceptable literate practices. The lower threshold articulated in William's case even presents the same distinction between memory of texts and the capacity to vocalize from the page, but the subordination in his case was the opposite: value here was placed on his ability to sing without the book. Having begun the proceedings by noting William's tardiness in presenting himself for examination, the chapter goes on to conduct the examination itself.

Idem dominus locumtenens de consensu ipsius capituli et ad peticionem eiusdem Willelmi eundem in psalterio de psalmo Quam bonus, in ympnario, Tu civitatis vnitas [*sic*],[67] in antiphonario, de responsorijs ad matitutinas in octauas sancti Johanni Euangeliste et de alijs in psalterio, ympnario et antiphonario examinauit. Qui sic examinatus nec psalmum nec ympnum nec responsorium vel unum vel aliud de quo tunc examinatus erat sciuit qui in aliquo dicere seu reddere sine libro.

[The president, with the consent of the chapter and at the petition of the said William, examined him in the Psalter, the psalm *Quam bonus*, in the Hymnal, *Tu ciuitatis vnitas*, in the Antiphoner, the responsories at matins on the octave of St. John the Apostle; and others in the Psalter, Hymnal, and Antiphoner. And he, having been thus examined, was able to say or render neither the psalm, nor the hymn, nor the responsories, not the one nor the other of anything in which he had been examined in any way without the book.]

The expectation of such extensive repertory knowledge—here, full memorization of the Psalter, Hymnal, and Antiphoner—was not at all uncommon. It could even function as a source of communal identity and pride, as at Lincoln Cathedral where the choir members even performed the lessons (usually read from the book) from memory.[68] Lack of knowledge, within this logic, was conversely a source of shame. William's examination was less a test than a form of public humiliation, as they tested his knowledge of the very responsories he had been unable to sing the day before.[69] Ultimately repertory knowledge served as a means of discipline, not simply in William's ritual shaming but in his punishment: he was ordered to spend the next five weeks learning his services, during which time he was not to wear a habit in church or receive commons, so that he might better accomplish the task. This temporary banishment from the choral community was a form of penance; only after fully submitting himself to the sovereign text would he be allowed to reenter the group.

The testing of required knowledge hints toward a transformation similar to that seen in benefit of clergy hearings in that knowledge becomes a prerequisite to group membership. Memorization had been an ideal of the choral community for some time, but consistent testing of that ideal, as well as imposing punishment for failure, is another matter. Although the frequency of such tests is impossible to ascertain, extant records suggest that textual discipline of this sort was strategically deployed rather than uniformly upheld. It was, furthermore, deployed especially in relation to this service class in ways that betray investments beyond a desire for vocal concord. William Elys, after all, had gone for years without taking his examination and was only forced to take it because the chapter perceived him to be a troublemaker. And while his disciplinary memorization seems to fit his crime, the same punishment was prescribed for other erring vicars whose inability to render the services is not mentioned (let alone tested). In 1385/6, Roger Gydy received a similar injunction to learn his services after impregnating a certain "Agnes" in town, as did John Hullyng, on account of his own *lapsus carnis*, compounded by his frequenting of taverns.[70] Memorization was in these cases considered a way to stabilize both bodily and moral vagrancy. Both of these types of vagrancy were, however, subordinate to (and metonymic of) the potential vagrancy of the mind that mercenary reading and singing might engender. The full embodiment of texts they hoped would result—the ability to render any chant given only the incipit—was meant to guarantee the continuity of the relationship between performer and text. Those who depended on the page had only a transitory connection to the text, one that ended with the completion of the service. Such a transitory relationship bore too much resemblance to other forms of "alienated" verbal labor, whether the chantry priest to his mass or the chancery clerk to the texts he copied, or perhaps even to the criminous "clerk" who, after convincingly rendering the neck verse, might never read—or sing—it again.

Vicars choral could be in either major or minor orders, but those who were priests were marked with an ambiguity similar to that of the minor clergy, since they had no title or benefice that situated them securely within the ecclesiastical structure. Given that they partook of the liminal status that defined the various *clerici* discussed earlier in this chapter, it is significant that the vicars alone were made to bear the onus of memorization and performance. Canons or prebendaries, whose positions entitled them to an ecclesiastical living and "a stall in the choir," were not always required to perform at Mass and Office and were not expected to know their services completely—or at least it was openly acknowledged that they did not: at Wells Cathedral, canons were given the coaxing incentive that they might have books and lights if they attended matins, provided that they did not allow the vicars to cheat by looking on with them.[71] Vicars choral differed from other ambiguous classes of clergy, however, because they did have a connection (albeit not one of enfranchisement) to a choir with all its discursive associations and because they could be considered as a body within that community.[72] Perceived as the performing body within the larger group, vicars choral at these institutions could indeed be said to have functioned as vicarious choirs—as a group that served to contain and control the higher clergy's emerging preoccupations with their own relationship to sacred texts and the place of the liturgy within competing temporal and spiritual economies. To the degree that the textual disciplining of vicars choral did serve such a purpose, the anxieties that provoked those strategies were similar to those that generated the reading tests for claims of benefit of clergy. Although the practices isolated opposite skills, they were both motivated by the clergy's fears about the fragmentation of literacies and clerical communities as well as how this fragmentation might ultimately destroy the foundation of clerical hegemony.

The skills of "reading and syllabifying" practiced by successful claimants of benefit of clergy provide a clear example of the unmooring of ritualized, performative scriptural reading from its original institutional context. The memory tests and textual discipline visited upon vicars choral, however, present a different dynamic that provides useful nuances to the process of "unmooring." Textual knowledge and performance remain within the choral community, but were manifested as more aggressive assertions of performative ability that defined the lower boundary of legitimate knowledge on which membership in the choral community depended. These assertions were responses to what were perceived as new and potentially disruptive textual practices within and beyond the choir. The instability that textual discipline sought to regulate was (as I argued in the case of benefit of clergy tests as well) not the product of lay usurpation but rather a necessary effect of the extension of the forms of power the discourse of choral community invested in the choir. The "unmooring" to which I refer is meant to distinguish this extension from narratives of supplantation that have been prominent in histories of literacy, yet this "unmooring" did not involve dislocation as much as it involved diffusion into new institutional contexts where "reading and singing" might ritualize different kinds of social relations. Liturgy remained a central cultural practice and a central practice of literacy, since as long as clerical power was derived from ecclesiastical stewardship of sacred texts, it would continue to be located and reproduced in institutions of reading. What had changed was the nature of the relations enacted by the performance of texts, which in turn would affect the relationship of the performer to the text itself. These relationships would become critical to the dialectical self-definition of both the clergy and the laity.

3

Legere et non intellegere negligere est:
The Politics of Understanding

IN 1387, SEVENTEEN YEARS after he had started proceedings against the masters of St. Cross, William Wykeham made a visitation of the monastic cathedral of St. Swithun's, Winchester. Among the injunctions he delivered to the monks was a complaint about the performance of divine service.

Item quia nonulli conmonachi et confratres ecclesie nostre predicte minime sapiunt in litteratura, non intelligentes quid legant, sed quasi prorsus ignorantes dum psallent vel legunt accentum breuem pro longo ponu[n]t pluries et econtra, et per nemora gradientes sanam scripturarum intellectum adulterant multociens et peruertunt fitque vt dum scripturas sacras non sapiant ad perpetrandum illicita prouiores reddant.[1]

[Also, because some of the co-monks and co-brethren of our church aforesaid know very little of grammar, not understanding what they read, but rather as if ignorant of letters, they put a short syllable in the place of a long one, and contrariwise, while reading and singing and, straying to the wilderness, frequently adulterate and pervert the sound meaning of scripture, such that, since they do not know the sacred scriptures, they are more likely to turn to illicit things.]

Wykeham's condemnation of his wayward monks invokes the concerns for correct execution elaborated in the discourse of choral community, yet the correspondence he posits between syllable length and understanding participates in a different economy of verbal exchange from that articulated in the Titivillus myth. Although Wykeham similarly focuses on the integrity of the syllable, the lapse for which he faults the monks differs from the transgressions against communal synchrony—the sins of the *overleper*. Whereas the *overleper*'s misdeed cheated God of the syllables due to him, the negligence of the monks of St. Swithun's is turned inward and affects the individual monk's spiritual health. Syllables are important to Wykeham

not because of the material nature of God's *verba* but because misaccen-
tuation impedes the reduction of *verba* to *res*. What they render to God,
in turn, stems from the faith derived from knowledge of *res*. The verbal
economy implied by emphasis on understanding, in other words, depends
on a discourse of interiority in which the performer's interior becomes the
site of exchange.

Wykeham's injunction thus seems to represent a change in the
way people imagined their relationship to the performed Word. At first
glance, this change might seem the opposite of what I have been describing as "unmooring." The requirement of an interiorized relationship to
liturgical texts appears to demand a more integrated form of compliance
with textual discipline, a response more thoroughly grounded in the institutions of *grammatica*, if not of choral community, than the verbatim
recall required of William Elys. Such a connection to grammatical discourse is only underscored by Wykeham's mandate for formal grammar
instruction for the "insufficiently lettered" of the cathedral community
to resolve the problem.[2] By invoking *grammatica*, he is able to call upon
the sense of organic unity with which it links the skill of *lectio* governing the monks' accentuation of their texts with broader knowledge of
litteratura, such that knowledge of one implies knowledge of the other.
Ironically, accentuation, as informed by the principles of grammatical
lectio, was reducible to a set of rules that could be learned independently
of the semantic and syntactic knowledge that would enable the monks
to construe meaning from the words they read and sang.[3] This irony
calls attention to the tenuous nature of his position, suggesting that his
assertion of the grammatical is a reaction to the danger of errancy that
reading and singing allows.

More critical than the motivation is the focus of his efforts. In calling
attention to syllable length, Wykeham seeks a criterion for distinguishing
learned from unlearned performance. More important, learned performance
involves the possession of "understanding," for which syllable length serves
as audible indicator. He even prefaces the final part of his injunction with a
quotation from the opening of the elementary grammar text, the *Disticha
Catonis*, with which he neatly sums up the problem: "legere et non intellegere negligere est"—"to read without understanding is to neglect" (lit.
"not to read at all").[4] This *sententia* betrays a second, more important irony
in his position: while it represents understanding as a self-evident necessity,
Wykeham's rendering of the passage registers for us the unacknowledged
slippage in the definition of understanding between the time of the *Disticha*

and his own. Since the aphorism's original audience presumably consisted of native Latin speakers, the quality of the estrangement characterized as "neglect" was not the linguistic incompetence Wykeham seems to have in mind. His accusation, in its self-conscious effort to restore understanding to St. Swithun's choral performances, acknowledges the radical separability, in addition to the malleability, of "understanding" in the performance of sacred texts. By admitting the possibility of uninformed performance, his complaint, and many others like it, adumbrated a concept of "understanding" that characterized a discrete relation to sacred texts, one that mere familiarity, or even the capacity to perform them, did not necessarily presume. Within the terms of grammatical methodology, understanding had been the irreducible product of training in *litteratura*—an accomplishment more than a competence. By the late fourteenth century, however, Lollard controversies, the Oxford translation debates, and other late medieval conflicts I have thus far loosely characterized as "hermeneutical struggles" make clear that "understanding" had become a site of contest, a textual relation potentially separable from both latinity and clerical identity, and one more urgently in need of monitoring.[5]

This separability is usually associated with appropriations of understanding to the vernacular and with the capacity of those outside clerical institutions to master religious texts and theological concepts. Injunctions like Wykeham's, however, remind us that the latinate practices of reading and singing also played a role in determining the parameters and value of "understanding." Instead of appropriating understanding to new audiences and linguistic environments, those engaged in the practices associated with reading and singing tended to explore the consequences of and compensations for the absence of understanding. This exploration has received little attention in modern scholarship, possibly because it was represented as the rejection, rather than the cultivation, of certain textual practices. More specifically, it was represented as the rejection of absence itself. The equation of understanding with grammar suppressed questions of precisely how much textual, syntactic, or lexical knowledge one needed to understand, as is particularly apparent in Wykeham's totalizing litmus test. Concerns were rather centered on the presumption of complete ignorance and inner absence. Alongside the opprobrious labels contrived for those who "overlept" syllables, an analogous list of vernacular nonce-verbs arose to describe absent-minded performances of prayer that lacked the proper interior investment: *mumeling, blabbering, bumbling.* Marked by reduplicated bilabial consonants, these verbs signify "mindless" repetition by figuring the lips as a bodily impediment to the pure vocality—the vocative "O"—of spiritual invocation.[6]

In this respect, complaints such as Wykeham's might appear to spurn what anthropologists refer to as "formalism," yet such a characterization would be misleading. "Formalism" is a problematic concept, since even its most neutral uses identify as "form" an exteriority that is generally equated with the absence of interior motivation—an equation that reinstalls the opposition of thought to action. It is even more problematic to apply to textual practices, since the absence some lamented in liturgical practice was not the product of orality or ritual, with which formalism is chiefly associated, but of writing itself. The liturgy was the principal demonstration of the centrality of writing to the Christian community. As such, there was always the possibility that it could display writing's deficiencies—its capacity merely to "repeat without knowing," as Derrida put it.[7] The very possibility of "mindless" repetition is a performative realization of the idea that scripture, as a substitute for the voice of God, can acknowledge the absence of the divine rather than serve as the medium of its presence. The terms in which such a lack was perceived, however, were subject to change—as the difference between iterations of the *Disticha Catonis* attests—as were the social meanings attached to it. Complaints about the neglect of understanding are thus not a rejection of formalism but an articulation of exteriority against which an interiorized relationship of understanding is implicitly figured as superior.

"Understanding" is no more unitary than literacy; like literacy, it takes different forms in different social settings. The exteriorized relationship to sacred language lamented as a lack of understanding in liturgical performance was not simply the obverse of the interiorized mastery associated with experiments in vernacular hermeneutics. That which was mourned in such complaints was not the intellectual mastery we associate with hermeneutical enfranchisement but a counterpart to it. The discourse of spiritual interiority exemplified in Wykeham's injunction, despite the hope it places in *grammatica*, is an extension and transformation of an older construction of liturgical practice. This construction of felicitous scriptural interaction is centered in the Liturgy of the Word and involves the publication of scripture for the purposes of instruction. Louis Althusser's concept of "interpellation" is helpful in describing the performative dynamics upon which this construction depends.[8] In his analysis of political subject formation, Althusser states that subjects recognize themselves as integrated beings in the process of being "hailed" or "interpellated" by ideology. Interpellation is for him a way to acknowledge the pervasiveness of ideology, its formative effects on unconscious as well as conscious thought. The simple act of recognizing oneself as the addressee of a policeman's "Hey, you there!" constitutes us as subjects in ideology.[9] The value of Althusser's discussion for my purposes, however, lies in the fact that "ritual"—specifically Judeo-Christian ritual—is among the chief conceptual vehicles he uses to describe these unconscious compulsions.[10] The policeman's power is modeled on that of the divine voice that "makes what it names, but … also subordinates what it makes."[11] At some risk of circularity, my use of his terminology to analyze ritual practice effectively reverses the conceptual polarity of his analysis—tenor for vehicle, as it were—though my aims are similar to his in my effort to focus on aspects of social (and in my case, textual) practice that may lie outside conscious thought. Whether or not the divine voice is a useful model for the workings of modern ideology,[12] it is precisely this power that liturgy ritualizes in its performance of the divine voice as preserved in scripture. Examining this performative dynamic illuminates a particular model of understanding that complements that produced by grammatical discourse and thus lends insight into the complex processes by which ritualized textual practice mediates social relations.

The mode of scriptural interpellation to which I refer has its clearest exemplification in *The Confessions*, when Augustine contextualizes the moment of his conversion by telling the story of St. Anthony.[13] Upon entering a church during the gospel lesson, Anthony heard a passage from Matthew that he perceived as an urgent mandate from the Lord: "Go home and sell all that belongs to you … then come back and follow me" (Matt. 19:21). Understanding the words to be directed specifically to him, Anthony sold his possessions and began a life of renunciation and solitude. Augustine's recollection of the story, in turn, prompts him to interpret the preternatural voice telling him to "take it and read" as a call from the divine to allow scripture to hail him as well, whereupon he allows his Bible to fall open at random and reads the first passage he sees. The dynamics of both of these interpellative moments are modeled on "the divine power of naming"[14]—the response to the call of the sacred voice, by which the subject is constituted in relation to the divine presence (the "Other Subject"), as when God hails Abraham or Paul by calling their names, compelling their subjection. But whereas in these paradigmatic moments of biblical interpellation God does indeed name his subjects, Augustine shows God hailing Anthony through the gospels. Anthony, in other words, recognizes the immediacy of the divine presence in the voicing of the text—a presence who speaks directly and specifically to him in that particular moment—and subjects himself to its authority. Although this recognition involves interpretive acts of particularization, recontextualization, and internalization, understanding arrives as *Gestalt*, synonymous with hearing itself. It is the hearing of those who have ears.[15]

The understanding I am describing as interpellation is therefore not the product of self-conscious hermeneutical activity. Indeed, the ultimate desire that Augustine, among others, expresses is for the immediacy of divine revelation that obviates the need for hermeneutics altogether, even though that immediacy is still experienced in relation to the written word. This necessary desire for subjection to the Word was as important to the distribution of power in late medieval religious politics as the desire for mastery associated with hermeneutics. Liturgy dramatizes both of these desires simultaneously. On the one hand, it ritualizes the publication of scripture, thereby dramatizing its potential to interpellate subjects. On the other, it demonstrates the act of publication as the exclusive prerogative of clerics, affirming the textual mastery on which their stewardship is predicated. The very nature of clerical authority dictates that the two desires be in tension. Because clerical forms of domination were exercised by means of an institutional authority to which one was permitted access, as opposed to a sovereign power that one embodies, clerical subjection to the institutional performance of the Word was as important as lay subjection to clerical authority. Commentaries on the liturgy frequently mention the silent and respectful attention that those in the choir should give to lessons, in particular to the reading of the gospel, as the scripture most closely associated with the *vox Dei*.[16] Wykeham's complaint, as well as the rigorous oversight of the Chapter of Salisbury,[17] shows how liturgy was a venue for regulating the behavior of errant clerics, but the mandate to submit oneself to the text applied to everyone. At the same time, however, the sanctity of scripture as the primary resource of clerical authority had to be perpetually affirmed through ritualized publication—a process that required both stable liturgical institutions and authorized clerics to oversee them. Clerical mastery was therefore necessary to sacralize the very text to which they were to subject themselves.

This tension is evident in Augustine's anecdote in ways that suggest more was at stake than protecting clerical power. In both Anthony's and his own case, the divine source of their hailing is authenticated by the fact that it arrives at a time or place not structured by human institutions or intentions. Anthony simply "happened" to enter the church while the gospel was being read and Augustine is converted in a garden whose symbolic, edenic associations place it outside ecclesiastical structures entirely. Both stories serve to show God's power and the power of scripture to interpellate subjects unaided, thereby establishing a divine presence whose authority exceeds that of the ecclesiastical institution founded upon it. Yet both conversion stories still derive some of their authenticity not simply from scripture but from the authorized publication of scripture. What Anthony heard seemingly at random was nonetheless an institutional performance; and even though Augustine heard the divine command to read outside of that setting, he cites St. Anthony's story as an authenticating precedent in order to associate his reading of the epistles with the publication of the gospel. These veiled invocations of institutional authority are not intended primarily to maintain ecclesiastical dominance but to serve the more critical purpose of sacralizing the voice that each hears, situating it definitively outside quotidian experience and thus at a distance from the subject's interpretive agency. In doing so they fend off the potentially devastating disenchantment lurking beneath all acts of sacred reading that acknowledge the reader's interiority: the possibility that meaning derives from the subject rather than from the divine presence.[18]

If the threat of disenchantment lay at the heart of the tensions surrounding understanding, it was almost by definition an issue not admissible to conscious speculation. More commonly the matters that arose around the delicate balancing of sacralization and regulation were assimilated to the already politicized dialectics of Latin vs. vernacular and clergy vs. laity. The terms in which such matters were debated were furthermore subject to change under different social and economic pressures. "The politics of understanding" refers to the debates and practical explorations in which the topic of "understanding," with all its inner tensions, became a focal point in determining how and what kinds of social and economic relations would be enacted by textual and literate practice—above all, for my purposes, in liturgical and devotional performance. In the first part of this chapter, I will consider understanding as it relates to the increasing attention paid to the status and content of lay speech during divine worship as well as to the cultivation of devotional speech as a private, and distinctively lay, counterpart to the public, clerical performance. The bifurcation of the liturgical and the devotional put particular pressure on the tension between mastery and subjection in the ritualized speech of the clergy. In the second part of this chapter, I will turn to the concerns about clerical understanding related to this development—concerns that were, as I will show, also strongly influenced first by new forms of liturgical endowment and the new socioeconomic relations they forged and then, much more intensely, by the socioeconomic upheavals of the Black Death.

The Manner of Hearing Mass and Constructions of Lay Speech

The same period that saw a growing interest in choristers at choral institutions also saw a more self-conscious interest in the laity and their participation in the faith, as exemplified by the promulgation of the Lambeth Councils of 1281, in which Archbishop Pecham set forth the minimal knowledge of the faith the laity should have.[19] Though the nature of participation in the Mass was not explicitly part of Pecham's program, it nonetheless was on the minds of writers of pastoral literature. Roughly contemporary with texts designed to convey the elements of faith in Pecham's Syllabus, various writings devoted to instructing layfolk on proper conduct during Mass begin to appear in English from the early fourteenth century.[20] That such instruction was thought necessary stands to reason. If part of the motivation behind Pecham's Syllabus was to assert the terms of Christian textual community more broadly, such a project required that even layfolk gain some familiarity with the faith's most basic constitutive texts, especially those sacralized in liturgical performance. Put another way, part of the process of strengthening the faith that sustained the Christian community involved finding more effective ways for its members to be interpellated. The liturgy, which ritualized interpellation, would be a logical point of departure for achieving this goal. Yet the liturgy also set lay performance and reception of sacred texts in close proximity to clerical performance and reception. Considering this proximity forced the issue of understanding and its potential contradictions. Since efforts were being made to familiarize the laity with at least some of the sacred repertoire that constituted clerical literacy, understanding became an even more important symbol of the clergy's exclusive mastery of that repertoire. The clergy's proprietary claims to understanding, however, created a pastoral dilemma: if the laity by definition cannot understand, how can they be interpellated?

Treatises on "the manner and meed of the Mass" attempt to resolve this dilemma. They survive in English in at least thirty manuscripts, from which several versions have been collated in the Early English Text Society's editorially titled volume, *The Lay Folks' Mass Book*.[21] They appear to envision various audiences: some imagine a noble audience, some a more general one, and at least one imagines an audience of religious.[22] Though these audiences are not exclusively lay or even, in some cases, exclusively illiterate, they are primarily linked by the fact that they do not actively participate in the celebration of the Mass and are thus constituted by the dialectic of clergy and laity (or *lerid* and *lewid*) as enacted in the liturgy. *The Lay Folks' Mass Book* might be considered one of the early fourteenth-century "harbingers" of vernacular theology, yet these Mass treatises did not try to erase the distinction between illiterate and literate, as has been said of later texts associated with that label.[23] Although they share with other vernacular religious texts the generative conceit that they offer guidance to the *lewid* who do not understand Latin,[24] their discussions could scarcely be called speculative and involve little in the way of translating authoritative Latin texts. Guidance, rather, generally consists of advising their audiences how to react to the words they do not understand. In this manner they seek to fulfill the dual purpose of inventing forms of engagement in the Mass for the laity while affirming the distinctiveness of the clergy's own performance.

The first level of engagement for those who do not perform in the Mass is to "hear" it, hence the common description of the topic of these treatises as "how to hear Mass." This "hearing," however, is not the interpellative hearing synonymous with understanding. It does not imply any capacity for linguistic discrimination (i.e., it does not require "listening"). Nor does it even require the hearer to engage the language of the Mass at all but refers to juridical "hearing," in the sense of acting as witness to the sacrificial event. Insofar as it might pertain to the language of the Mass, "hearing" involves attending to its illocutionary force and its perlocutionary effects.[25] Readers are told how to modulate their attention in accordance with the ceremonial rhythms of the service—what to attend to, what prayers they might say at any given moment, and for whom to pray. "Hearing" Mass, therefore, does not even require the hearer to be silent, though lay speech is generally synchronized to function as a private and inaudible counterpoint to the public speech of the service. Most important, "hearing," in this sense, provides a meaningful connection to the ritual that does not require grammatical understanding.

This connection, however, still falls short of interpellation. At the very least, it fails to account for the specific moments in the service in which interpellation is most clearly ritualized. Chief among these moments was the reading of the gospel, to which a special status was accorded. Not only was it the closest approximation of the *vox Dei* whose presence underwrote the authority of all other speech acts in the service, it was for this reason also the most obvious symbolic reiteration of interpellation. The ritual decorum particular to the gospel lesson underscores this interpretation. Latin commentaries on divine service, for example, state that the choir should remain seated during other lessons, but stand at the gospel.[26] In similar ritual acknowledgment of the primal authority of the divine voice ventriloquized in the gospel lesson, vernacular treatises teach the laity, who are told to pray during most other parts of the service, to remain silent during the reading of the gospel. A version of the *Lay Folks' Mass Book*, found in British Library MS Royal 17 B.xvii, instructs, "Whils hit is red, speke þou noght,/bot þenk on him þat dere þe boght" (B. 183–84). The advice to let the mind dwell upon Christ rather than attend to the lesson itself, however, suggests that the writer is primarily concerned with maintaining the ritual decorum of the moment by having the laity provide the outward appearance of listening rather than with the laity's understanding as such.

Mimicking the external appearance of understanding is part of the compromise this writer arrives at after sorting through the conflicts inherent in understanding. The Royal MS treatise introduces its discussion of the gospel lesson by stressing that all are subject to the words of Christ.

> bothe þo reders & þo herers
> has mykil nede, me þenk of lerers,
> how þai shulde rede, & þai shulde here
> þo wordes of god, so leue & dere.
> Men aght to haue ful mikel drede,
> when þai shuld here or els hit rede. (B. 163–68)

The "hearers" would presumably include all who were not reading, whether cleric or lay. Together with the reader, described as "an erthly mon" (B. 161), they all submit to the power of the Word. This communal submission, however, is not left to imply a lack of differentiation between clergy and laity. The insignificant distinction between reader and hearer is soon replaced by a significant opposition within the community of hearers:

> bot syn oure matir is of hering
> þer-of newe shal be oure lering.
> Clerkes heren on a manere,
> bot lewed men bos anoþer lere. (B. 171–74)

To maintain the privileged status of clerical hearing, the writer offers a different, compensatory mode of hearing. Unmoored from the structures of grammatical, locutionary meaning, the "meaning" to which layfolk should attend is that generated by the charisma of the *vox Dei* ventriloquized. Though the unlearned hearer is instructed to pray to receive the Word ("Bi gods worde welcome to me" [B. 181]), she is also provided with a vernacular prayer to repeat internally ("in þi mynde") throughout the lesson (B. 185–92). The laity were thus encouraged to cultivate their own inner voices to compensate for the words of the gospel they could perhaps hear but not hear as clerics do. The prayer itself does, in some sense, respond to the Word, but instead of responding to its content, it responds to its illocutionary force with an optative expression of future obedience: "graunt mi þi grace,/... þi word to kepe" (B. 187, 189). The writer of the Royal MS treatise thus imagines the laity to participate in the ritual but not in ritual language. The lay participant is told to cultivate an attitude of external attention that figures an interiorized, indirect engagement in the text, one that allows a greater degree of involvement than that of a witness but a lesser degree than is implied by "comprehension."

Since there was no expectation that the laity *should* understand the words of the gospel lesson, the writer of the Royal MS treatise most likely considered his compromise to be an act of inclusion rather than one of exclusion. Other versions provide similar advice that imagines and invites various degrees of engagement in the language of ritual performance while simultaneously guarding against the possibility of lay mastery. One such text, found in the Vernon Manuscript, goes further than the Royal MS treatise in considering how the laity might respond to God's Word, if only by its implicit supposition that the laity's silent attention to the gospel lesson requires further explanation. The lay hearer in this case is not directed to inner prayer but is told to attend to the lesson itself.

Al ʒor lykyng þer-on leiþ
To wite what þe prest seiþ,
   Holliche þat ʒe here hit.
Þauʒ ʒe vnderstonde hit nouʒt,
ʒe may wel wite þat god hit wrouʒt,
   And þerfore wisdam were hit
For to worschupe al godes werkes
To lewed men þat be none clerkes:
   Þis lesson now go lere hit.[27]

Yet despite the greater degree of linguistic involvement this writer imagines, the elaboration of his advice performs a similar gesture of exclusion.
The hearer is effectively instructed to listen, as if to "know" or discern
"what þe prest seiþ," yet all he can "know" in the end is the presumptive,
illocutionary knowledge that the words were made by God. The "lesson"
the audience learns is that of the clerical writer, not the gospel, and what
they derive from it constitutes experiential "wisdam" (*sapientia*), not formal
knowledge (*scientia*). While *sapientia* was frequently set forth in texts of
vernacular theology to diminish the prestige of *scientia*,[28] here it would seem
to have the opposite effect. At best it compensates for the lack of clerical
scientia from which it is distinguished.

Clerical ambivalence comes across even more forcefully in the exemplum proffered by the writer of the Vernon treatise to illustrate the efficacy
of hearing without understanding. The dynamics of illiterate listening, the
writer claims, can be likened to the relationship between a snake and its
charmer.

> He[o] vnderstond no þing þi speche,
>   Whon þou hire enchauntes,
> Neuerþeles heo wot ful wel
> What is þi menynge eueri-del
>   Whon þat þou hire endauntes. (441–45)

The exemplum is meant to express the interaction between God as the
author of the Word and the sinner, and insofar as it does, it suggests an
intensity of relation that exceeds language. Yet the image itself is obviously
at odds with the passage's reassuring claims. Considering that the clergy
performed the role of charmer in God's stead, the exemplum seems also
to express tension between clergy and laity, envisaged as a delicate and
dangerous negotiation of power. Even though the writer momentarily
imagines a specific "menynge" discernable by means other than speech,
this meaning is quickly assimilated to a more generalized economy of
"vertu," or power, which is provided not merely as an alternative to
meaning but as the only alternative to the linguistic exchanges involved
in understanding: "So fareþ þer vndirstondyng fayles, / Þe verrey vertu
ȝow alle avayles" (446–47).

Emphasis on *vertu* rather than understanding prevailed in many Mass
treatises. The "merits" or "virtues" of the Mass included benefits rang-
ing from forgiveness of venial sins to prevention of illness, hunger, and

aging. For Raymo, treatises expounding the merits of the Mass "tastelessly exploit the simple piety of the laity."[29] Yet though some contemporaries like Jean Gerson objected to promises of magical reward,[30] we should not be too quick to assume that the piety of all clerics rested on such a fully intellectualized sacramentalism as his, nor that the clergy strategically played upon a piety they felt was inappropriately unreflective. It is true that they courted the laity's self-interest, but the principle of exchange that encouraged such self-interest was scarcely foreign to the principles of *commercium sacrum*.[31] Dismissing the desire for such merits as "magical thinking" can draw attention away from those moments, such as the gospel lesson, when these exchanges intersect with the linguistic exchanges of ritualized speech. In such moments, *vertu* might be considered as part of "that surplus of meaning which gives [ritual language] its 'illocution-ary force.'"[32] Just as the clergy had an interest in subjecting themselves to the Word, so too did they have an interest in cultivating this surplus. The danger, of course, was the almost inevitable result that this surplus might come to circulate independently of the words to which it was so tenuously attached, creating a symbolic economy unregulated by grammar or clerical control.

One response to the problem of lay understanding in the reception of sacred language was to consider alternative means for their interpellation. Levation prayers arguably served this function.[33] Although there is no indication that the rise in popularity of these prayers or their form resulted from coherent ecclesiastical strategies, prayers designed for recitation at the Elevation of the Host encouraged the same self-interest underlying the merits of the Mass. Their performance, however, also ritualized interpellation in that it transferred the medium of subjection to the Other from the aural and linguistic relation to the *vox Dei* enacted during the reading of the gospel lesson to an ocular and corporeal relation potentiated by viewing the *corpus Christi*. Visual representations of prayer at the Elevation of the Host have been documented from the thirteenth century,[34] but most extant collections of the prayers themselves, particularly prayers in the vernacular, date to the fourteenth and fifteenth centuries.[35] The practice was perhaps a logical extension of the Elevation itself, a ritual technology developed in the late twelfth century that focalized the intervening presence of God in a specific moment and in a specific object.[36] Dramatically displayed to be made visible to the congregation, the Host became the means by which all might be touched by the divine in common. The moment of the Elevation was generally regarded as a moment of respectful self-abasement and of petition. Levation prayers were thus acts of subjection in which one acknowledged and submitted oneself to God's authoritative power.

Though the prayers were said in common, they were not said communally. The majority of these prayers—especially those in the vernacular—use the first person singular, and those that use the first person plural form in the address to "our Lord" often shift to the singular in the supplication itself.[37] The other most common and distinctive feature of levation prayers is the inclusion of a vocative "hailing" in the opening salutation: "Hail," "Ave," or "Welcome," generally followed by a series of descriptive appellations, such as "Hayl, þu in forme of bread." Like all vocatives, this hailing "posits a relationship between two subjects,"[38] but as another form of naming, it obviously has a different status from the interpellative naming of the divine voice. It is the hailing of tribute and therefore concedes sovereignty instead of assuming it, but it performs a similar function: it serves to punctuate the temporal and physical specificity of the Eucharistic incarnation, marking the immediacy of the divine presence otherwise contained in the ventriloquized *vox Dei* of the gospel lesson. In his own act of hailing, the suppliant acknowledges that divine presence, which the Eucharist makes available to all, specifically in relation to himself. He thus constitutes himself as a Christian subject in relation to that presence in a gesture of appropriation not unlike St. Anthony's recontextualization of the gospel.

Focusing on levation prayers as an alternative moment of interpellation might seem to take care of the problem of lay understanding by replacing the laity's reception of ritual language with their production of speech. Yet the prospect of lay speaking created some problems of its own. As speech uttered during the ritual, levation prayers were distinct from other forms of participation because they responded to, rather than merely supplemented or accompanied, a particular liturgical action and because they were held to be particularly efficacious. If listening to the gospels seemed to tread upon the domain of clerical understanding, the utterance of one's own levation prayer and petitions, as a specific instance within the rite that allowed lay performative speech acts, might well appear to grant to the laity not simply mastery of sacred language but also the power of ritual language, which they could not legitimately wield.

Such license was a special concession, made in spite of a more general anxiety about lay speech in liturgical settings. While all unlicensed speech was problematic, whether it came from the laity or from clerics like William Elys,[39] lay speech was suspect almost by definition. Layfolk were, it is true, counseled to say prayers during the service, but the primary purpose of these prayers was to help the parishioner focus her attention appropriately; they were not meant to have any claim on the attention of other participants in the service. It was not simply a matter of noisily distracting the priest, though that was frequently listed among the dire consequences. Illicit lay speech was usually represented as misdirected speech—as conversation or gossip with another transgressor. Such utterances asserted smaller, factional social relations—disruptive social bonds that threatened the transaction between God and the whole of the Christian community and thus defied the verbal economy of both the ritual and the relations of power it performed. Treatises on the Mass make a special point of warning the laity to "holde no parlyment / Wiþ no cristen man" during the service (Vernon, 281–83). Representations of lay speech as conspiratorial gossip or content-less chatter serve to characterize it as *un*productive, but it is arguably the *counter*productive relations they posited that were problematic, for to acknowledge the factional relations of gossip is to acknowledge the capacity of lay speech to produce that relation.

Depictions of gossip often betray a fear that congregational voices could, in fact, be productive and, far from disrupting the economy, had the potential to participate in it. Such is the case with a lay version of the Tutivillus story that emerged to parallel that of the sack-carrying devil.[40] In the lay version, Tutivillus patrols the nave rather than the choir but attends as precisely to the congregation's words as he did to the clerics'. As related in the Vernon Mass treatise, Augustine of Canterbury (or a similarly authoritative cleric in other versions) found himself distracted from his reading of the gospel lesson by two women gossiping in the congregation (281–376). Near them, he spied a devil, copying their every word on a roll. So garrulous were they that he ran out of space on the parchment and, while attempting to stretch the roll with his teeth to make more room, slipped and knocked his head against the wall. Augustine, astounded by the noise, burst into laughter, a disruption in the service he later had to explain to his superior, St. Gregory. The ostensible focus of the story is the fact of disruption, as shown not only in Augustine's indecorous laughter but also by setting the story during the reading of the gospel, when all but the reader are commanded to remain silent, as well as by assigning the infraction to women, the most unlicensed of speakers. But it is nonetheless significant that the gossips are exposed by a counterpart of the devil (and in many versions the same devil) who had assigned material value to each syllable emitted from the choir. In some fashion, lay words are accorded a value that makes them worthy of God's attention and which renders the speaker accountable for them: "god may wreke / Euerich word þat we speke" (395–96), counsels the Vernon treatise.

As is often the case, however, the parallel serves to differentiate, since the speakers are accountable for commission rather than omission. Thus the inclusion of the congregation in an economy of verbal exchange serves to give their words a negative value that is the precise converse of that of ritual speech. Indeed, the story partly functions to make the thought of including lay speech a joke—punctuated by a bit of demonic shtick—that renders as absurd the idea that such excessive and unproductive words would be granted the fixity and solemnity of the writing in the first place. Ultimately, the only significant "writing" that results from the women's gossip appears not in the devil's ink but in his blood, for it is by that telltale mark left on the wall where he struck his head that Augustine was able to prove the truth of his story to Gregory. (Such forensic evidence, we are told, was clearly the result of divine forbearance, since devils generally do not bleed.) Gregory thus takes the mark as a sign to make all mindful of the devil's surveillance, thereby granting it "public" and sacramental meaning that stands in contrast to the garrulous women's "private" and mundane speech. Indeed, the purpose of the exemplum is to make this very distinction between private and public—gossip and gospel. "Public," in this context, seems to function in terms of the "representative public-ness" that Jürgen Habermas associates with premodern Europe.[41] In this conception, "public" gestures are essentially synonymous with the display or performance of political power permitted to those with the authority to command public attention. This publicness is "limited and representative rather than expansive and inclusive."[42] It is "representative" in that display is meant to signify, "to make something invisible visible,"[43] be it lordship or sacramentality. That which is "private," by contrast, does not enter into the field of representation; it is "private in the sense in which the private soldier was excluded from representation and from military honor, even though he had to be a 'part.'"[44] The women are required to bear witness to the clerical performance of textual and sacramental mastery, but their words cannot partake of this mastery themselves.

The "public" nature of liturgical performance, however, differs from the displays of sovereign power and noble status that Habermas has chiefly in mind. I will discuss the differences and their implications more fully in the next section, but here it is useful to note that whereas the sover-eign represents the power that he himself embodies, the cleric represents the institutional power with which he has been invested, as well as the divine power that underwrites it—power, in other words, to which he has subjected himself, relinquishing self-interest. In order to guard against the threat of disenchantment, the representable is defined as that which does *not* emanate from the self.[45] This determination, necessary to signify both institutionality and sacramentality, affects the way in which meaning is assigned as well as how it circulates. The demon's parchment and the demon's blood are both static, visible signs, but in the latter case, Gregory, by virtue of his clerical authority, grants the sign a surplus of meaning—a meaning beyond itself and, more important, in excess of the intention of the demon who produced it.[46] The validity of that surplus is further supported by the miraculous nature of the medium, which stands as further proof both that the sign is not a product of the devil's intention and that the surplus is not a product of Gregory's intention, for the cleric's job is merely to identify and disseminate surplus meaning, to make it available for others to appropriate. In the context of the liturgy, the same surplus of meaning is generated by its complex, cyclical form. The liturgy's impersonal structure, constantly changing in accordance with multiple combinatory cycles of seasons and feasts to produce varying juxtapositions of scriptural texts, is not attributable to any single human "author." Its authority stems instead from the divinely inspired *cursus* to which its clerical performers have subjected themselves. The clerical performers, for their part, do not therefore speak in their own voices or wield authority in their own persons. Within the economy of liturgical performance, personal intention cannot generate surplus meaning, nor can it bear ritual or public authority. Augustine's laughter is inappropriate not solely as a general transgression of ritual decorum but because it originates in Augustine himself.

This distinction between public and private speech comes to determine the place of levation prayers. The prayers prescribed for the laity, like clerical speech acts, were structured by the forms of the ritual—indeed, one of the functions of such instruction was to help articulate the ritual form of the Mass for the laity to appreciate. They also had a surplus of meaning by virtue of being votive utterances within ritual time and space. But they were distinguished from public speech in important ways. First, the regimen of levation prayers is offered as pastoral advice, which makes adherence to that advice a response to the clerical author's specifiable intention. Second, the treatises consistently provide their audience with choices among possible actions. The more directly the action might participate in the ritual, the more personal choice is stressed. Levation prayers emphasize this choice to a greater degree than other suggested prayers.

The directions for the Elevation in the Royal MS treatise, for example, make the choice of prayer depend on the congregant's "lyking."

> swilk prayere þen þou make,
> als lykes best þe to take.
> sondry men prayes sere,
> Ilk mon on his best manere. (B. 418–21)

To provide "sondry men" with a supply of texts from which to choose, levation prayers proliferated and were frequently collected, either by devotional connoisseurs or by priests catering to them. These texts were distinguished still further from official forms in that they were particularized in terms other than those of ritual structure. Their rubrics often state the occasion of their writing or associate specific names with them, as is the case with one of the more popular Latin prayers—*Domine Ihesu Christe qui hanc*—which the conventional rubric states was written by Boniface VIII at the request of King Philip IV.[47] Like many levation prayers, this one has an indulgence attached to it, though it is more potent than most, promising two thousand years of indulgence for those who say it between the Elevation and the third *Agnus Dei*. Thus in addition to having a particularized origin, several promise benefits that will accrue to their users in a manner much more specific than that of the generalized *vertu* that accompanied the gospel lesson. This particularity situates lay speech in a different system of exchanges from that of clerical speech.

By communicating that there was no ordained or obligatory prayer for the Elevation, and that each of the possible prayers had a specific effect or served different needs, the Mass treatises ensured that the prayers would be chosen through the parishioner's conscious intention, as an expression of self in her own person. Such personalizing gestures made clear that when layfolk engaged sacramental language, it was to appropriate its surplus meaning or to assimilate themselves to that meaning but not to publish it in the manner of clerical, public speech. Levation prayers thus served two purposes. They enacted the symbolic interpellation of the laity as Christian souls, which was at some level a gesture of inclusion that momentarily set them, along with the clergy, before the unmediated presence of the divine. Yet because their voices were the instrument of their subjection, their prayers also served to determine the status of their speech. Paradoxically, uttering their personally selected prayers in their own voices deprived them of authority in this ritual setting. The effect of this scripting was to create "a pandemonium of vernacular prayers and supplications" at the Elevation[48]—a throng of simultaneous, private utterances, more likely to be perceived (particularly by reformers) as ocular consumption and inarticulate idolatry than as speech at all.[49]

The opposition of clerical and lay speech inscribed in the performance of levation prayers is that between liturgy and devotion. The categories themselves, of course, were ancient, but when brought to bear on Christians' relationship to sacred language in congregational worship, they were transformed. Within monastic traditions, liturgy and devotion were merely two registers of expression practiced in a life entirely given over to renunciation. Devotion focused on the individual will, celebrating the free will's ability to impose its own discipline. Liturgy was informed by devotion but was further a practice of community that fulfilled humanity's obligation to God on behalf of others as well as oneself. Treatises on the manner of hearing Mass grafted dialectical social roles onto these registers, defining liturgy as a distinctively "public," clerical activity by allowing devotion to serve as its distinctively "private," lay counterpart. As the laity were increasingly encouraged "to be a 'part'" of liturgical celebration in secular settings, registers that were ideally continuous were as a result figured, as they are in the Derby Psalter, as simultaneous and in competition with each other.

For the laity, this transformation enhanced the cultivation of devotional interiority popularized by trends of penitential piety.[50] Unlike the interiority of monastic traditions, theirs had its boundaries audibly pronounced by public, clerical voices and thus was private rather than solitary. Those with "private" interiors were not necessarily incapable of forging social bonds (or even the factional relations the clergy disapproved of), but the dialectic of public and private speech acts that fostered such interiors placed the laity in a more self-conscious relationship with the liturgy, the clergy, and the concept of understanding. There are certainly aspects of disenfranchisement in this kind of privatization, as well as in the cultivation of mechanisms of interpellation to substitute for grammatical understanding. Yet both of these developments invited the laity to appropriate surplus meaning produced in ritual settings, thus allowing them to participate in the symbolic economy of divine service in ways that were in fact more difficult for the clergy to control. As I will describe in the next chapter, this kind of participation could produce its own set of anxieties and would ultimately alter the social and symbolic economy of the liturgy itself.

Yet it was not solely lay participation, nor even the calculus of inclusion and exclusion in the clergy's attitudes toward the laity, that brought about

these alterations. Though stories like the lay Titivillus myth and images
like that in the Derby Psalter evince contemporary sentiments that the
laity was encroaching on clerical domains, beneath this politicized dialectic
lay complex socioeconomic developments that are not easily reducible to
conflict between clergy and laity. These developments were connected to
the new forms of liturgical endowment mentioned in Chapter 1, forms
that complicated the terms of representation in liturgical speech acts. The
emphasis on the public, institutional nature of liturgical speech implicit in
discussions of lay devotion may have called attention to the alienation of
speech from self required by those who spoke *in persona ecclesie,* but to a
greater extent it was the negotiations involved in these new kinds of endowments that prompted concerns about the act of representation itself.
No longer simply a matter of what something meant or even whether its
status as "public" was legitimate, representation in "contractual" liturgy
turned on the questions of who speaks in whose voice on whose behalf. It
was through the cultivation of this type of liturgy by laity and clergy alike
that the cleric's verbal productions came to seem for some a suspect form
of alienable labor power that did not rely on the performer's subjection to
or understanding of the words he produced.

Contractual Liturgy

The distinctive features of the *clerical* "publicity of representation" are not
acknowledged by Habermas. For him, "ecclesiastical lords" participated
in the same structures of representation as did sovereigns and nobility. If
there was a difference, it was that ecclesiastical representation was more
stable and enduring, such that the Church remained a site of vestigial
representation even after the advent of the public sphere: "In church ritual,
liturgy, Mass, and processions, the publicity that characterized representation has survived into our time."[51] The terms of liturgical representation,
however, were not as stable as is often assumed. One could even argue
that the rise of liturgy funded by and dedicated to particular individuals
turned ritual practice into a locus of change rather than stasis. "Private" or
"peculiar" liturgy, as it was called, involved a complex restructuring of the
socioeconomic relations that supported liturgical production—the development of a system of material and spiritual exchanges that grew alongside
and often intersected with the celebration of the *opus Dei* in the discourse
of choral community. This restructuring took place over several centuries.

Though "peculiar" masses are often associated with the privatization and commodification of the autumnal Middle Ages, many shifts associated with these labels—for example, the specification of the recipient of spiritual benefit or the exchange of temporal for spiritual goods—occurred earlier. Votive masses dedicating spiritual benefits to particular purposes or persons had been in use from late antiquity. By the ninth century, the practice of celebrating anniversaries had been fully cultivated.[52] Prayer fraternities—voluntary associations of secular and religious clergy as well as layfolk who promised spiritual support to each other with masses and prayers—have been recorded from the eighth century. In connection with these fraternities, a list of equivalences assigning specific monetary and penitential values to masses and psalms survives from circa 800.[53] Innovations of the late medieval period center more on attempts to specify and formalize the relations between retained mass priests and their patrons in terms of their obligations and compensations. These changes were not independent of other social developments; they are, not coincidentally, contemporaneous with the formation of contract law in the thirteenth century.[54] I describe these later forms of patronage as "contractual" liturgy to call attention to this connection because of the emphasis it places on the socioeconomic relations and social expectations formed through liturgical contracts. Although contemporaries referred to individually endowed masses as "private," the privatization of liturgy proceeded differently than the privatization of devotion. Though the two were clearly related, liturgy was still by definition a "public" act and therefore prompted more self-conscious speculation about the social relations it performed.

Although these changes did not lead directly to the formation of a Habermasian "public sphere,"[55] they did involve the structures of representation. By "representation," I do not refer solely to the act of signification ("re-presentation") but also to the act of "speaking for."[56] According to Habermas, the latter meaning is not a part of representative publicness: "Representation (*Vertretung*) in the sense in which the members of a national assembly represent a nation or a lawyer represents his clients has nothing to do with this publicity of representation."[57] Yet the refraction of authority and the necessary self-abnegation required in ecclesiastical performance resulted in speech and gestures that ipso facto represented someone else's interests. Clerical representation, in other words, was always vicarious representation.[58] A sovereign may have derived his authority from God, but he was not Christ's vicar. Contractual liturgy exploited this second sense of representation in particular and did so in a way that altered the structures of obligations and interests at the heart of parish and choral communities alike.

*   *   *

Contractual liturgy achieved its greatest formalization in the perpetual chantry. Though these institutions accounted for only a fraction of contractual liturgy, they were the model for other forms of endowment. The problems that surfaced in the course of their evolution, furthermore, were those that most clearly isolated clerical labor—specifically verbal and sacramental labor and its representational power—as a topic of speculation. Chantries became attractive in the thirteenth century because the Mass and above all the Eucharist were accruing more sacramental power that could be appropriated.[59] Yet chantries, as perpetual institutions, became necessary because just as the power was multiplying along with the masses themselves, the Church restrained both consumers and producers of this power by limiting priests to celebrating one mass per day. Though there had been earlier decrees against multiple celebration, only that of Innocent III in 1206 seems to have been universally heeded.[60] As a result, the Mass was resituated from a surplus economy in which its fecundity threatened to devalue it to a scarcity economy in which to engage a priest was potentially to deprive others of his ministrations. The scarcity economy, like any structure of exchange that dealt in quantifiable and particularizable spiritual benefit, was potentially in conflict with notions of God's infinite capacity for grace and mercy—the very benefits that masses were thought to solicit. Although this dilemma could have constrained the prestige and the representational power of masses, thinkers like Aquinas resolved the contradiction between immeasurable sacramental power and quantifiable benefit by distinguishing between the power of Christ, which is infinite, and the efficacy of the Mass, which was limited and therefore enhanced by repetition.[61] Such a distinction was the first step in creating a market for liturgical labor in that it made the job security of priests a function of their inefficiency as mediators.

The chantry as an autonomous institution arose as a solution to the problem of supply and demand created by simultaneously encouraging the multiplication of masses while limiting the means of their production. Patrons found that they could reap spiritual rewards by supplying a living for a personal chaplain whose full attention could then be devoted to celebrating masses over time without detriment to a cure of souls. Such arrangements generated both new institutional forms and new kinds of socioeconomic affiliation. Although there were precedents both for arranging services in perpetuity and for retaining personal chaplains, the chantry priest established a unique combination of the two. Anniversaries commemorating the death of a patron had been endowed in perpetuity since the ninth century, but these services were generally founded at pre-existing institutions, such as monasteries, that had the stability to sustain them. Since they were only yearly commemorations, anniversaries also did not require the full resources of a priest, and the service itself often featured additional elements, such as doles to the poor, that did not require sacerdotal authority.[62] Chantries, by contrast, did not simply require a priest's services but appropriated his entire vocation. Though chantry chaplains were often given pastoral or parochial duties beyond the singing of masses, the nature of their contract made liturgical labor the most central part of that vocation. Such would be the case with a member of a household chapel choir, but the relationship between patron and chaplain differed in the case of the chantry. The chantry chaplain did not provide services for his patron directly—for her own spiritual consumption, as it were—rather he performed services on her behalf. Because he was situated in the chantry itself, his affiliation was not supported by the day-to-day workings of the *familia* and had to be sustained outside it. Such agreements therefore isolated liturgical performance from other social activities as the foundation of socioeconomic relation. These arrangements might seem to impoverish the more complex social bonds of the household, but it should be kept in mind that the relationship between chantry chaplains and their patrons was not a transformation of preexisting socioeconomic ties. As dispositive documents, liturgical contracts effectively created such relations as sets of autonomous obligations and entitlements where there had been none before.

The idea that private liturgy existed as agreements between persons was important to retain, since supporting a priest rather than paying for the services themselves guarded against the commodification of masses. Yet maintaining these agreements in perpetuity created new problems, as it involved not merely sustaining this relationship after the death of the patron but also reproducing it after the death of the chaplain. This reproduction required both a perpetual supply of priests who would agree to fulfill preexisting obligations to a deceased patron and a secure source of income to support them. While the former issue created concerns about chaplains' investments in their obligations, the latter created concerns

about the entitlements of both chaplain and patron in this new socioeconomic relation. The most problematic of all were the cases in which this
relation was situated within the already complex and socially embedded
system of exchanges that constituted benefices.[63] Normally a benefice was
considered the most secure way to guarantee an income, yet chantries
supported in this manner were felt to be especially susceptible to abuse,
leading patrons to explore ways to ensure that the funds dedicated to
sustaining the chantry and its chaplains would not be misappropriated.
If lands were entrusted to the chaplain, the concern was that he might
deplete the endowment by appropriating it for his personal use, just as the
masters of St. Cross Hospital had done. If, however, lands were entrusted
to a third party or to the Church, there was no way to prevent them from
diverting funds that allowed the chantry priest to support himself to some
other purpose. Far from the simplification of exchange that often goes
under the rubric of "commodification," the institution of chantries often
called attention to the complex gift economy of the liturgy and the ways
in which it could be manipulated.

The most extreme result of patrons' legal efforts was an institutional
form far removed from the mutual agreements of prayer fraternities. Over
the course of the late fourteenth and early fifteenth centuries, chantries
were increasingly granted corporate status, thereby lending these institutions a kind of "fictitious personality" (*persona ficta*) by which rights to
land could be secured in the name of the chantry itself. In the case of
chantry colleges, corporate status required no stretch of the imagination,
since there were many reasons why any group might wish to exercise rights
and responsibilities as a collective entity rather than as individuals. By the
1440s, however, the similar rights and privileges that had been gradually
accruing to chantries consisting of only a single priest had reached a stage
of codification in what Frederic Maitland referred to as "that unhappy
freak of English law," the corporation sole.[64] Granting corporate status to
a single priest, corporations sole allowed chantry priests to pursue their
legal interests while maintaining the boundary between office and person.[65]
Contractual liturgy in this instance maintained its emphasis on the relation
between persons rather than quantifying the value of particular services,
but it could do so only by disembodying the notion of the "person" who
performed those services.

Though corporations sole had not evolved in the fourteenth century, patrons' tinkering with various forms of endowment participated
in a developing conceptual affinity between the juridical category of the

persona ficta—an ancient legal concept that had been elaborated in canon law to represent the collective rights of religious houses[66]—and the position of chantry priests. More specifically, in relation to chantry priests, the *persona* went from an instrument of representation to an instrument of entitlement predicated on alienation. The distinction is one of emphasis, since exercising corporate rights generally requires one to relinquish personal claims, but the emphasis on prior alienation that played a larger role in chantry foundations created complicated resonances between this juridical use of *persona*—describing the relationship of chantry chaplains to their entitlements—and a related notion of the *persona*: that used to describe the relationship of speaker to utterance in the register of ritual authority. When invoked in the phrase "in persona ecclesie," this ritual *persona* allowed the speaker to represent the collective authority of the church. The bifurcation of liturgy and devotion discussed in the previous section, however, had the potential to emphasize the incompatibility of devotional and liturgical utterances, even to the point of suggesting that those who performed *in persona ecclesie* must suppress private, devotional speech. In 1337, John Grandisson enjoined the choir of his collegiate foundation of Ottery St. Mary from inappropriate devotional speech in his statute against "private prayers said during Mass ... and during the Elevation."[67] Wykeham, in the statutes for Winchester and New colleges, also expressly prohibited scholars, priests, and clerks from "saying matins or any hours in a low voice by themselves or with several fellows or anyone in the choir of the chapel, or saying anything else in private while the divine services are being sung."[68] In contrast to the Mass treatises that encouraged such devotional participation, these patrons and others categorized devotional utterances on the part of those who served in the choir as unlicensed speech—*garrulaciones, strepitus indiscreti,* and so forth.[69] Like the juridical *persona,* the *persona ecclesie* was an instrument of entitlement, giving access to authoritative language, yet also like the juridical *persona,* its entitlements depended on prior alienation—a relinquishing not only of self-interest but of self-representation.

Such prohibitions, however, generally occur in statutes for collegiate churches, which funded choral performance of the *opus Dei.* Chantries, whose primary function was the celebration of masses dedicated to particular souls, presented a different set of concerns. Both kinds of institutions were "contractual" in the sense that specific patrons determined the terms of the foundation, but chantry founders inserted their interests in the structure of liturgical obligations in ways that complicated the divisions between

personal and representative that these collegiate foundations sought to
clarify. The performance of the Mass, I have claimed, produced a surplus of meaning that all were invited to appropriate. Chantry patrons,
however, made proprietary claims on the intention of the masses they
funded. By appropriating liturgy as a means of self-representation before
God, they confused the distinction between public and private speech.
Public, institutional authority was necessary to give the Mass its salvific
powers, but an authority that patrons, acting *in propria persona*, might
appropriate to their own personal demands is not really institutional
authority at all. Any particularizing of the intention of a mass at some
level had to stem from the chaplain's personal will. For this reason, the
specter of self-interest that haunted the financial arrangements of chantries and the performance of the *opus Dei* surfaced in a very different form
in discussions of chantry masses. Critics were less concerned with the
possibility that chaplains would insert their own devotions than with the
idea that the self-abnegation required to speak *in persona ecclesie* might
allow for alienation from ritual language altogether instead of alienation
of one's own voice. Complaints about the mindless act of *blabbering* in
this context represent anxiety about a withdrawal of self-interest that was
more disturbing than the inappropriate investment of self-interest enacted
by speaking *in propria persona*.

Patrons were not alone in expressing such anxieties, nor were they the
only ones to assert their own interests within the institutional structures
of representation and obligation. Those in the communities in which contractual services were celebrated also found in them models and means for
their own manipulations. Chantry services were not "private" in the sense
of being a withdrawal from communal celebration. Although "private"
appropriately marks the peculiar intention of these masses, the chaplain still
performed them in his public authority as priest. The contractual nature of
these services, in fact, left them open to enforcement by means of public
scrutiny, such that liturgy performed through such agreements was a palpable presence in parish communities. Bishops, executors, and even parishioners were sometimes entrusted with overseeing the priest's activities. Some
founders arranged to have their statutes displayed or read aloud in the parish
church.[70] Returns from parochial visitations conducted by John Trefnant,
Bishop of Hereford, in 1397 show that parishioners were aware of whether
chantry priests were fulfilling their duties.[71] Quite apart from the parochial
duties chantry priests were often expected to perform,[72] parishioners could
often partake of their ministrations, however "peculiar" their masses. In

1385, John Gilbert, Bishop of Hereford, complained that the parishioners of the church of Ledbury would arise early on Sundays and feast days to hear the low masses celebrated by chantry priests so that, having fulfilled their obligation, they might spend the rest of the day consorting in the tavern.[73] Complaints of this sort were frequent enough to suggest that the difference between private and parochial masses was not very meaningful to some of the more pragmatic parishioners who felt free to interpret the terms of their obligations as they saw fit.

The perpetual chantry was the most fully institutionalized form of contractual liturgy. The vast majority of liturgical contracts were far more modest in their ambitions, often taking the form of short-term agreements of a month or a year to celebrate trentals or annuals. Though based on the same objectification of liturgical labor that underwrote the chantry, these more affordable options explored the other extreme of obligation from the perpetual agreement. Although they required the full resources of a priest, they provided only temporary support rather than a living. The positions were most suited to unbeneficed priests as a short-term source of income, yet their popularity encouraged some unbeneficed priests to support themselves entirely by means of these ephemeral relations, objectifying their capacity to celebrate masses as a form of liturgical representation still further. Non-Eucharistic liturgical performance could also function in this burgeoning economy, as members of the minor clergy were funded in exchange for performance of votive antiphons and commemorations.[74] These smaller benefactions did not have the autonomy of masses and were frequently funded as accretions to preexisting conventional or contractual services. Their potential to turn liturgical representation into a means to assert the interests of the performers, however, can be seen in gestures like that of the vicars choral of York Minster, who in 1394 agreed to sing the antiphon *Inter natos* daily in the name of Richard II in exchange for his granting them corporate status.[75]

As this economy grew, the nature, not to mention the recipient, of the "service" provided by "divine service" became a complex matter. The chantry priest was still, on the one hand, answerable to God and still represented the community of the faithful, but, on the other hand, he simultaneously represented his patron, to whom he was also answerable. These obligations differed significantly from the established relations of the parish between the parson and his cure. Despite the potential confusion about ecclesiastical authority and the representational power of ritual speech and despite the fact that contractual liturgy had financial drawbacks in that it "support[ed] current expenditure in the form of stipends, rather than increasing capital assets,"[76] there is no indication that the Church discouraged it in any way. Ecclesiastical authorities, rather, seem to have been equally invested in manipulating the structures of representation and obligation. Given that the earliest chantries were founded by bishops, one might even say they invented the idea. Though there was some concern about the multiplication of chantry masses, there is little in the first half of the fourteenth century to suggest conflict or competition between the two economies. In the aftermath of the Black Death, however, the conflicts inherent in contractual liturgy would come to take center stage as socio-economic disruptions precipitated a crisis of representation in which the concept of understanding would play a crucial role.

The Crisis of Clerical Representation in the Wake of the Black Death

Gilbert's complaint about his errant parishioners and their strategic atten-dance of chantry masses is indicative of the air of hostility that became more frequent in discussions of contractual liturgy after the arrival of the plague. There had been complaints before this time, to be sure, but they were of a different character. As early as 1320, Roger Martival mandated that chantry masses could not be sung in the parish churches of Wiltshire until after the gospel lesson of the parish High Mass to avoid interruptions.[77] In 1348, the Chapter of Salisbury Cathedral similarly instructed a chantry priest to celebrate only at the altar of St. Martin so that he would no longer dis-rupt the cathedral's services.[78] These injunctions address competition over the institutional resources of ritual time and space and are less interested in curtailing practices than in managing their proliferation effectively. By contrast, Gilbert's concern with competition over audience share betrays a fear that contractual liturgy had the potential to disrupt bonds of the parish community. While this case differs from other complaints I will consider here in that it is the parishioners who are at fault, it underscores a prevalent sentiment in postpandemic England: that contractual liturgy encouraged opportunism—the pursuit of self-interest—at the expense of obligation, both individual and communal.

The Black Death affected all aspects of clerical labor as acutely as it affected manual labor.[79] Whereas every additional death was one less mouth to feed, it was one more act of extreme unction to perform and one more requiem mass to sing. This ever-increasing need was matched by a high death rate among priests, which created a considerable shortage.[80] For clergymen who survived, the sudden depletion of tithes and rents threatened the solvency of their benefices and chantries. With the degeneration of forms of income based in communal relations or other long-term arrangements, many priests sought ways to supplement their income or, in some cases, support themselves entirely. Among the various types of clerical piecework such men could engage in, contractual liturgy gained considerable notoriety as a technically legitimate yet morally indefensible form of employment. Chantry chaplaincies were said to be luring parsons from their cures. More suspect still were unbeneficed mass priests supporting themselves with short-term contracts for annuals and trentals,[81] whose abbreviated commitments were considered to be a threat to the socioeconomic order comparable to that posed by agrarian workers who favored day labor over manorial obligation. Yet it was not solely the socioeconomic transgressions attributed to these clerics that captured the imagination of critics and reformers. They saw this lack of social and spiritual responsibility as intimately connected to a lack of understanding of the ritual language that formed the tools of the mass priest's trade. Conflating what we would now consider two distinct kinds of representation, critics equated the mass priest's failure to represent the interests of patron, parish, and institution with a failure to signify in ritual language.

Disparagement of *lewid* priests was a stock complaint, but differences arise in designations of both the priests who offended and the precise nature of their offense. Insofar as illiterate priests were considered a cause for concern in the first half of the fourteenth century, it was the unbeneficed clergy in general who bore the brunt of public criticism. Unbeneficed clergy could fill a number of positions beyond that of chantry service:[82] they could function as parish vicars, vicars choral, household or civil servants, or private chaplains, to name only a few of the possibilities. Neither cantarists nor mass priests were singled out as objectifiable problems worthy of particular scrutiny. Suspicion was rather broadly manifested in a connection between the more contingent relationship of stipendiary clerics to the people they served and their more tenuous relationship to ritual language represented by illiteracy or lack of understanding. This illiteracy was almost always figured in terms of liturgical performance, but liturgy tended to be represented within the context of the parish, where it was perceived to function within parochial structures of obligations to which stipendiary labor was subordinate. The early fourteenth-century

poem *The Simonie* provides one example in its enumeration of the sins of
a hypothetical parson.

> And if þe persoun haue a prest   of a clene lyf
> Þat be a god consailler   to maiden and to wif,
> Shal comen a daffe and putte him out   for a litel lasse,
> Þat can noht a ferþingworþ of God,   vnneþe singe a masse
>   But ille.
> And þus shal al þe parish   for lac of lore spille.[83]

Although the *lewid* priest momentarily becomes the focus of attention,
the fault in this situation lies chiefly with the parson, who is ultimately
responsible for tending to the spiritual needs of the parish. In an attempt
to retain a greater percentage of his income, he allows the "daffe,"
whose function in the complaint is largely instrumental, to take the place
of the morally upright and knowledgeable vicar. The "daffe" is clearly
blameworthy for usurping the occupation of a more legitimate practitio-
ner, but the illegitimacy of his performances does not correspond directly
to an illegitimate material exchange. Despite *The Simonie*'s titular concern,
it is not the fact of payment for spiritual services that is problematic here or
even the incommensurability of such payments—quite the opposite, the
problem is that one gets what one pays for with the "bargain" vicar, whose
sin lies in asking for less, not more, money.

The exchange does, however, become an occasion for denouncing
illiterate priests in general.

> For riht me þinkeþ hit fareþ   bi a prest þat is lewed
> As bi a iay in a kage   + þat himself haþ bishrewed:
> God Engelish he spekeþ,   ac he wot nevere what;
> No more wot a lewed prest   in boke what he rat
>   Bi day.
> Þanne is a lewed prest   no betre þan a iay. (103–8)

While the complaint continues to reflect on the parson and his miserly,
inappropriate choice of vicar, the concerns it raises overpower the
description of performative and pastoral incompetence to which it is
connected. The jay—whose English seems to be better than the Latin of
the vicar he analogizes—is proverbial, but its connection here specifically
to priestly illiteracy raises the specter of absence inherent in writing in

relation to liturgical performance. The criticism of rote performance does not serve to promote self-originating language (as in the modern reflex of this analogy, "parroting"), but it is at least outwardly concerned with speakerly self-presence. Self-presence, in turn, depends on knowledge; failure is therefore a matter of incompetence, in contrast to the problem of the *mens vagans*, which was primarily a matter of self-discipline. The distinction between the two is no doubt related to the presumption of group membership in the discourse of choral community versus the significant lack of any prior affiliation on the part of the stipendiary cleric. In the latter case, the focus is less on the intention or motivation of the vicar than on the inevitable yet unpredictable incompetence of some priests: "Þer beþ so manye prestes, hii ne muwe noht alle be gode," laments the poet directly after this analogy (110). That this situation leaves the parish at the mercy of the parson who selects the vicar helps explain the analogy's subtle investment in maintaining the integrity, or at least the felicity, of the ritual speech act, no matter the speaker. The jay may lack the rationality to understand its own speech, but this lack is worthy of proverbial commemoration because the jay nonetheless manages to curse itself. Thus the proverb implies that the illocutionary act does not depend on the performer's self-presence for its efficacy even as it disapproves of such illiterate performances.

Unbeneficed mass priests, their inner motivations and failed representations, take center stage after the plague as they became central characters in a powerful narrative of postpandemic fraudulence. In one of the most detailed versions, Henry Knighton states that a surplus of priests before the plague had required the unbeneficed, like the *lewid* vicar in *The Simonie*, to accept lower wages to compete for clerical positions. The postpandemic shortage, by contrast, led these same clerics to plumb the depths of moral turpitude by taking advantage of others' misfortunes and overcharging for their services. Motivated more by a desire to profit from price-gouging opportunities than by the pastoral crisis caused by the lack of priests, a large number of men took holy orders, including many who were unqualified, until there was once again a surplus of priests, though this surplus was paradoxically still able to demand inflated wages.[84] The shortage and resulting inflation in wages is supported by contemporary documents. Bertha Haven Putnam, furthermore, found a pronounced increase not so much in the number of ordinations but in the number of dispensations given for those ordinations to excuse ordinands from requirements of age, legitimate birth, literacy, and more,[85] which suggests that many who would otherwise have been disqualified were being ordained.

For Knighton, however, it is insufficient literacy above all that indicated the illegitimacy of the new clergy: "Within a short time, a great number of men whose wives had died in the plague rushed to take orders, many of whom were illiterate, and like mere laymen, except that they knew how to read somewhat, though without understanding."[86] These illiterate priests were worse than the less costly vicar mentioned in *The Simonie*: neither was fully legitimate, but whereas the vicar occupied an improper place, the new clerics were perceived as having no place at all. Like so many other elements of postpandemic England that seemed to represent the unraveling of the social fabric, these clerics tended to be depicted in motion, usually toward the nearest source of money.

In contrast to the disruptive yet aimless wandering associated with the *mens vagans*, these priests were perceived to be moving away from the parochial ministry of the cure of souls to engage in mercenary liturgical contracts. Whatever coexistence traditional and contractual liturgy had managed before the plague became outright opposition after it. This opposition may have derived in part from competition over resources, but it was fueled primarily by a politicized conceptualization of contractual liturgy as a rejection of community.[87] For while many cures were indeed without priests, there is little to support the claim that they had been abandoned by beneficed clerics who, unlike Chaucer's virtuous Parson, had gone to London "to seken ... a chaunterie for soules" (*CT*, 1.509–10). It is, in fact, unlikely, since the incomes of chantries were usually less than those of benefices.[88] This is not to say, however, that contractual liturgy did not provide opportunities for those who needed to support themselves. Those without cures to abandon or benefices to exchange were apparently congregating in urban centers like London where concentrations of wealth were more likely to provide demand for their services.[89] Although here, as elsewhere, there were several options open to unbeneficed clerics, contractual liturgy, especially one-year contracts for the singing of masses, became the most prominent, and most scandalous, form of employment. Those "annuellers" who supported themselves entirely by such means could be found gathering at St. Paul's with other prospective mass priests offering their services.[90] The singular "daffe" who had infiltrated the parish had evolved into an urban underclass of clerical mercenaries who had willingly left the parish in pursuit of financial gain. It is possible that priests had supported themselves with such piecework before the plague, but if they did no one paid them much attention. In the postpandemic economy, however, the annueller became the symbol of the mercenary cleric who provided services to the highest bidder. If the rise of chantries allowed priestly vocations to be considered more as occupations, the plague allowed priestly occupations to be considered something closer to alienable labor power.

Annuellers soon gained a reputation as the clerical equivalent of agrarian laborers who had rejected manorial ties to work on short-term contracts. As with laborers who were perceived to be upsetting the socioeconomic order, the terms of annuellers' employment were subject to regulation. In 1350, the year after the Ordinance of Laborers set maximum wages and compelled fulfillment of preexisting contracts in secular domains, Simon Islip, Archbishop of Canterbury, issued its ecclesiastical counterpart, *Effrenata generis humanis cupiditas*, which limited the yearly stipends paid to unbeneficed clerics and required them to accept cures if offered.[91] The mandate covered all manner of unbeneficed clerics—including private chaplains and those serving as vicars in cures—yet Islip's introduction, like other contemporary accusations, focuses entirely on those who, he claimed, were setting a poor example for lay workers by neglecting their cures and choosing instead to celebrate annuals and other "peculiar" obsequies.[92] If Knighton's account is to be believed in this regard, curates and chaplains had also been demanding high wages to fulfill their duties within the parish,[93] and they were arguably in a better position to do so since they provided essential services rather than the luxury goods of mass priests. Itinerant mass priests, however, were a more visible target precisely because they represented the emergence of a new, luxury economy structured by contractual representation of patrons instead of by parochial obligation—an economy that was precipitating the unmooring of liturgical practice from the communal structure, and needs, of the parish.

If the contractual bases of their labors made mass priests targets of ecclesiastical criticism, the explicit discussion and practical regulation of those labors using the language of contract law called greater attention to the nature of the work itself and its distinctions from other kinds of labor. Often such discussions occurred in secular contexts, for until the end of the reign of Edward III, chaplains could be prosecuted in secular courts under the contract clause of the Ordinance of Laborers.[94] In an especially illuminating case brought before the court of common pleas in 1376, Henry B. Parson claimed that Thomas F. Chaplein, whom he had retained to serve as seneschal and parochial chaplain, had departed from service before the end of term. While one justice refers to the more complex structure of obligations that govern a chaplain, pointing out that he is first and foremost a "servant of God," more discussion is devoted to the nature of the labor in question. Despite the claims of a dissenting justice who notes that a chaplain had many duties to perform, such as visiting the sick, the argument ultimately focuses entirely on the singing of masses and hinges on distinguishing this activity from manual labor.

car chescun auter servant s'il soit en sanite et power de corps, il est tenus de faire son service, et son labour de jour en jour, mes le Chaplein n'est tenus de chaunter chescun jour, s'il ne voille, pur divers causes que gissent en son conscience, et issint poet cesser de chaunter par un demaine ou deux, issint que il est tout en auter degree que labourer ou artificer.[95]

[for another servant, so long as he has health and power of his limbs, is bound to do his service and his labor each day, but the Chaplain is not bound to sing each day, if he does not want to, for various reasons that pertain to his conscience, and therefore can stop singing for a day or two; thus he is in a completely different category than a laborer or artisan.]

The chaplain's labor is described as spiritual rather than manual and therefore not dependent on the health of his body but on his inner state. Conscience is mentioned as playing a role, but since only the chaplain himself can judge his inner disposition, the final arbiter becomes his will, such that he may choose not to sing if he does not want to ("s'il ne voille") and is thereby exempt from the statutes compelling other kinds of work. The singing of masses, in fact, would ultimately become exempt from the contract clause. Though cases involving clerics tried under the ordinance usually concerned parochial chaplains who had left service and tended to focus on the various administrative or pastoral duties the chaplain had agreed to perform, this exemption led some chaplains to claim (in a manner similar to that of the former masters of St. Cross Hospital) that celebration of divine service was their primary obligation, no matter what else they had agreed to do.[96] By the close of Edward III's reign, chaplains were exempted from the ordinance as a group, at least in part because their duties had come to be so strongly associated with liturgical performance.

The privileging of will over contractual obligation that made liturgical labor distinctive, not to mention attractive to those who did not wish to fulfill their contracts, derives from elsewhere. Similar clauses qualifying the priest's obligation to sing only "when he is so disposed" appear frequently in chantry statutes and other forms of liturgical contract.[97] The qualification served primarily to prevent the commodification of the Mass itself, both by ensuring that the agreement would not be mistaken for a simoniacal exchange of money for masses and by making clear that the liturgy had been ordained by God and could not be manipulated by mortals as currency to secure their salvation. Like the conceptual manipulations that surrounded the development of the *persona*, part of its purpose was to ensure that the exchange retained the complex structure of the gift as underwritten by divine and ecclesiastical power rather than devolving into the pursuit of mundane self-interest. In this juridical context, however, this same privileging of the will had the effect of granting stipendiary chaplains control over the terms of their contractual obligations. The will that determined whether or not the chaplain would perform the duties he had promised was treated in terms comparable to the "will" denied to manual laborers, who in 1381 were said to have demanded that "no one be compelled to serve any man except by his own will (*volunte de mesme*) or by free covenant (*covenante taille*)."[98] Under this logic, securing the chaplain's right not to celebrate might seem an institutional gesture made less in deference to God's will than to the will of a priest whose motives could be questionable. Instead of preventing the pursuit of self-interest, the emphasis on the will appeared to give the unbeneficed mass priest the legal means to do so.

With the acknowledgment that the chaplain's will was governed by interior motivations that could not be compelled, the patron or employer was placed at the mercy of a will that was inscrutable and therefore unmanageable. As a result, discipline and intention once again became central concerns, though critics were now more interested in errant wills than errant minds. These matters are palpable even in the first promulgation of the *Effrenata*, as its point of departure makes clear: "Effrenata generis humanis cupiditas"—"the unbridled cupidity of the human race." By the time that the *Effrenata* was reissued in 1362 and 1378, the reputation of mass priests had worsened considerably, making them even more emphatically the prime target of indignation. Still succumbing to their unbridled desires, such priests warranted a more passionate execration.

sacerdotesque praedicti sic cupidi et delicati salariis excessivis hujusmodi farcinati, evomunt, indomiti delirant, et deficiunt, ac eorum nonnulli post ventris ingluviem, et varias carnis illecebras spumant in libidinem, et tandem in malorum voraginem funditus demerguntur.[99]

[These priests—voracious and addicted to pleasure, stuffed by such excessive salaries and unbridled—vomit, rave, and pass out, and some of them, after overindulgence of their bellies and various enticements of the flesh, foam into lust, and finally drown at the bottom of the abyss of vice.]

Whereas the primacy of the mass priest's will had been secured in part by defining his labor as disembodied, his failings are here figured in terms of an immoderate use of the body that desecrates those labors. Annuellers betray an ethical posture incommensurate with responsible enactment of their juridical will, yet in equating this irresponsibility with cupidity that exceeds even the body's capacity for pleasure, the revised versions of the *Effrenata* recast the conflict as a more fundamental struggle involving the free will granted by God and squandered by undisciplined clerics.

Apart from making their behavior all the more inexcusable, the *Effrenata*'s depiction intimates that these mass priests, engaged as they are in acts of concupiscence that rival Augustine's pre-Christian lifestyle, have not been effectively interpellated as officers authorized to speak on behalf of the Church or even as Christian subjects. Considering the accusation in these terms offers one explanation why these clerics become the group most frequently castigated for their illiteracy in postpandemic England. Though this illiteracy is figured, as it was before the plague, as a lack of understanding, the problem is not so much one of competence or mastery over the texts of the services as it is the priest's failure to subject himself either to those texts and their institutional power or to the interests of the parishioners or patrons their performance was meant to convey to God. In the emptiness of the mass priest's utterances—an emptiness indicative of willful neglect—the two senses of representation coalesce as he refuses to participate both in ecclesiastical or parochial structures of obligation and in grammatical systems of meaning. Just as the image of abandonment reflected the wayward priest's rejection of communal ties, complaints of priestly ignorance suggested the willful relinquishing of ties between the *persona* and ritual language as well as the ties between ritual language and meaning. The demand for an interiorized relationship of understanding in such cases reflects the institutionally motivated sentiment that only as Christian subjects, and only from the stable, focalized position of their cures, are priests able to oversee the proliferation of surplus meaning effectively. These unbeneficed clerics were, by contrast, floating signifiers, threatening to upset the delicate balance of economies enacted in liturgical performance by destabilizing the relationships between the clergy, the laity, and the Word altogether.

At roughly the same time that Henry B. Parson was pursuing his claim at the court of common pleas, John Gower was examining the stakes of liturgical representation in his *Mirour de l'Omme*. Similar to *The Simonie* in its estates satire form, the *Mirour* provides a much more extensive treatment of the entire clergy, in which Gower pursues the nature of their obligations more relentlessly, but the *Mirour's* differences concern more than length. Gower's text exemplifies many of the shifts in attitudes I have described. Within his catalogue of secular clergy, the unbeneficed clergy are discussed at the very end of a hierarchical list, ranked only above "clergeons," and are described solely as "autre prestes Annuelers, qui sont sans cure."

> Ils sont auci pour noz deniers
> Prestres qui servent volentiers,
> Et si n'ont autre benefice,
> Chantont par auns et par quartiers
> Pour la gent morte, et sont suitiers
> Communement a chascun vice.[100]

> [There are also priests who, for our money, serve willingly and have no other benefice. They sing by the year or by three-month periods for the dead; and they are commonly followers of every vice.][101]

With the words "servent volentiers" Gower sets up his satiric portrayal such that it turns on the multiple registers in which the annueller's will can be interpreted. Considered as simple desire, the annueller's willingness to serve is immediately suspect due to its appearance only after the topic of "deniers" (arranged in the line to emphasize the rhyme with "volentiers") has been introduced. "Volentiers," however, also invokes the language of contract, a register that is sustained throughout much of the discussion and one that, as we have seen, has special relevance for the annueller. Within this more restricted context, the term refers to service rendered without formal agreement,[102] though given the irony that has already been established about the character of the priest's voluntarism, the lack of a formal agreement seems more likely to serve the priest than his patron. The priest's willingness resonates still more powerfully with the legal "will" that allowed priests more control in establishing the terms by which they might fulfill liturgical contracts. After noting the annuellers' lack of benefices, Gower goes on to mention the typical length of the liturgical contracts that they substitute for them: "par auns et par quartiers." In emphasizing the exceptionally brief periods to which such priests are willing to commit, Gower establishes ephemeral and self-serving loyalty as the first of their vices.

Gower thus invokes the language of contract not to exempt annuellers from fulfilling their agreements but to castigate them for engaging in them in the first place. The fact that priests who comport themselves in such a manner are unlikely to keep their end of the bargain is simply presumed.

> Qui prent louer d'autri vivant,
> Par resoun doit servir atant,
> Ou autrement souffrir destresce
> Du loy, si l'en n'est pardonnant.
> Quoy dirrons lors du prestre avant,
> Qui pour chanter la sainte messe
> Les biens du mort prent a largesce,
> Mais pour luxure et yveresce
> Ne puet tenir le covenant
> A l'alme ardant peccheresse? (*MO*, 20533–42)

[Whoever accepts wages from another living person must logically render corresponding service or else (unless excused) suffer legal punishment. What shall we say, then, of the priest who takes the wealth charitably bestowed by the dead for chanting holy masses and, because of lechery and drunkenness, does not keep his covenant with the sinful burning soul?]

In the course of this censure, Gower's invocation of contract allows him to move rhetorically from the volition that exempted clerics from legal reprisal to the obligations that bind him in any event. The terminology, in fact, serves primarily as conceptual leverage to foreground a more binding claim on the priest's actions. His contract is not with the patron himself but with his soul, which broadens the ethical framework of his commitment. The mass priest's withholding of services not only adds to the purgatorial torment of the deceased benefactor but more fundamentally constitutes neglect of his greater covenant by withholding priestly services from the Christian community more broadly conceived.

As far as Gower is concerned, annuellers fail in all aspects of their obligations. It is precisely at this juncture that he cites their failure in regard to language as well.

Comment auci bien priera
Qui point n'entent ce qu'il dirra?
Car ce nous dist saint Augustin,
Qe dieus un tiel n'escoultera. (*MO*, 20545–48)

[Also, how can anyone pray effectively who does not understand what
he is saying? Saint Augustine tells us that God will not hearken to any
such person.]

Where *The Simonie* invoked the proverbial jay to illustrate the sins of ignorance, Gower invokes an equally conventional *sententia* from Augustine.[103]
As in *The Simonie*, there is a mismatch between the familiar passage and
the situation on which it is brought to bear. No more concerned with the
obstacles of linguistic alterity than the writer of the *Disticha Catonis*, Augustine was not addressing illiteracy as much as hypocrisy and insincerity.
For Gower, however, hypocrisy and illiteracy are intimately connected,
not simply because both obstruct any direct correspondence between intention and meaning but more fundamentally because one cannot effect
the interior disposition appropriate to prayer without first having been
interpellated, without having understood. The connection is evident in
Gower's Anglo-Norman term for "understand," "entent." Like its modern French reflex, *entendre*, the word refers to hearing as well as to understanding—indeed, it is the hearing of those who have ears. At the same
time, insofar as the mass priest is representing and pursuing his patrons'
interests, the meaning of "entent" shades into the semantic field of Latin
intentio and its Middle English counterpart, *entente*. The latter is, however, predicated on the former.

In the absence of this prior subjection, Gower supplies his own interpellative gesture in its stead. Shifting to the vocative, he names the offenders
and their crime.

O prestre lays, di quoy serra
De toy, q'ensi par mal engin
As pris l'argent de ton voisin
Pour ton office q'est divin
Chanter, et tu n'as a cela
L'entendement de ton latin?
Trop serras hontous au fin,
Qant dieus de ce t'accusera (*MO*, 20549–55)

[O lay priest, what shall become of you, who by evil trickery have taken the money of your neighbor to chant your divine office, without your having any understanding of your Latin? You will be much shamed in the end, when God shall accuse you of this.]

The oxymoronic appellation "prestre lays" presumably refers to the combination of clerical pretension and lack of learning that define the annuellers' misbehavior.[104] There is, however, a paradoxical accuracy in the label in that the interpellative dynamic of understanding that Gower wants to inform these priests' utterances is that which had come to be more visibly aligned with devotional practice and with the laity. This paradox helps explain how Gower is able to cite Augustine's thoughts on infelicitous prayer, which were usually invoked to discuss private devotions, to examine the obligations that inhere in the authorized speech acts of the liturgy. Though much of this conceptualization of understanding as an isolatable dynamic of textual interaction had been elaborated to compensate for the laity's exteriorized relationship to ritual language, the demands of contractual liturgy called attention to the necessity of understanding for the cleric as well. The author of *The Simonie* also felt this, yet by the time Gower was writing, the stakes of understanding had been raised considerably. Whereas the *lewid* vicar's illiteracy was deplorable, the same failing in the annueller is disastrous, for the felicity of the speech act depends on his understanding.

Contractual liturgy was not the only kind of ritual performance in which understanding was a concern. Wykeham, as we saw, had similar worries about the understanding of the monks of St. Swithun's. Yet within the more conventional structures of the monastery, still shaped to some extent by the discourse of choral community, Wykeham was able to call upon grammatical discourse, making it accommodate his anxiety over the relationship between self and sacred text that was the basis of textual community. The performances satirized by Gower took place outside those structures and constituted a new kind of textual relation. There is still a connection to the discourse of choral community in that Gower imagines a final reckoning, just as Titivillus had threatened, but the transaction that will be audited is not one involving syllables rendered to God, nor one involving money exchanged for masses. It is an exchange of money for *entendement*. Because it functioned in the exchange itself, *entendement* could not be defined solely as reception, as an exchange of *verba* and *res* that takes place within the confines of one's interior. The outward gesture of representing someone else's interests before God made "intention" central as well. As such, it could not be so easily governed by grammatical discourse. *Grammatica* might be invoked to discern the *intentio auctoris* of the words that were read and sung—the meaning to which the priest, acting *in persona ecclesie*, should assimilate himself—but it could not account for the particular intention of the contractual Mass—by which it was dedicated to interests that the priest was ethically required to assimilate to himself. Still less could it govern a priest's personal intention, which had become the object of perpetual suspicion.

This suspicion was, in the end, metonymic of broader suspicions concerning the new kinds of textual relations forged by contractual liturgy as well as the manner in which these textual relations were imbricated in the socioeconomic relations of textual community. Contractual liturgy was one of several practices that stressed the surplus of meaning—sacramental or profane—that is produced in the ritualized performance of sacred texts and the excesses of intention that accompany the performance of "textualized" language, as Ong calls it.[105] Whether in the unlettered performance of annuals or in private recitation of the Hours, these practices allowed the circulation of meaning that was not always reducible to grammatical meaning and transactions of power that did not require mastery of Latin. The necessity that all subject themselves to the text led some to imagine sacred language in terms that would no longer allow the simple equation, presumed by Wykeham, that understanding is automatically conveyed by grammatical instruction. The socioeconomic circumstances after the plague made itinerant mass priests visible targets of criticism, allowing them to be cast as the villains of a new and unstable market in liturgical services, yet they were only one part of a larger shift in the ways that the performance of sacred texts was reshaping the terms and relations of the Christian textual community.

4

Extragrammatical Literacies and the Latinity of the Laity

Extragrammatical Literacies

DURING THE HALF CENTURY following the plague, among the fragmentation of latinate literacies and emerging liturgical economies, England also experienced a period of accelerated vernacular literary production. Though the fiction of Chaucer and Gower is the best-known evidence of this phenomenon, Nicholas Watson has underscored the importance of contemporary religious texts by writers such as Walter Hilton, Julian of Norwich, and the author of *The Cloud of Unknowing*—a body of writings to which he has influentially applied the label "vernacular theology."[1] These texts played a crucial role both in the development of English as a language capable of presenting topics normally reserved for *litteratura* and in the imaginative construction of a broad "public" of vernacular readers. Characterized as "a huge cultural experiment involving the translation of Latin and Anglo-Norman texts, images, conceptual structures—the apparatus of textual authority—into ... English,"[2] many of the texts associated with the label attempt to reconfigure both forms of knowledge and social identities. In this respect, they contributed significantly to the redistribution of intellectual and material resources at the heart of this study.

Watson's discussions of this "cultural experiment" are geared toward explaining trends in Middle English writing and are connected to the concept of "vernacularity" that has been such a central focus of Middle English studies in recent years.[3] Yet the label "vernacular theology" links literary production not simply with language choice but also with religious experience, placing English writing in a larger social and political context that invites questions about the relationship among writing, textual authority, and spirituality. Within this context, vernacular writing has been presumed to be uniquely enabling. Many writers of English, according to Watson, assumed a posture that had "at least the potential for a wholesale democratizing of the spiritual life" in that they invited the *lewid* to entertain "hard religious questions or the desire for theological knowledge."[4] This aligning of the vernacular with democratizing intellectualization, however, is not without its qualifications. Some scholars, including Watson, have warned that assessments of the vernacular should not devolve into "a crude narrative of oppositionality, with the vernacular in the role of the plucky underdog,"[5] but even these cautions have been focused on acknowledging that not all vernacular texts necessarily espouse democratizing goals. Given the complex and competing sets of spiritual, social, and economic values I have been describing as the "politics of understanding," however, one might ask not only whether vernacular texts are liberating but also what constitutes "liberating." The cerebral endeavors of vernacular theology may have allowed those not in positions of clerical authority to have some measure of control over their spiritual fortunes, but focusing solely on this aspect runs the risk of equating challenges to ecclesiastical hegemony exclusively with abstract intellectualization and hermeneutical mastery. It runs the further risk not simply of aligning such challenges exclusively with the use of the vernacular but also of locating the power of the vernacular primarily in its seeming ability to render theological concepts transparent.

The transparency implicitly accorded to the vernacular and the celebration of intellectual engagement with the ideas it encoded stands in stark contrast to attitudes toward the Latin texts of liturgy and devotion. Modern discussions of devotional and liturgical recitation tend to represent it as an alienation from language, such that Latin texts become meaningless strings of phonemes to the unlettered who perform them.[6] The ungrammatical friend of Chaucer's *litel clergeon* epitomizes this alienation to the degree that his admission of grammatical incompetence has itself become an ossified text, subject to almost obligatory quotation in accounts of the history of educational practice, as I have noted.[7] Its repetition bespeaks the seemingly irreducible alterity associated with the idea of encountering the letter in pure exteriority. Scholars of late medieval religious writing sometimes take this perception of exteriority a step further as they pursue their more sympathetic interest in the cultivation of spiritual interiority. Writers like Julian of Norwich, for whom the "literature of interiority" was a vehicle for speculative theology,[8] are figured within a tradition that is opposed to the "formalism of authoritative structures developed in Latin"[9] that the *clergeon*'s unlettered singing exemplifies. While instances of the former tradition, whether situated under the rubric of vernacular theology or not, are generally described as impressive examples of spiritual self-determination, "formalism" tends to be associated with inauthentic piety, as in Lee Patterson's reading of the *Prioress's Tale*, which figures the *clergeon*'s illiterate performance as an example of "mindless ventriloquism" consonant with a mode of Marian devotion that "fosters a lack of spiritual struggle by short-circuiting the inwardness and penitential self-examination of true religious transformation."[10] In the most extreme articulations, descriptions of formalism, in the guise of liturgical and more generally sacramental practice, are based on the implicit opposition not so much of thought and action but of thought and inaction, in which authenticity becomes a function of engagement in the labor of interiority.[11]

In terms of textual practice, such an opposition is difficult to maintain. However we imagine lay or *lewid* performance of Latin prayer, there is little evidence that the champions of vernacular theology saw it as opposed to or fundamentally incompatible with more speculative endeavors. Even a writer like the author of *The Cloud of Unknowing*, who scorns the performance of "any longe sauter vnmyndfuly mumlyd in þe teeþ," makes clear that his alternative contemplative exercises were not meant to replace the texts and practices ordained by Holy Church.[12] Though such cautionary statements might be deemed efforts to avoid the censure of orthodox institutions, they are consistent with the fact that the rise of vernacular theology is contemporaneous with the development of Books of Hours and other technologies of Latin prayer. Evidence of book ownership, further, suggests that this burgeoning market catered to the same audience as that of speculative vernacular texts.[13] Though based, in Watson's phrase, on "authoritative structures developed in Latin," the use of these texts cannot be classified as a traditional practice that was discarded in favor of theological speculation but must be considered an emergent practice that developed in tandem with it, effectively complementing vernacular theology rather than opposing it. Considered in these terms, an act such as the devotional rehearsal of the Hours, even when performed by the unlettered, becomes a practice defined less in terms of inability and disengagement than in terms of the facet of textual authority it isolates and exploits, namely, the power of ritualized language and the ennobling sense of obligation and responsibility that ideally characterized performance of the Office. If the attraction of vernacular theology was the power it gave the *lewid* over their own spiritual fortunes, the ability to wield ritualized language in fulfillment of a commitment made to God would seem similarly to grant a measure of spiritual agency. In pointing to this possibility, I do not intend to substitute performativity for theologizing as a resource of empowerment; I would like to suggest, however, that the "theological" emphasis implicit in some discussions of vernacular theology tends to privilege intellectualizing textual and spiritual strategies in ways that can hamper the analysis of textual authority.

The label "vernacular theology" is most productively used, to use Watson's phrase, as a "catch-all term" for all manner of writing in English,[14] that is, as a synthetic, rather than analytic, concept used to classify under a single rubric texts that scholars had formerly isolated in accordance with their own generic and theological assumptions. When these texts are viewed together as an insular corpus rather than variously as imitations or continuations of continental traditions, one sees the outline of an emerging literary discourse in English—one of an intellectual vitality capable of addressing complex theological questions. Yet to appreciate the capabilities of this discourse fully, to elaborate on the heterogeneity of texts labeled "vernacular theology," as Watson suggests, vernacular religious writing needs to be situated within a broader ranger of contemporary textual practices—which could include both Latin prayer and vernacular fiction—under the rubric of literacy. In this approach, the primary object of analysis is "the apparatus of textual authority" itself. The very possibility of vernacular theology—indeed the possibility of translation of any kind—is contingent on the disarticulation of this apparatus, the unity of which had been sustained by grammatical culture. Textual strategies, such as the intellectualizing gestures that vernacular theology often exemplifies, are derived from isolating constituent elements of textual authority (e.g., the monopoly on abstract nouns) and appropriating them as a way of gaining access to the symbolic capital associated with clerical letters. Insofar as such appropriative gestures come to be systematized—that is, repeatable, communicable, allowing at least the possibility of strategic use, even if not necessarily self-consciously "literate" use—they can usefully be considered literacies; to the degree that they are not elaborated under the auspices of the formal grammatical curriculum, they might be termed "informal" or "extragrammatical" literacies. Since extragrammatical literacies can be based on any aspect of textual authority that can be imaginatively isolated, one could potentially generate a long list of them that might include not only vernacular theology but also certain modes of reading and singing and even secular practices, such as "pragmatic" literacy with documents, as described by Malcolm Parkes.[15] Yet taxonomy as such is of less value than the premise that would underlie such a list: a recognition of both the multiplicity and the pervasiveness of textual authority as well as the correlative breadth of the range of strategies by means of which people might poach from that authority.

This chapter will examine practices involving Latin prayer as extra-grammatical literacies.[16] My goal, however, is not simply to name or define these practices but also to investigate how practices derived from Latin prayer participated in the politics of understanding. In the case of Latin recitation, pursuing these issues is especially complicated because of the degree to which the politics of understanding surrounding *modern* literacy has infiltrated discussions of medieval practice. Taking their cue from documentary references to acts of reading "without understanding," modern scholars have hypothesized a discrete, lower-level literacy skill involving the generalized ability to "sound out" words on the page. Paul Saenger has even provided a label for this skill, "phonetic literacy," and situates it among the competencies lay readers brought to Books of Hours.[17] There is evidence, as mentioned in Chapter 1,[18] that early pedagogy within the grammatical curriculum did isolate phonemic recognition of syllables as one of its first elements. There is far less evidence that owners of Books of Hours were regularly exposed to this formal training,[19] but modern perceptions of "phonetic literacy" are, I suspect, based less on medieval evidence than on our own experience of, for example, learning to pronounce words in languages we do not know or of similar modern practices involving the Koran from which we intuit a notion of decoding that is purely phonemic.[20] It is at this point that modern politics of understanding come into play, for this intuition is not a neutral observation of our cognitive experience. Modern literacy is such that the multiple and redundant strategies we use for word recognition (which can involve recognition of phonemes, morphemes, "word-shapes," and so forth) are deployed unconsciously; "skilled" reading behaviors almost by definition cannot be observed.[21] Our intuitions are rather guided by modern ideological constructions of writing that maintain it as a transparent reflection of speech. This point is worth dwelling on. In calling attention to the perception that writing is simply speech represented in a visual medium, I am not adverting to the fundamental opposition of speech and writing undergirding Western metaphysics but rather to the more pragmatic (and more modern) notion that literacy is solely a matter of word recognition, an ability achieved in a language—usually a mother tongue—in which one is already conversant.[22] Such a definition effectively conceals the *discursive* labor of comprehension: if you can recognize (sound out) the words, you are presumed to understand them (unless they belong to a "specialized" language requiring its own discrete discipline, such as literature or law). Modern literacy is thus a *finite*, as well as a minimal, skill, preferably acquired in one's youth; *litteratura* becomes something one does with one's literacy, not a facet of literacy itself. This notion of a finite skill with general application is one that we inevitably bring to our assessment of medieval literacy.

Still more important, this construction of literacy isolates the phonemic as the realm of the discursively and even semantically neutral, thereby articulating an area of knowledge that is perceived as universally accessible and unlimited in its applications. This perception is a critical component of the democratizing powers attributed to literacy (while simultaneously critical in producing the "functionally illiterate" as a categorically anomalous group). To some extent, it underwrites the democratizing powers attributed to vernacular theology as well, insofar as the act of rendering theological concepts in the vernacular is implicitly assumed to be sufficient (not merely necessary) to make them widely accessible. In a similar fashion, historians of education once assumed that those who possessed "phonetic" literacy in Latin would ipso facto be literate in their native languages,[23] though most would now acknowledge this as a misconception. The isolation of the phonemic, however, has ramifications for our perception of Latin prayer as well. If this notion of decoding makes vernacular writing seem transparent, it has the opposite effect on unfamiliar languages of rendering them utterly opaque. Historians of education have been less extreme in their description of pedagogical practice (of varying degrees of formality), usually claiming that aspiring readers were taught to "pronounce (i.e., read) … Latin, although not necessarily to understand it grammatically."[24] Saenger, by contrast, identifies "phonetic literacy" as a skill possessed by lay users of Latin devotions specifically to distinguish it from "comprehension literacy," which he equates with silent reading. Though he acknowledges that a positive value was granted to the act of giving voice to sacred texts, he describes the ability to do so as a lower "level" of literacy that he presumes those (far fewer) who have attained "comprehension" literacy must automatically possess.[25] Yet if one pursues the logic of a "comprehension" literacy that is a second, more advanced level that follows acquisition of "phonetic" literacy, the implication is that one can only enter the textual domain of Latin prayer by first stripping words of their meaning.

Lending priority to performance—to the voicing of a text—is in this formulation virtually equated with self-absence. While this description is not particularly judgmental in its evaluation of devotional practice, linguistic alienation remains its defining feature. Even when some semantic knowledge of the texts being performed is granted, it is figured not as fully legitimate but as based on "extraneous sources" that would include a vernacular translation, but not Donatus.[26] Medieval sources, such as the treatises on the Mass discussed in Chapter 3, do place aids created for the *lewid* in a distinct category, yet the sources on prayer consulted by Saenger do not always characterize estrangement from the language of performed texts as the result of inability or illiteracy, as we shall see. The implicit connection on Saenger's part creates a boundary between comprehension and phonetic literacy that can only be crossed with the acquisition of new skills, which further implies that it can only be crossed in one direction. Though he claims that the two literacies existed "side by side," they are ultimately figured as an opposition: in this case, a linguistic instantiation of the opposition between thought and action. Because it is connected to notions of language, this version of the opposition resonates almost invariably with post-Enlightenment constructions of "free speech," in which language is the vehicle and expression of thoughts that originate in the self. The perpetuation of this construction goes a long way to explain the alterity of the little *clergeon*'s friend, whose ignorance runs counter to the basic premise that one should at least have semantic control over one's speech, even if one is not the "author" of one's words.

In suggesting that scholarly accounts of devotional practices have been influenced by these modern constructions, I do not mean to imply that the phenomena scholars have described are simply fictitious. Again, medieval grammatical discourse did isolate the syllable as a discrete, potentially separable phonemic aspect of written language. Yet even though our own isolation of the phoneme is the legacy of *grammatica*, there were different reasons to capitalize on its separability in medieval culture. As I argued in Chapter 2, the skill designated *legere aut sillabicare* in benefit of clergy examinations did make it possible for a greater number of men to claim clerical status, yet I also proposed that this gesture represented a reassertion of ecclesiastical jurisdiction over literate skills—a far cry from the gestures to the universal, unaffiliated access to writing connected with modern alphabetic literacy. "Reading or syllabifying," further, had different ideological motivations from the articulation of *scientia legere et cantare*, even where this ability constituted a portable, marketable skill. These differences—both those between medieval and modern and those within either period—need to be acknowledged. Only by attempting to discern the interests that might be served by the complaints, instructions, and cautions concerning the practice of Latin prayer will it be possible to imagine beyond reading strategies articulated by and within grammatical discourse and ultimately to understand the social implications of extragrammatical reading.

Vocal Prayer, Public Speech, and the Elaboration of Attention

In popular thought, the Church's insistence on Latin as the primary language of religious experience has placed it among the foremost mechanisms of disenfranchisement in late medieval religious culture, more specifically, as the propagator of rote or mechanical experience devoid of individual agency or responsibility. While there is no denying that intellectual and even affective experiences mediated by the vernacular had enabling potential, nor that the Church perceived some facets of this potential as threatening, it would be at best an overgeneralization to claim that the Church advocated disengaged recitation of Latin texts. There is little evidence that ecclesiastical institutions promoted the devotional rehearsal of Latin prayers found in Books of Hours and miscellanies by those who were utterly ignorant of their meaning—not, at least, in the same way that Gaytryge's translation of Thoresby's *Catechism* (1357) was commissioned or Love's translation of the *Meditations on the Life of Christ* (1409) was specifically endorsed for lay use,[27] or that vernacular levation prayers were actively encouraged as a performance of lay status. This is not to suggest that the Church in any way discouraged the use of Latin prayer books by the laity, nor even that they objected vociferously to illiterate performance; clearly the Church tolerated the practice and on a few occasions even defended it when the polemical stakes were high.[28] Yet attending to the specifics of precisely which practices were discouraged, for which performers, and in what settings yields far greater insight into the kind of authority that was invested in Latin as well as how sacralized language enacted this authority.

Discussions in vernacular Mass treatises that instructed the *lewid* in how and why they should attend the reading of the Latin gospel demonstrate that the Church saw no problem in the laity's *hearing* words they purportedly did not understand, but these treatises do not advise their lay audiences to *say* them. Boy choristers, as we have seen, were often in the position of having to perform the liturgy in Latin before they had

learned grammar, yet insofar as this arrangement may have given license
to ignorant recitation in some cases, it was only because the requirements
of performance necessitated it and was likely viewed as an excusable failure
due to youth and inexperience, rather than promoted as a model of piety
(by those other than Chaucer's Prioress). This accommodation for lack of
knowledge in youth, however, underscores the most important distinction
in determining the necessity of understanding: that it was not as critical
to the performance of liturgy as it was to devotion. Such an assertion may
seem a contradiction in light of the complaints about illiterate priests I
discussed in Chapter 3, yet in this case, I refer to a different group of performers. Whereas illiteracy was clearly a failing in an ordained priest and as
such could become the symbol of other failures of responsibility, liturgical
performers who were not necessarily expected to possess such knowledge
offered the possibility to explore the nature of sacred speech acts from a
different perspective. Even more than choristers, women religious were
such a group.[29] Nuns were required by their rules to perform the Office
daily, thus their performances did bear official, liturgical authority. Grammatical training, however, was not consistently expected of them, and some
clearly had very little education at all. Though similar to the boy choristers
in terms of formal knowledge and limited access to clerical authority, their
marginality in male ecclesiastical culture was permanent. In part also as
a result of their cloistered lifestyles—the voluntary social alienation that
allowed them to become objects of speculation and recipients of (written)
pastoral advice—their textual practices became typical starting points for
explorations and rationalizations of licit unlettered performance.

   One such exploration occurs in *The Chastising of God's Children*, a
late fourteenth-century devotional manual written for a group of women
religious. In discussing the value of illiterate liturgical recitation, the writer
invokes terms similar to those used in Mass treatises that appealed to the
vertu of sacred speech.

If ʒee wil aske how ʒe shuln preie deuoutli in preier whiche ʒe vndirstonde nat, I
answere ʒou þerto and seie þat for þe uertu of þe wordis and ʒoure lownesse and
obeisaunce to holi chirche, wiþ a feruent desire upward to god aftir ʒoure entent,
þouʒ ʒe vndirstonde no word þat ʒe seie, it may be to ʒou more medeful, and
more acceptable to god þanne grete deuocioun þat ʒe wene ʒe haue in oþer preuy
deuocions.[30]

"Uertu" in this context, however, circulates differently than it did for the
parishioner who merely bore witness to its performance in the gospel,

for the nuns are in effect responsible for its production as well as for its consumption. The character and meaning assigned to the act of voicing *vertu* imply that the stakes of this performance are not precisely the same. Like the hearing of the gospel, the recitation of divine service demands an act of subjection, but in this case (closer to that encouraged in the discourse of choral community) subjection involves the fulfillment of vows made to Holy Church. The women's performance is thus defined more in terms of a prior commitment than in terms of interpellation as such. Yet even if this kind of recitation is figured as a quasi-clerical act, the value attached to understanding is precisely the obverse of that assigned to it in contractual liturgy. In contrast to the unlearned annueller, whose illiteracy stood for the pursuit of self-interest and a refusal to subject himself, illiteracy itself becomes a vehicle of subjection as it is opposed to the self-indulgent desire for "grete deuocioun."

In this fashion, the writer uses the marginal position of women religious to examine explicitly the distinction between liturgy and devotion that was only implicitly articulated in Mass treatises addressed to lay audiences. The discussion in which the quoted passage occurs begins by pointing to the importance of liturgical prayer: "Preieþ þanne ententifli in tyme of preier of ʒoure diewe seruice, for to þat preier ʒe bien most bounden" (220/5–6). Invoking the familiar regulations of choral performance, the writer admonishes his readers to say their services at the appropriate time, to say them "ententifli," without rushing, and to say them in Latin. The very possibility of lapses in this regard hints at the motivation for spelling out these distinctions. Potential latitude in the choice of prayer (even if taking advantage of that latitude could be perceived as a failure to observe one's vows) and other details of advice (as, for example, when the sister having difficulty maintaining attentive focus is advised to perform her services "wiþ a felawe" [224/8]) suggest that the sisters of this house did not perform their services *in choro* or even communally. Lacking the more visible characteristics of choral performance, the liturgical needed to be distinguished from "preuy deuociouns" or "special praiers" by other means (224/14). As a result, the liturgical becomes a type of speech act that can be enacted, even by those without sacerdotal authority, in a number of different settings. Ultimately, it comes to be defined by exteriority—a gap between speaker and speech that can be measured temporally (services are not the immediate exclamations of the devout soul but externally regulated services) and linguistically (services must be performed in Latin rather than in English). The writer disdains the possibility of "sautir and matyns of oure ladi" in English but does not object to their use under all circumstances. His interest, rather, lies in assigning the use of English to the realm of private devotion.

"Exteriority," then, does seem a fitting term to describe the speaker's relationship to the words she utters in this case because the writer assumes that the reluctance to give up "preuy deuociouns" and the desire to rehearse services in English is due to the sisters' complete ignorance of the meaning of the Latin words and thus the total absence of semantic control. Whether this assumption was accurate is another matter that I will take up in the next section. It is, in any event, worth remarking that in spite of this presumed ignorance, the Latin words of the service are capable of bearing an "entent," even if that "entent" is a "feruent desire upward to god" that is not directly related to the grammatical meaning of the words. There is even a subtle implication that Latin words are better at conveying *entent* or transmitting desire, for *deuocioun* is generally described as a form of spiritual pleasure ("goostli likyng" [220/11])—as something one feels or receives rather than gives or intends. In this respect, the passage is related to a much more common topic concerning "vocal prayer" in which the various modes of attention or intention that can be invested in ritualized speech are elaborated and codified. The treatises in which this topic is discussed have not received extensive scholarly attention as a group. What attention they have received has focused on the degree to which they appear to advocate exteriority and justify ignorant recitation, as the *Chastising* passage appears to do. This tendency is especially marked in Saenger's discussion, in which oral prayer is strongly aligned with "phonetic" literacy, which is in turn equated with a lack of comprehension. In his account, this "older oral mode" of prayer comes to be distinguished from "the newer mode of silently reading prayers" that spreads as more layfolk acquire comprehension literacy.[31] A closer inspection of these sources, however, allows a different reading, one that is more consistent with the liturgical trends I have charted in late fourteenth- and early fifteenth-century England (where Saenger's interests are predominantly in fifteenth- and sixteenth-century France) and less consistent with the modern politics of understanding that is quick to connect liturgy with exteriority, a lack of semantic mastery, and "oldness." For though the sources do speak variously about silence in prayer and meditation, the concerted attention and labor bestowed upon oral prayer suggests a new interest, however old the practice. The degree to which this interest takes the form of definition and codification specifically in regard to oral prayer does not signal the emergence of a single, discrete, competing practice such as silent prayer as much as it suggests a proliferation of textual practices involving sacred texts—whether silent reading, English recitation, or a newly emerging repertoire of Latin devotions—from among which the authorized, "public" practices of the liturgical needed to be firmly distinguished.

One feature that distinguishes the liturgical is the priority given to performance over semantic mastery. Yet many discussions figure the lack of such mastery as a temporary state resulting from a failure of attention, not as a permanent condition stemming from a lack of literacy. Lapses of attention were not peculiar to liturgy, but because liturgical utterances were regulated by external means to which the well-intentioned but way-ward soul was to subject itself, they were more forgivable in liturgical performance. In his *Scale of Perfection*, Walter Hilton urged patience for the women religious addressed in Book 1 should they find themselves hin-dered by vain thoughts in vocal prayer: "For wite thou weel that thou art excusid of thi dette, and thou schalt have meede for it as for anothir good dede that thou doost in charité, though thyn herte were not thereupon in the doynge."[32] The language of debt recalls the discourse of choral community, upon which these discussions draw so heavily. At the same time, however, care is always taken to distinguish these illocutionary acts from those that do not stem from an externally imposed obligation. Jean Gerson, in his treatise *De valore orationis et de attentione* (1416–17), makes a point similar to Hilton's that mandated prayers need not be repeated if the speaker has been troubled by inadvertent wandering of the mind away from the words or meaning of the text, yet he also makes a point of noting that the same did not apply to personal prayers (*voluntariis*).[33] Only the liturgical, in other words, was marked by a distance that made attention an act of discipline.

As an effect of this distance, attention was rarely singular. Just as the gap between speaker and speech in the chantry priest allowed his words to bear multiple intentions, discussions of vocal prayer became the occa-sion to explore the less threatening, but closely related, multiplication of attention—that is, the many aspects of the liturgical speech act to which one could direct one's intention. Gerson, who defines *attentio* as "the direction of the heart's intention" (*intentionis cordialis directio*), is typical in his enumeration of three types of attention: *actualis*, *habitualis*, and *virtualis*. "Actual" attention concerns itself with the sounds or the words, "habitual" with the meaning of the words, and "virtual" with "neither the forms of words nor the meaning … but in any feeling (*affectus*) that

tends toward heavenly or divine things."[34] Gerson does claim that of these
the third alone suffices for effective prayer, which leads Saenger to point
to the low priority oral prayer places on understanding.[35] Of greater interest, however, is the manner in which Gerson characterizes the first two
as insufficient rather than unnecessary (2:184–86). Precise attention to
sounds or words is insufficient, he claims, in the same way that counting
the precise number of steps one takes on a pilgrimage does not sufficiently comprehend the meaning of the act. Attention to words is insufficient because meaning does not regulate intention, just as one can go on
pilgrimage on account of greed. Virtual attention, by contrast, is said to
lead to the others. Derived from *virtus* (ME *vertu*), virtual attention involves the power that motivates the heart of the one who prays, directing
the prayer on its path in the same way that a bow directs an arrow, such
that it will remain on course even if the heart should later waver. Gerson's
concern is not to trivialize grammatical meaning but to elaborate and
codify the spiritual and cognitive processes that are rendered visible for
him in all their richness by the estrangement of liturgical speech from its
performer.

     These processes could be arranged in a number of different ways. In
the *rationale* of the Divine Office created for the Brigittine nuns of Syon
Abbey, *The Myroure of Oure Ladye* (second quarter of the fifteenth century),
Gerson's "virtual" attention is simply labeled "entent" and placed in a
different category from the first two.[36] These two are divided into two categories each to create four manners of "entendaunce" in prayer. Attention
to the sounds and words is articulated as two distinct groups that separate
exteriority from ignorance. One manner of *entendaunce* is "to kepe the
mynde vpon the selfe wordes wythout eny vnderstandynge" (49), but this
manner is distinct from ensuring that "all the seruyce be sayde as yt oughte
to be bothe, psalmes, responces and lessones, and verse" (50). Attention
to the meaning of the words is divided into that given to the "lytterall
vnderstondynge" and that given to the "gostly vnderstondynge" (49).
The mention of spiritual senses is somewhat unusual in this context, even
ambitious in comparison to Gerson, who acknowledges the practical and
intellectual obstacles that might impede even the more able theologians
from fully understanding language so rich and inexhaustible in meaning
(2:187). Very likely, the inclusion of spiritual senses is related to contemporaneous fifteenth-century debates surrounding the uses of scriptural
translation and vernacular hermeneutics.[37] Although this particular site of
contention lies beyond the scope of this study, it is worth noting that the

writer of the *Myroure* does not imagine that access to spiritual meaning required extensive grammatical training, or even the ability to parse, for he intends his vernacular translation and commentary on the service to make such meaning available. More important, it is worth noting that in this case, as in others, liturgical performance often facilitated such debates rather than serving as a refuge from them.

Even from these two examples, in fact, it should be clear that the concept of attention in vocal prayer served not as a way to subordinate understanding but as a way to examine the nature of understanding itself, specifically as it related to public speech. Or, it might be more accurate to say, public speech—liturgical speech—was in part defined by the emphasis it placed on the relationship of the performer to sacred language, a relationship that could include the mastery of grammatical meaning we now describe as "understanding" but that encompassed much more. The *Myroure*'s choice of the word *entendaunce* is particularly instructive in this regard. The term is more closely related to the Anglo-Norman term *entendement* used by Gower to chastise unethical annuellers and opens up a similarly complex field of semantic agency involving hearing, understanding, intending, and attending (in the sense of both "paying attention to" and "serving").[38] Further, it effectively erases the subtle distinctions between intention and attention Gerson tried to maintain, creating even greater ambiguity in terms of subject and object in speech. The writer is fully aware of the various shades of meaning, as he makes clear in his introductory remarks: "For god lyste not to here his prayer that hereth not hymselfe ne takyth not hede to that he sayth" (49). In this formulation, as in others, the liturgical is defined by an estrangement from language that does not alienate, yet it can make one the audience of one's own speech. This estrangement was partly a function of ritualization in general and thus served to sacralize scriptural texts. The prominence of such issues specifically in discussions of liturgical speech acts, however, points more strongly to the homologous relationship between this estrangement and the gap between speaker and speech that allowed performers to inhabit the *persona ecclesie*. It was therefore also critical to the reproduction of ecclesiastical power in ritualized speech. Such a privileged mode of speech might be said to disenfranchise the laity, yet if so, it accomplishes the task through a far more complex means of regulating language and lettered practice than a dichotomy between opacity and transparency can account for.

*   *   *

Extragrammatical Devotion and the *Lewid*

Not all discussions of the services of women religious focused on matters of understanding or attention connected to the liturgical nature of their speech. Thomas Walsingham, for example, in his *Gesta Abbatum*, describes the reading and singing of nuns in terms that align them more closely with the *lewid* laity. While recounting Abbot Thomas's disapproval of the poor standard of literacy at the Benedictine House of St. Mary des Prez, he claims that "the nuns for the most part had formerly been illiterate and performed nothing of their services, but instead substituted Lord's Prayers and Angelic Greetings [sc. aves] in the place of the Office."[39] These women, it would appear, did not have the luxury of modulating their attention except, perhaps, in regard to the two inappropriately deployed texts they did know. Though their illiteracy, unlike that of the laity, is clearly a failure in need of remediation, its centrality in Walsingham's account makes his discussion a useful starting point to examine the parameters of illiteracy as they were defined for the non-cleric. Understanding these parameters will in turn help us consider the abilities and the lettered prospects of the unlearned layperson engaged in Latin devotion.

Perhaps the most striking feature of illiteracy in Walsingham's discussion is the textual terminology in which it is couched. The illiterate are those who know only their *paternoster* and *ave*, in contrast to those who have access to the texts of the Office and other services. Literate status for the nuns would seem to depend on neither their understanding of Latin texts nor their ability to decode these texts from the written page, even though both of these skills may have been involved. The question of whether or not the *paternoster*, or the Office for that matter, is understood simply goes unasked. The task of decoding likewise receives no mention in the proposed solution to the nuns' situation. The remedy to illiteracy, as Walsingham reports, was not to insist on grammatical instruction nor to provide primers or other materials for learning letters but to supply the nuns with "professional" service books—breviaries and ordinals, which the abbot donated from the abbey's own collection (much to the consternation of the precentor and others who objected to the alienation of the abbey's property).[40] We might presume that those few who knew their services could use the books to teach the others, but the means by which this might have been accomplished is of no concern to Walsingham and possibly even to Abbot Thomas. Within this context, at least, having the books and knowing the texts are essentially conflated.

Discussions of Latin devotions used by the laity exhibit the same definitions and ambiguities. Because it was the one text that all were presumed to know, the *paternoster* becomes a marker of *lewidness*. When Hilton advises the audience of Book 2 of the *Scale* on "the most special praiere that the soule useth and hath most confort in," he makes the same distinction between *lewid* and *lettrid* and prescribes different texts for each: "Pater Noster for lewid men, and psalmes and ympnes and othere servyce of Holi Chirche for lettred men."[41] Similarly, one Mass treatise, anticipating an audience of both literates and illiterates, counsels this universal substitution for any text that lay outside the boundaries of *lewid* knowledge: "If þou kan noghte rede ne saye/Þy pater-noster rehers always" (C.89–90). Here, as elsewhere, the matter of understanding is not broached. Jean Gerson, when speaking about the insufficiency of "actual" attention (that is, attention to words and sounds), offers an exemplum that highlights this ambiguity. A man wanting to make clear the instability of the heart in a peasant (*rusticam*) whom he suspected of feigning devotion and attention promised to give him an ass if he could recite the Lord's Prayer without thinking about anything else. Taking up the challenge, the peasant found himself distracted by thoughts of his forthcoming financial gain, whether he might also have a saddle, and so on, such that his inner wandering was undeniable.[42] On the one hand, Gerson considers the peasant to be a fitting example of one who attends to words and sounds alone, yet within the paradigm he has set up, this is the only category under which any lapse of attention may be discussed regardless of knowledge. If his exemplum contains a slur against peasants, it is only that they are examples of distractibility, not necessarily that they lack knowledge. On the other hand, it is unclear what character of attention a well-disciplined peasant might have, given that for Gerson the only form of attention that is sufficient is "virtual" attention directed toward the power and intention of the prayer. Like the distinction between having the book and knowing the texts, the distinction between knowing grammatical meaning and knowing basic intention is largely irrelevant to Gerson in this context.

Such a lack of distinction is not entirely foreign to modern culture. American children, for example, are taught to recite the Pledge of Allegiance with a similar indifference to precise "grammatical" or semantic meaning. The comparison is useful in allowing us to complicate our thinking about linguistic opacity and transparency, for while we would generally not imagine a seven-year-old (and, likely, some adults) to know the meaning of the word "indivisible," neither do we presume that she experiences the Pledge as completely exteriorized or meaningless. While any connection we imagine to those words is based on the familiarity we presume the child to have with the language in which it is recited (English, in this case), there is reason to believe that Latin may not have been quite as opaque to the late medieval laity as we assume. The drama *Mankind* presumes a certain degree of morphemic knowledge on the part of its audience in Mischief's comic rendering of a poorly written document: "Here is '*blottibus in blottis, / Blottorum blottibus istis.*'"[43] Though *Mankind* is a much later text (c. 1465–70), the amount of knowledge required to get the joke is minimal and not implausible for a lay population that at least *heard* a good deal of Latin.[44] Far more complex is the morphemic and syntactic play at work in Mischief's earlier faux-*sententia*, "*Corn servit bredibus, chaffe horsibus, straw firybusque*" (57), though in this case the speaker "translates" his joke to accommodate Mercy's and the audience's "leude undyrstondinge" (58) and thereby makes the principles on which his joke is based available. The point is that lack of grammatical training did not necessarily doom the untutored layperson to encounter Latin texts as made up of only undifferentiated vocal sounds and unrecognizable words. Cognizance of Latin morphemes, sounds, and vocabulary, however unsystematic, would come into play in the assimilation and retention of sacred texts, whether learned by means of the written page or not. Even this degree of knowledge had the potential to make the recitation of these texts meaningful in some way.

Quantitative terms like "degree" can in fact be misleading, particularly when applied to those whose experience of letters was not hierarchically structured by institutionalized curricula. Forms of knowledge need to be assessed instead in terms of how they may have functioned within broader perceptions of the cultural function of letters and texts. The emphasis on textual knowledge in this case once again invokes the distinction I have introduced between repertory-based and skilled-based literacy.[45] The comparison to the Pledge of Allegiance further helps clarify that the distinction is more heuristic than strictly historical, its primary function being to illuminate how textual practices are regulated in different cultural settings. In realms beyond the Pledge, the skill acquisition more closely associated with "literacy" in modern settings is geared toward the capacity to decode unfamiliar material at sight (what musicians refer to as "sight reading"), a cognitive organization that anticipates a hypothetically infinite amount of unfamiliar material. Skill-based literacy is, in other words, a literacy of things that have yet to be written. Those deemed "literate" are furthermore expected to participate in the production of these unfamiliar materials and skills are transmitted to this end. Writing is privileged as the active aspect of literacy as opposed to the passive reading ability with which it is felt to be continuous, hence, "grammar" in modern pedagogy deals primarily with proper writing and speaking. The repertory-based literacy that characterized liturgical and devotional practice was, by contrast, a literacy of things to be read, one that imagined a finite number of texts that collectively constituted a resource of infinite meaning. This difference in telos permits different cognitive organizations and potentially even a different hierarchy of skills and strategies that readers brought to texts. While these differences have implications for the formally trained reader, as I will discuss, they have even greater implications for how we imagine the reading activities of those without formal training, who develop their "skills" unconsciously in the very act of textual performance.

The kind of unsystematic knowledge I have projected for lay readers, for example, is not the kind of knowledge that would enable instantaneous word recognition of unfamiliar texts. Yet Books of Hours and other Latin devotional materials—which generally consisted of a limited number of familiar, frequently repeated texts—do not necessarily require this ability. It is in fact unlikely that unschooled users of sacred Latin texts would be interested in acquiring such an abstract skill. Layfolk were probably far more motivated to learn to read the single book or prayer roll they had acquired than to possess a generalized skill. Even layfolk with ambitions to extensive clerical knowledge aspired to the accomplishments of "clerkes that konne manye bokes," as Langland puts it, rather than to the abstract potential of a clerk that *could read* any book (*PP*, B 11.455). Learning to read a Book of Hours (among other books) in the terms of a repertory-based literacy was a social practice, whereby texts were transmitted from person to person as much as they were transmitted from page to person.[46] Images of the "Education of the Virgin" that depict St. Anne or the Virgin pointing to a written text with a fescue or finger may well represent an informal tutorial in word recognition by which such textual assimilation might have been achieved (Fig. 5).[47] What precisely Anne or, in many cases, the Virgin points to—whether to letters, syllables, words—is most likely unrecoverable, just as one can only speculate about the possible word recognition strategies used by someone who has not fully internalized the "alphabetic principle" (the basic concept that individual letters stand for sounds) or is not possessed of "phonemic awareness" (the capacity to

Figure 5. The Education of the Virgin, 1420s, Church of All Saints, North Street, York. The Virgin uses a fescue to point to specific words. Reproduced by permission of All Saints Church, York.

discriminate phonemes).[48] Though both of these types of knowledge are indispensable to modern literacy acquisition, a literacy based on a limited number of familiar and frequently repeated texts might involve other, less "efficient" strategies. Such a task would also involve memorization, though there is no reason to think that the distinction between page and memory mattered, as it did in the benefit of clergy examinations, nor that this kind of memorization was undertaken independently of the written page. Insofar as any of these strategies enabled the rendering of texts, they represent engagements with the Word, however unsystematic. Even if we cannot describe the precise means by which an unschooled reader might recognize "χρι" as the visual symbol for *Christi*, it is worth acknowledging such abilities in positive terms rather than grouping them collectively under rubrics of disengagement, such as "rote" memorization.

Acknowledging forms of linguistic awareness beyond the phonemic as well as textual strategies beyond those taught in formal grammatical instruction opens up new areas of inquiry concerning the kind of sense-making that might have been achieved in the practical world of lay devotion. For those without formal training, the bases of understanding might run from semantic (if not syntactic) knowledge of individual words gained from translations to more generalized knowledge of gist or affect to purely idiosyncratic associations the performer might attach to the words she voiced. Some of these mechanisms might yield meanings "accurate" enough to rival those produced through grammatical instruction. Indeed, though critics looked down on translation as a substitute for Latin scriptures, scruples about their fallibility are less prominent in liturgical and devotional contexts, where translated passages or even translations of entire services like those in the *Myroure* are legitimated precisely because they inform rather than replace Latin performance. Yet however similar the meanings may have been to those generated by grammatical training, extragrammatical strategies differed in character. Grammatical discourse conveys the capacity to infiltrate the Word through the anatomizing gestures of parsing and subsequent resynthesizing gestures of construing. Its primary methodology, as taught in the sequence of *officia* that enabled readers to isolate discrete structural elements of syntax and morphology, is that of reduction to the signified. Extragrammatical strategies, while not adverse to the similar kinds of reduction implicit in the act of translation, tend to assign meaning by association, apposition, accretion, and other nonanalytic gestures. Often the first to come to mind in this respect is the assigning of particular "virtues" to the performance of certain prayers, either through the complex mechanism of indulgences, or through more direct promises that recitation will ensure that the performer will not die unconfessed (to cite one example).[49] Yet sense-making strategies such as these, which append to the words an illocutionary force that has no relation to their grammatical meaning, represent only a fraction of the many ways of making performance meaningful outside grammatical structures.

There is little direct evidence of the precise techniques unschooled readers used. We can, however, gain a rough idea of some of these strategies through contemporary treatises on and translations of Latin texts. These writings were clerical productions, disseminated by priests through parish communities or procured from a burgeoning market of devotional texts. My goal, however, is not to locate a lay literacy or lay piety that is more authentic or oppositional because it is untouched by the clergy. Extragrammatical literacies were derived from the discursive resources of latinate textual authority the clergy made available. The surviving written documents that evidence the transmission of such resources (representative of the more extensive oral transmission within parishes) have often been cast as the clergy's denial or repression of the laity's intellectual resources—the substitution of less threatening "emotional" or "superstitious" engagements with the sacred. My purpose here is to consider some of these texts more seriously in terms of how they may have informed the experience of Latin texts as meaningful objects. Like all species of spiritual guidance produced in this period—Latin or English, "theological" or "affective," whether their promoters imagined themselves to be freeing or curtailing lay imaginations—texts of and advice about Latin prayer were enabling in some respects and limiting in others.

One might begin by noting that there is potentially a difference between a Mass treatise that offers *vertu* as a *substitute* for understanding said to be beyond the abilities of layfolk ("So fareþ þer vndirstondyng fayles,/Þe verrey vertu ȝow alle avayles")[50] and extragrammatical meaning (whether *vertu* or some other type) that is offered as a *kind* of understanding. One text that claims to provide the latter is the mid-fourteenth-century Middle English translation of *De spiritu Guidonis*, a tale in which a revenant soul from Purgatory explains the "privatese" of various prayers and masses for the dead.[51] *The Gast of Gy*, as it is titled in some manuscripts, sometimes aligns prayers with quasi-catechetical knowledge—the five psalms and five antiphons of the Vespers for the Dead are said to stand for the Ten Commandments, for example. Yet even such vaguely appositive meanings can be connected to the actual words of the text. In discussing the efficacy of reciting the Seven Penitential Psalms and the Litany, both Latin and Middle English versions describe how each psalm has been assigned a sin against which it is particularly helpful. Where the Latin text merely lists the psalm's incipit and the sin it guards against, however, the Middle English version demonstrates the psalms' effectiveness in this regard by providing a gloss for the first penitential psalm, Psalm 6, which is said to atone for the sin of pride.

> And þus to vnderstand it es:
> "Lord, deme vs nought in þi wodenes,
> Als þou dyd Lucifer, þat fell
> For his pryde fro Heven to Hell." (1083–86)

The gloss does begin by translating the psalm itself (*Domine ne in furore tuo arguas me*) but then departs to provide an alternative version of the text's supplication—a paraphrase of the basic intention that has been assigned to the psalm. Such glosses are not offered as translations, nor do they preclude awareness of grammatical meaning. At the same time, however, they do not require it and thus help distinguish sacred, scriptural language from other kinds of official language as that which can bear such appositive intentions in addition to the grammatical. These intentions, furthermore, were not merely vague pious sentiments that could be attached to any prayer; an effort is made in these treatises to connect meanings to particular texts, even if they are not the meanings the *bene litterati* would assign to them.

The form of direct speech in which the paraphrase is given in this case evinces the embodied nature of textual interaction encouraged by these aids to prayer. Similar gestures occur in a translation of the Hours of the Cross found in the Vernon Manuscript. The greatest effort is expended translating the hymns unique to each of the Hours, such as the following hymn sung at Sext.

> Hora sexta cristus est cruci conclauatus
> Et est cum latronibus pendens deputatus,
> Pre tormentis siciens felle saturatus;
> Agnus crimen diluit sic deificatus.[52]

> [At the sixth hour, Christ was nailed to the cross and consigned to hang among thieves. Thirsting for his torments, he was slaked with gall; the Lamb thus deified washed away sin.]

The versified English translation that accompanies the Latin text in the manuscript follows the original more closely than the casual paraphrase of *The Gast of Gy* yet shows a similar tendency to depart once its verbal correspondence to the Latin has been established.

> At Midday Ihesu hondes : þei nayleden to þe Rode,
> Bi-twene twey þeues : þei him hengen as wode;
> þei ȝeuen him galle and Eysel : Ihesu þat blisful fode.
> Serewful were boþe Marie an Ion : þer þei bi him stode,
>   As folk þat were mad.
> Whose þenkeþ on Marie serwe : May he neuere be glad.[53]

Here, the translator replaces the more abstract theological claim about the Lamb to extend the narrative scene, inviting the performer's affective participation. Many such Middle English lyrics based on Latin devotions are marked, according to Alexandra Barratt, by a "vividness" not found in the Latin texts.[54] While this imagery clearly departs from the grammatical, and to some extent the theological, meaning of the words, the elaboration of affect could be said to constitute a narrative troping of the text more than the abandonment of or alienation from its grammatical meaning.

This predilection for the concrete goes beyond narrativizing. The texts themselves are nominalized, such that their incipits become synechdotal names of discrete, countable texts: *aves*, the *credo*, the *Veni creator*, and so forth. I refer to this cognitive gesture as "nominalization" to distinguish it from "objectification." To objectify is to articulate something as an object apart from the self that can be possessed, mastered, or subject to scrutiny, or any other intellectual operation that falls under the rubric of "critical distance" as well as commodification. Objectification tends to produce *Orationes dominicas* and *Salutationes angelicas* rather than *paternosters* and *aves*. To nominalize, by contrast, is simply to convert the abstract and inert into material entities with which one can interact—in effect, to name the speech act itself. An abstraction that has been nominalized can perhaps be counted, but it also has a capacity for worldly agency that objectification does not allow for. The mid-fifteenth-century devotional poem known as the "Pety Job" demonstrates the process of nominalization.[55] Another example of troping, this poem creates a twelve-line stanza translating and expanding upon each verse of the first lesson of the *Dirige* (Job 7:16–21), using the incipit of the lesson—*Parce mihi, domine* ("Spare me, o Lord")—as a refrain. The first stanza represents the refrain as performed speech: "I

nat what I may synge thare/But *Parce mihi, domine*" (11–12). The second
stanza, however, converts the incipit into a noun: "I wote nothyng that
helpe may/But *Parce mihi, domine*" (23–24). Whereas the phrase served
as the object of the verb "synge," it now becomes an agent that can itself
"helpe." As John Alford has pointed out, the phrase refers to the result of
the prayer in that salvation depends on God's response to the supplication.[56]
More accurately, the incipit names the act of supplication upon which the
hope of salvation relies and in so doing lends both agency to the speech act
and responsibility to the suppliant. Though there is evidence that lay devotional practice did objectify and commodify prayers, this aspect has vastly
overshadowed the manner in which it simultaneously produced an entire,
charismatized repertoire of such nominalized texts—*paternoster, ave, credo,
Placebo* and *Dirige*—that allowed for such creative interactions.

Nominalization of this sort is often considered an unsophisticated
form of engagement, yet it is not entirely inconsistent with the textual
interactions of high literates. Medieval scholars objectified texts whenever
they "alleged" an "auctor" in support of a claim. Representing authoritative words as the words of another, they engaged in the practice we now
refer to as "quotation" and signify with quotation marks that essentially
delineate words or phrases as alienable property. Alongside such textual
practices, however, were those particular to scripture, in which texts were
"voiced" rather than "alleged." In such cases, textualized passages, while
they are clearly the speech of another, are not as palpably objectified but
performed *as if* they were one's own speech. The way in which St. Augustine weaves passages from scripture throughout *The Confessions* is a salient
example of this intellectual habit. When, for example, Augustine describes
his failure to conceive of an immaterial God in terms of a wound caused
by his pride, he expresses himself by inhabiting the subject position of the
Psalmist, who provides the images with which he can elaborate upon his
predicament: "for *You have humbled the proud one as if he were a wounded
man*, and by my wound I have been separated from You."[57] Such a gesture
may seem the opposite of nominalization, given that Augustine assimilates
himself to the text instead of interacting with a text that has its own name,
as it were. Yet both strategies rely on the embodiment of texts rather than
on critical distance, on textual performance rather than on textual study.
They are to textual practice what borrowing and code-switching are to
linguistic practice.[58] Both of these sociolinguistic terms describe ways of
shifting between languages within a single utterance: "borrowing" (analogous to nominalization) refers to the act of simply importing words from

a second language into a first; "code-switching" (akin to the Augustinian example), to a switch between languages that involves both the words and the syntax of the second language. The practices differ in the forms they produce, but both are forms of language contact. Similarly, one might say that these two strategies of "voicing" texts are forms of "textual contact," where contact occurs between the text and the subject interpellated by means of its performance. In this respect, both could also be said to explore conceptions of agency in sacred language that grammatical study does not cultivate.[59]

The associations that the unschooled may have attached to the texts they performed—whether these associations stemmed from commentaries, pastoral advice, or pious conversation—likely did not possess the rhetorical cleverness of Augustine's psalmic rhapsodies, yet the logic of their textual interactions may not have been as far removed as we are inclined to think. This performative disposition—what Walter Ong would refer to as a preference for the "empathetic and participatory rather than [the] objectively distanced"[60]—is a central feature of the literacy of things to be read. It was not, however, uniformly cultivated in relation to all texts but specifically directed toward the practices that helped sacralize canonized texts as divine. Sacred texts were those to which one was obligated to give voice to allow the eternal Word to be enacted in worldly time and space. Possessed of inexhaustible meaning, sacred texts were appropriate to an infinite number of worldly contexts that could be assimilated to them through figuration, apposition, and troping. Liturgical performance, with its own juxtapositions of texts and seasonal alignments, encouraged these types of associations. Indeed, one of the functions of the Liturgy of the Word as an institution was to ritualize these appositive and metonymic styles of sense-making. Devotional recitation seems to have followed the liturgical in this regard. The same nonanalytic interpretive gestures that allow the five psalms sung in the *Placebo* to signify the Five Wounds of Christ, as they do for William Durandus in his *Rationale divinorum officiorum*, also allow them to signify half of the Ten Commandments, as they do for the translator of *The Gast of Gy*, as well as the five senses, as they do for both writers.[61] Given the similarity of these gestures, and given their similar lack of dependence on grammatical meaning, it would be unwise to immediately brand texts that provide extragrammatical alternatives as patronizing. At the same time, insofar as these extragrammatical alternatives were legitimized as valid participation in the Christian textual community, one might wonder about their "democratizing," let alone "oppositional" potential. To associate this kind of reading with the *lewid* is not to claim it is a grassroots movement. It is, however, meant to point out that some kind of Latin prayer was available to most Christians who participated in the religious life of their communities; to perform these texts was not necessarily a cessation of cognitive activity, nor did it necessarily mute spiritual or political will.

Even if *lewid* readers of these translations and treatises obediently followed the advice offered therein, depictions such as those in the Derby Psalter, which associated reading from private volumes with the "old song" of the Jews, do insinuate some perceived tension between devotional and liturgical recitation and imply that not everyone was comfortable with the idea of a world in which "simple and sophisticate could kneel side by side, using the same prayers and sharing the same hopes."[62] Though lack of surviving evidence may prevent us from ascertaining the oppositional content of lay readings of Latin texts, there are more general indications that the very act of lay recitation was felt by some to be in need of regulation. It is in this context that we should place the appearance of images of the Education of the Virgin in early fourteenth-century England. These images, like the contemporaneous interest in boy choristers with which they are no doubt connected, draw attention to the entry into literate discourse and practice, evincing an interest in the unarticulated threshold of understanding. Insofar as they depict a reading lesson,[63] the content of that lesson is as much about the appropriate uses of scripture as it is about word recognition. The emergence of the image is contemporary with the rise of the cult of St. Anne,[64] but it is also contemporary with a gradual reconception of the iconography of the Annunciation, with which the Education of the Virgin was frequently paired.[65] Over the course of the fourteenth century, the image of Mary engaged in reading when Gabriel appears to her underwent a concretizing and narrativizing of its own. The presence of the Book at the Annunciation becomes not merely a symbolic reminder of the prophecy the Virgin is about to fulfill nor a signifier of her wisdom but is imagined to be the object the Virgin is actually engaged (or had engaged) in reading when Gabriel appears.[66] An early fifteenth-century translation of Aelred of Rievaulx's *De institutione inclusarum* provides a meditation on the Annunciation in which the recluse is advised to picture the Virgin in her chamber, "beholdyng bisely hou she was occupied with redynge of such prophecies in the which weren profecyed Cristis comynge thorugh a maydens birthe."[67] The Annunciation is thus refashioned as the apotheosis of scriptural (as well as angelic) interpellation, the ultimate gesture of self-actualization in subjection. St. Anne's tutorial becomes the precursor to this moment, a representation of the Virgin's introduction to scriptural practice that will later enable her to comprehend fully the gravity of Gabriel's announcement.

The naturalistic detail with which the pedagogical scene is often portrayed associates the Virgin's reading with current devotional practice. This connection extends to the text that is used: the window in All Saints, York, shows the Virgin reading Psalm 142, the last of the Penitential Psalms; the fifteenth-century Burnet Psalter even depicts the Virgin learning to read the *ave* itself (Fig. 6), which, apart from creating a paradoxical figuration of salvation history, is also one of the most common and recognizable devotional texts. Marian images such as these represent an idealization of devotional reading—a gendered domestication in which textual assimilation is overseen by wise and divinely prescient mothers.[68] Viewed together with the image of reading in the Derby Psalter, they suggest an attempt to impose unity and imaginary oversight on the variety of devotional practices that were proliferating throughout the period. In this regard, however, it is worth noting that Mary's subjection to God (a subjection that is an example to all Christians, not simply women or layfolk)[69] is enriched by her comprehension of the text. If such domesticated images serve dominant ideology, then it is not an ideology that promotes a fully exteriorized relationship to sacred language but one invested in controlled and properly directed understanding.

From this perspective, those said to "vndirstonde no word þat [they] seie" should be identified as those who did not understand according to the parameters—implicit or explicit—of valid participation in the Christian textual community. Given how broad those parameters seem to have been by modern (grammatical) standards, we might do well not to take such pronouncements at face value, as indicators of mindlessness or meaningless exteriority. Attaching meanings to words, however, was only one aspect of textual engagement that might fall under the rubric of "understanding" or even *entendaunce* in lay devotional and liturgical practice. Beyond semantic control, there was the possibility of mastering and learning to manipulate in some fashion the larger structures within which sacred language signified and, even more influentially, the modes of sacramentality in which it participated. These possibilities were precisely those that presented themselves as devotional practice moved beyond the realm of the domestic and as the signs and signifying power of the liturgy came to be appropriated to ends that were by no means independent of, yet were no

Figure 6. St. Anne and Virgin reading from the "Burnet Psalter," first half of the fifteenth century. The text "Ave Maria gra" is visible on the page. Aberdeen University Library, MS 25, f. 24v. Reproduced by permission of Aberdeen University Library.

longer as decisively rooted in, ecclesiastical institutions or the more traditional social structures of the parish.

Reading and Singing as Public Discourse

According to Habermas, the Church's use of Latin—its "*arcanum*" or "secret at the inner core of publicity"—was one of the means by which the laity were relegated to the "surroundings"—the realm of the private rather than the field of representation.[70] In fourteenth-century England, however, one could claim that the lay use of Latin devotional and liturgical texts was one of the means by which the laity did in some measure gain access to that more public site. The Eucharist, which has received much scholarly attention, had its own place in this field; as a central Christian symbol, it gave rise to a symbolic language that was appropriated to various ends, prompting questions about the nature of signification in the process.[71] The appropriation of Latin texts was homologous with this development but created a slightly different set of issues. The Eucharist was the only part of divine service designated as a sacrament in the strictest, ecclesiastical sense of the term—as a particular conduit of God's grace, authentically mediated only by priests, and necessary for salvation. The ritualized performance of sacred texts, by contrast, did not require priest's orders and had a devotional counterpart that was encouraged for the laity. Prayer, nonetheless, possessed supplicatory and intercessory powers. More specific than mere sanctity or sacramentality in its broadest sense—that is, the quality that endowed words or objects with meaning beyond themselves, making them signs that signaled the presence of the divine—sacred words were endowed with *vertu* that could be directed, lent intention in excess of the *intentio auctoris* perceived in the words themselves. If the promotion of Latin prayer for the laity served to sacralize the language and texts over which the clergy had power, it also endowed the layperson with knowledge of even a limited number of texts with a means of access to the divine and even in some cases the ability to direct the numinous *vertu* of sacred texts to particular intercessory ends. Latin recitation could thus allow layfolk to wield a power that had formerly been the preserve of public institutions.

This power was, furthermore, vested in verbal language. More specific than symbolic language, appropriations of sacred texts focused self-conscious attention on textualized, institutional language, prompting questions about agency and meaning. These questions are difficult enough when they concern performative utterances that in some sense "do what they say," that is, perform a specific action that is clearly related to its locutionary meaning, like the Eucharistic words of Institution (*hoc est corpus meum*).[72] They become still more complex when this correspondence does not obtain—when, for example, the performance of a psalm in the Office of the Virgin is said to shorten the time of a specific soul in purgatory. Fourteenth-century sources evidence a growing interest in and speculation on what words could do. The transmission history of the ghost story I referred to in the previous section, *De spiritu Guidonis*, is a particularly illuminating example. Based on a reported encounter with a spirit that took place in 1323 in Alès, the text first appeared in the form of a brief Latin "Report," recounting the event in which the Dominican Jean Gobi questioned the deceased Guido about his experience in purgatory. While Guido's answers in the report affirm the importance of suffrages for the dead, this topic receives much greater elaboration in a longer Latin version of the story that was circulating by the 1330s.[73] Several questions and responses concerning the most helpful kinds of suffrages as well as their effects are added in this recension. Masses are considered unquestionably the most useful to souls in purgatory, yet, perhaps because the Mass was so unequivocally efficacious, the writer does not go into detail about how masses help souls. Guido's spirit does, however, discuss the benefits of the seven penitential psalms, which are mentioned only briefly in the report, as well as the Office of the Dead, which is new to the expanded version. The utility of these non-Eucharistic suffrages seems to require explanation and Guido's spirit goes so far as to reveal the "misterium" of the *Placebo* and *Dirige* in order to make their benefits clear (64). It is not simply the case that the five psalms and five antiphons of the *Placebo* symbolize the Ten Commandments but, more specifically, that alluding to the Ten Commandments in this fashion benefits the soul in purgatorial torment.

in placebo sunt 5 psalmi et 5 antiphone, qui reficiunt animas, pro quibus dicuntur, quoad X precepta dei, que, dum fuerunt in hac vita, compleuerunt, saltem quantum ad suos effectus, set non quantum ad officium eorum in omnibus. (64–65)[74]

[In the *Placebo* there are five psalms and five antiphons, which restore the souls for whom they are said with respect to the Ten Commandments of God that they obeyed while in this earthly life—yet only to the extent of their performance of them, and not as much as it was their duty (to follow them) in all things.]

Whereas Durandus, speaking of the psalms of vespers in general, is content merely to point to their numerological association with the five senses, the excess meaning of a votive office must have its own illocutionary intention or be directed toward a particular end, even if the precise logic of the symbolic economy in which it functions is obscure, as is the case here.

This interest in the power of ritualized utterances that do not require sacerdotal authority carries over into the earliest vernacular translations of the text (all of which are in English),[75] including a prose version found in the Vernon Manuscript, which follows the Latin fairly closely, and a slightly freer verse adaptation preserved in two mid-fourteenth-century manuscripts.[76] Unlike the prose version, the verse translation explicitly claims to have been created for the benefit of "lewed men, þat kan les" than "clerkes þat kan of lare" (5–7).[77] Writing for this lay audience, whom he clearly presumes to be familiar with the texts of Office of the Dead, the verse-translator pursues the matter of ritual efficacy more relentlessly, if no more successfully. In reference to the five psalms and five antiphons of the *Placebo*, he states,

þa ten togeder, when þai er mett,
For þa saul er þusgat sett,
For to restore, wha to þam tentes,
Vnto þe saule þe ten comandementes;
þai sall mak mynde, how he þam dyd,
So þat his mede sall nought be hyde. (1109–14)

Though "restore" is the translator's rendering of *reficiunt*, here the Ten Commandments, not the soul, are its direct object, which only raises further questions as to the function of the speech act—what, that is, referring to the Ten Commandments is meant to accomplish. Similarly, the phrase "wha to þam tentes," seemingly added simply to fill out the rhyme, raises questions of agency that are further exacerbated by the explanation that the recitation of the psalms and antiphons will "mak mynde" of the soul's adherence to the Commandments. The idea that the soul will be rewarded insofar as he obeyed them remains, yet the matter of who needs to be reminded of this (presumably not God) and why remains unspecified. Most likely it is the soul, who might then take comfort in the promise of eventual compensation for his past good behavior.[78] Yet if this is the case, it would seem to limit the *vertu* of the utterance such that its powers—those of comforting—do not invoke divine intercession. Such speech is not sacramental and illocutionary (though its transmission might require sacred assistance) but is, rather, personal and perlocutionary, even if the perlocutionary effects are not related to the grammatical meaning of the utterance.[79]

If such an alteration is indeed being made, it may signal a clerical effort to distinguish between liturgical and devotional speech, since the Office of the Dead was gradually becoming a regular part of the charismatized devotional repertoire found in Books of Hours. It may also be an attempt to affirm the intercessory powers of the Office of the Dead while maintaining the connection to interiority associated with devotion. At stake in either case, however, was the possibility of representative speech that had otherwise been reserved for public, institutional performances. Though devotional performances of the *Placebo* and *Dirige* were not "public" in the sense that they were performed before others and though they did not enter the field of "representative publicity," they did allow layfolk in some small measure to wield the kind of power that this publicity was meant to represent. Such practices furthermore encouraged a familiarity with, and even a connoisseurship of, textual performance, whether devotional or liturgical, that could extend to their patronage of performances that were public. Beyond the desire to multiply masses, varieties of non-Eucharistic benefaction gained widespread popularity alongside contractual liturgy involving masses. Because these charitable exchanges were not subject to the same types of regulation and institutional strictures regarding performer and performance as the Mass, they became sites of greater creativity in which patrons were often free to select the texts they wished their beneficiaries to perform. Simultaneously with the voicing of pejorative attitudes toward chantry priests, whose purportedly unscrupulous greed made them the focal point of fears about the failure of representation in virtually all senses of the term, patrons from different social strata used forms of non-Eucharistic benefaction to explore the possibilities of liturgical representation, not simply in the sense of having their interests represented to God but also as representations of individual and corporate spiritual identity before a liturgy-loving and textually savvy "public."

Non-Eucharistic benefactions varied widely in their forms and putative functions. Some, like the myriad performances of the Office of the Dead requested in wills throughout the period, had obvious intercessory ends even as they allowed those not in priests' orders to fulfill charitable bequests. Others, however, though they clearly sought divine grace in the form of prayer, seem to have attracted benefactors for reasons beyond a desire to reduce suffering in purgatory. Chief among these was the votive antiphon.[80] The singing of a single Marian antiphon with a versicle and a few prayers after compline was practiced widely at monasteries from the early thirteenth century. By the fourteenth century, the votive antiphon had become a regular part of the liturgy, mandated by statute at many secular cathedrals, collegiate churches, chantry colleges, and convents, where their performance was often deputed at the request of a patron to choristers, clerics in minor orders, or nuns.[81] Because they were not officially a part of the liturgy of secular uses but true luxury items that allowed patrons a broad range of choices concerning the text and location, they had the potential to signify something about the patron's spiritual identity. Although a priest could say only one mass per day at an altar, antiphons could be endlessly multiplied and choreographed. The statutes of Fotheringhay College, founded in 1415 by Edward, Duke of York, and Henry IV,[82] require that the entire college end compline in the choir by singing *Inter natos*, the antiphon of St. John the Baptist, with the usual psalm and prayers, after which they were to proceed to the step before the high altar and, kneeling, sing the Marian antiphon of the season, a single chorister responding with an *ave*. At this point, the older members of the choir left, leaving the choristers to say a series of prayers for Edward, to line up on either side of his tomb to say the *De profundis* and *Kyrie*, then to sing the antiphon *Benedicta* before the two images of the Virgin, and finally end by singing antiphons of SS. Michael and Thomas the Martyr at their respective altars.[83] What was a simple devotion was thus elaborated to become essentially a new service, one that allowed Edward to map the geography of his devotion onto the floor plan of his church.

Antiphons did not need to be attached to chantries or commemorations for the dead. Richard II gave the members of his Chapel Royal extra compensation for their daily performance of the antiphon *Inter natos*—a performance that allowed Richard to display his devotion to his patron saint, John the Baptist, before the court.[84] At the other end of the social scale, the St. Mary guild of St. Magnus the Martyr, London Bridge, each paid a halfpenny per week in 1343 to support the nightly performance of *Salve regina*.[85] Whereas for Richard the additional antiphon was an extravagance, for the members of the St. Mary guild it was an affordable way to enhance the ceremony of their parish worship. Unlike similarly modest endowments, such as the funding of a taper, the funding of a Marian antiphon expressed the corporate devotion of the guild in a manner both more specific and more temporally focalized (and thus noticeable) than could be accomplished with a taper. Though they represent only one of several different kinds of non-Eucharistic benefactions, votive antiphons are particularly salient examples of how both clergy and layfolk could exploit even small amounts of textual knowledge garnered through devotional practice as well as the very terms of representation in which the liturgy operated.

These newer forms of liturgical endowment were informed by a sense of connoisseurship—an aesthetics of consumption—in regard to liturgical celebration. Manipulations that might affect this consumption could go beyond the textual and could involve larger formal considerations that signaled the public, institutional status of the liturgical, such as time and place. The chantries of York that came to be overseen by the mayor and council provide an example of civic interests informing both the time and place of liturgical celebration. In the 1320s, four chantries (three founded by clerics) appeared in a chapel on Ouse Bridge, which had formerly held none.[86] Though none of the founders was a member of the council, the chantry was strategically situated next to the council's chambers. Barrie Dobson has speculated that "within a few years, and almost certainly as a result of deliberate policy rather than of the vagaries of individual benefaction, the mayor and council had equipped themselves and their city with a team of chaplains, of *oratores*, directly at their service,"[87] a team that was maintained through the end of the fifteenth century. The mayor and council not only had the right of visitation but used the oversight that had been granted to them eventually to regulate the times at which masses were sung "in order to suit the convenience of councillors attending meetings and of other inhabitants of the town crossing the bridge on their daily business."[88] Civic control of performances, to an even greater degree than privately endowed services, made possible the appropriation of this pubic fund of texts, narratives, and images to signifying ends beyond, though not necessarily in conflict with, the ecclesiastical. Miri Rubin speaks of a "gradual insertion of political meanings" into Corpus Christi processions during this period, singling out the second half of the fourteenth century as a time when civic corporations and guilds involved themselves more in their staging, "as the symbolic possibilities inherent in the ritual unfolded."[89] At this point, one might say the aesthetics of consumption and the familiarity with texts and forms it engendered became an aesthetics of production.

Among the most lavish products of this aesthetic were the civic pageants of the "royal entry" staged in London, as they were in continental cities, to mark significant royal occasions.[90] Though Anne Lancashire has found traces of such pageantry as early as 1207,[91] the evidence in general is too inconsistent in the amount and type of details it records to determine either when precisely these traditions began or when and how the symbolic associations of the liturgy came to play a role in their imagery. With the 1308 entry of Edward II and Queen Isabel, however, there is the first definitive reference to representations of the New Jerusalem[92]—an image that Gordon Kipling has linked to the hymn *Urbs beata Ierusalem*, which is sung in the Office of the Dedication of a Church.[93] Later, more detailed accounts, most notably Richard Maidstone's description of the pageantry that accompanied Richard II's reconciliation with the city of London in 1392,[94] suggest that the ceremonial of dedication was linked with the liturgy of Advent to create a complex overlaying of narratives that associated Richard with Christ and his entry into the city with the Second Coming. In a later description of Henry V's royal entry of 1415, celebrating his triumph at Agincourt, Kipling similarly sees imagery based on a narrativization of the Office of the Dead.[95] While royal entries may have borrowed imagery from the liturgical texts, the account of Henry V's Agincourt entry even claims that banners with brief Latin scriptural texts played a role in the ceremony as well.[96] The texts do not have liturgical uses that link them to specifiable services, but are drawn mostly from the Psalter; linked to the repertoire of reading and singing, they are not obscure. Performances such as these may have participated in what John Bossy refers to as "migrations of the holy,"[97] the shifts in sociocultural focus by which signification and sacramentality came to be transferred from ecclesiastical institutions to other realms. Yet insofar as they did so, the "migration" did not so much involve sovereign power, which was already endowed with its own aura of sacramentality; rather it was the civic community itself that was newly sacralized in such displays—the *corpus reipublicae*, as Kipling calls it, who performed their power to signify as a group as much as their subjection to a sovereign.

One could say that liturgical texts, images, and gestures come to be unmoored from their institutional settings in these celebrations. It is for this reason that I categorize the practice (along with the other extragrammatical practices I have discussed in this chapter) as a species of reading and singing, though contemporaries would not refer to it in these terms. Yet, as I suggested at the end of Chapter 2, this unmooring involved not simply dislocation, but reconfiguration, for which "migration" is as useful a descriptor as any in this context. The most important migration in these civic ceremonies was that of the locus of articulation: the producers of royal entries defined a site from which to signify that was "public" in the sense of having a claim on the attentions of "folk" in general, yet not decisively ecclesiastical or royal in that claim. In the process of this migration, however, the dynamics of articulation changed. Those who performed did so not "in the person of" but rather "in the name of" their company; the mask of the *persona* was replaced by livery badges that signaled a corporate, not institutional, voice. The content of their expression can scarcely be said to be oppositional, though examples of oppositional liturgical expression can, of course, be found.[98] Both the oppositional and the merely alternative, however, shared strategies of voicing and sense-making that arguably only extended the logic already inherent in liturgical practice: the recontextualization and narrativization of scripture, or the apposition, accretion, and subsequent conflation of narratives, to name a few. Liturgical texts and images made up the primary symbolic language that was likely to resonate with all—indeed it was perhaps the synthetic ambitions of the liturgy that many found so compelling. As I have already suggested, however, the synthetic ambitions that underwrote the desire to include more people in liturgical celebration invariably led to its diffusion into the various practices of reading and singing—yet this diffusion was precisely what made these texts and images sites of cultural vitality as well as social conflict.

"Þe lomes þat y labore with": Vernacular Poetics, *Clergie*, and the Repertoire of Reading and Singing in *Piers Plowman*

Public Poetry and Reading and Singing

THE EXAMPLES of royal entries and civic Corpus Christi processions make clear that even as critics fretted over the crisis of representation that they saw embodied in the annueller of popular mythology, many were availing themselves of the expressive opportunities that this fluidity in signification afforded. Civic pageantry that appropriated the texts and ceremonial forms of the liturgy reconfigured the dynamics of representation at all levels: the social identity of the performers (who speaks?), the social and institutional locus from which they spoke (in whose voice?), as well as the interests that were represented in performance (on whose behalf?). The extragrammatical literacies that generated such signifying acts thus isolated and exploited not simply the texts of the liturgy but the representational power and potential that was granted to their performance. The attraction of this mode of authoritative speech was no doubt the capacity it gave to its performers and patrons to participate actively in a symbolic economy—to create meaning that would resonate beyond the grammatical content and immediate context of the utterance (what I have been calling "excess" or "surplus meaning") to a general audience that could be imaginatively expanded to include the entire Christian community.

Though vernacular making seems a very different enterprise, the aspirations of writers such as Langland and Chaucer could be couched in similar terms. The Ricardian poets who cultivated large-scale forms of vernacular fiction did, it is true, focus their extragrammatical efforts on translating aspects of textual authority into English rather than on isolating aspects of that authority as it continued to inhere in Latin texts, as did those who staged civic pageantry. Yet the use of English as such in imaginative writing was not the only or even the primary innovation these poets made. Narratives had, after all, been produced in English before this period. Even if these writers can be credited with developing the literary forms of sustained fiction in English, their attitudes toward the language were complex, at times even appearing ambivalent in comparison to earlier vernacularizing undertakings. Where an earlier text might contain an earnest apology for English as a language of inclusion,[1] Gower's *Confessio amantis* announces its vernacular poetic project in Latin verse: "Qua tamen Engisti lingua canit Insula Bruti/Anglica Carmente metra iuuante loquar" [Nevertheless, in Hengist's tongue, sung in the island of Brutus, I will, with Carmenta's aid, speak English verses]" (*CA*, Prol.).[2] Rather than promote the universal accessibility of English to the *lewid* as a "native" tongue, the poet places his singing in a chiastic balancing act between the dual Germanic and classic pedigrees ("Engisti lingua . . . insula Bruti") he bestows upon the vernacular.[3] Similarly, Langland's occasional translations of the Latin tags of *Piers Plowman* are often explicitly marked as concessions to the *lewid* readers of his poem, yet these concessions, while neither comically nor even patently ironic, are never unproblematically earnest, as we shall see. The prominence of Latin in both of these writers' texts suggests that they imagined English as a counterpoint to, not a replacement for, Latin. While such linguistic gestures are less conspicuous in the writings of Chaucer and the *Pearl*-poet, it is nonetheless clear that their perception of the sociolinguistic landscape was too complex for them to envision their inventiveness as simply a matter of language choice.

Ricardian poets are rather distinguished by their attempts to situate English writing in the realm of public representation. Anne Middleton's influential essay, "The Idea of Public Poetry in the Reign of Richard II," identifies this feature of late fourteenth-century poetry, describing it as both a mode of address and a particular sensibility—characterized by "impassioned direct address," public poetry was "defined by a constant relation of speaker to audience within an ideally conceived worldly community, a relation that has become the poetic subject."[4] The imaginative construction of that audience and of the poet's relationship to it situated the poetic voice such that it actively and explicitly engaged the dynamics of representation. For those who sought to represent the "common voice," the questions of who speaks in whose voice on whose behalf were constant preoccupations, generally centered in the highly self-conscious narratorial voices that typify public poetry.[5] It is in this respect that the emergent practices of vernacular making most closely resembled the many emergent practices of reading and singing. The fact that the two vernacular texts I will discuss in this chapter and the next—*Piers Plowman* and *The Canterbury Tales*—both invoke modes of sacred, ritualized speech, often at critical moments of poetic self-definition, shows that Langland and Chaucer were aware of this similarity and creatively exploited it.

The similarity was not due to an organic relationship to the liturgy, as was the case with civic pageantry (and all practices I have placed under the rubric of reading and singing). These writers rather perceived an affinity between the status of vernacular making and the status of reading and singing as modes of verbal performance in the variability surrounding the dynamics of representation. In public poetry and reading and singing, Langland and Chaucer saw both the problems and the possibilities of entering the field of representation and, more specifically, of making claims to public authority in the absence of a clear institutional locus of articulation. Vernacular writers created works that aspired to the status of institutionally sanctioned *litteratura* in a language that lacked the fixity, authority, and institutional supports characteristic of Latin. While liturgy did have a clear institutional location, the proliferation of practices associated with reading and singing allowed the skills and texts of the liturgy to be used in an increasing number of settings, thereby destabilizing perceptions of their institutional use. In other words, if vernacular making had in some respects no proper place, reading and singing had too many.

Reading and singing, by virtue of its unmoored status, also allowed unlicensed speakers to participate in public signification. As vernacular makers who needed to justify their pretensions to enter this field (however small a corner of it they may have occupied in reality), Langland and Chaucer seem to have identified with these performers. Their most self-referential allusions to the practices of reading and singing, in fact, tend to involve the marginally clerical—nuns, *clergeons*, clerical piece-workers in minor orders. With such depictions, Chaucer and Langland aligned their authority not with those whose sacerdotal powers would automatically authorize their speech but with those whose authority stemmed from temporary license realized primarily in performance. At the same time, Ricardian poets, in their desire to speak for the common,[6] articulated representational ambitions more closely associated with the unbeneficed clergy, contractual liturgy, and the ethical issues that attended the practices of performers and patrons alike. The concerns expressed in Ricardian poetry about the social and spiritual value of vernacular making, as well as the kind of social identity such labor might confer upon the maker, had much in common with the concerns surrounding the verbal labor of unbeneficed priests. Though not connected as exclusively to the practices of reading and singing, priestly speakers, like Chaucer's Nun's Priest, with his emphasis on voice and song,[7] or Langland's "lewed vicory" (B 19.412ff.; C 21.409ff.), which I will discuss in the next section, call attention to the potential self-interest and hypocrisy of authorized performers in ways that suggest similar temptations for the public poet. In portraying speakers motivated by desires and interests beyond those dictated by ecclesiastical institutions, both writers were able to examine the privileges and the responsibilities connected with public representation in all its meanings.

In liturgical settings, public, performative authority was vested in the *persona*. Those licensed to speak *in persona ecclesie* were enabled to speak in a voice that was not merely personal but had a claim on public attention with a capacity to sustain excess meaning. "Public" speech therefore had as much to do with the relationship between speaker and speech and with the closely related dynamics of representation (who speaks in whose voice on whose behalf?) as it did with the question of audience (to whom does one speak?). Put another way, it required a locus of articulation from which to speak as well as a particular conception of the audience of one's speech. The *persona ecclesie* was one such locus, one that was articulated by means of vicarious and representative textual performance. It was only one of several loci that vernacular writers explored, alongside those of the prophet or the courtly "advisor to princes," for example.[8] To claim that writers explored the *persona ecclesie* is not to maintain that they aspired to inhabit it. Neither Langland's nor Chaucer's verbal productions pretended to the authority or ritual efficacy of the unbeneficed priest's Mass. Their interest not only in marginally clerical performers but also in less formal modes of performance—in devotional display and non-Eucharistic benefactions—suggests that they were more interested in the authoritative locus of articulation such a *persona* symbolized as well as the ways in which emergent liturgical and devotional practices had transformed it.[9]

The *personae* of ecclesiastical or legal discourse—the *persona ecclesie* or *persona ficta*—were, after all, specifically institutional loci of articulation. One might even say that these *personae* are technologies of institutionality itself in that they abstract "personality" from particular bodies to create a generalized, transferable category of institutional identity.[10] Langland and Chaucer, by contrast, seem to have imagined their public vernacular enterprise as one that generally avoided relying on the resources

of authority vested in single institutions, ecclesiastical or otherwise, and
instead appealed to the more tenuous and multiple authority of a variety of
institutions as well as that of collective experience—the "common voice"
or the differentiated voices of the "felaweshipe."[11] Consequently, though
they used the tools made available to them by institutional discourses
(both the uses and abuses thereof), they adapted their loci of articulation, restructuring them for their own purposes. In a manner similar to
the cleric whose liturgical utterances were performed *in persona ecclesie*,
vernacular poets adopted a fictive "I" that was potentiated by an awareness
of the gap between such an "I" and the authorial "I" who performed it.
Yet whereas a felicitous liturgical utterance *in persona ecclesie* depends on
the negation or complete subordination of performer's own voice as it is
subsumed in the voice of institutional authority, the locus of articulation
cultivated by Chaucer and Langland (though we tend to associate it primarily with the former) depends not on the extremes of negation but on
disavowal, by which one voice disclaims responsibility for its speech (often
in the very act of claiming authority) such that its presence continues to be
felt. Chaucer's ironic representation of himself as mere reporter of others'
words is the most obvious example of this technique, yet Langland also
experiments with this form of "double-voicing" with the framing device of
the dream vision and his use of Latin tags, as I will argue.[12]

    The gap was not one between two distinct "persons," if we under-
stand this term to refer to fully constituted speaking subjects. As a locus
of articulation the *persona* authorized liturgical speech acts by locating
the origin of the utterance outside the speaker and outside the immediate
context of the utterance. It is the separation of speaker and speech that
allows words to enter the field of representation.[13] The practices of reading and singing, however, problematized this gap. In addition to civic
display and its destabilizing effects on the dynamics of representation,
complaints about itinerant mass priests and their suspect motivations and
intentions signaled a concern that the gap between speaker and speech
that authorized liturgical speech acts had become desacralized to the extent
that it was as likely to represent the hypocrisy of a duplicitous speaker as
the ritualized performance of ecclesiastical authority. For Langland and
Chaucer, however, this gap, perhaps because it had been desacralized,
became a site of experimentation, as critical to the development of what
we now call "literary voice" as the gap between author and narratorial
persona. The fictive locus of articulation and forms of refracted discourse
we now describe in terms of the literary "persona" were thus derived in

part from the vexed status of the institutional *personae* that allowed for public representation.

In pointing to forms of liturgical and devotional practice as models for vernacular poetics, I do not mean to disregard the more "literary" antecedents of vernacular narratorial personae that writers surely drew upon, such as that used in the *Roman de la Rose,* which David Lawton has connected to Chaucer.[14] Such models, however, were developed in courtly settings for courtly audiences. Since they are much more appropriate to Chaucer than to Langland, they can obscure the similarities between these two writers, especially in the challenges both faced in imagining an audience beyond their immediate circles of readers. "Public poetry" required an expansion of possible loci of articulation beyond those of courtly literature. Both *Piers Plowman* and *The Canterbury Tales* explore the poetic potential of different loci of articulation—of different voices or, rather, of different ways of voicing. Forms of double-voicing served them as a way of distancing themselves from institutional loci while maintaining enough of a connection to ensure the recognition of their gestures. Both, as we shall see, also depict practices associated with reading and singing to explore the structure, status, and purpose of their poetic voice. Focusing on this engagement allows me to place both Langland and Chaucer in a larger literary-historical moment in which language with representative potential was, in certain social and religious spheres, migrating away from the institutions designed to maintain and define its use.

In charting these similarities, I do not mean to overlook the differences between the two poets. Each began from different starting points; for neither writer did reading and singing immediately present themselves as vehicles for poetic exploration. In addition to their French courtly pedigree, Chaucer's early works show his greater sense of affiliation with the institutions of *grammatica.* Langland, for his part, attempted to orient himself and his voice in relation to the much more problematic abstraction regulating linguistic production, *clergie*—a concept that for him incorporates a much larger variety of textual practices and social identities than does reading and singing. It is only later in their careers that both writers turn to these texts and practices and their anomalous status when considering the stakes of verbal performance. For Langland, with his more clergially minded background, they come to play a central role as he lists the titles of reading and singing repertoire as the tools of his labor when accounting for his activities in the famous poetic *apologia* of the C Version. Chaucer's more secular-minded pursuits did not lead him to focus quite as intently on reading and singing, yet *The Canterbury Tales* show his later interest in experimenting with clerical and religious voices, embedding his own poetic performance among a high concentration of such performers (Prioress, Monk, Nun's Priest).[15] With the pairing of the marginally clerical Prioress and Second Nun, reading and singing do become a major topic of speculation—speculation that, I will argue, is metapoetic as well as social and spiritual—yet they lead Chaucer to a strikingly different conception of poetic voice and of vernacular poetics than they do for Langland.

This chapter will treat the role of reading and singing in *Piers Plowman*. I begin by examining Langland's earliest imagining of vernacular poetics, which is closely linked to his integration of Latin tags throughout the poem. As he cultivates a variety of extragrammatical strategies to incorporate these preexisting texts, English appears to broaden the possibilities of textual performance almost in an effort to restore the unity undone by a fragmented latinity. This project—so evocative of the discourse of choral community—does not, however, proceed without a consideration of the status of his own singular voice in these performances, which I detail in the next section. *Clergie*, the concept in which this consideration is centered—most explicitly in the poem's difficult Vision Three—proves a frustratingly unstable category for such an endeavor, despite its institutional affiliations. Finally, in the C Version's poetic *apologia*, Langland focuses instead on the texts of the reading and singing repertoire as a way of obviating, or, at any rate, avoiding, many of the questions of intention and self-interest that plague his pursuit of *clergie*. These "tools" of his labor become a metonymy for vernacular making in terms of the claims to legitimacy, social utility, and "common" status that can be made in defense of their repeated performance.

Extragrammatical Voicing and the Discourse of Choral Community

Langland's persistent incorporation of textualized Latin phrases within his narrative has received a good deal of scholarly attention.[16] These words and phrases have often been termed "quotations"—a term that has the virtue of acknowledging that the non-English elements of the poem are generally perceived as having a textualized existence anterior to it and that this prior existence is invoked with a self-consciousness that concepts such as "intertextuality," "code-switching," or "macaronicism" cannot fully acknowledge. Yet, as I suggested in Chapter 4, our modern perception of the act of quotation (as designated by the use of quotation marks) is closely linked to objectification. Langland does indeed objectify some of these phrases by marking them (even in the absence of quotation marks) as the speech of another, for example: "And þerof seiþ þe Sauter in a Salmes ende: / '*In quorum manibus iniquitates sunt; dextra eorum repleta est muneribus*'" (B 3.248–49). In other cases, however, preexisting passages are incorporated into the speaker's utterance in a manner closer to that discussed in Chapter 4 in relation to Augustine: "And þere I sauȝ sooþly, *secundum scripturas*, / [Where] out of þe west coste a wenche, as me þouȝte / Cam walkynge in þe wey" (B 18.112–14). The distinction is textual, not linguistic. While in both of these examples Latin signals a gesture of invocation, the rehearsal of a prior text, textualized status is distinct from the use of Latin as such. Passages can be objectified as the speech of another even when they are not wholly in Latin, for example: "'*Reddite Cesari*,' quod god, 'þat *Cesari* bifalleþ, / *Et que sunt dei deo*, or ellis ye don ille'" (B 1.52–53).[17] Both this passage and "*secundum scripturas*" employ code-switching—that is, they shift between Latin and English while preserving the syntax of each language.[18] Yet despite the similar linguistic strategies, the passages differ in the relationship they posit between the speaker and the text she or he voices.

The range of relationships exemplified in *Piers Plowman* extends beyond these two possibilities to include those produced by the nominalizing strategies discussed in the previous chapter. The poem even seems to explore the poetic possibilities of extragrammatical techniques that acknowledge the distance between speaker and text without fully objectifying the latter in the manner of quotation. These techniques include treating incipits of discrete texts as synechdotal labels, that is, as names, capable of functioning as nouns ("He kan portreye wel þe Paternoster and peynte it with Aues" [B 15.181]), but extend far beyond this commonplace example. Phrases from other familiar texts—not always *incipits*—are similarly nominalized, as when the Dreamer invokes the Apostles' Creed to describe his vision of the Harrowing of Hell: "I drow me in þat derknesse to *descendit ad inferna*" (B 18.111). In this instance, the entire phrase is treated as a place-name; in still others, words or phrases are similarly converted to nouns and momentarily personified, as when Christ describes the fate of those who sin: "They shul be clensed clerliche and [keuered] of hir synnes / In my prisone Purgatorie, til *parce* it hote" (B 18.391–92). Here *parce*, an invocation of Job 7:16 from the Office of the Dead, as in the *parce mihi domine* poem discussed in the previous chapter,[19] becomes the agent of a self-referential command to spare the prisoner. Such a gesture is related to the formal techniques of personification allegory but is distinguishable in important ways. The verb *parce* does not itself name an abstract concept or institution, such as Ymaginatif or Cyuyle, that is examined in any sustained manner by assigning it narrative agency or motive. Its presence in the text is generated as much by its immediate alliterative possibilities as by any desire to consider the concept of "sparing" as such. The imperative form rather stresses the activity and efficacy of verbal performance itself, especially by invoking a text thought to have particular intercessory powers for souls in purgatory, as *The Gast of Gy* made clear.[20] As an incipit, it stands not for a concept but for a familiar and recognizable text in the manner of *paternosters* and *aves*. It thus participates in Langland's experimentation with the various ways of integrating these texts—his playful exploration of the possibilities of both grammatical and extragrammatical renderings of socially important texts to see what their manner of invocation might signify.

In this case, as in others, *parce* does not stand simply for a longer text but also for a particular *use* of that text. *Parce* invokes the passage from Job that serves as the first lesson in the Matins of the Dead, as we have seen. This allusion to the repertoire of reading and singing underscores the possibility that textual practices as well as texts can be cited. The study of quotation tends to focus solely on identifying the passage's origin, often seeking to isolate discrete textual sources to the exclusion of others. Such an emphasis can overlook the possibility that a single passage can participate simultaneously in different textual practices and even different literacies. This is the direction taken by Robert Adams, for example, who, in an effort to dampen many of the liturgical resonances earlier scholars had heard within the poem, accepted as liturgical quotation only the scriptural passages that appear in forms unique to the Breviary.[21] At the root of such an argument lies an assumption on his part and on the part of those he cites that the Vulgate and the Breviary and Missal are different texts potentially in competition with each other—that the liturgy represents a departure from scripture rather than a performance of it. While it is true that the Missal contains texts not found in the Vulgate and vice versa, it is difficult to imagine that a medieval cleric would perceive the scripture he read and sang to differ fundamentally from the concorded scriptural passages that helped generate his sermon. Singing and sermonizing rather represent two textual practices; the fact that the Bible can sustain both practices merely underscores the plenitude of sacred scripture. Langland's use of textualized Latin phrases suggests that he sought to re-create this sense of plenitude in his vernacular poem. The number of textual practices that have been detected as informing the structure of various sections of the poem—not only those based on scriptural texts, but also those related to legal discourse and documentary culture—points to a more ambitious project of integrating a range of disparate latinate literacies.[22]

In this respect, the poem seems designed to serve a unifying function similar to that which choral performance served within the discourse of choral community. As much a formal project as a response to any sense of cultural crisis, the use of the vernacular to frame and align various literacies allows it to participate in the excess meaning that marks public and sacramental language. The linguistic features and poetic traditions of English are often instrumental in the process of this unifying. Most obviously, the native alliterative form Langland adapts creates links between Latin and vernacular,[23] allowing the collocation of "prison" and "purgatory" that occurs throughout the poem to be linked with the *Dirige* text, *parce*, or "derknesse" to be linked with the creed phrase, *descendit ad inferna*. On occasion, an entire Latin passage, whether by accident or design, adheres to Langland's metrical contract, most tellingly when the Dreamer complains about "overleaping" priests who compromise the metrical integrity of scriptural language in liturgical performance. The paraphrase of James 2:10 the speaker "alleges" in support of his censure creates a perfect alliterative long line—*Qui offendit in vno in omnibus est reus*, "Whoever fails in one point is guilty in all" (B 11.309; C 13.122α)—that associates Langland's own metrical integrity with that of scriptural language.[24] Beyond alliteration, the extragrammatical strategy of nominalization is arguably facilitated by the ease with which English, as a largely uninflected language, allows the syntactic conversion of words, though Langland's predilection for momentary personification obviously extends beyond the simple conversion of verb to noun. The many Latin and French legal formulae translated entirely into English allow the vernacular to represent public, textualized language, as when Wareyn Wisdom and his companion Witty seek advice from Reason on how they might pursue a frivolous lawsuit that might "saue hem[seluen] from shame and from harmes" (B 4.31; A 4.28), which translates the legal formula *damage e huntage* that covered slander, among other offenses.[25] All of these unifying gestures are performed simultaneously in Langland's invocation of the *Dirige* lesson, where alliteration and nominalization are combined with a translated legal formula used to announce the term of punishments,[26] allowing the speaker, Christ, to represent his power to dispense justice and mercy in connection with ritual speech. The complexity of these gestures suggests that Langland sought both to bridge a gap between Latin, French, and English and to use English to align a number of lettered practices that were coming to be seen as increasingly fragmented.

In acknowledging this fragmentation, Langland represents official forms of Latin and French as heteroglossic—as internally differentiated and stratified according to social uses.[27] I would, however, argue that the goal of these complex invocations and rehearsals is ultimately synthetic, not dialogic. He is less interested in creating a dialogue that will underscore conflicts or competition between various discourses than in creating a sense of heterophony among them—the experience of different voices sounding in unison. This is not to say that the poem is devoid of conflict or dialogue. At the formal level, as Anne Middleton has pointed out, the poem progresses chiefly by means of conflict.[28] The disputes that generate much of the poem's action, however, are not those between competing institutions, or even between particular textual and discursive practices generated by institutions; conflicts rather arise out of the difference between practices structured by institutions, with all of their limitations, and the necessary deficiencies and excesses of their actual performances and performers. Even as Langland attempts to represent a "common voice" that expresses a "common will" instead of an institutional mandate, there is still an acknowledgment that making must be made from the discourses or textual practices that assure public intelligibility and public interest. If his repeated attempts to distance the poetic voice from the institutions that govern these discourses provoke crises of authority, these crises arise out of a persistent desire for the unifying framework such authority might provide.[29]

Of all possible institutional resources that might consistently bestow that authority, liturgy arguably holds the greatest promise of doing so in a manner that will resolve the tensions between competing performances, creating at a formal level the kind of heterophony to which he so often aspires in his integration of textualized words. This promise is most evident in Visions Five, Six, and Seven, much of which is structured by the liturgy.[30] From the fall of the first apple from the Tree of Charity (B 16.73ff.; C 18.100ff.), the narrative shifts from the didactic exposition of a static image to a series of events assimilated to the relentless forward progression of salvation history. In alluding to the Fall then to Abraham and Moses the poem gestures to the recital of Old Testament history (Genesis and Exodus) that structures the lessons read at matins from Septuagesima through the first weeks of Lent.[31] The liturgy for the thirteenth Sunday after Trinity provides even more specific connections between Abraham, Moses, and the Good Samaritan.[32] Langland thus takes his cue from the liturgy's predilection for associative accretions and narrative assimilation to synthesize strands of his own narrative, combining exposition, history, and lived experience. It is this combination that underlies the "dynamic reading of Scripture" James Simpson has noted as structuring Passus 16–19. In Simpson's account, this reading, in its retelling of the founding of Holy Church, "finally produces a newly imagined institution that can contain the common will evoked by the poem."[33] Liturgy is critical to this imagining, as becomes clear in Visions Six and Seven. In these dreams, based on the liturgy of Holy Week,[34] textualized passages are more frequently objectified as quotation, yet this objectification is related to their representation as communal acts performed within the narrative, from the *Gloria laus* and *Osanna* sung by young and old at the beginning of Vision Six (B 18.7, 8; C 20.6, 7) to the climactic moment when the Dreamer joins "many hundert" in a rendition of the Pentecostal Hymn, *Veni creator spiritus* (B 19.210–12; C 21.209–11).[35] Such heterophonic song is for Langland both the expression and the image of a "common will." Though Langland's ideal vision of the Church might be newly imagined in the context of the poem, it is also an image deeply indebted to the discourse of choral community.

Like all human institutions in the poem, and like all striving toward *communitas*, the song of those gathered in the barn called Unitee ultimately fails. Whereas the failure of the ideal community of Unitee is announced by an uncooperative brewer (B 19.399–405; C 21.396–402), the failure of the institution of Unitee is announced by that metonymic spokesman for ecclesiastical hypocrisy, the "lewed vicory" (B 19.412ff.; C 21.409ff.). His speech unsurprisingly details the failings of ecclesiastical officers, yet more important to Langland's conception of himself as public poet is the speaker's vicarious status. In this respect, he represents not simply ecclesiastical hypocrisy but also the specter of self-interest that haunts those who commit themselves to representing the interests of another. There is thus a connection between the two loci of articulation inhabited by vicar and public poet—a connection underscored by the "lewed vicory's" brief reappearance at the end of the Passus, as if his departure "fer hoem," with the agnostic refusal of the communal enterprise it implies (B 19.480; C 21.480), is responsible for waking the Dreamer and disrupting his poetic vision.

At this juncture in the poem, the mention of the vicar and the difficulties of representation he embodies serve primarily to show the limitations of liturgy's synthetic ambitions by allowing him to represent, vicariously, the self-interest that seems invariably to intrude on the choral ideal, yet the end of the vision subtly hints at the analogous limitations of Langland's own synthetic ambitions for his poetic voice. A more explicit exploration of this aspect of poetic voice, however, occurs in the successive revisions of Vision Three. In this central and difficult vision, Langland self-consciously attempts to situate his poetic voice in relation to *clergie* more broadly conceived as a way of establishing as well as scrutinizing the loci of articulation he can inhabit.

Clergie in Vision Three: Langland's Scrutiny of the Poetic "I"

The visions of liturgical unity that mark the final Passus of the poem come only after Langland has done some scrutinizing of his poetic project and its relationship to abstract forms of knowledge and institutions. At this critical juncture in the poem, Langland follows up his already ambitious bipartite allegorical narrative by setting a new poetic agenda. Whereas the first two visions rely on narrative tropes of courtly intrigue or pilgrimage to provide broad social commentary, the ethical inquiry underlying the search for Dowel represents a more speculative project—one whose procedures are meant to be internalized as well as represented. As such, it would appear to be an undertaking more suited to a treatise of vernacular theology than to sustained vernacular fiction, for even if the quest has a self-evident conceptual telos, it has no clear narrative trajectory. Indeed, at the point at which the A Version of the poem ends, the vision shows few signs of adhering to the narrative form of a *vita*—the title assigned to it in some manuscripts[36]—but threatens instead to become a formless colloquy of personified abstract nouns. More important, it precipitates a crisis of authority not simply among the speakers within the narrative but for the poetic "I" itself. Part of the appeal of the allegorical dream vision, for Langland as well as for others, is that it tempers claims to authority, not only because of the potentially spurious nature of dreams or the manner in which the retelling of the dream situates the "I" of the poem as a mere observer of events but also because the allegory within the dream can adhere to narrative rather than expository logic, creating its own momentum of cause and effect that seems more plausibly independent from authorial invention. Vision Three's focus on the "I's" active search for Dowel potentially negates these advantages. Without the interventions of narrative logic beyond mere seriality to provide a sense of motivation, the views expressed in the individual speeches the "I" encounters become more transparent as forms of authorial ventriloquism. Even among these ventriloquized positions, the "I" who must ultimately provide closure to the poem seems destined at some level to become the final arbiter of what it means to do well.

In the A Version of the poem, Langland's attempts to divorce his poetic voice from the authority his internalized ethical inquiry has thrust upon it causes the poem to stall.[37] Following the speeches of Wit, Study, Clergy, and Scripture, the poetic "I" engages in a reflection that distances him from the very advice he sought.

> 3et am I neuere þe ner for nou3t I haue walkid
> To wyte what is dowel witterly in herte.[38]

Though the speech boundary is marked only by a contrastive "3et," the passage's first person allusion to the peripatetic inquiry initiated in the waking scene of Passus 9 situates it outside the fictive framework of the dream. From this vantage point, the speaker eludes the problem of discerning the nature of Dowel from among the various definitions he has heard by disavowing the enterprise altogether, expressing an ambivalence toward his project that borders on retraction. In order to accomplish this gesture, however, Langland introduces the concept of *clergie* as a collective category of the waking world, to some extent distinguishable from the personification, Clergie, with whom the speaker conversed in the dream. Used in roughly the same way as Latin *scientia*,[39] the idea of *clergie* is used to group together his inquiries about Dowel and the responses he receives (to say nothing of the poetic project as a whole) as a single, questionable form of knowledge. As the speaker equivocates about the value of such knowledge, he notes that "clergie of cristis mouþ comendite [was hit] neuere" (A 11.294). Insofar as *clergie* serves as an English term for *scientia*, this is a fairly conventional vernacular maneuver: a turn away from the knowledge of human institutions to embrace a superior, sapiential wisdom perceived as widely accessible.[40] *Clergie*, however, possesses shades of meaning that set it apart from the abstraction *scientia*—above all, its inextricable relationship to ecclesiastical institutions and authorized performers. More problematically for Langland, it represents both the authorizing institution that generally validates his subject matter as worthy of public attention and the institutional locus of articulation from which he wants to distance his poetic voice.

The problems *clergie* poses for vernacular poetics are especially visible in the final lines of the poetic "I's" reflection. In what in many extant manuscripts is the last passage of the A Version, the speaker "alleges" St. Augustine as *auctoritas* for his renunciation of *clergie*.

> *Ecce ipsi ydiot[e] rapiunt celum vbi nos sapientes in infernum*
>   *mergemur.*
> And is to mene in oure mouþ, more ne lesse,
> Arn non raþere yrauisshid fro þe riȝte beleue
> Þanne arn þise [k]ete clerkis þat conne many bokis,
> Ne non sonnere ysauid, ne saddere of consience,
> Þanne pore peple, as plouȝmen, and pastours of bestis,
> Souteris & seweris; suche lewide iottis
> Percen wiþ a paternoster þe paleis of heuene
> Wiþoute penaunce at here partyng, into [þe] heiȝe blisse.
>   (A 11.305–13)

Augustine's *sententia* is a significant choice since it approaches the question of *clergie* not only by means of its comparative efficacy but also in terms of social identity and the affiliations it voices, privileging the simplicity of *ipsi ydiote* while claiming membership in the "we" of *nos sapientes*.[41] Langland's translation reveals a desire to manipulate this social dynamic. Apart from assigning specific professions to the *ydiote* and the *sapientes*, it also attempts to reorient the relations of speaker and audience to formal knowledge. The "I" both associates himself with those vernacular speakers who require translation into "oure mouþ" and distances himself from "þise [k]ete clerkis" (a reversal also played out when the active seizure [*rapiunt*] of heaven by the ignorant is transmuted into the passive ravishing ["yrauisshid"] of the distinguished clerics). Yet if the "I" does not align himself with the clerics, neither does he claim membership among the various professions that constitute "suche lewide iottis." In contrast to the Augustinian *sententia* that emanates from a stable sense of the social location of both speaker and audience, Langland's vernacularization manifests both an evasion of the institutional authority that underwrites the clergy and an evasion of disingenuous claims to *lewidness*. It is a voice in search of a location.

The unstable nature of *clergie* and the speaker's relationship to it haunts all further versions of this transitional vision as Langland attempts to resituate the poetic "I" and its function in his vernacular undertaking. In the B Version, this equivocal (and potentially hypocritical) denunciation of *clergie* becomes a point of departure for exploring these very issues in both narrative and narratorial terms. Langland initiates the narrative reconfiguration of his project by placing the speech with which the A Version stalled within the fictive framework of the dream. No longer a general response to the vision, the questioning of *clergie* is situated as a continuation of the vision—as an irritable reaction to Scripture's "long lesson" and its negligible returns (B 10.377–78). Because it is the first extended speech by the poetic "I" to be so situated, it could be argued that this gesture creates the "Dreamer" as an entity specifically of and within the fictive frame. Though "Will" had earlier been named by Wit as a participant-observer within the vision (B 8.125–28; A 9.117–18),[42] it is only at this moment that he becomes one of the subjects of the poem—one who instigates the productive conflict by which the poem has proceeded.[43] In this case, the Dreamer's temper tantrum precipitates the inner dream of self-reflection—a narrativizing of the contemplative imperative to "know thyself"[44]—that allows the poem to continue. Inasmuch as the inner dream rehearses the motifs of the first two visions, as Anne Middleton has demonstrated,[45] it represents an internalization of the events of those visions by the Dreamer. In this manner it exemplifies ethical responses to issues raised in them, making the process of internalization the subject of narrative representation. Authorial signatures (such as the "land of longing" itself) that give this fictive "I" a specific identity suggest that if this "I" is meant to be exemplary, he is no Everyman.[46] Rather, he represents the particularity of lived experience in a way that is not so personal and context-bound as to hinder its capacity to bear excess meaning that his narrative might offer.

Context-bound or not, however, the matter of the poetic "I's" social location and social identity still needs to be clarified, or at least examined more fully. To do so, Langland seizes on an earlier passage in the vision to allow the Dreamer's pretensions to resonate with similar moments both before and after his tirade, thereby integrating his self-representation with concerns expressed in the poem as a whole. In the A Version, Study had complained generally (though she surely had the undeserving wisdom-seeker, Will, in mind) about misleading theological sophistry conducted by "Clerkes and [k]ete men" as well as "Freris and faitours," who "carp[en] aȝens clergie crabbide wordis" (A 11.56–65). In the B Version, this section is revised to form a narrative and expository frame for the Dreamer's complaint—one that emphasizes the difficulty of isolating the social and institutional resources that might authorize public speech concerning serious ethical and spiritual matters. While the mixed group of clerical and lay beguilers continues to cater to the egos of "proude men" in this version, those who assail *clergie* with "crabbede wordes" are specifically said to be "heiȝe men"—pretentious layfolk who "Carpen as þei clerkes were" (B 10.104–7). To contextualize this armchair theologizing, Langland adds a discussion of their lack of charity in preferring to take their meals in private chambers instead of sharing their wealth in the great hall. In addition to stressing that the intellectual posturing of such "heiȝe men" is authorized, or at least underwritten, in their eyes by their material wealth, the convivial, postprandial setting of such theological conversations makes clear that they are a form of facile amusement, not earnest inquiry. It is, however, amusement with a purpose. Their discussion questions the logic of Original Sin and, in particular, objects to the idea that they should bear any responsibility for it (B 10.108–16α). Though the Dreamer is never represented as a "heiȝe" man in any sense of the word, a parallel is implied between the pretensions of these layfolk and his uppity dismissal of *clergie* as similarly motivated by a desire to evade responsibility. Viewed from the perspective offered by Study, the Dreamer's outburst suggests that though he claims to search for Dowel, he would just as soon not do anything at all. His dismissal of *clergie* is thereby exposed as an illegitimate use of *clergie* by one who is not truly authorized to use it.

The parallel is made explicit by Study's unusual anticipatory mention of Ymaginatif as one who will in some sense provide Will with a response to the "crabbede wordes" of the "heiȝe men": "Ymaginatyf herafterward shal answere to [your] purpos" (B 10.119). The insertion links this part of Study's speech to the later moment in the vision, in which Ymaginatif justifies his long excursus on the value of *clergie* by claiming that it responds to the Dreamer's own "crabbed wordes": "Why I haue tolde [þee] al þis, I took ful good hede / How þow contrariedest clergie wiþ crabbed wordes" (B 12.155–56). This verbal repetition, aligning the Dreamer's behavior with that of the pretentious laymen, creates an arc of narrative exposition that frames the inner dream, refocusing attention on the issue of *clergie*—above all, the poetic "I's" relationship to it—without disrupting the larger trajectory he has set up with the search for Dowel, a search that now continues beyond the boundaries of this single vision.

Because of *clergie*'s unstable nature, the issues surrounding it are complex. It is not simply a matter of attitudes toward *clergie*—indeed, the Dreamer's stated position championing the plowman's *paternoster* is not far from the position taken by Study in reaction to the offending armchair theologizers: "*Non plus sapere quam oportet*"; "do not understand more than is appropriate" (B 10.121). The connections between the Dreamer and the "hei3e men" implied by the label "crabbed wordes," I have suggested, have more to do with the questionable motives behind the *use* of *clergie*. More to the point, they pertain to a certain kind of *performance* of *clergie* from an inappropriate social location. The speech of the "hei3e men" is not only distinguished from the sycophancy of clerks and friars but also elaborated to represent a particular rhetorical style. Newly seasoned with Latin quotations "alleged" in support of spurious theological claims, their speech clearly mimics the textual practices of those to whom they consider themselves intellectual equals.

> "Here lyeþ youre lore," þise lordes gynneþ dispute,
> "Of þat [ye] clerkes vs kenneþ of crist by þe gospel:
> *Filius non portabit iniquitatem patris &c.*
> Why sholde we þat now ben for þe werkes of Adam
> Roten and torende? Reson wolde it neuere!
> *Vnusquisque portabit onus suum &c.*" (B 10.112–160α)

The invocation of textualized Latin phrases here calls attention to their potential misappropriation in ways that divide rather than unify the Christian community. Underscoring such divisiveness is the use of direct address: "youre lore." From this rhetorical position, the "hei3e men" define themselves as a group precisely by their opposition to the very clerics whose learning they imitate. The "lore" itself, in turn, may involve transcendent truths, but in the hands of these armchair theologizers, it becomes an object that is, as they suggest by their appropriation, portable—a notion ironically reinforced by the concording Latin verb *portabit*, which they use to deny their own burden of Original Sin.

Similar, though not synonymous, gestures are added to the Dreamer's outburst. His discussion moves from pondering the value of seeking out and possessing *clergie* to decrying the hypocrisy of clerics who are supposedly *clergie*'s authorized practitioners but who rarely live up to its ethical precepts. With a comparable addition of Latin and French phrases to his discourse, Will likens the fate of such clerics to the ignominious end of the carpenters who built Noah's ark. His criticism, like that of the "heiȝe men," culminates in "crabbed wordes," newly added in the B Version, that define the speaker's social position through direct address to the offending body.

> The *culorum* of þis clause curatours is to mene,
> That ben carpenters holy kirk to make for cristes owene beestes:
> *Homines & iumenta saluabis, domine, &c.*
> [At domesday þe deluuye worþ of deþ and fir at ones;
> Forþi I counseille yow clerkes, of holy [kirke] þe wriȝtes,
> Wercheþ ye werkes as ye sen ywrite, lest ye worþe noȝt þerInne].
>   (B 10.415–19)

This use of direct address, however, differs significantly from the earlier example. Taking it upon himself to "counseille" clergy rather than merely dispute with them, the Dreamer obviously claims much greater authority.[47] This authority, furthermore, is closely related to the positioning of his voice. Those engaged in postprandial theologizing do so after having withdrawn from the great hall to take meals in their own chambers, with the subtle implication that they are emboldened by the freedom that their privacy affords them. Will, by contrast, addresses the clergy from the standpoint of a prophet, a position that, while it similarly defines itself in opposition to institutional loci of articulation, is nonetheless public by its very nature. It is also a rhetorical position taken up by different speakers throughout the poem, part of the apocalyptic visionary tradition that informs the work.[48] Though this was a tradition that authorized non-clerical speakers, Langland here makes it the subject of self-conscious representation, submitting its procedures to scrutiny. Connecting it to the "crabbede wordes" of pretentious laymen earlier in the vision helps bring out the parodic potential in what elsewhere in the poem is a serious rhetorical gesture. The effect is only enhanced by placing this performance in the context of the Dreamer's temper tantrum. In this manner, Langland turns a speech that in the A Version had been a final contemplation in the "voice of the poem" into a parody of his own performance that questions the terms by which this narratorial voice has been constructed.

The parodic elements are not sustained. Though Langland does objectify the narratorial voice, he does not create a discrete "persona," in the literary sense of the term, that is consistently maintained throughout the poem.[49] It is, rather, a locus of articulation he can strategically inhabit. In this respect, it is like the institutional *persona ecclesie* but has the opposite purpose of calling attention to the speaker's self-interested motivations instead of requiring their suppression. Langland has taken a disavowal of his poetic enterprise, figured as a search for *clergie*, and transformed it into a disavowal of voice that focuses attention on narratorial activity as a critical component of public representation. This gesture self-consciously engages the problem of positioning the vernacular poetic voice and of locating its resources of authority. The instability of *clergie* is in many ways the root of this problem. From one perspective, *clergie-as-scientia* is articulated as objectified knowledge, which is represented throughout the poem as an alienable possession: "And be we noȝt vnkynde of oure catel, ne of oure konnynge neiþer, / For woot no man how neiȝ it is to ben ynome fro boþe," the poetic "I" advises (B 11.211–12). As a possession, *clergie* is also separable from clerical identity. The "fracture between *clergie* and the clergy" effected by this objectification, as Wendy Scase puts it,[50] is a necessary precondition of a lay poetics. At the same time, however, this fracture is far from complete. Langland's choice of the term *clergie*, I have already suggested, reinforces the ties between knowledge and clerical identity as well as those between authoritative knowledge and ecclesiastical loci of articulation. These ties are almost ineluctably realized in the performance of *clergie* in ways that raise critical questions for Langland's vernacular poetics: first, whether it is possible to perform clerical knowledge without performing clerical identity; and second, whether there is spiritual knowledge worthy of public attention that would not qualify as *clergie*.

The inescapable yet conflicting affiliations of *clergie* manifest themselves not merely in the irony that speakers like the "heiȝe men," who are said to "carpen ayein cler[gie]" are, almost by virtue of that activity, also said to "carpen as þei clerkes were" (B 10.107, 105).[51] More critically and self-referentially, the Dreamer's explicit rejection of *clergie* is exposed as a kind of clerical performance. As Scripture criticizes him, she points to a distinction between "vain *scientia*" and the knowledge of self the Dreamer lacks: "*Multi multa sciunt et se ipsos nesciunt*" ("Many know many things, yet do not know themselves").[52] Castigating him for his impatience and pretension, Scripture's admonishment implies that his tirade was itself a performance of vain *scientia* rather than the embracing of sapiential wisdom he pretends to. As he is subsequently "rauysshed" to the Land of Longing (B 11.7), he appears less the uppity layman than one of the "[kete] clerkes" he claimed were so easily "yrauisshed fro þe riȝte bileue." Vertiginously, this straying is imagined in the ensuing inner dream as the result of the Dreamer's rejection of "Clergie" (B 11.16). The contemplative tradition Scripture invokes to initiate the inner dream was one that, in its vernacular instantiation, often advocated knowledge of self as an alternative to the speculative sophistry that *clergie*-as-*scientia* can become.[53] The Dreamer's relationship to *clergie* more broadly conceived, however, is equivocal. On the one hand, his decision to disregard *clergie* to follow Fortune and the enticements of the flesh is clearly a sign of Will's impetuousness; on the other hand, equally ill conceived is the trust he places in the clergial ministrations of the Friars with their abuse of the sacrament of confession.

One could argue that Will has simply abandoned a legitimate and objectified form of knowledge—*clergie*—and entrusted his soul to those illegitimate clergy (indeed, friars rather than secular clergy as such) who abuse the institutional power that governs its use. Yet his complaint about their behavior—their obvious self-interest in favoring lucrative confessions over baptisms (11.75–83)—stresses their sacerdotal (as opposed to strictly fraternal) activities, specifically their performance of the sacraments, in ways that complicate the issues of identity and legitimacy. Knowledge of the sacraments is an important part of *clergie*, as Ymaginatif's recuperation of the abstraction will later make explicit (B 12.85–86); the sacraments are also performative practices in which knowledge, clerical identity, and institutional authority are not as easy to separate. They are, furthermore, "public" in the sense that they have a social and spiritual utility and thus involve responsibilities that extend beyond "private" contractual agreements with individual souls for confession or burial rites. Precisely because the Friars are "free agents" who do not operate within parochial systems of obligations, this greater responsibility is intensified. In choosing confession and burial over baptism—the sacrament that essentially creates the Christian community—they betray not only the trust that Will had placed in them but also their duties to the community of the faithful as a whole. It is this greater betrayal that motivates Will to speak on behalf of the betrayed, allowing his particular experiences to bear meaning beyond that of his own salvation. Will thus enters the realm of public discourse by situating himself in opposition to *clergie*/clergy, as Lewtee gives him license to publish his indignation.

> It is *licitum* for lewed men to [legge] þe soþe
> If hem likeþ and lest; ech a lawe it graunteþ,
> Excepte persons and preestes and prelates of holy chirche.

It falleþ noȝt for þat folk no tales to telle
Thouȝ þe tale [were] trewe, and it touche[d] synne. (B 11.96–100)

Associating *lewidness* with the power of latinate legal terminology (*licitum, legge*), Langland thus imagines the possibilities for a lay, vernacular poetics with comparable (and in some ways compensating and restorative) utility to the performative obligations that the Friars have failed to uphold.

Lewtee's speech even appears to reverse the relationship between clerical/lay identity and public/private speech: *lewid* men, such as Will, have *exclusive* license for public speech, while parsons and priests are seen as inappropriate conveyors of such truths. This reversal stems partly from the particularity of lived experience that Langland has made the subject of this vision. Generalized *exempla*, presumably, would not hold the same risk of scandal in clerical speech. Because parsons and priests represent Holy Church, however, to broadcast particular wrongs, suffered or witnessed *in propria persona*, threatens to become an indecorous misuse of the power to speak *in persona ecclesie*—the substitution of gossip for gospel. *Lewid* men are also prone to the inappropriate assertion of self-interest, whether vengeful, supercilious, or sycophantic in motive, but the danger for them is not as great precisely because their speech carries no institutional authority. Nonetheless, the status of such complaint as worthy of public attention depends on establishing the same gap between speaker and speech that defined the institutional *persona*, though in this case that gap is established by ensuring that the poet merely rehearses that which has already been said.

Ac be [þow] neueremoore þe firste [þe] defaute to blame;
Thouȝ þow se yuel seye it noȝt first; be sory it nere amended.
[Th]ynge þat is pryue, publice þow it neuere. (B 11.103–5)

With this warning, Lewtee appears to create a non-clerical locus of articulation that, while still reformist in tenor, is less presumptuous than the prophetic mode enacted by the Dreamer in his tirade. Relying on the "common vois" as a resource of authority (a term more prominent in the works of Chaucer and Gower, in which "vois" often translates Latin *fama*), this speakerly position seems to solve the difficulty of *clergie* in a vernacular poetics.

Problems remain, however, with such a locus of articulation. Its primary use is largely limited to the satirical detailing of clerical and other abuses. Because of its affiliation with *lewidness*, to move beyond satirizing, to take up matters of *clergie* considered as knowledge rather than solely as social identity, creates the same potential for disingenuousness that marked the Dreamer's translation of Augustine. These limitations become clear when Lewtee's pronouncement is confirmed by Scripture, whose clergial reaction receives comment from the poetic "I."

> "He seiþ sooþ," quod Scripture þo, and skipte an heiȝ and preched.
> Ac þe matere þat she meued, if lewed men it knewe,
> Þe lasse, as I leue, louyen þei wolde
> [The bileue [of oure] lord þat lettred men techeþ]. (B 11.107–10)

Speaking from outside the narrative economy of both dream and inner dream, the "I" also positions himself outside the binary opposition of *lewid* and *lettred*—as a mediator or, rather, as one who gives voice to the rupture that divides them. Using language that displays his familiarity with sermon conventions, he states that he "took ful good hede" of Scripture's "teme and hir text" (B 11.111). In so doing, he reestablishes the poetic "I's" capacity for explicit metapoetic commentary because maintaining the fiction that the "I" always speaks as the Dreamer who experiences events in the narrative as they occur has its own risks of disingenuousness, to put it in narratorial terms. In terms of social identity, the "I's" informed attention to Scripture's sermon situates him in the position of disinterested witness, not unlike the position of the *viri litterati* consulted in the St. Cross proceeding who were authorized by their lettered competence.[54] It is also similar to the pardon scene, in which the "I" makes a point of establishing his physical proximity to Piers, the priest, and the pardon, stating that he "bihynde hem boþe biheld al þe bulle" (B 7.110). This, one might argue, is Langland's ideal locus of articulation for public poetry—over the shoulder, as it were, of clergy and lay.

Such an ideal, however, still does not situate the poetic voice clearly. It shifts the issue only by demonstrating that the poetic "I" does not position himself solely in opposition to *clergie* (unlike the "common voice" described directly before the intrusion). Both connected and distanced from *clergie*, this locus of articulation, however ideal, still lacks a stable and recognizable social position. It is perhaps significant in this regard that the speaker of the long speech on poverty that ends the first half of the inner dream is not unequivocally identified—the origin of the utterance, even its place in the nested narrative economies of the inner dream, is unclear.[55]

But no matter the speaker, the expository movement of this passage traces a chain of associations regarding *clergie* that lead to the practices associated with reading and singing—practices that place knowledge in a similarly undefined and often suspect relationship to ecclesiastical institutions. The speaker (whom I identify as the poetic "I," accepting Kane and Donaldson's determination of speech boundaries) takes up Trajan's rejection of *clergie* as necessary to salvation. Categorizing *clergie* among the wealth of this world, the speaker advocates poverty as an alternative. While considering those who value worldly wealth inordinately, the proverbially materialistic and greedy unbeneficed clergy enter the discussion, specifically those who "[nyme] siluer for masses" (B 11.291). The ethical failings of this group, as we have seen, were strongly associated with their purported ineptitude and illiteracy—an association the speaker retraces as he berates "overskipperis" and the priest "þat konneþ noȝt *sapienter* / Synge ne psalmes rede ne seye a masse of þe day" (B 11.310, 313–14). In this retracing the speaker has thus moved from a position rejecting the necessity of *clergie* to one lamenting its absence, a shift caused by the fact that his primary focus has moved from *clergie*-as-*scientia* to "clergy" as social identity and authoritative locus of articulation. From this new vantage point, the clergy's lack of *clergie* is indicative of a larger social ill underlying the debate over *clergie*'s value: that *clergie*'s portability, its ability to be appropriated, results from a "fracture" between knowledge, social identity, and authority that threatens the ideals of choral unity at the heart of his poetic project.

Langland registers the disquieting effect of this train of thought by marking its final point as a digression: "This lokynge on lewed preestes haþ doon me lepe fram pouerte" (B 11.318). This explicit admission—so striking in a poem that few would characterize on the whole as focused or linear—results in an expository stutter in the ungainly transition between the first and second parts of the inner dream that is virtually the opposite of the momentum achieved in Passus 16–19. One might be tempted to dismiss such an odd moment were it not that the second extensive treatment of *clergie*—Ymaginatif's speech—follows a similar pattern of free associative logic that results in conceptual reversal. Chastising Will for his "crabbede wordes," Ymaginatif sets out to recuperate *clergie* by describing its many valences and values. After extensive exemplification of the benefits of *clergie*, a discussion described by Derek Pearsall as "burr-like" in its logic,[56] he picks up on the Dreamer's invocation of the thieves who were crucified with Christ, connecting their fate with the possession of clerical knowledge.

Wel may þe barn blesse þat hym to book sette,
That lyuynge after lettrure saue[d] hym lif and soule.
Dominus pars hereditatis mee is a murye verset
That haþ take fro Tybourne twenty stronge þeues,
Ther lewed þeues ben lolled vp; loke how þei be saued!
    (B 12.187–91)

The irony of Ymaginatif's reference to the literacy tests for benefit of clergy is so incongruous that Pearsall takes the sentiment as sincere: "Imaginatif clearly regards the practice [of benefit of clergy] not as a gross abuse of the law, but as an instrument of God's mercy to the sinner."[57] The sarcasm of "murye verset," however, seems to me to make such a reading implausible.[58] This shocking deflation hinges on the meaning of the word "saued" but is enabled, once again, by focusing on performative practices that threaten the unity of clerical knowledge and clerical authority in the service of the community of the faithful. In this case, the problem is that knowledge, identity, and authority are indeed equated, yet only through self-interested manipulation that belies any sense of organic unity.

    The ethically dubious or illegitimate practitioners of *clergie*—the illiterate mass priest and the criminous claimant of benefit of clergy—are depicted as manifestations of institutional deterioration, worthy of consternation. Structurally and rhetorically, however, these passages stand out from other citations of clerical abuses, occupying pivotal positions. The passage on *lewid* priests, as I have said, demarcates the first part of the inner dream. The passage on benefit of clergy, its thematic recursivity punctuated by the final exclamation, marks the end of Ymaginatif's exemplification of *clergie* and the beginning of his more carefully reasoned assessment of the events immediately before and within the inner dream. With this gesture Langland also links illegitimate performative practice with the parodied performance of public poetry that preceded the inner dream. A similar connection to narratorial activity is hinted at by the vague similarity between priestly lapses of attention in "ouerskipping" and poetic lapses of attention in expository "leaping" in the earlier passage. Despite the fact that these *lewid* priests and spurious clerics, like the "lewed vicory" of Passus 19, could be viewed as the polar opposite of a learned layman, as the Dreamer/poetic "I" generally represents himself, a subtle, problematic affinity persists—one that causes rhetorical stutters and ethical impasses. These performers ultimately typify both the fissures of *clergie*/clergy that make a vernacular poetics possible and the questionable legitimacy and patent self-interest of those who take advantage of these fissures. Langland, with his pretensions to public speech and authority, as well as his aspirations to *clergie*, remains at risk of accusations of self-interest. With Vision Three, Langland focuses attention on voice and performance as the most critical components of public poetry, yet as long as he continues to orient these components exclusively in relation to the unstable concept of *clergie*, he is unable to justify his poetic activity.

Vernacular Poetics and the Repertoire of Reading and Singing

As was the case with B's revision of the A Version, the C Version turns a site of impasse into a point of departure. The latent identification of vernacular making with illegitimate clerical performance is made explicit in the poetic *apologia* inserted between the first two visions in the C Version. Some scholars have associated this waking episode with an interrogation under various labor legislations from 1349 to 1388.[59] Most extensively, Anne Middleton has suggested a parallel between the Cambridge Statute of Laborers of 1388, which, among other things, compelled those not trained in a "necessary" craft to manual labor at harvest time, and Reason's questioning of Will.[60] In this interpretation, Langland uses this mock juridical setting to redefine, once again, the terms of his poetic project and the social identity his verbal performance confers upon him. His explicit assertion of clerical status as means of exemption from the statute is comically spurious, combined as it is with similarly unconvincing excuses, such as claiming his height as a disability that should exempt him from stoop labor (C 5.23–25).[61] Among these dubious claims, however, the pretension of clerical identity plays a central role in this aggressive gesture of self-justification. Whether or not it preemptively dismisses any claims to sacerdotal authority, as Middleton suggests,[62] Langland's response to Reason effects a shift in his strategies of self-positioning. Instead of trying to situate himself in relation to *clergie* in its unstable totality, Langland uses pressing ethical issues surrounding labor legislation to refocus his attention more specifically on the gray area of the *clerici* and away from the institutional authority of the *presbyteres* and *sacerdotes*. This refocusing, as we shall see, ultimately enables a more powerful reimagining of the poetic voice less in relation to the institutional abstraction *clergie* than in relation to the concrete texts of the reading and singing repertoire.

* * *

The changes made to Vision Three in the C Version suggest that Langland sought to disentangle the narratorial experiment of situating his poetic voice within nested narrative economies from the debate over the nature and value of *clergie*. The tirade against *clergie* that in the B Version established the "Dreamer" as a sustained, fictive locus of articulation is reassigned to the "I's" more specifically and allegorically characterized alter ego, Rechelesnesse, and placed within the narrative economy of the inner dream. The shift in part simply accommodates the fact that the narratorial function assigned to the speech in B has been obviated by the C 5 *apologia*, which now performs the gesture of creating the Dreamer, "Will" (who in the C Version is defined not merely by the desire manifested in his dreams but also by those of his waking life and is thus situated still more firmly in the realm of lived experience). Yet the change also aligns this first extended speech on *clergie* with Rechelesnesse's second speech on poverty and the unbeneficed clergy (C 12.89–13.128). No longer marked as a digression, the comments on illiterate priests are linked to the immediately preceding passage on poverty, such that lettered knowledge now exemplifies the kind of responsibilities incumbent upon those (in this case entitled priests) who are not utterly impoverished. More important, the passage now also serves a recursive function. Returning to Rechelesnesse's preoccupation with *clergie* as a whole, it provides the most immediate referent to the demonstrative in the line that replaces B's admission of digression: "Thus rechelesnesse in a rage aresenede clergie" (C 13.129). This framing gesture is reinforced by several added references to Clergie/*clergie* and, to a lesser extent, Scripture, throughout the inner dream (C 11.199, 202, 222, 312, 13.129, 131). While these additions emphasize the topical centrality of *clergie* to the vision—possibly even the *textual* aspects of *clergie* stressed by Scripture's presence—refocusing the topic through Rechelesnesse distances it from the poetic "I's" performance.[63] In his later recuperation of *clergie*, Ymaginatif continues to chastise Will, not Rechelesnesse, for his "crabbede wordes," making clear that it is the poet's relationship to *clergie* that is at stake. What Rechelesnesse provides is a way to separate this examination from one that considers the relationship of *clergie* to the poetic voice.

The C 5 *apologia* explores the possibilities of the poetic "I" much earlier in the poem, at the point at which the poem distinguishes itself from the more conventional single-vision allegorical form.[64] Isolated in its own brief waking episode, Will's encounter with Reason and Conscience more self-consciously separates the relevance of *clergie* to poetic production from its relevance to salvation more generally. Due to this disarticulation, the discussion hinges less on the value of *clergie* than on the value of verbal performance as a legitimate form of labor, though both clerical knowledge and clerical identity play an important role. Will mentions both his early clerical education—his knowledge of holy writ—as well as his current donning of "longe clothes"—the habit that asserts his clerical identity (C 5.35–41). He describes his current occupation, however, in terms of the texts he performs.

> The lomes þat y labore with and lyflode deserue
> Is paternoster and my prymer, *placebo* and *dirige*,
> And my sauter som tyme and my seuene p[s]almes.
> Th[u]s y s[yn]ge for here soules of such as me helpeth,
> And tho þa[t] fynden me my fode fouchensaf, y trowe. (C 5.45–49)

This list of texts is useful to Langland not because they support Will's claim to clerical status but because they short-circuit the binary opposition between clerical and lay performance and identity.[65] All of the texts had both liturgical and devotional uses. As popularized by early reading and singing pedagogy, this repertoire marked the lowest level of clerical literacy; as popularized by Books of Hours and other devotional materials, the repertoire also functioned as a canon of charismatized devotional texts. Yet Langland's citation of these texts goes beyond merely replacing the ambiguities of identity that marked Vision Three. Concentrating on performed texts, and above all on this particular group of texts, turns attention away from the sacerdotal pretensions and contractual obligations of the mass priest (the very affiliation this passage is often thought to express) and onto the much more complex gift economy of informal, non-Eucharistic benefaction—a system that in its oblique forms of exchange more closely resembled the modes of patronage that governed vernacular literary production. Within this economy and the kinds of signification it enabled, Langland seems to find an imaginative focus better suited to articulating the terms of his poetic enterprise and the "I's" relationship to it.

Arriving at such a conceptual vantage point was simply a matter of following a different strand of associations already embedded in A and B. The A Version's musings ended by opposing *clergie* and the making that results from its pursuit to the *lewid* recitation of the *paternoster*. In the B Version, this opposition loses some of its overt metapoetic force as its sentiments are refracted through the fictive "I" within the narrative economy of the dream. It is, however, supplemented by Ymaginatif's more explicit (and oft-cited) criticism of Will's misuse of his time.

And þow medlest þee wiþ makynges and my3test go seye þi sauter,
And bidde for hem þat 3yueþ þee breed, for þer are bokes y[n]owe
To telle men what dowel is, dobet and dobest boþe,
And prechours to preuen what it is of many a peire freres.
　　(B 12.16–19)

While the opposition of rehearsal and *inventio* is similar, the substitution of the Psalter introduces some complicating elements. Though the *paternoster* is decisively *lewid* (perhaps the only Latin text that designates *lewidness*), the Psalter has clergial potential at least. These clerical pretensions are nonetheless acceptable because they are directed toward the specific end of praying for others. Rehearsal of the Psalter does not simply secure one's own salvation but is socially productive. Its productivity is furthermore linked to its very nature as sanctioned and sacralized text, which lends it a capacity to bear repetition profitably, as opposed to Will's making, which errs not only in its pretensions to clerical authority but in its redundancy. Upholding Psalter recitation as a model of useful verbal labor, against which Will is only able to categorize his making as "solace" and "play" (B 12.22, 24), resonates with the curiosity, exemplified in *The Gast of Gy*, about the potential intercessory powers of nonsacerdotal performance. Closely related to this power, and more relevant to vernacular making, is the possibility of sacramentality in such performances and the excess meaning it generates, as well as the possibility of public signification that capitalizes on the multiplicity of intention these texts can sustain. Though these possibilities remain unexamined in this brief exchange, they become central to Langland's reevaluation of vernacular making in the C 5 *apologia*.

In what was his most emphatic gesture of self-justification, Langland undoes the opposition between rehearsal and *inventio*. When asked to give an account of himself, Will does not explicitly mention his making at all but, apparently having taken Ymaginatif's advice, claims his informal reading and singing activity as his primary occupation. Given the context of this claim and Will's investment in using this activity to exempt himself from prosecution under secular labor legislation, his motives are immediately suspect. It would appear that Will has listened to Ymaginatif not only in regarding Psalter recitation as a more justifiable use of his time but also in putting his knowledge of the Psalter to self-interested uses, as he himself adduces the "murye verset"—*Dominus pars hereditatis mee*—in support of his claim to clerical entitlements (C 5.60α). But it is not solely clerical texts that receive this treatment. In Will's last attempt at righteous indignation, he returns to the *paternoster*.

> "Forthy rebuke me ryhte nauhte, resoun, y ʒow praye,
> For in my Consience y knowe what Crist w[o]lde y wrouhte.
> Preeyeres of a parfit man and penaunce d[iscret]e
> Is the leuest labour þat oure lord pleseth.
> *Non de solo,*" y sayde, "for sothe *viuit homo,*
> *Nec in pane [nec] in pabulo*; the paternoster wittenesseth
> *Fiat voluntas dei* fynt vs all thynges." (C 5.82–88)

Hedging his bets, Will enlists his conscience—the final arbiter of clerical labor, as we have seen[66]—and, at the same time, defers to the devotional nature of his performances, effectively replacing the opposition between labor and idleness with the implicit, and more flattering, opposition between Mary and Martha. His use of scripture to demonstrate the implications of the better part that he has chosen, however, betrays the duplicity of the sentiment in its ellipses and insinuations. Will may not live by bread alone, but he does, in a much more material fashion, live by every word that flows from the mouth of God. Not only does he trust in God's will to sustain him; he trusts in his own performance of the *paternoster—fiat voluntas tua*—to support him financially (as well as spiritually).

Insofar as Langland embraces this textual repertoire, then, it is because of the excesses of intention that invariably inform its performance, allowing rehearsal to become *inventio*—a source of making rather than the antithesis to it. This potential for invention perhaps adds a third layer of meaning to the final line of the passage above, which attributes to the *paternoster* the power "to *fynt* … alle thynges." More accurately, it attributes this power to his extragrammatical nominalization of the *paternoster* passage, *fiat voluntas tua*—to his most distinctive and marketable poetic trademark, one might say. The reading and singing repertoire become in this poetic *apologia* a metonymy for vernacular making. While it may seem counterintuitive to affiliate English poetry with Latin texts, for Langland, the essence of vernacular poetics, its capacity to produce "public" meaning or the polysemy that dignifies *litteratura*, does not necessarily derive from its use of the English language. His interest lies not in the ossified English text that commingles with or even rivals Latin *litteratura* but in the extragrammatical gestures that wrest socially and spiritually important texts from the complacency and abuses their institutional settings have engendered. Such gestures are not always performed *in* English. In addition to the nominalization of *fiat voluntas tua*, the passage above relies on Langland's rearrangement and augmentation of the Latin gospel passage ("non in pane solo vivet homo" [Matt. 4:4, which is itself an invocation of Deut. 8:3])[67] as well as the nominalization of the *paternoster* verse "fiat voluntas tua." English, tellingly, comes into play with the semantically gratuitous but usefully alliterating "y sayde" that fills out the alliterative long line by emphasizing Will's performance, his "voicing," of the text. This stress on vernacular, extragrammatical performance, in turn, endows the nonce phrase "for sothe" with ironic overtones—excess meaning—it otherwise would not possess concerning the actual truth value of Will's defense.

The passage is as witty and evasive as any of Chaucer's self-deprecating claims. Yet Chaucer's ironies tend to stem from his representation of the verbal performances of other speakers—performances, whether those of the Prioress or of Lollius, to which he has privileged access. Langland's ironies, by contrast, derive from his performance of "common" texts with potentially public status. In the case of the repertoire of reading and singing, they are authorized, but not specifically or singly authored, texts: always already refracted because they are someone else's words, yet (ideally) always already personal because their recitation is an act of subjection, an expression of one's own will. While the heterophonic chorus of the Easter Passus remains the ideal expression of Christian community, the solitary, yet heteroglossic performance of C 5 becomes a more fitting figure for vernacular making precisely because it represents the particular yet generalizable Will (with its unavoidable self-interest) first articulated in Vision Three of the B Version. Though Reason and Conscience remain unconvinced by Will's claims, the penance they advise him to perform is one of reiteration. Will's private, devotional act, "S[yh]ing for [his] synnes, seggyng [his] paternoster" (C 5.107), causes him to fall asleep and continue the vision that issues in public poetry.[68] Whereas in the A Version, his deferral to the superior efficacy of the *paternoster* seemed to obviate his poetic endeavors, making communication with God a private matter that did not warrant representation before others, in the C Version the same speech act is figured as generative of and continuous with the signifying project of vernacular making.

6

Reading, Singing, and Publication in
The Canterbury Tales

Reading versus Singing:
The Dialogue between the Prioress and the Second Nun

LANGLAND'S TURNING TO THE repertoire of reading and singing was a logical, if not inevitable, step, given that his concern with *clergie* bespeaks an interest in loci of articulation related to ecclesiastical institutions. The clergial connections of the loci Langland explored are for many scholars what set him apart from Chaucer and his "courtly" personae. It is a significant distinction. Chaucer's early works in particular show him positioning himself not in relation to *clergie* but in relation to that other, more prominent, authorizing abstraction of Ricardian poetry, Love. Love governs a different speech dynamic—one more invested in displaying sovereign allegiance than in claiming vicarious representation or prophetic authority. Though (fictively) anyone can speak in Love's name, no one can speak in his person. The speaker rather adopts the persona of the Lover, whose unfulfilled desires place him in the position of suppliant. This positioning provides narrative impetus while distancing the poetic voice still further from any claims to authority. Less explicitly reformist in stance, the ambitions of "courtly" poetry were complex. Though frequently marked by appeals to "common love,"[1] works produced under Love's aegis, as Lynn Staley has noted, "seem to participate in a highly coded and private conversation among men who style themselves as bumbling lovers and, simultaneously, in public forms of address that are meant to be overheard, if not completely understood, by the mighty."[2] Public courtliness, in such cases, vacillates between the ambition to produce texts with import worthy of the attention of larger groups and the desire for an expressive language enabled by the established relationships of a "coterie," not only for its safety but also for the controlled production of excess meaning such a language affords.[3]

Yet even some of Chaucer's early works at times situate themselves in relation to institutions explicitly charged with the reproduction of language that might transcend discrete communities of familiars or even the larger community of the court. In contrast to Langland, with his liturgical leanings, however, Chaucer tended in such cases to look to *grammatica* and its canon of classical texts.[4] His particular self-positioning was in part a result of his perception of the sociolinguistic landscape. Whereas Langland's use of English was among the extragrammatical strategies he employed for its potential to help synthesize latinities he perceived as variegated, Chaucer's invocations of *grammatica* more often show his concern for the vernacular's comparative instability. The anxieties he voices through his cursing of Adam Scriveyn and his apprehension about "gret diversite/In Englissh" at the end of the *Troilus* betray an investment in preserving his own texts as ossified verbal objects (*TC*, 5.1793–94)—an investment that Langland seems not to have shared to the same extent.[5] For Chaucer, *grammatica* and the classical canon serve at times as a fantasy of stability, in which architectural imagery represents the institutional constraints that preserve the books of Homer and Statius as ossified verbal objects. The House of Fame is the most salient example of this imagery and the poem that describes it can be read as an articulation of the difficulties of vernacular poetics conceived of as an extragrammatical project. The many allusions to grammatical discourse that Martin Irvine has identified in the text, in fact, sort themselves into a narrativization of extragrammaticality.[6] The poem begins with Virgil's *Aeneid*, safely enshrined within the Temple of Glass. Whatever we might think about "Geffrey" as a reader of that text, as he translates the story of Dido into his own vernacular narrative idiom, his reading is enabled by this structure and its preservation of the *Aeneid* as a verbal object. In contrast to both the Temple and Fame's edifice, the world of contemporary *tydynges* figured in the Whirling Wicker are subject to the vagaries of oral transmission associated with English.

Chaucer's early focus on *grammatica* as the institutional resource in and against which he might situate his broader signifying ambitions (for all the anxieties it may have caused him) gives his writing a "secular" character for modern readers. Yet if the Whirling Wicker can be imagined as a resource of extragrammatical making, it is one with difficulties similar to those described in the B Version of *Piers Plowman*. Pointing to the value of profitable rehearsal of the Psalter, Ymaginatif branded Will's making as unproductive in that it merely repeated the advice given by others. In Chaucer's Whirling Wicker, repetition and rehearsal are similarly central activities. The potential for productivity is hinted at as each repetition of the various *tydynges* heard therein is said to grow "evermo with more encres / Than yt was erst" (*HF*, 2074). This "encres," however, is described in destructive, not productive terms: "As fyr ys wont to quyke and goo / From a sparke sprong amys, / Til al a citee brent up ys" (2078–80). Augmentation, furthermore, invariably involves the corruption of truth value—its commingling with *lesynges*. Such an outcome is not as devastating as it would be within Langland's reformist ethics, but the Whirling Wicker does envisage the stuff of making as frenetic speech that in its variousness and instability cannot signify publicly, as gossip that can never command the public attention or the public intelligibility of gospel. One could argue that the problem, as in *Piers Plowman*, is one of location. Though the Whirling Wicker is a "place," it is one whose boundaries are defined by their porousness, with its folk variously situated "some wythin and some wythoute" (2036). The most concrete location within the House of Rumor is the courtly "halle / Ther men of love-tydynges told" (2142–43). Though this hall holds the promise of an interlocutor—the "man of gret auctorite"—who might bestow intelligibility on the proceedings (2158), it is precisely at his entrance that the poem stalls.

The Canterbury Tales represents a reconfiguration of Chaucer's extra-grammatical project, one that situates the text's articulations somewhere between meaning governed by a singular man of authority and the chaos of conflicting accounts. An experiment in modes of double-voicing, the *Tales* evince an exploration of the various loci of articulation—from the courtly to the clerical to the mercantile—that one could imagine inhabiting in the late fourteenth century. The framing concept of the tale-telling contest replaces the decontextualized *tydynges* of the Whirling Wicker with a poetics that embraces the "situatedness" that modern scholars have found characteristic of much vernacular writing.[7] It is in the context of this experiment that Chaucer examines the practices of reading and singing, most explicitly in the dialogue between the pilgrimage's two women religious, the Prioress and the Second Nun. With this dialogue, he considers the possibilities and problems inherent in modes of reading and singing as textual practices that involve public performance and claims of authority by otherwise unlicensed and unlikely speakers. While these practices and the ethical questions they elicit form topics of speculation in their own right, the interplay between the Prioress and the Second Nun, as we shall see, ultimately figures in the *Tales'* metapoetic dialogue as well. As the issues brought up by the women religious resonate within Chaucer's more explicitly self-referential tales, such as *The Tale of Sir Thopas* and *The Tale of Melibee*, one sees Chaucer's interest in and scrutiny of the stakes of more public signification that were so central to Langland's writing. Further, it becomes clear that an exploration of reading and singing allows Chaucer to contemplate facets of his vernacular enterprise that a consideration of courtly loci of articulation alone would not permit.

* * *

While it is generally accepted that *The Second Nun's Tale* began its existence as the independently circulated "lyf of Seynt Cecile" (*LGW*, F 426) and that the state in which it survives in the *Tales* shows little evidence that it was edited to accommodate the tale-telling frame, its assignment to the Second Nun seems designed to invite comparison to the tale of her companion pilgrim, the Prioress; several critics have already taken up the invitation.[8] Professing the only occupation among the tale-tellers with two representatives, the women religious are figured as doubles of each other. With elaborate prologues that announce their devotional ambitions, the two together form a pious counterpart to the Wife of Bath's unrepentant spiritual mediocrity. This piety is expressed in large part by means of the liturgical texts underlying both tales. Of the two, *The Prioress's Tale* is more self-conscious in its liturgical references, both in its use of the Marian antiphon *Alma redemptoris mater* as an important plot device and in the thematically central allusions to the liturgy of Holy Innocents throughout the tale.[9] Yet the Second Nun's tale of St. Cecilia has its own, albeit less explicit, liturgical invocations. In *The Second Nun's Prologue*, for example, the *clergeon*'s singing of *Alma redemptoris mater* is matched by echoes of *Salve regina*, another Marian antiphon.[10] More substantially, the story of St. Cecilia is translated from Jacobus de Voragine's *Legenda aurea*, which, although it was not itself used for performance, still recalls the liturgical roots of the *legenda*—the hagiographical narrative read as lessons at matins on the feast days of saints.[11] Chaucer's rendering of this particular legend furthers the association by following, at least initially, the distribution of the liturgical version of the narrative over the nine *lectiones* of matins in his stanzaic divisions—above all, keeping intact within a single rime royal stanza the text of the well-known first responsory sung after the first *lectio, Cantantibus organis*: "And whil the organis maden melodie,/To God allone in herte thus sang she" (8.134–40).[12] The two tales are thus linked by the very repertoire that would presumably link their narrators within their convent community.

More accurately, the tales are linked by their narrators' unmoored usage of these texts—in other words, by their reading and singing. The Prioress's expertise in "service dyvyne" (1.122) and the Second Nun's legendary knowledge are used outside the official institutional context of the *opus Dei*: the Marian antiphon with which the Prioress associates her narrative "song" is sung independently of the liturgy as an act of devotion and the Second Nun translates her legend from an extraliturgical source made for private consumption. That these institutionally decontextualized performances take place within the "liminoid" space of the pilgrimage and its impromptu tale-telling contest only enhances the effect.[13] To an even greater degree than Will, the Prioress and Second Nun have at best only a marginal affiliation with clerical institutions, their knowledge of liturgical repertoire being one of the only resources of clerical authority regularly available to them. Their institutional identities as nuns may be less ambiguous than that of Will's conflicted clerkliness, but as women any access to ecclesiastical or literate authority their affiliation might grant them would be severely circumscribed. Unlike Langland's Will, neither the Prioress nor the Second Nun can make any meaningful claim to clerical status, whatever the extent of their knowledge might be. Just as other writers thought about women religious to consider the various relationships that might obtain between performers and liturgical speech acts,[14] Chaucer uses them to consider the potential gaps between speaker and speech, as well as those between speech and meaning, in less institutionally regulated settings.

Chaucer fictively capitalizes on the exclusion of such non-clerical speakers to examine resources of authority that are potentially separable from clerical identity. In addition to providing rhetorically self-conscious prologues with elaborate justifications for their narration, both the Prioress and the Second Nun significantly offer tales featuring protagonists who, like them, lack institutional authority. The issues that these characters raise within their tales are then sharpened still further by the presence of contiguous tales—*The Shipman's Tale* and *Canon's Yeoman's Tale*—that juxtapose these unauthorized protagonists with unscrupulous members of the clergy—the lascivious Daun John of *The Shipman's Tale* and the scheming Canon of *The Canon's Yeoman's Tale* (to say nothing of his "mark," the proverbially greedy annueller). Chief among these issues is the use and dissemination of knowledge. Forms of privileged knowledge explicitly marked as secret are in fact central to all four tales, whether it is the transforming alchemical knowledge of *The Canon's Yeoman's Tale* or the transforming spiritual knowledge of *The Second Nun's Tale*; or whether it concerns the "privitee" that Daun John convinces the Merchant's Wife to confide to him by swearing an oath of secrecy on his breviary or the lessons the *clergeon* receives "prively" from his friend that entice the young scholar to ignore his primer, even at the risk of punishment, to learn the antiphon (7.164, 131–33, 544). Yet whereas the anti-clerical stereotypes of *The Shipman's Tale* and *Canon's Yeoman's Tale* use knowledge only for sexual gratification and material gain—the kinds of self-interest of which clerics were most often suspected—the *clergeon* and St. Cecilia seem designed to exemplify an authentic piety and purity of motive that show them to be more deserving custodians of spiritual truths.

In both *The Prioress's Tale* and *The Second Nun's Tale*, this custodianship ultimately issues in forms of verbal performance. Both the *clergeon*'s singing and Cecilia's preaching receive particular emphasis by their miraculous prolongation after the speakers' throats—the instrument of vocalization—have been cut.[15] With this emphasis, the Prioress and Second Nun engage in a dialogue over the appropriate uses of textual knowledge—what can and should be done with pious, sacralized words. This dialogue is grafted onto the collocation "reading and singing," evoking and redefining its elements literally. The *clergeon* not only sings but has also rejected the reading of his primer to do so. Cecilia's *legenda*, conversely, shows her rejecting the song of the pagan marriage ceremony (the *cantantes organi*) to engage in evangelical activity more closely associated with reading and grammar. Though Cecilia herself begins with a private, internal song, the most vivid description of conversion in the tale is Valerian's reading of the sacred book that magically appears as the instrument of his interpellation (8.200–215). "Reading" and "singing" thus come to represent two opposing projections of the ideal Christian utterance. The Prioress champions Latin song as a pure speech act—as objectified language selflessly rendered to God to which understanding is subordinated. The Second Nun's vernacular translation of the legend of St. Cecilia conversely stresses the educative function of the *lectio* as a form of preaching designed to convey transforming understanding.[16] Whereas the Prioress upholds adoration of the ineffable for its own sake, the Second Nun concerns herself with avoiding idleness by means of the productive labor of translation. As in Will's C 5 defense of his "clerical" occupation as beadsman, the opposition between the two women is figured in terms analogous to the gospel debate between Mary and Martha, with the Prioress's "contemplative" and the Second Nun's "active" utterances in competition with each other.

In both cases the stakes of such verbal performances are especially high, as their fatal consequences testify. That both protagonists suffer such violent repercussions for their actions is a function of the "public" nature of their utterances, both in terms of the knowledge they convey and their mode of transmission. The spreading of the Word in the nuns' tales creates an immediate contrast to the contiguous *Shipman's Tale* and *Canon's Yeoman's Tale*, in which knowledge is essentially private and unofficial. In keeping with Chaucer's habit, noted by Staley, of situating larger social issues within these more intimate settings,[17] knowledge is transacted within domestic spaces in these mens' stories. Even more to the point, the tales depend on their (institutionally sanctioned) protagonists withholding knowledge from others. *The Prioress's Tale* and *The Second Nun's Tale* are unusual in that their climactic moments involve public performances in the sense that they occur before unfamiliar—indeed, hostile—audiences in spaces outside the domestic.[18] The content of their knowledge is also public—not solely in that it warrants the attention of these broader audiences, but also because knowledge is figured in relation to the dominant institutions that attempt regulate its dissemination, as the insubordinate *clergeon* shuns his primer to learn the antiphon by unauthorized means and the dissenting St. Cecilia refuses to submit to idolatry. Singing and reading in these tales thus dramatize the very act of publication. In the distinction between the two, Chaucer imagines different ways of perceiving language with the capacity to signify publicly and, ultimately, with the capacity to interpellate.

Repetition, Intention and the Song of the *Clergeon*

From the outset of her prologue, the Prioress distances the performances of her *clergeon* from *clergie*. Introducing her tale with a loose translation of Psalm 8,[19] she characterizes her protagonist's unlettered singing as an act of prelingual innocence.

> O Lord, oure Lord, thy name how merveillous
> Is in this large world ysprad—quod she—
> For noght oonly thy laude precious

> Parfourned is by men of dignitee,
> But by the mouth of children thy bountee
> Parfourned is, for on the brest soukynge
> Somtyme shewen they thyn heriynge. (7.454–59)

The Prioress expends the most labor translating the psalm's second verse: *ex ore infantium et lactantium perfecisti laudem,* "from the mouths of infants and sucklings you have perfected your praise." By rendering *infantium* as "children," she loses the paradoxical force of the Latin, which has praise come forth from the mouths of non-speakers—a gesture that allows the association of these "children" with the school-age *clergeon*.[20] Yet she reinscribes the more restricted meaning of *infans* when she implicitly compares the *clergeon*'s song to her own narrative performance: "as a child of twelf month oold, or lesse, / That kan unnethes any word expresse, / Right so fare I" (7.484–86). So it is not merely childish praise but infantile praise—both the *clergeon*'s and her own—that she compares (invoking an opposition not found in the original psalm) to that performed by "men of dignitee."[21] Although her rendition of the psalm offers infantile praise as a mere addition to dignified performance, she ultimately asserts that it is better when she describes the ineffable qualities of the Virgin: "Lady, thy bountee, thy magnificence, / Thy vertu and thy grete humylitee / Ther may no tonge expresse in no science" (7.474–76). In claiming the insufficiency of "science," she implies that infantile devotion, undefiled by human knowledge (Lat. *scientia*), comes closest to praising the ineffable Virgin. It is, in fact, more valuable than performances by men of dignity, the implicit possessors of "science."

Yet the *clergeon,* as his appellation implies, is himself a nascent man of dignity. He could even be said to stand for them, as one poised to cross the threshold of clerical knowledge. With her redundantly diminutive "litel clergeon" (7.503), the Prioress partly seeks to neutralize the power such knowledge might have over her when actualized in a male cleric, as if her obsessive use of diminutives in referring to the boy and his learning ("A litel scole," "This litel child, his litel book lernynge" [7.495, 516])[22] might demonstrate her superiority over them. Yet to a greater extent, she represents the *clergeon*'s piety as antithetical to lettered knowledge; what authority he does bear is in fact predicated on his rejection of clerical *science*. From this perspective, the *clergeon* performs a kind of vicarious wish fulfillment. As a future cleric, he would be allowed access to and, in some cases, be expected to pursue fields of literate knowledge not always available to women like the Prioress. His insubordination in substituting his own strategies of textual assimilation for whatever authorized strategies are offered in the school constitutes a voluntary refusal that allows the Prioress to recast her own circumscription as an affirmative, pious act.

Such praise of unlearnedness is reminiscent of Langland's anti-clerical discussion of the plowmen who "percen wiþ a *paternoster* þe paleis of heuene," which he used to question the value of his search for Dowel (A 11.312; B 10.468; C 11.294). Yet the Prioress's focus on the child's un-lettered recitation changes the terms of this conventional sentiment as well as the definition of innocence. As was the case in Gerson's discussion of prayer,[23] there is no reason to think that the plowmen and the other "lewede iottis" to whom Langland refers do not understand their *pater-noster* (A 11.311; B 10.467; C 11.293); the virtue of their simplicity lies in their lack of spiritual or repertory pretensions rather than in their lack of grammatical knowledge as such. The *clergeon*, by contrast, *does* have such pretensions: he sees the *Alma redemptoris mater* as a form of praise supe-rior to the *ave* his mother taught him. Given the textual, latinate object of the *clergeon*'s desire, these pretensions are not synonymous with those connected with the promotion of an ideal, experiential wisdom (*sapientia*) that trumps the efforts of book learning in attaining understanding of the divine. The Prioress, rather, seeks to establish a realm of Latin praise that is somehow innocent of *scientia*. Such a gesture requires her to manipulate the very definition of "book learning"—to realign the opposition between the infantile and the informed such that the performance of the *Alma redemptoris mater* as well as her own linguistic performance in translating Psalm 8 (among other texts) fall outside the realm of *science* and become paradoxically aligned with the natural and instinctive act of suckling. The Prioress thus does not merely champion unlearned praise; she defines unlearnedness to situate her protagonist's and her own authority.

The school where children learn "to syngen and to rede" provides the Prioress with the opportunity to determine what, precisely, defines learn-ing and what forms of praise can be said to be innocent of *science*. Though historians have tended to view her description of it as a transparent rep-resentation of medieval practice, it is critical to note that many of the details she conveys about early schooling are calculated to sanctify her pro-tagonist, granting him motives unsullied by desire for what she defines as institutionalized knowledge. Whatever we imagine the clientele of schools like the *clergeon*'s to have been, the Prioress's representation of its cur-riculum as general, elementary practice, "as smale children doon in hire childhede," underwrites the idea that her *clergeon*'s singing is motivated by his unique piety rather than by his privileged access to Latin texts (7.501). Her desire to distinguish the boy's knowledge from that gained by means of the written page similarly leads her to show the formal assimilation of chant as entirely book bound and distinct from the "rote" learning of her *clergeon*. Ultimately, the Prioress's representation of her *clergeon*'s knowledge is not just implicitly anti-clerical (or anti-*clergie*) but explicitly extragrammatical, as she takes pains to divorce the boy's singing from the formal structures of *grammatica*. The *clergeon*'s fellow performs this gesture, not only with his confession, which alludes to grammar only to signal its absence from his studies, but also by himself serving as an ungrammatical conduit of textual knowledge. By calling upon resources defined in opposition to grammar to teach his friend the song, the nameless fellow ensures that the *clergeon* is twice removed from the structures of grammatical discourse.

By focusing so intently on the unconventional assimilation of the Latin antiphon, the tale suggests that the *clergeon*'s purity stems less from his rejection of all clerical letters than from his poaching them from their proper institutional settings or, put another way, from his rejection of the grammatical and ecclesiastical discourses that govern their assimilation and use. This rejection figures the boy's singing as devotional and gratuitous rather than liturgical and vicarious, despite his "public" performance. As a result, the illiteracy that was a moral failing and evidence of hypocrisy in the illiterate priest and the illiteracy that was a sign of obedient self-abnegation in the women religious of the *Chastising* takes on a different meaning. It is precisely because he does not claim to speak *in persona ecclesie* or on anyone's behalf that illiteracy becomes in the "litel clergeon" a sign of innocence and purity of motive. To underscore the *clergeon*'s poaching, however, is not to suggest that the tale is not deeply interested in the power of institutional language and its capacity to interpellate and unify audiences. It is rather that *grammatica* and *clergie*, and the human institutions they underwrite, are for the Prioress inextricable from the ethical corruptions so frequently associated with liturgical performance, particularly those involving self-interest and material gain. Her idealizing of the *clergeon*'s singing attempts to define a mode of public verbal performance that can somehow be purified of those corruptions.

The Prioress's world is one in which linguistic exchanges, especially those of sacred words, always threaten to become mired in other forms of monetary and material exchange. While contemporary complaints about greedy annuellers show that this was a prevalent concern, the commingling of commercial and linguistic exchanges is more concretely thematized in *The Shipman's Tale*. The Shipman's bawdy fabliau is a tale in which monks trade money for sexual favors and use breviaries for swearing oaths, and in which the only "song"—the Wife's plaintive "allas and weylawey" (7.118)—merely registers worry over monetary and marriage debts that go unpaid. The tale progresses by a series of exchanges within a commercial economy sustained by *creaunce* (a rather material form of belief), such that by the tale's resolution, as Lee Patterson has pointed out, money seems to have grown merely by circulating,[24] though this circulation is, of course, heavily informed by Daun John's crafty withholding of knowledge. Patterson connects the economic order of *The Shipman's Tale*—an order in which exchanges are determined by a system of equivalences based on immediate need rather than a stable referent—to the tale's language. The Shipman's abundance of puns and double entendres force the audience to be aware of the multiple interchangeable signifieds that can be assigned to a single signifier, as is most vividly exemplified in the use of the term "taillynge"—"a triple pun that correlates the orders of sexuality, commerce, and tale-telling into a mutually reciprocal system of interchangeable values."[25] *The Prioress's Tale* might be said to put paid to such notions of language. By making her *clergeon* ignorant of Latin grammar, the Prioress removes him from the world of linguistic exchange. Though such a turn from commerce to Latin liturgy might lead us to label her reaction conservative or nostalgic, her tale does not attempt to reinstall either the economy of the *opus Dei* or the values associated with the choral community. Her invocation of Latin song guards against the dangers of sliding signification not so much by restoring the stable referent that unifies interpretive gestures, as one might expect in the discourse of choral community, but by proclaiming the sufficiency of the signifier alone, thereby eliminating the need for the signified altogether.

The Prioress responds to such commercialism by creating a world in which any desire for profit is deeply suspect. Though she begins her prologue by describing how God's name is "ysprad" throughout the world (a verb not found in the Latin psalm)[26] and ends the tale with a prayer that God "his grete mercy multiplie" (7.454, 689), the Prioress describes mortal attempts to effect such multiplication as presumptuous. Despite the financial or career incentives there might be for any contemporary *clergeon* to sing, the Prioress takes pains to eliminate any financial motives on the part of her protagonist. Analogues of the tale, in fact, sometimes present the boy's singing as a source of income ("Þe child non oþer Craftus

couþe / But winne his lyflode wiþ his Mouþe," states the version of the
miracle found in the Vernon Manuscript),[27] but her *clergeon*'s song is
described as a gratuitous offering with no expectation of repayment from
mortal or divine. All such commercial desires are instead displaced onto
the villainized Jews of the tale and recast as the "foule usure and lucre of
vileynye" the Prioress claims is their primary social purpose in the Asian
city (7.491).[28] She is invested in the verbal performances of mortals only
insofar as they lack productivity and makes clear at the outset that her own
song does not presume to "encressen" the honor of the Virgin (7.464).[29]
With this rejection of *encress* she implicitly invalidates the desire for "the
increase of divine service" that was the formulaic motivation behind so
many liturgical contracts.[30] Although the *clergeon* rehearses his antiphon
twice daily (more than the single daily performance of most endowed
votive antiphons), and although the text clearly possesses an excess of
meaning that lends it sacramentality, the Prioress shuns the cumulative
excesses produced by ritualized performance, imagining instead a sacramentality born of purity of motive and lack of grammatical engagement.

These manipulations are for the Prioress deeply connected to the
grammatical modes of understanding practiced by "men of dignitee."
For if the Prioress objects to the morality implicit in the economy of *The
Shipman's Tale*, she objects especially to the behavior of Daun John, who
clearly is not "an hooly man, / As monkes been—or elles oghte be" (7.642–
63). Her reaction conflates the corruptions she perceives in commercial
exchanges with those she perceives in grammatical methodologies that
produce meaning by reduction to the signified. For the Prioress, all forms
of exchange entail corruption and loss.[31] Guarding against such loss, she
fills her tale with images of intactness that leave both performer and text
whole. The *clergeon* himself is not utterly ignorant of the song's purpose
and intention. When he sings, we are told, "On Cristes mooder set was
his entente" (7.550), which suggests that he gives the text the kind of
"virtual attention" that does not require grammatical knowledge.[32] The
ideal form of attention is that which leaves the verbal surface of the text
intact and therefore requires the utmost interpretive passivity on the part
of the performer. Contemporary writers of contemplative manuals offered
similar images of passivity as models of self-abnegation. Walter Hilton,
for example, spoke of the ideal prayer as that in which the body becomes
a mere "trompe of the soule," through which one might "bloweth swet
nootes of goostli lovynges to Jhesu."[33] The Prioress's version, however, is
still more extreme, requiring not mastery over the body but the surrender

of all agency to the song itself, such that the *clergeon*'s throat becomes a mere conduit: "Twies a day [the song] passed thurgh his throte" (7.548), just as, ideally, the *clergeon* himself would pass unimpeded through the Jewry said to be "free and open at eyther ende" (494).[34] The ideal Christian utterance is thus defined by the Prioress as unsullied not only by grammatical meaning but by human intention altogether.

It is understanding, a grammatical form of *entendement*, that interrupts the journey of both the song through the *clergeon*'s throat and the *clergeon* through the Jewry. The Jews who violently interrupt the boy's singing do so because they have, at Satan's instigation, attended to the "sentence" of the *Alma* (7.563), whereas for others in the tale, the song (which remains untranslated) functions more broadly as a sign, first of the boy's piety then of the miracle visited upon him by the Virgin. In one respect, the Jews' disruption is figured as a violation of the conduit itself: the hired assassin, focusing on the site of the boy's transgression, slits his throat. Yet Chaucer, following one tradition of the tale, also has the Jews dispose of the ruptured body by throwing it in the privy, where, the Prioress comments, they "purgen hire entraille" (7.573)—an image that in this version of the story resonates with the rejected textual strategies used by "men of dignitee" by invoking the commonplace of the *lectio divina* that figures reading and interpretation as chewing (*ruminatio*) and digestion. With this image, the Prioress displaces these high literate strategies onto the Jews to demonize them. Extrapolating the logical end of the metaphor, she creates a nightmarish parody of the *lectio divina*, in which the ultimate fate of digested texts is figured as excrement.

In the apostrophe that follows this episode, the Prioress attempts to restore the intactness of the *clergeon*'s body by stressing his virginity (7.579). But despite the rhetorical resurrection of the *clergeon* implicit in her apostrophizing, the miracle of the tale resides in the restoration of the text more than of the *clergeon* himself. The grain is the figure of this restored text—an image that invokes yet another high literate commonplace: that of the fruit and the chaff. For the Prioress, however, the grain remains intact, much like the precious stones—the emerald of virginity, the ruby of martyrdom—she associates with the *clergeon*'s body (7.609–10).[35] No longer the object of grammatical winnowing, the text becomes the object of perpetual performance, each repetition re-presenting the verbal surface of the text. Louise Fradenburg marks the desire for the intact text as the desire for "pure repetition," that is, repetition without difference, and connects it to the tale's poetics—a poetics based in repetition of

vocabulary, alliteration, and other purely formal features.[36] This investment
in formal features is what marks the Prioress's piety as conventional in
its formalism for some scholars,[37] yet Chaucer's characterization is both
distinctive and extreme in its depiction of textual interactions. Contemplative writers like Richard Rolle were also interested in language's surfaces
and relied on alliteration as an extragrammatical and anti-ecclesiastical strategy; texts like *The Cloud of Unknowing* advocated the repetition of single
words as a devotional practice.[38] These techniques, however, sought to
gain access to excess meaning—to sacramentality that could be attained
through, but not encoded in, human language. The Prioress, by contrast,
is more interested in stasis than excess; the repetition that Fradenburg
calls attention to leads only to circularity and emptiness—what modern
readers would label repetition compulsion rather than reiteration. By these
means, the Prioress represents "language that can barely make any space or
articulate any distance that would allow the play of presence and absence
that constitutes meaning."[39] While interest in ritualized rehearsal of texts
and in meaning that resides beyond grammatical reduction to the signified
could certainly fall under the label "conventional," the phobic defensive-
ness of the Prioress's language is unconventional enough to require further
investigation.

Despite its seeming emptiness, the Prioress's language, as well as the
clergeon's textual performance, are not ineffective and have even been described as "powerful."[40] Their effects, however, are registered not within
the performer's soul but on the *clergeon*'s and the Prioress's various publics.
Though the Prioress's emphasis on praise and devotion marks her path as
contemplative, and though she distances her *clergeon*'s performance from
institutions, much of what is explored in the tale in terms of the speaker's
relationship to his speech is more closely related to contemporary discussions of liturgical, or public, speech. Both the elaboration of intention and
the elaboration of attention discussed in previous chapters focused on the
potential gap between speaker and speech as well as its implications for
liturgical performance. Here, despite the lack of a liturgical setting, that
gap is reinforced by the *clergeon*'s illiteracy. Furthermore, whereas in the
case of mass priests that gap had become desacralized, in the *clergeon*'s case
it has been resacralized with a vengeance, creating an idealized linguistic
performance with interpellative power. While this power is unwittingly
exercised to disastrous effect in the interpellation of the Jews within the
story, it finds its idealized counterpart in the uncharacteristic choral unanimity of the pilgrims' reaction to the tale.[41]

This idealized speech, however, is in tension with aspects of the tale that undermine the possibility of a mode of public signification that is based on pure repetition and distanced from institutions. In spite of the anti-clerical agenda to which the Prioress alludes in her prologue, it is significantly the Abbot—the man of greatest dignity in the tale—who finally retrieves the grain. Ultimately his actions do more to recuperate men of dignity than to condemn them, for the Abbot serves the important function of authorizing the miracle, which in turn authorizes him as a "hooly man" for having recognized the divine intervention. Whatever sense of competition was implied at the beginning of the tale thus gives way to an acknowledgment that even in the absence of grammatical meaning in the narrowest sense of the term, men of dignity still preside over texts and remain the final arbiters of miracles.[42] Similarly, although the *clergeon*'s song itself does not appear to require translation to have an effect, the child's *performance* of the antiphon does require some narrative glossing by the *clergeon* himself at the end of the tale. While he does not intrude on his own funeral service, as he does in some of the analogues,[43] his explication of his plight takes place "Biforn the chief auter" and takes on a decidedly clerical tone as he describes Christ's will "as ye in bookes fynde" (7.636, 652). One might consider the *clergeon*'s miraculous learning an indicator of his receiving grace in the form of superior knowledge,[44] yet the primary function of this knowledge is the ability it gives him to grant meaning to his story for others. It is once again only within the context of ecclesiastical institutions that such meaning may be assigned.

The Abbot's retrieval of the grain also calls attention to a different tension underlying the *clergeon*'s gruesome plight and the Prioress's need to assign some sort of meaning to it. Within the logic of the tale, of course, the reason for retrieving the grain is that it will release the *clergeon*'s soul. That such a kindness is necessary calls attention to a conflict between the resurrected text and the resurrected body that gives it voice. While the Prioress continues to restore the *clergeon*'s gemlike, inviolate condition rhetorically—even to the extent of enclosing his body in "a tombe of marbul stones clere" after his death (7.681)—the *clergeon* himself affirms the violence that has been done to him as soon as his own speech has been entreated by the Abbot's conjuring: "My throte is kut unto my nekke boon" (7.649). While the statement confirms the miraculous nature of the *clergeon*'s singing, it also calls attention to the corruptible materiality of his body as well as to the violence upon which the miracle is predicated.[45] The fact that his singing in this instance was initiated by the sprinkling of holy water, and his speech enabled by the Abbot's conjuring, underscores the *clergeon*'s lack of agency.[46] The passivity that marked the *clergeon*'s singing during his natural life thus becomes more profound in his preternatural life, wherein his singing is no longer a devotional act of the will but a command performance at the direct bidding of the Virgin.[47] In effect, he becomes an instrument of divine expression, as the Prioress exclaims in her next narrative intrusion: "O grete God, that parfournest thy laude / By mouth of innocentz" (7.607–8).[48] The Prioress would surely celebrate this kind of instrumentality,[49] and yet this prolongation of the *clergeon*'s life is potentially in tension with the fate she proclaimed for him after his throat had been slit: "*Now* maystow syngen, folwynge evere in oon / The white Lamb celestial" (7.580–81, my emphasis).[50] This seemingly contradictory description of the *clergeon*'s fate is merely the rhetorical product of the narrator's capacity to move seamlessly between the "now" of the story and the "now" of the telling, but introducing the boy's ultimate reward so early in the tale nevertheless underscores the incompatibility of the earthly song that he must continue to sing and the new song that he eventually will be allowed to join in.

If, then, the desire for the inviolate text and pure repetition require the indefinite deferral of reduction to the signified, it also requires the indefinite deferral of closure for the *clergeon*. The already multivalent grain symbolizes this predicament as well, since martyrdom is associated with fallen grain in the liturgy of martyrs through the reading of John 12:24–25: "unless the grain of wheat falling to the ground dies, it will remain alone; if, however, it dies, it will bring forth much fruit."[51] Still more specific in its extrapolation of the metaphor is a responsory commemorating the death of Thomas of Canterbury that is sung on the Feast of Holy Innocents.

> Jacet granum oppressum palea,
> justus caesus pravorum framea
> Caelum domo communtans lutea

> [The grain lies crushed from the chaff, the just man felled by the sword of sinners, changing his house of clay for heaven.][52]

At the most basic level, the "chaff" in the responsory refers to the "house of clay"—the mortal body that has imprisoned the spirit, yet like all metaphors involving the fruit and the chaff, it is guided by the logic of the new song, that is, by a logic of rebirth and transformation (and expulsion) rather than one of pure repetition. Although the Prioress goes to great lengths to resist change of any kind, much of her narrative labor is expended on drawing parallels that render the events of her tale as reenactments of prior biblical narratives: figural references to the new song and the "new Rachel," most obviously, but also her association of the Holy Innocents with the *clergeon*, herself, and that most recent Innocent, Hugh of Lincoln. These are the kinds of figural accretions that liturgical celebration of the events of sacred history invite. The fact that the *clergeon*'s decontextualized, extragrammatical performance still participates in these cyclical narratives underscores the impossibility and, to some extent, the undesirability of pure repetition even within the Prioress's world.

The notion of pure repetition attempts to invest form with ethical and spiritual value, if not meaning, and with the capacity to command universal assent. The manipulations required to define what aspects are "pure" and undefiled by the kinds of corruptions the Prioress associates with intellectual engagement are, however, too complex to label her efforts as "formalism." Similarly, the relationship between interior and exterior that "form" articulates should not be taken for granted. For all the tale's contemplative leanings, the *clergeon*'s interior is remarkably opaque, so unlike the excessive and unruly interior writers like Hilton imagined their would-be contemplative audiences to possess.[53] This simplicity and opacity is necessary insofar as intention in the Prioress's ideal utterance is located in its form. The *clergeon* is connected to his song only by a vague, "virtual" intention that might (as the various analogues show) connect him to any number of Marian antiphons. In contrast to the image of the arrow offered by Gerson, in which the momentum of one's intent remains even if one cannot attend to the meaning of the words in performance, the *clergeon*'s attention to Christ's mother figuratively results in his heart being pierced by the sweetness of the antiphon (7.550, 555);[54] the song itself is endowed with momentum, sustained in the boy's preternatural singing long after he has lost his capacity for intention. One might claim that this disregard for individual intention is the hallmark of formalism, yet it is perhaps more appropriately viewed as the price of an ethically pristine utterance. The detachment of the text from speakerly intention lent the power of public signification even to—or, rather, especially to—the unauthorized, yet it was power without the ability to shape or even direct one's meaning. Taken in these terms, it is a fitting irony—and possibly one not wholly unanticipated—that all questions of motive and intention have deflected off the *clergeon* onto the Prioress herself, establishing her as, if not the most "rounded," then unquestionably the most pathologizable of Chaucer's narrators—a speaker whose intentions seem both disturbingly "phobic" and yet elusive.[55]

Translation, Work, and the Preaching of St. Cecilia

If song renders the *clergeon*'s interior opaque, it has the opposite effect on the protagonist of *The Second Nun's Tale*. St. Cecilia's one moment of song is described in terms that figure her singing as a private and fully internalized expression: "And whil the organs maden melodie,/To God allone in herte thus sang she" (8.134–35). Cecilia has the spacious interior of the contemplative—a site in which inner dialogue and sacred conversation can resonate. Her inner song is figured as uniquely her own. Its dissonant simultaneity with the external song of the pagan marriage ceremony symbolizes her estrangement from those around her. Once her internal convictions have been established, however, inner song is passed over for verbal performances that breach the boundaries of the body even as they claim the more authoritative status of "conseil" (8.145). While the Second Nun depicts Cecilia as a dutiful daughter of Holy Church, in contrast to the mildly insubordinate *clergeon*, she goes even further than the Prioress in representing a speaker whose verbal performance is meant to be venerated precisely because of her defiance of received authority. Whereas the Prioress showed her *clergeon* choosing not to follow the formal course of study in the "litel scole of Cristen folk," the legend of St. Cecilia is set in pagan Rome, when the Church was not yet a dominant institution with the wealth or political security to regulate ritual observance or formal education. Pope Urban, living in hiding on the outskirts of town, may perform the sacraments, but Cecilia remains at center stage as the primary custodian and disseminator of the "wise loore" of the Christian faith (8.414), performing the preaching duties that would eventually be institutionalized in the priesthood. Her preaching is situated within a progression from inner to outer, beginning with her words to her husband, within the modest domestic space of the marriage chamber, then progressing to increasingly public settings until the prefect Almachius summons her to a formal inquisition. With this reversal of spatial dynamics, Chaucer sets the stage for a very different notion of language use and very different kind of extragrammaticality.

Translation is the basis of the Second Nun's extragrammatical project. In contrast to the Prioress's desire to keep the verbal surface of sacred Latin texts intact, the Second Nun has no qualms about the linguistic exchanges involved in translation. It is worth noting, however, that her translating project is first cast as a private, devotional activity, designed not to edify a larger audience or to make accessible the truths obscured by the language or learning but to provide her with "leveful bisynesse" that will protect her from the dangers of Idleness (8.4–5). As the prologue moves from this confession to the etymological explication of Cecilia's name, translation takes on precisely the function of revealing truth encoded in unfamiliar languages as a learned and authoritative service she performs for others. The *Prologue* thus mimics the spatial dynamic of the *Tale* in its movement from inner to outer that establishes her sincerity and lack of worldly ambition before initiating the transition from private to public. Her emphasis on the virtues of labor, when juxtaposed with the Prioress's insistence on devotion, further hints at an analogy to Mary and Martha, with the Second Nun unapologetically taking on the cause of Martha.[56] The progression of *The Second Nun's Prologue and Tale* is not only one from inner to outer but also from contemplative to active.

That activity is embodied in language itself. Where the Prioress created a language designed to prevent change, the Second Nun's ideal Christian utterance is that which effects it. Both tales focus on verbal performances that can interpellate subjects, but *The Second Nun's Tale* emphasizes interpellation that marks radical transformation, specifically conversion. Conversion is a conspicuous absence in *The Prioress's Tale*—it is the one area in which the Prioress (perversely, some might say) is successful in preventing change. In contrast to several of the analogues, the child's singing causes no conversions among the Jews whose understanding of the song interpellates them *as* Jews.[57] Unable to be saved in a world where sanctity is associated with hermeneutical virginity, they are violently dispatched within a single rime royal stanza. Insofar as the *clergeon* bears witness to the Virgin's miraculous actions, he does so within the walls of a monastery, "preaching" literally to the choir. Conversion, however, is the main business of *The Second Nun's Tale* and, indeed, the chief preoccupation of Fragment Eight as a whole, if "conversion" is understood to refer to substantial transformation, whether of souls or of metals.[58] Privileged knowledge is a key element of both *The Second Nun's Tale* and *The Canon's Yeoman's Tale*, but more important still is their interest how these pursuits of the mind might issue in transforming "work," a key term in both tales of Fragment Eight.

The Canon's Yeoman's Tale, despite its narrator's interest in "clergial" and "queynte" terms,[59] emphasizes the withholding of knowledge, partly as a deceitful strategy and partly as a duty incumbent upon custodians of privileged knowledge, "That they sholden discovere it unto noon, / Ne in no book it write in no manere" (8.1465–66). This withholding only reflects back on *The Second Nun's Tale*'s focus on transforming revelation—on verbal exchanges that are meant both to be and to do work.[60]

That such verbal work should result in *encrees* is an idea taken for granted rather than something to be denied. The Second Nun makes clear that one of the chief problems of idleness is its lack of productivity: "ydelnesse is roten slogardye, / Of which ther nevere comth no good n'encrees" (8.17–18). Though a great deal of attention has been paid to the unity and simplicity of *The Second Nun's Tale* in relation to the fixation with "multiplicacioun" that marks *The Canon's Yeoman's Tale*,[61] a comparison with *The Prioress's Tale* shows that the Second Nun's sense of unity is generative. As if in response to the *clergeon*'s irreducible grain, Pope Urban praises the "seed of chastitee" that God has planted in Cecilia and refers to Valerian as the "fruyt"—the first of many converts (8.193).[62] Thus while the unifying aspects of truth are stressed throughout the tale in contrast to the duplicity that marks *The Canon's Yeoman's Tale*, the ultimate fate of this truth is its dissemination. The paradox of generative virginity dominates the imagery of prologue and tale, replicating still further the spatial dynamics of inner to outer. In her prologue, the Second Nun describes the conception and birth of Christ, moving from an image of enclosure—Christ's taking on of flesh "Withinne the cloistre blisful of [the Virgin's] sydis"—to an image of movement outward across a boundary, though without violence to the boundary itself: "and thou, Virgine wemmelees, / Baar of thy body—and dweltest mayden pure—/ The Creatour of every creature" (8.43, 47–49). This image gives added meaning to Cecilia's singing "To God allone in herte" (8.35), suggesting that she, too, conveys the Word she has conceived within herself to others in progressive acts of publication. While *The Prioress's Tale* contains a preponderance of images of containment that stress interiority (like the Virgin's inviolate womb)[63] or nondirectional, recursive movement (like the passage in the Jewry that is "free and open at eyther ende"), movement in *The Second Nun's Tale* always progresses outward toward revelation, just as Cecilia sends her converts to the Apian Way that leads out of the city to the hiding place of Pope Urban. This outward movement is figured rhetorically in the prologue, where the speaker provides the etymology of Cecilia's name. Etymologizing relates the ideal of productivity to language itself: beginning with a single word then crossing boundaries of related words and languages, it is an instance of rhetorical *dilatio* that exemplifies the controlled proliferation of meaning—the cumulative *encrees* that was missing from the Whirling Wicker.[64]

For Patterson, the inner space of St. Cecilia and the Second Nun that is the origin of *encrees* indicates only that they "lack all signs of personality: they are mere agencies, empty vessels for a power beyond" that stand in contrast to the Canon's Yeoman's "claustrophobically subjectivized discourse."[65] Yet again, when contrasted to the Prioress's *clergeon*, it is precisely Cecilia's agency (empty or otherwise) that stands out. Matching the *clergeon*'s preternatural singing with her own miraculous performance, Cecilia spends her final days, her neck similarly "ycorven," teaching the faith and preaching (8.538–39). Unlike the *clergeon* with his command performance, however, Cecilia asks specifically for a three-day extension to her mortal life, fully conscious of its all too apparent discomforts, for the purpose of commending particular souls to Pope Urban and founding a church (8.542–46). This self-awareness and the awareness of the effect of her words on others underscores Cecilia's awareness of the public nature of her activities—an aspect of verbal performance to which the *clergeon* was fatally oblivious. Agency and self-awareness, of course, are quite different from "personality," nor, in a genre like hagiography, with its basis in exemplarity, should one expect to find "personality" as much as one encounters a *persona* that one might emulate and inhabit. The various shades of agency in and through language that emerge from a juxtaposition of the Prioress and Second Nun suggest that Chaucer's subject was not always the subject but, in the case of his two women religious, was rather the speech that can be performed by subjects and that had the power to configure selves in a variety of ways.[66]

Both tales are also deeply invested in the politics of understanding, specifically how verbal performance can make subjects through interpellation. The way in which the choral unanimity that meets the Prioress's tale resonates with the declamation of faith made "with o voys" by Almachius's recently converted ministers shows an additional interest in the interpellation of communities (8.420). The notion of linguistic immediacy that critics have found in both tales registers the sense of *Gestalt* that characterizes interpellation.[67] *Entente*—as a form of intention / attention / understanding—is critical to the process in both cases, yet the tales differ in where they locate it. In *The Prioress's Tale*, *entente* resides in the text's *vertu*, which the

Prioress associates with its verbal surface. "Entente" in *The Second Nun's Tale* is a central and complex term that embodies the full semantic range of *entendaunce* we have encountered elsewhere. As Russell Peck has pointed out, *entente* is both "Man's purpose" and "God's purpose"[68]—in other words, what one intends and what one should attend to, the enactment of mastery-in-subjection that produces the interpellated subject. The true transforming power of verbal performance, however, ultimately lies in its *sentence*, or meaning, as the internalized truth that informs *entente*. *Sentence* bears its own authority. The term is, in fact, most frequently used in the tale to denote the penalty Almachius declares for those who will not sacrifice, until his own ministers univocally appropriate the term in the service of their own defiant belief: "'Crist, Goddes Sone, withouten difference, / Is verray God—this is al oure sentence'" (8.417–18). Though the internalization of *sentence* is connected to reading in Valerian's paradigmatic interpellation, it is not connected with hermeneutics or grammatical reduction to the signified. The immediacy of Valerian's assimilation of the *sentence* of the message presented to him contrasts strongly not only with the *clergeon*'s rote assimilation of the antiphon but also with the arduous process of formal schooling that of necessity stands between subject and sacred text in the Prioress's world, allowing her to figure derivation of *sentence* as a form of corruption and to find in virtual *entente* an alternative resource of authority. The Second Nun's depiction of language as an instrument of redemption relies heavily on the perceived transparency of a mother tongue that renders schooling unnecessary and more easily promotes a sense of self-evident fidelity between signifier and signified generally encapsulated in the term "trouthe," another key term in the tale.

The mother tongue foregrounded by the Second Nun, of course, is English, as she defines her opening topic as that which "men clepe in Englissh Ydelnesse" (8.2). The centrality of translation in *The Second Nun's Prologue*, as a useful labor that can expose the knowledge latent in the name of St. Cecilia, among other things, intimates a belief in the transferability of the authorizing mechanisms of latinate discourse to English or, at the very least, in the efficacious substitution of vernacular wisdom for latinate *scientia* through translation. The importance of interpellation, however, betrays a more complex politics of understanding. For all the Second Nun's efforts at the translation by which she makes truth perceptible—her "work" under the sign of Martha—the critique that Fradenburg directs at the Prioress could stand equally for the Second Nun: "if meaning is an issue at all, it is possessed magically, not striven for."[69] Yet though it might be true that understanding conveyed through language is immediate in the tale, it is not exactly because language is transparent. Knowing the truth is equated with knowing the deceptive nature of earthly signifiers and their incommensurability with sacred signifieds. If the Prioress declares the sufficiency of the signifier, the Second Nun declares the sufficiency of the signified. Such knowledge, however, is only for those who have ears. When Tiburce is given access to the smell (through Valerian's prayer), but not the sight, of the two crowns, Valerian promises him,

> So shaltow seen hem, leeve brother deere,
> If it so be thou wolt, withouten slouthe,
> Bileve aright and knowen verray trouthe. (8.257–59)

Tiburce's will and lack of sloth are clearly important, yet they are dependent on the impersonal condition "If it so be" that mitigates both his agency and his assiduousness. Such gestures save the Second Nun from the charge of Semi-Pelagianism with which she flirts, but they also curtail the claims that can be made for the good of translation. The Second Nun's implicit claims for the power of rhetoric are so strongly felt that one scarcely notices that her most stirring rhetorical performance fails to convert Almachius.

The incommensurate relationship between signifier and signified and the dependence of understanding on God's grace both unsettle any direct correspondence between *entente* and expression that might reside within the individual subject. This gap—corresponding roughly to that between speaker and speech that I have discussed throughout this study—may be more disappointing to modern critics who hope to find democratizing vernacularity than it would have been to a contemporary audience. As scholars have pointed out, even the Wycliffites who supported biblical translation perceived their revelatory intervention not as giving responsibility for understanding to layfolk but as making understanding contingent on the working of grace in the upright individual.[70] More disturbing still is that this separation, that with its antihermeneutic gives power to those otherwise unauthorized and allows women to preach, is not that distant from the antihermeneutic that underwrites the Prioress's anti-Semitism. The distinction that Chaucer likely saw in the story of St. Cecilia was that insofar as its protagonist has agency, she uses it to make her will adhere to God's *entente*, matching intent and expression, inner and outer, thereby creating verbal performances that signify without communicating self-interest.

The sentiment that this sort of will to fidelity is rare among the contemporary authorized spokesmen of Christianity is suggested by the entrance of the Canon, whose very ecclesiastical garb hints at his duplicity: "clothed ... in clothes blake,/And undernethe ... a whyt surplys" (8.557–58). *The Second Nun's Tale*'s possible flirtation with ideas associated with Wycliffites, however, should discourage us from viewing the tale as nostalgia for an idyllic past. Indeed, Staley has called attention to the way in which Cecilia's final bequest to commit her earthly wealth to the founding of a church, "In which, into this day, in noble wyse,/Men doon to Crist and to his seint servyse" (8.552–53), can be said to announce her originary patronage of the modern institutional church, even if the Canon appears to be a disappointing return on that investment.[71] *The Second Nun's Tale* and its counterpart, *The Prioress's Tale*, introduce distance, whether temporal or geographical, to create less threatening sites for exploration into the potential resources of authority and potential power of public speech that does not speak in the person of specific institutions. It is at such sites that the questions that plagued Langland, concerning the social or spiritual function of such speech, as well as the claims to authority it entailed, were considered by Chaucer as well.

Reading, Singing, and Vernacular Making

My discussion thus far has focused on the idea of public speech as a broadly social and spiritual act. While it should be clear at this point that verbal performances that claimed the power and authority of sacramentality were a topic of general interest in this historical moment, there is reason to believe that the explorations of public performance in *The Prioress's Tale* and *The Second Nun's Tale* had particular relevance for Chaucer's sense of himself as vernacular maker. Within the two nuns' dialogue, reading and singing, as descriptors of opposing versions of the ideal Christian utterance, are also connected in each tale to narratorial activity. Just as the Prioress refers to her narration as a "song," the Second Nun, in a momentary suspension of the tale-telling fiction, begs the indulgence of the audience that "reads" what she has written (7.486, 8.78).[72] In itself these connections are not terribly striking: narratorial self-referentiality can be found in any of the tales, especially if one is looking for it. More compelling is the degree to which the terms of debate that emerge in the juxtaposition of the Prioress and Second Nun are mirrored in the juxtaposition of Chaucer's own two tales, *Thopas* and *Melibee*. Both pairs pit a tale highly conscious of its orality against a tale whose "writtenness" has yet to be edited out to fit the fictive framework of the tale-telling contest (cf. 7.964, 8.78).[73] Both pairs, to further the analogy, juxtapose "singing" and "reading." Furthermore, in both cases this juxtaposition associates song with form (with "drasty rymyng" [7.930], in the case of *Thopas*) and reading with *sentence* (7.946, 947, 951, 961, 963).[74] Such similarities prompt further examination of the terms in which these two sets of tales are matched as well as how they inflect each other.

It is not difficult to see the parallels in *The Tale of Melibee* and *The Second Nun's Tale*. Both tales feature female protagonists, endowed with authoritative wisdom and loquacity, who try to convince men in power to change their ways.[75] Given these points of comparison, one might see in St. Cecilia's evangelical success and moral courage a distant and idealized counterpart to Prudence's relentless (and to some, tedious) reasoning in her more domestic and courtly setting.[76] Parallels between *The Prioress's Tale* and *The Tale of Sir Thopas*, however, seem more problematic. Several critics have noted them, usually singly and in passing: both tales have male protagonists described as "children"; upon hearing a song (the antiphon for the *clergeon*, a bird song for Thopas [7.773]), both are inspired to love an otherworldly woman (the Virgin Mary, the Elf Queen), yet whereas the *clergeon* is inspired to sing without ceasing, Thopas is given over to a similarly compulsive "prikyng" as he searches for the object of his desire (7.774, 775, 798). Scholars have nonetheless been reticent to pursue these similarities, unwilling to attribute to Chaucer parodic intentions that seem "irreverent or perverse."[77] Mary Hamel, who has done the most extensive examination of the parallels between the tales, finds the parodic potential irreverent and incongruous enough to liken it to the comedy of Monty Python.[78] Though some, like Hamel, would like to see in such an apparent act of *quyting* Chaucer's refutation of the Prioress's anti-Semitism, the implicit comparison of the *clergeon*'s piety and Thopas's oversexed desire seems to court blasphemy.

It is possible, however, that the object of parody is not the Prioress or the piety she promotes (or, alas, her anti-Semitism) but the idealized poetics her tale exemplifies. The *clergeon*'s performance represents the monologic utterance—a singly-voiced song that stands in contrast to the double-voiced poetics that make up *The Canterbury Tales*. Though, as I have suggested, Chaucer considers the potential tensions and inner contradictions of such a monologic fantasy within the tale itself as well as in its dialogue with *The Second Nun's Tale*, I do not think he was impervious to the allure of such a powerful form of expression and the universal, perhaps even choral assent it seems to command. He does, however, appear to distinguish between what can be performed imaginatively by a *clergeon* in distant "Asye" and what can be performed by an aspiring vernacular poet from the courtly loci of articulation closer to home. Like Langland, he counters a devotional and liturgical ideal with a profoundly self-conscious representation of his own poetic activity that highlights the material realities of making and his own limitations. For Chaucer it prompts the question, If the *clergeon* represents the degree of self-abnegation, surrender of agency, and textual innocence required to ensure ethical authenticity, what does this say about a maker who lost his hermeneutical virginity long ago?

Chaucer's performance serves in part as a response to this question—a response tempered not only by the textual knowledge and pretensions necessary to producing poetry but also by the material realities of verbal production. As Richard Firth Green has shown, the positions of minstrel and advisor to princes in *The Tale of Sir Thopas* and *The Tale of Melibee*, respectively, survey the social extremes of courtly loci of articulation;[79] Chaucer thus further takes into account the discursive restraints of the institutional loci from which he is arguably attempting unmoor himself with the Canterbury project. In general these elements conspire to make innocent monologic utterance impossible and double-voicing a viable formal and ethical solution. Yet in the context of *Sir Thopas*, the hypervalidation of form over meaning that was redemptive in *The Prioress's Tale* becomes an aesthetics of form in a variable literary marketplace that is as oppressive and unforgiving as the *clergeon*'s audience. Harry Bailey's infamously scatological appraisal of Chaucer's poetic performance "Thy drasty rymyng is nat worth a toord!" recalls the similarly scatological assessment of the Jews of *The Prioress's Tale*, who turned *sentence* into excrement in a similarly interruptive gesture (7.930). It is, however, the *form*, not the *sentence*, that the Host objects to and which he invests with material, rather than ethical or spiritual, value. A similar reversal occurs when the Jews, who in *The Prioress's Tale* were associated with grammatical winnowing—with the inner *sentence*—reappear in *Thopas* (more amiably integrated into a chivalric economy, it would seem) as the makers of the outermost layer of Thopas's armor: the "hawberk" that is "al ywroght of Jewes werk" (7.864). The exteriority articulated by this elaborate armor stands in contrast to the innocent opacity of the *clergeon*, as it is designed to prevent the "percynge of [the] herte" that spiritually afflicted him (7.862). The various demands and constraints of his performance combine to make the question of productivity inescapable, even if it is difficult to define what kind of productivity is required. In the end, Chaucer finds himself reprimanded with the most Langlandian of ethical accusations: "Thou doost noght elles but despendest tyme," which recalls Reason's inquisition of Will in the C 5 *apologia*, particularly Will's own forced confession that he has "ytynt tyme and tyme myspened" (C 5.93). The accusation in Chaucer's situation seems an especially ornery assessment, given that the purpose of the tale-telling game was to *kill* time. Such assessments, however, depict the various and variable demands that mark larger, more public fora as well as Chaucer's self-deprecating and possibly disingenuous claim that he is unable either to anticipate or to meet such varying demands.

*   *   *

In bringing marginally clerical loci of articulation and the ethically and spiritually valuable speech that can issue from them to bear on his own poetic project, Chaucer does not simply perform an homage or allusion to Langland but participates in a larger discursive framework Staley has referred to as "postures of sanctity." As Staley has defined it, this discourse dealt with social and political power: "In their efforts to jockey for political leverage, the king, the church, and Parliament each sought to appropriate the language of devotion."[80] This study provides the background for such posturing, as well as a different context for understanding it. It was not that there was a preexisting "language of devotion" accessible to all, waiting to be appropriated. It was rather a language that emerged from the proliferation of the texts and practices of reading and singing—a proliferation that extended beyond those in power to create innumerable forms of posturing and social signification. Chaucer did more than refract performances of such posturing within this discursive framework; he participated in the formation of this language. Both he and Langland created their own postures and personae of sanctified speech as they indulged in their shared predilection for investigating the social positioning of their own narrative performances. It is an aspect of vernacular poetry we have overlooked perhaps because the language of devotion had become so diffuse and pervasive by the time Chaucer and Langland were experimenting.

I offer one final poetic passage as an index of just how diffuse and pervasive reading and singing, as critical formative components of the "language of devotion," had become. In the oft-quoted valedictory at the end of the *Troilus*, Chaucer unconsciously invokes the liturgical collocation as he considers the future of his writing. Just after the narrator has sent his "litel bok" off to kiss the steps of the grammatical fellowship of Virgil, Ovid, and others, he once again considers the instability of the vernacular.

> And for ther is so gret diversite
> In Englissh and in writyng of oure tonge,
> So prey I God that non myswrite the,
> Ne the mysmetre for defaute of tonge;
> And *red* wherso thow be, or elles *songe*,
> That thow be understonde, God I biseche! (*TC*, 5.1793–99, my
>   emphasis)

Chaucer's collocating of "reading" and "singing" is not a conscious reference to the liturgical. Though the origin of the collocation, here as elsewhere, is the reading and singing of the *opus Dei*, usage in both continental sources and in the works of Chaucer's circle show that it had migrated to participate in a bardic rather than liturgical register, as in *The House of Fame*, when Dido laments that her shameful acts will be "red and songe / Over al thys lond, on every tonge" (*HF*, 347–48).[81] It is a testimony to the processes of unmooring and recontextualization that such an unconscious allusion could arise. The existence of continental examples, furthermore, shows that such recontextualization was not limited to England. Though this broader migration is in itself important, Chaucer's usage here has additional features that tie it more specifically to the topics discussed in this study and thus to some distinctively English concerns. Chaucer's worries about metrical integrity and understanding give added liturgical resonance to his use of the collocation, invoking as they do the politics of understanding in terms similar to those used by William Wykeham (to give just one example) to critique the reading and singing of the monks of St. Swithun's. Such unconscious invocations arise not because Chaucer gives his work the status of scripture or expects it to be ritualized in the same manner. His focus is the fact of textual performance and, more specifically, textual publication. Knowing that both textuality and publicity require the separation of speaker and speech ("Go, litel bok" [*TC*, 5.1786]), Chaucer rehearses the same constellation of concerns and terminology connected to public speech that was officially and institutionally sanctified.[82] Thus while he refers to neither liturgy nor devotion, issues associated with liturgical practice that were so prevalent in late medieval England have insinuated themselves in the way Chaucer expresses himself about his vernacular poetic desires. One can, nonetheless, perhaps still see traces of the liturgical in Chaucer's desire for some kind of sanctification, perhaps even a degree of sacramentality, to reinforce the value and aid in the intelligibility of his words.

Notes

Preface

1. For a brief overview of the subversive potential that might, or might not, be attributed to the vernacular, see Ruth Evans, "Historicizing Postcolonial Criticism: Cultural Difference and the Vernacular," in *The Idea of the Vernacular: An Anthology of Middle English Literary Theory, 1280–1520*, ed. Jocelyn Wogan-Browne, Nicholas Watson, Andrew Taylor, and Ruth Evans (University Park: Pennsylvania State University Press, 1999), 366–70.

2. For a consideration of musical textuality, see Bruce Holsinger, *Music, Body, and Desire in Medieval Culture: Hildegard of Bingen to Chaucer* (Stanford, Calif.: Stanford University Press, 2001).

3. This isolation is purely heuristic and not intended to neglect the many valuable studies on the Eucharist, such as Miri Rubin, *Corpus Christi: The Eucharist in Late Medieval Culture* (Cambridge: Cambridge University Press, 1991); David Aers, *Sanctifying Signs: Making Christian Tradition in Late Medieval England* (Notre Dame, Ind.: University of Notre Dame Press, 2004); or more general studies, such as John Bossy, "The Mass as a Social Institution, 1200–1700," *Past and Present* 100 (1983): 29–61.

4. M. T. Clanchy, *From Memory to Written Record: England, 1066–1307*, 2nd ed. (Oxford: Blackwell, 1993); Richard Firth Green, *A Crisis of Truth: Literature and Law in Ricardian England* (Philadelphia: University of Pennsylvania Press, 1999).

5. Leo Treitler, "Reading and Singing: On the Genesis of Occidental Music-Writing," *Early Music History* 4 (1984): 181–97.

6. Eamon Duffy, *The Stripping of the Altars: Traditional Religion in England, 1400–1580, 2nd ed.* (New Haven, Conn.: Yale University Press, 2005), whose notion of traditional culture has been critiqued in David Aers, "Altars of Power: Reflections on Eamon Duffy's *The Stripping of the Altars: Traditional Religion in England, 1400–1580*," *Literature and History* 3 (1994): 90–105; Walter J. Ong, *The Presence of the Word: Some Prolegomena for Cultural and Religious History* (New Haven, Conn.: Yale University Press, 1967); Ong, *Orality and Literacy: The Technologizing of the Word* (London and New York: Routledge, 1982); Michel de Certeau, *The Writing of History*, trans. Tom Conley (New York: Columbia University Press, 1988).

7. One such critique, though it is more interested in the absences attributed to the "premodern subject" than the plenitude said to be experienced in the presence of the *vox Dei*, is David Aers, "A Whisper in the Ear of Early Modernists; or, Reflections on Literary Critics Writing the 'History of the Subject,'" in *Culture*

and History, 1350–1600: Essays on English Communities, Identities and Writing, ed. David Aers (New York: Harvester Wheatsheaf, 1992), 177–202.

8. Bruce Holsinger, "Liturgy," in *Twenty-First Century Approaches to Literature: Middle English*, ed. Paul Strohm (Oxford: Oxford University Press, 2007), 295.

9. Catherine Bell, *Ritual Theory, Ritual Practice* (New York and Oxford: Oxford University Press, 1992), 19–29.

10. Ibid., 74; see also 89–92.

11. See, for example, Gabrielle M. Spiegel, "Memory and History: Liturgical Time and Historical Time," *History and Theory* 41 (2002): 149–62. Holsinger discusses and offers alternatives to this point of view by promoting a "detheologizing" of liturgy ("Liturgy," 297–303).

12. On *communitas*, see Victor Turner, *The Ritual Process: Structure and Anti-Structure* (Ithaca, N.Y.: Cornell University Press, 1969), 96–97.

13. On grammar as "master discourse," see Rita Copeland, *Rhetoric, Hermeneutics, and Translation in the Middle Ages: Academic Traditions and Vernacular Texts* (Cambridge: Cambridge University Press, 1991), 5, 55–62.

14. Clanchy, *From Memory*, 186–87.

15. Nicholas Watson, "The Middle English Mystics," in *The Cambridge History of Medieval English Literature*, ed. David Wallace (Cambridge: Cambridge University Press, 1999), 539–65; Rita Copeland, *Pedagogy, Intellectuals, and Dissent in the Later Middle Ages: Lollardy and Ideas of Learning* (Cambridge: Cambridge University Press, 2001).

16. Anne Hudson describes a Latin mass performed by accused heretic William Ramsbury recorded in 1389 ("A Lollard Mass," in *Lollards and Their Books* [London: Hambledon, 1985], 111–23). Kathryn Kerby-Fulton, however, has suggested that the heterodox elements of his performance might signal his affiliation with the Heresy of the Free Spirit more than with Wycliffism (*Books Under Suspicion: Censorship and Tolerance of Revelatory Writing in Late Medieval England* [Notre Dame, Ind.: University of Notre Dame Press, 2006], 269–71).

17. See, for example, Sarah Beckwith, *Signifying God: Social Relation and Symbolic Act in the York Corpus Christi Plays* (Chicago: University of Chicago Press, 2001); Carol Symes, "The Appearance of Early Vernacular Plays: Forms, Functions, and the Future of Medieval Theater," *Speculum* 77 (2002); 778–831; Ruth Nissé, *Defining Acts: Drama and the Politics of Interpretation in Late Medieval England* (Notre Dame, Ind.: University of Notre Dame Press, 2005).

18. Katherine Zieman, "Playing Doctor: St. Birgitta, Ritual Reading, and Ecclesiastical Authority," in *Voices in Dialogue: New Problems in Reading Women's Cultural History*, ed. Kathryn Kerby-Fulton and Linda Olson (Notre Dame, Ind.: University of Notre Dame Press, 2005), 307–34.

19. Roger Bowers, "The Performing Ensemble for English Church Polyphony, c. 1320–c. 1390," in *English Church Polyphony: Singers and Sources from the 14th to the 17th Century* (Aldershot: Ashgate, 1999); Jo Ann H. Moran Cruz, *The Growth of English Schooling, 1340–1548: Learning, Literacy, and Laicization in Pre-Reformation York Diocese* (Princeton, N.J.: Princeton Unversity Press,

1985), 256–57; J. Heywood and Thomas Wright, eds., *The Ancient Laws for King's College Cambridge and Eton College* (London, 1850), 477–619.

20. Nicholas Watson, "Censorship and Cultural Exchange in Late-Medieval England: Vernacular Theology, the Oxford Translation Debate, and Arundel's Constitutions of 1409," *Speculum 70* (1995): 822–64; Jeremy Catto, "Religious Change Under Henry V," in *Henry V: The Practice of Kingship*, ed. G. L. Harriss (Oxford: Oxford University Press, 1985), 97–116.

Chapter 1

1. See, for example, A. F. Leach, *The Schools of Medieval England* (1915; repr., New York and London: Barnes and Noble and Methuen, 1969), 137–38; Nicholas Orme, *English Schools in the Middle Ages* (London: Methuen, 1973), 60, 63; Orme, *Medieval Children* (New Haven, Conn.: Yale University Press, 2001), 266; Orme, *Medieval Schools: From Roman Britain to Renaissance England* (New Haven, Conn.: Yale University Press, 2006), 59–60; John Lawson and Harold Silver, *A Social History of Education in England* (London: Methuen, 1973), 69; Moran Cruz, *Growth of English Schooling*, 60–61; William J. Courtenay, *Schools and Scholars in Fourteenth-Century England* (Princeton, N.J.: Princeton University Press, 1987), 18–19; Suzanne Reynolds, *Medieval Reading: Grammar, Rhetoric, and the Classical Text* (Cambridge: Cambridge University Press, 1996), 9.

2. *The Riverside Chaucer*, ed. Larry Benson, 3rd ed. (Boston: Houghton Mifflin, 1987), 7.536. All further citations of Chaucer's works will refer to this edition and will be cited parenthetically by title (or fragment for texts from *The Canterbury Tales*) and line number. With the exception of Reynolds, all of the studies cited in n. 1 quote the "smal grammeere" passage.

3. Moran Cruz, *Growth of English Schooling*, 56–62.

4. Orme, *English Schools*, 63.

5. I have borrowed the useful phrase "hermeneutical enfranchisement" from Rita Copeland, *Pedagogy*, 62.

6. Discussions on the parameters and definition of education can be found in Nicholas Orme, *Education and Society in Medieval and Renaissance England* (London: Hambledon, 1989), 1; the breadth of courtly education is examined fully in his *From Childhood to Chivalry: The Education of the English Kings and Aristocracy, 1066–1530* (London: Methuen, 1984). Joan Simon has emphasized broader definitions of education in *The Social Origins of English Education* (London: Routledge, 1970), 4–6, 48–54, 103, though her distinctions, couched in a linear narrative of development, presume the continuity of that which is deemed "intellectual."

7. Studies of Lollardy and its relation to intellectual resources are too numerous to name, but two useful recent studies that focus on hermeneutics are Copeland, *Pedagogy*, and Kantik Ghosh, *The Wycliffite Heresy: Authority and the Interpretation of Texts* (Cambridge: Cambridge University Press, 2002). The topic

of the Oxford translation debates has been discussed in Watson, "Censorship," 840–51; this article, together with Watson's "The Middle English Mystics," outlines the concept of "vernacular theology." On the 1381 rebellion, see Steven Justice, *Writing and Rebellion: England in 1381* (Berkeley: University of California Press, 1994). James Simpson also describes "a newly articulate vernacularity" that emerged in England after 1350 (*The Oxford English Literary History, vol. 2, 1350–1547: Reform and Cultural Revolution* [Oxford: Oxford University Press, 2002], 2).

8. On "textualized" language—i.e., language subject to a degree of stability and ossification generally lacking in purely oral languages—see Walter J. Ong, "Orality, Literacy, and Medieval Textualization," *New Literary History* 16 (1984): 1–12.

9. Eamon Duffy views the texts and practices of the liturgy as the core resource of "a repertoire of inherited and shared beliefs and symbols" of "traditional" religion (*Stripping of the Altars*, 3), whereas Nicholas Watson finds this version of "traditional religion" to have been "itself the creation of a movement of reform, a movement that was equally imposed on English society from above, equally held in place by decades of religious repression" ("Censorship," 859).

10. Spiegel, "Memory and History," 149–62.

11. Conceptual vocabulary of "residual" versus "emergent" is based on Raymond Williams, "Dominant, Residual, and Emergent," in *Marxism and Literature* (New York and Oxford: Oxford University Press, 1977), 122–24.

12. Leach, *Schools*, 136.

13. Ibid., 6–7.

14. Ibid., 7.

15. Ibid.

16. Leach, "St. Paul's School Before Colet," *Archaeologia* 62, pt. 1 (1910): 191.

17. Moran Cruz, *Growth of English Schooling*, 13.

18. Leach, *Schools*, 137.

19. Ibid., 138.

20. Although he does not discuss "song schools," Pierre Riché's discussion of continental schooling has the same dual categorization. In his *Écoles et enseignement dans le Haut Moyen Age: Fin du Ve siècle – milieu du XIe siècle*, 2nd ed. (Paris: Picard, 1989), he lists the teaching of song separate from, though clearly related to, reading, under the heading of "elementary education," where it served to help children memorize texts and introduced them to the liturgy (225). "Lectors and Cantors" are later described as those who received "specialized" education (237–42).

21. Orme, *English Schools*, 63; see also Orme, *Education in the West of England, 1066–1548: Cornwall, Devon, Dorset, Gloucestershire, Somerset, Wiltshire* (Exeter, University of Exeter Press, 1976), 2; and Orme, *Medieval Schools*, 63.

22. Lawson and Silver, *Social History*, 68.

23. Roger Bowers, "Choral Institutions Within the English Church: Their Constitution and Development, 1340–1500" (Ph.D. diss., University of East Anglia, 1975), 2038 n3.

24. Moran Cruz, *Growth of English Schooling*, 54. When describing a tentative methodology for the interpretation of testamentary evidence through the mid-

sixteenth century, Moran Cruz claims to take the wills "at face value": "Mention of [bequests to] scholars, without specific reference to grammar, suggests a reading school. Evidence for children singing suggests a song school" (95). The chronological parameters that define my study (fourteenth and early fifteenth century), however, produce a somewhat different picture: almost all schools before 1450 that Moran Cruz designates as "reading schools" (a virtually unattested term in earlier documents) are based on this kind of testamentary evidence. There is, in other words, little to corroborate the criteria that define "face value" for this earlier period. Moran Cruz's perception of literacy as the ability to decode unfamiliar material at sight ultimately leads her to place song outside the realm of "scholarship." Since the repertoire of song may have been memorized without recourse to the written page, "the degree of literacy attained in many song schools ... must remain questionable" and those who attended them would not be considered "scholars" (54).

25. James McKinnon, "*Gregorius presul composuit hunc libellum musicae artis*," in *The Liturgy of the Medieval Church,* ed. Thomas J. Heffernan and E. Ann Matter (Kalamazoo, Mich.: Medieval Institute, 2001), 683–84, provides this early date from the mention of a *prior cantorum;* tradition had it that Gregory I founded the scola before 597, but Joseph Dyer has shown this claim to be unsupportable ("The *Schola cantorum* and Its Roman Milieu in the Early Middle Ages," in *De musica et cantu: Studien zur Geschichte der Kirchenmusik und der Oper. Helmut Hucke zum 60. Geburtstag, ed.* Peter Cahn and Ann-Katrin Heimer (Hildesheim and New York: Olms, 1993), 19–40. Joseph Smits van Waesberghe is cautious about such early dating of the *scola*, pointing out that the term *scola cantorum* does not appear until the beginning of the ninth century and that prior to this there is mention of only an *ordo cantorum* (*Musikerziehung: Lehre und Theorie der Musik im Mittelalter,* Musikgeschichte im Bildern, vol. 3, ed. Heinrich Besseler and Werner Bachmann [Leipzig: Deutscher Verlag für Musik, 1969], 16–17). If the extant manuscript record does reflect a change in terminology, that change is contemporary with the Carolingian reforms that enhanced the choir's educative function, as well as that of the other *scole* modeled upon it. Which one was first called *scola* is not a critical point in this context.

26. For a discussion of the different meanings of *scola*, see Orme, *Medieval Schools*, 53–55.

27. McKinnon, "*Gregorius*," 686; Smits van Waesberghe, *Musikerziehung*, 17.

28. McKinnon, "*Gregorius*," 684. Andrew Hughes analogously sets chant developed in "institutions like Conservatories"—concerned with precise and discrete pitches and a linear melody unfolding over time—against a "florid" style of chant of imprecise, connected pitches in which melody was secondary to ornament. In Hughes's account both styles coexisted into the late Middle Ages, though only the former would be likely to be associated with the *scola cantorum* ("Charlemagne's Chant or The Great Vocal Shift," *Speculum 77* [2002]: 1069–1106).

29. In making this claim, I do not suggest that Christians did not sing before this time, since a long tradition of hymnody preceded this moment. "Song" refers to a specific repertoire of chant, performed for the most part by "ritual specialists" (see Bell, *Ritual Theory*, 130–40).

30. I am not concerned here with the mode of transmission, which was much debated among musicologists with the publication of Leo Treitler, "Homer and Gregory: The Transmission of Epic Poetry and Plainchant," *Musical Quarterly* 60 (1974): 333–72; it is merely the fact of and emphasis on teaching that is important to me at this point.

31. Epistola 30, *Monumenta Germaniae Historica: Epistolae Merowingici et Karolini aevi*, 8 vols. (Berlin, 1892–1939), 4:543, quoted in Riché, *Écoles*, 370, and discussed 237, 239.

32. For a description of the practices of the *lectio divina*, see Jean Leclercq, *The Love of Learning and the Desire for God: A Study of Monastic Culture*, 3rd ed., trans. Catharine Misrahi (New York: Fordham, 1982), 15–17 passim.

33. The term "textual community" was coined by Brian Stock in his *Implications of Literacy: Written Language and Models of Interpretation in the Eleventh and Twelfth Centuries* (Princeton, N.J.: Princeton University Press, 1983), 88–92 passim, and reconsidered in *Listening for the Text: On the Uses of the Past* (Baltimore and London: Johns Hopkins University Press, 1990), 140–58. I use it here to refer to the *scole* insofar as they are constituted by their use of a shared set of texts (rather than by a written rule, though this was probably also the case). What is critical to this study is not merely the presence of texts but how they are used. Where possible I use more specific terms to reflect the predominating practice (as in "choral community," below). I also use it in its broadest sense to refer to a conception of the Christian community insofar as their relations are regulated by a body of biblical, liturgical, and patristic texts and their licensed uses.

34. "Alternative" practices in this instance can be distinguished from "oppositional" practices. See Williams, "Dominant, Residual, and Emergent," 122–23.

35. The dynamics of the choir, or "choral community," will be discussed at greater length in Chapter 2.

36. Susan Rankin, "Carolingian Music," in *Carolingian Culture: Emulation and Innovation*, ed. Rosamund McKitterick (Cambridge: Cambridge University Press, 1994), 275–79.

37. Charlemagne proposes that "Psalmos, notas, cantus, compotum, grammaticam" be taught in every bishopric and monastery (rub. 72). The text of the *Admonitio generalis* can be found in *Monumenta Germaniae Historica. Leges. Sectio II: Capitula Regum Francorum, ed.* Alfred Boreti and Victor Krause (Hanover, 1883), 1:52–62, and is discussed in Riché, *Écoles*, 70–71.

38. Reynolds, *Medieval Reading*, 1.

39. Copeland, *Rhetoric*, 5, 55–62.

40. Martin Irvine, *The Making of Textual Culture: "Grammatica" and Literary Theory*, 350–1100 (Cambridge: Cambridge University Press, 1994), 13. For a full discussion of the Carolingian program, see pp. 305–33.

41. Irvine, *Making of Textual Culture*, 461.

42. Ibid., 287.

43. *The Use of Sarum*, ed. W. H. Frere (Cambridge: Cambridge University Press, 1898–1901), 1:283–85. See also Kathleen Edwards, *English Secular Cathedrals in the Middle Ages,* 2nd ed. (Manchester: Manchester University Press; New York: Barnes and Noble, 1967), 181–82. Margot Fassler has noted a similar

division in early monastic rules, where the cantor oversees the singing and the armarius the reading of the *opus Dei*. These two offices, however, had gradually become one by the beginning of the twelfth century ("The Office of the Cantor in Early Western Monastic Rules and Customaries: A Preliminary Investigation," *Early Music History* 5 [1985]: 43, 47).

44. Irvine, *Making of Textual Culture*, 287, 317.

45. Irvine quotes Notker's remark that Charlemagne reformed the liturgy because of his desire to support *scientia litterarum* (*Making of Textual Culture*, 311).

46. Ritva Jonsson and Leo Treitler have shown that concepts from *grammatica* informed the structuring of the musical language of song ("Medieval Music and Language: A Reconsideration of the Relationship," *Studies in the History of Music* 1 [1983]: 1–23). The melodic syntax that resulted generally set words in ways that upheld the principles of *lectio*, but the structure of melodic forms is analogous to, not reducible to, *grammatica*. Treitler has further claimed that neumes are not derived from Roman signs for *accentus* (the study of which was part of *lectio*) but rather that both neumes and medieval punctuation developed in parallel from Carolingian (liturgical) lesson signs ("Reading and Singing," 181–97).

47. See Chapter 2, pp. 43–47.

48. For studies of training in song on the continent, see Osvaldo Gambassi, *"Pueri Cantores" nelle Cattedrali d'Italia Tra Medioevo e Età Moderna: Le Scuole Eugeniames: Schole de Canto Annesse alle Cappelle Musicali*, Historiae Musicae Biblioteca 80 (Florence: Olschiki, 1997); and Martin Kintzinger, *"Varietas puerorum:* Unterricht und Gesang in Stifts- und Stadtschulen des späten Mittelalters," and Urs Martin Zahnd, "Chordienst und Schule in eidgenössischen Städten des Spätmittelalters: Eine Untersuchung auf Grund der Verhältnisse in Bern, Freiburg, Luzern, und Solothurn," both in *Schule und Schüler im Mittelalter: Beiträge zur europäischen Bildungsgeschichte des 9. bis 15. Jahrhunderts*, ed. Martin Kintzinger, Sönke Lorenz, and Michael Walter (Cologne: Böhlau, 1996), 299–326, 259–98.

49. *Historia ecclesiastica*, 3.18: "instituit scholam, in qua pueri literis erudirentur." Latin quoted from *Bede's Ecclesiastical History of the English People*, ed. Bertram Colgrave and R. A. B. Mynors (Oxford: Clarendon, 1969). All further citations of the Latin text will refer to this edition.

50. *Hist. eccl.* 2.20: "Qui, quoniam cantandi in ecclesia erat peritissimus … magister ecclesiasticae cantionis iuxta morem Romanorum seu Cantuariorum multis coepit existere."

51. McKinnon, *"Gregorius,"* 692. See also Bede's description of Theodore's unifying episcopacy (in which the spread of singing plays an important role) during which Putta was installed in the see of Rochester; Putta's knowledge of singing is authenticated by the fact that he learned from "the disciples of the blessed Pope Gregory" (4.2).

52. *Hist. eccl.* 4.18: "cursum canendi annuum, sicut ad sanctum Petrum Romae agebatur, edoceret."

53. The register of the canons regular of Huntingdon has an entry in which "Henry, archdeacon of Huntingdon … who entered upon his archidiaconate in 1109 or 1110, makes known that he has given back and offered on the altar to the canons of Huntingdon the song school [*scolas de cantu*] which is known to be

theirs of right" (Mary Bateson, "The Huntingdon Song School," *English Historical Review* 18 [1903]: 710–2). From Hastings, there is a fourteenth-century copy of a confirmation (*temp*. John) of the value and lands of the prebends of the collegiate church founded in the castle by Robert, Count of Eu, where "the rule of the *scole cantus*" is listed along with the titles of lands associated with one of the prebends. The "rule of the grammar school" is similarly listed under a different prebend (A. F. Leach, ed., *Educational Charters and Documents, 598 to 1909* [Cambridge, 1911; repr. New York: AMS, 1971], 68–69). In Canterbury, the Charter of the Priory of St. Gregory (1086) lists "scolas urbis et uiculorum eius tam grammatice quam musice" as the responsibility of the Augustinian canons of the house (*The Cartulary of the Priory of St. Gregory, Canterbury*, ed. Audrey Woodcock [London: Royal Historical Society, 1956], 1–2). There is no further explicit mention of a song school for the town of Canterbury, but a dispute over an adulterine schoolmaster in 1321 suggests that if there were such instruction, it was presided over by the archbishop rather than the priory of St. Gregory (C. E. Woodruff and H. J. Cape, *Schola Regia Cantuariensis: A History of Canterbury School* [London: Mitchell, 1908], 16–44; Orme, *English Schools*, 69, 168–69).

54. For Wells, see H. E. Reynalds, *Wells Cathedral: Its Foundation, Constitutional History and Statutes* (Leeds, 1881), 45, 55 (at Wells, the precentor is known as the "Cantor"). York's statutes, dated by Edwards to "before the mid-thirteenth century" (*English Secular Cathedrals*, 154), can be found in *Statutes of Lincoln Cathedral*, ed. Henry Bradshaw and Christopher Wordsworth (Cambridge, 1892), 2:95, 96. For St. Paul's, see *Statutorum et Consuetudinum Ecclesiae Cathedralis Sancti Pauli Londoniensis*, ed. W. Sparrow Simpson (London, 1873), 22. Lichfield's statutes can be found in *Statutes of Lincoln*, 2:17. For Salisbury, see *The Use of Sarum*, 1:3–4, 8.

55. For the 1214 statutes, see *Statutes of Lincoln*, 2:137–42; *"The Registrum antiquissimum" of the Cathedral Church of Lincoln*, ed. C. W. Foster (Lincoln: Lincoln Record Society, 1931), 1:262–63.

56. Smits van Waesberghe, *Musikerziehung*, 16.

57. "Ad illum pertinet puerorum instruccio, et disciplina, et eorundem in choro admissio et ordinatio" appears under the office of the Precentor in the statutes of Wells, York, Lichfield, Salisbury, and London. All of these statutes are derived from the *Institutio Osmundi* of Salisbury, dated 1091, in which neither the song school nor the duty to instruct boys is mentioned, though the chancellor's duty "in scolis regendis" is (*Statutes of Lincoln*, 2:9).

58. Orme, *English Schools*, 64.

59. Bowers, "Choral Institutions," 2041.

60. Printed in A. F. Leach, ed., *Early Yorkshire Schools, Yorkshire Archaeological Society Record Series* 27, 33 (Leeds, 1898–1903), 1:22–3.

61. Several disputes over adulterine schools occurred in Lincoln, which are described in Leach's article in *The Victoria History of the Counties of England: Lincolnshire*, ed. William Page (London: Constable, 1906), 2:421–40. At Bury, the first mention of an adulterine school is dated 1268 in a document translated by Leach (*The Victoria History of the Counties of England: Suffolk*, ed. William Page

[London: Constable: 1907–11], 2:309): "By long custom it had been granted and it had from time whereof there is no memory peacefully obtained that no one should dare to teach boys their psalters or singing without the license of the master of the Assembly of Twelve (*congregacionis duodene*)." Leach gives no satisfying explanation of the "Assembly of Twelve" (Orme presumes it to be a religious guild [*English Schools*, 119]). We know of this document because it was copied as precedent for a similar dispute in 1370, in which it is mandated that no one should teach boys in psalter or song (*psalteria vel cantum*) without license from the master of the song school (*magister scolarum cantus*).

62. While I have not yet been able to consult the documents pertaining to St. Leonard's history, the mention of the song school first seems to appear in a list of personnel provided for a royal inquisition into the affairs of the hospital, where it mentions "a master for teaching boys and a master of the song school" (quoted in Angelo Raine, *History of St. Peter's School, York*, A.D. *627 to the Present Day* [London: Bell, 1926], 42). See note 92 below. As I will show in my discussion of a similar dispute at St. Cross Hospital in Winchester (see Chapter 2, pp. 50–56), terms that appear in such lists are heavily invested in institutional definitions of precisely this type.

63. The document containing the rivalry between the grammar master and the song master at Warwick is printed in Leach, *Educational Charters*, 272–75. Leach's date of 1316 has been corrected by Bowers ("Choral Institutions," appendix A5) to sometime between c. 1314 and c. 1333. For several different interpretations of the incident, see Bowers, along with Orme, *English Schools*, 65, 69; Moran Cruz, *Growth of English Schooling*, 52, 55; and Leach, *History of Warwick School* (London, 1906), 62ff.

64. Clanchy, *From Memory*, 44–81 passim.

65. Paul F. Gehl, *A Moral Art: Grammar, Society, and Culture in Trecento Florence* (Ithaca, N.Y.: Cornell University Press, 1993); and Robert Black, *Humanism and Education in Medieval and Renaissance Italy: Tradition and Innovation in Latin Schools from the Twelfth to the Fifteenth Century* (Cambridge and New York: Cambridge University Press, 2001).

66. For a similar observation on fifteenth-century chantries, see Clive Burgess, "'For the Increase of Divine Service': Chantries in the Parish in Late Medieval Bristol," *Journal of Ecclesiastical History* 36 (1985): 46–65; and Burgess, "Strategies for Eternity: Perpetual Chantry Foundation in Late Medieval Bristol," in *Religious Belief and Ecclesiastical Careers in Late Medieval England: Proceedings of the Conference Held at Strawberry Hill, Easter, 1989*, ed. Christopher Harper-Bill (Woodbridge, Suffolk: Boydell, 1991), 1–32.

67. Compare, for example, the statutes of William Wykeham in his foundation of Winchester College, discussed below, to those of the college founded by Katherine de Berkeley in Wotton-Under-Edge (printed in *A Calendar of the Register of Henry Wakefield, Bishop of Worcester, 1375–95*, ed. W. P. Marett, Worcestershire Historical Society, n.s., 7 [Leeds: Maney, 1972], 85). In the latter, the patron reserved the right to appoint the priest and scholars under the rule of the Bishop of Worcester while she lived, after which point the right would pass to Thomas de Berkeley and his heirs, unless he died without issue, in which case the right would

pass to John de Berkeley (and so on). The modes of affiliation found in the Berkeley college most closely resemble the right of the precentor to admit boys to the choir in secular cathedrals.

68. Given that many of the details in the statutes of newly founded institutions were the work of more than one individual and that lay founders were no doubt advised by clerics with experience in such matters, my attribution of motives to "the founder" is meant largely as an interpretive expedient (a "founder-function," on the model of Foucault's "author-function," if you will) that presumes (a) that founders were not completely oblivious to the details of their foundations; and (b) that, at any rate, the desires expressed in the statutes are, for the purposes of this study, more important than the person(s) from which they emanate.

69. There is an earlier continental tradition producing pedagogical treatises in music—including Guido of Arezzo's *Micrologus* (c. 1026)—that professed as their enabling conceit the need to provide a systematic method of transmitting chant to boys. Guido, for example, claims that his method enabled boys (*pueros*) to sing "at first sight chants they had not seen or heard"—"invisos et inauditos cantus ita primo intuitu indubitanter cantabant" (*Hucbald, Guido, and John on Music: Three Medieval Treatises,* trans. Warren Babb, ed. Claude V. Palisca [New Haven, Conn.: Yale University Press, 1978], 58; *Guidonis Aretini Micrologus,* ed. Jos. Smits van Waesberghe, Corpus Scriptorum de Musica, vol. 4 [(Rome): American Institute of Musicology, 1955], 85). His methods, however, were not solely intended for boys (whose literacy, as with their older counterparts, is presumed). The tradition responds more to intellectual concerns rather than the pragmatic concerns at issue here. For some of the material and ideological consequences of this intellectual tradition, see Holsinger, *Music,* 259–92.

70. *Reg. ant.,* 2:102–3.

71. Ibid., 2:137–38; Gravesend's ordinances are discussed in Edwards, *English Secular Cathedrals,* 211–12.

72. The grant appears in *The Register of Walter Bronescombe, Bishop of Exeter, 1257–1280, ed.* F. C. Hingeston-Randolph (London, 1889), 77–78. See Nicholas Orme, "Education and Learning at a Medieval English Cathedral: Exeter, 1380–1548," *Journal of Ecclesiastical History* 52 (1981): 265–83 (repr. in Orme, *Education and Society*).

73. "Statuimus et ordinavimus statuendo ut in domibus infra clausum ecclesie nostre Sar' ad hoc secundum ordinacionem piam predecessoris nostri predicti constructi omnes pueri choriste ecclesie nostre predicte una cum magistro suo viro honesto et in gramatica bene fundato qui eos litteris et moribus valeant perpetuis temporibus simul vivant in communi sub custodia perpetua" (*Registrum Rogeri Marivital,* ed. C. Y. Erlington, Canterbury and York Society 58 [London: Canterbury and York Society, 1972], 413–14).

74. When discussing proper behavior and attire in the choir, it is stated that if one of the fellows goes through the ambit in secular attire, he thereby will lose that attire to either the proctor or the boys of the college (T. C. Peter, *History of Glasney Collegiate Church, Cornwall* [Camborne, Cornwall: Camborne Printing, 1903], 42–43).

75. William Dugdale, *Monasticon Anglicanum, Enriched with a Large Accession of Materials,* ed. J. Caley (London, 1817–30), vol. 6, pt. 3, 1330; see David Knowles and R. Neville Hadcock, *Medieval Religious Houses* (New York: St. Martin's, 1971), 442; and *The Victoria History of the Counties of England: Berkshire,* ed. P. H. Ditchfield and William Page (London: Constable, 1906–27), 2:103–6.

76. Dugdale, *Monasticon Anglicanum,* vol. 6, pt. 3, 1339.

77. A few of the earliest examples include the colleges at Tormarton (1344), Ottery St. Mary (1339), and St. Mary in the Newarke, Leicester (1355) (*A Calendar of the Register of Wolstan de Bransford, Bishop of Worcester, 1339–49,* ed. R. M. Haines, Worcestershire Historical Society, n.s., 4 [London: H.M.S.O., 1966], 84–86; John Neale Dalton, ed., *The Collegiate Church of Ottery St. Mary* [Cambridge: Cambridge University, Press, 1917], 93; A. H. Thompson, "Notes on Colleges of Secular Canons in England [Appendix: The Statutes of the New Collegiate Church of St. Mary, Leicester, 1355–6 and 1490–1]," *Archaeological Journal* 74 [1917]: 203; Thompson, *The History of the Hospital and the New College of the Annunciation of St. Mary in the Newarke, Leicester* [Leicester: Leicester Archeology Society/Backus, 1937], 45).

78. *Register of John Grandisson, Bishop of Exeter, 1327–1369,* ed. F. C. Hingeston-Randolph (London: Bell; Exeter: Eland, 1894–99), 2:1154.

79. Knowles and Hadcock, *Medieval Religious Houses,* 442.

80. The statutes, promulgated in 1422, are printed in Dugdale, *Monasticon Anglicanum,* vol. 6, pt. 3, 1418–19, from which all passages have been quoted.

81. Most commonly the collocation takes the form of *litteras et mores* (as in the provisions for the Salisbury choristers, quoted above, n73). For more on "in letters and in manners" at early continental cathedral schools, see C. Stephen Jaeger, *The Envy of Angels: Cathedral Schools and Social Ideas in Medieval Europe, 950–1200* (Philadelphia: University of Pennsylvania Press, 1993), esp. 2–17.

82. "Sintque praedicti vicarii et clerici in plano cantu et discantu sufficienter instructi ad voluntatem decani. Etiam caeteri ministri dicti collegii, ad continuam et personalem residentiam sit vinculo juramenti instructi."

83. For both original and revised statutes, see A. H. Thompson, *The English Clergy and Their Organization in the Later Middle Ages* (Oxford: Clarendon, 1947), 256, 267; see also Thompson's discussion in *Song-Schools in the Middle Ages,* Church-Music Society Occasional Papers 14 (London: Society for Promoting Christian Knowledge and Humphrey Milford, 1942), 22–23; and Moran Cruz, *Growth of English Schooling,* 271.

84. "in diebus cum vacare poterit parvulos parochie illius qui addiscere litteras voluerint in hiis instruat et informet" (Thompson, *English Clergy,* 267).

85. The text of the statutes can be found in *Documents Relating to the University and Colleges of Cambridge* (London, 1852), 2:121–46.

86. Rubric 29 of the Winchester College Statutes, as printed in T. F. Kirby, ed., *Annals of Winchester College from Its Foundation in the Year 1382 to the Present Time* (London, 1892), 502. All further citations will refer to this edition.

87. Rubric 8 (481–82). Choristers were fed primarily from the table scraps of the fellows and scholars; they prepared the priests' beds, and helped serve at meals.

88. The foundation is described in Leach's article on schools in *The Victoria History of the Counties of England: Lincolnshire*, 2:427–28. I was able to confirm some of the details through reference to Roger Bowers, "Musicians of Lincoln Minster, 1090–1642" (typescript, n.d.), which he generously allowed me to read.

89. Each chorister was required to be a boy lacking means, at least eight years old, "qui adminus sciat suum Donatum et probabiliter sciat cantare" (quoted in *The Victoria History of the Counties of England: Lincolnshire*, 2:427).

90. The original statutes (1393) can be found in *Literae Cantuarienses: The Letter Books of the Monastery of Christ Church, Canterbury*, ed. J. Brigstocke Sheppard, Rolls Series 85 (London, 1887–89), 3:15–21, from which all quotations have been taken. The revised statutes (1398) are in Dugdale, *Monasticon Anglicanum*, vol. 6, pt. 3, 1391–93. See Orme's discussion in *English Schools*, 183–84.

91. The statutes state that there should be two scholars, "uterque eorum cum competenter legere et cantare sciverit, et non ante, nominetur et praeficiatur per Magistrem et Scolarem dicti colegii in Socium et Scolarem cantarie sive colegii praedicti" (17).

92. "Cum bene legere, cantare, et construere, ac viginti quatuor versus uno die de una materia componere, sciverit, cum licencia dicti Capellani, permittimus eundem Scolarem in dicta ecclesia divina celebrare" (19).

93. "Et capellani seculares et pueri chori simul conveniant ad ecclesiam ad horas decantandas, et ingrediantur ad ostium versus porticum beatae Virginis, quod statim post ingressum et egressum eorundem claudantur" (Dugdale, *Monasticon Anglicanum*, vol. 6, pt. 1, 607). Though the actual documents still need to be verified, the patterns of references to boys at St. Leonard's seem to emphasize their status as choristers more in the fourteenth century than previously. The list of personnel from 1280 (see discussion above) refers to "14 boys wearing habits and five others" in the grammar school. The wearing of "habits" probably signals a choral function, but it is not emphasized. In 1299 we hear of "13 scholars and various other boys," which suggests a stable group of thirteen boys who probably functioned as choristers along with others who did not. In 1365/6, however, thirty choristers are mentioned, more than a choir is likely to have maintained. It is possible that in this categorization of the personnel, the additional "choristers" are boys from the orphanage maintained by the hospital who attended services, for in 1395 we are once again told of twelve choristers. All of these accounts of the personnel, however, come from the many inquisitions that arose in St. Leonard's somewhat shady administrative history (see the account in *The Victoria History of the Counties of England: Yorkshire*, ed. William Page [London: Constable, 1907–13], 3:336–44, for details) and are each likely to be informed by the institutional interests of the inquisitors.

94. The evidence comes from an inquisition carried out by William Wykeham in 1372, in which witnesses claimed that "consueuerunt esse in hospitali predicto septem pauperes pueri litterati qui … vocabantur choriste et solebant interesse et ministrare omnibus diuinis officijs ac horis canonicis in ecclesia hospitalis predicti et illis expletis solebant scolas exercere in dicto hospitali" (Oxford, New College Archives MS 3691, f. 23v). See Chapter 2, pp. 50–56.

95. *Calendar of Patent Rolls 1441–6*, 110–1; F. W. Weaver, ed., *Somerset Medieval Wills, 1383–1500*, Somerset Record Society 16, 19, 21 (London, 1901–5), 2:204. The original endowment provided for several chaplains and six scholars supported by the hospital who were to assist the chaplains in the daily office. Bowers ("Choral Institutions," 5009–10) notes that Thomas Bekynton, who had been master of the hospital from 1440 to 1446, left money in his will of 1464 to the chaplains, *clerks*, and *choristers* of the hospital and has speculated that the hospital had acquired the clerks in order to complement a chapel staff that contained six scholars who already functioned as choristers, and that Bekynton, who secured several rights for the college, was the most likely agent of this putative refoundation (see, for example, *CPR 1441–6*, 110–11, in which he secures additional income and privileges for the staff as originally stipulated in 1442).

96. "Ordinamus quod in dicta ecclesia sint sex pueri choriste ponendi ... qui eciam in capis nigris et superpeliciis in ecclesia incedant antedicta et ministrent in eadem iuxta modum choristarum ecclesie Sarisberiensis." Thompson, "Notes," 213. See also Bowers, "Choral Institutions," 3004–7. The statutes are clearly based on those of Salisbury Cathedral, with the duties of the succentor assigned to the sacrist.

97. This does not mean that there were no singers at court before this date but that at this point the word *capella* clearly refers to a body of resident singers, defining a new institutional identity. The term *capella* at first referred to the effects of the chapel such as vestments and relics and therefore underwent a semantic change similar to that of the *scola* in which its "institutionality" is transferred—in this case, from its material instruments to its personnel. See Ian Bent, "The English Chapel Royal Before 1300," *Proceedings of the Royal Musical Association* 90 (1963/64): 77–95.

98. Ian Bent quotes a document in which Edward, the Black Prince, sent a messenger to Windsor "to procure five boys from there for service [*pro capella ... deserviendi*] in the Prince's *capella*, at court in Warnborough [Hants], at the feast of Christmas" ("The Early History of the English Chapel Royal, ca. 1066–1327" [Ph.D. diss., St. John's College, Cambridge, 1968], 230). This evidence only implies the presence of such boys to loan to the prince, but clear (and aggressive) recruitments of boys (usually from outside the household) are documented for later dates. See Andrew Wathey, *Music in the Royal and Noble Households in Late Medieval England: Studies of Sources and Patronage* (London and New York: Garland, 1989), 140–41, 286–87.

99. The boys of Bury's chapel appear on an account roll of Durham Cathedral Priory. See Bowers, "Choral Institutions," 2061. Although no systematic search has been done, Bowers has found evidence that the following ecclesiastical magnates maintained chapels that included boys (I give the date of the evidence here, which is frequently the date of a will): Ralph Shrewsbury, Bishop of Bath and Wells, 1363 (2061); Thomas Arundel, while Bishop of Ely, 1381–84; William Wykeham, 1388; Richard Young, Bishop of Rochester, 1418; Henry Bowet, Archibishop of York, 1423; John Fordham, Bishop of Ely, 1425; and John Wakerying, Bishop of Norwich, 1425 (4036). Frank Ll. Harrison has also noted William Courtenay, Archbishop of Canterbury (*Music in Medieval Britain*, 2nd ed. [London: Routledge,

1968], 25). My own casual and unsystematic search has yielded evidence for John Waltham, Bishop of Salisbury, 1395 (*The Register of John Waltham, Bishop of Salisbury, 1388–1395*, ed. T. C. B. Timmons, Canterbury and York Society 80 [Suffolk: Canterbury and York Society, 1994], 215); Richard Mitford, Bishop of Salisbury, 1406/7 (C. M. Woolgar, ed., *Household Accounts from Medieval England* [Oxford: Oxford University Press, 1992–3], 1:261–429); and Edmond Stafford, Bishop of Exeter, 1413/4 (*The Register of Edmond Stafford, Bishop of Exeter, 1395–1419*, ed. F. C. Hingeston-Randolph [London and Exeter, 1886], 405, 421).

100. For Ogard's chapel, see Bowers, "Choral Institutions," 5031–32. Again, there has been no systematic search for these chapels, but Bowers has found evidence of chapels that included boys in several royal and noble households: Edward Woodstock, Prince of Wales, 1355; Richard of Bordeaux, 1376; John of Gaunt, 1376 (3030); John Holland, Earl of Huntingdon, 1401; Thomas, Duke of Clarence, 1418 (4033–34); and Ralph Baron Cromwell, 1453/4 (5031–32). Wathey also mentions Thomas, Duke of Exeter (*Music in the Royal and Noble Households,* 52n7). There is, of course, evidence of many other household chapels in which there is no mention of boys.

101. "uno alphabeto pro paruo Thomelino addiscendo" (*The Household Book of Queen Isabella of England for the 5th Regnal Year of Edward II*, ed. F. D. Blackley and G. Hermansen [Edmonton: University of Alberta Press, 1971], 120–21).

102. Bowers, "Choral Institutions," 4035; Orme, *English Schools*, 39, 322; Margaret Aston, *Thomas Arundel: A Study of Church Life in the Reign of Richard II* (Oxford: Oxford University Press, 1967), 247, 411.

103. See Brian Trowell, "Music Under the Late Plantagenets" (Ph.D. diss., Cambridge University, 1960), 226–27; Wathey, *Music in the Royal and Noble Households*, 73–74.

104. The relationship of the children of the chapel to King's Hall has been examined by Alan B. Cobban, *The King's Hall Within the University of Cambridge in the Later Middle Ages* (Cambridge: Cambridge University Press, 1969), and more recently by Wathey, who has given some indication of the fortunes of these children: of the twenty-four names of boys that survive during the reign of Richard II, eighteen went to King's Hall; of these, two died and seven came back to the chapel (*Music in the Royal and Noble Households*, 87–88). Wathey has also paid close attention to the documentary vocabulary used to denote boys of the chapel and has suggested that the "decline" in scholars sent to King's Hall in the second half of the fifteenth century may in fact signify a change in the relationship between the chapel staff and the scholars.

105. Wathey, *Music in the Royal and Noble Households*, 88–89; Cobban, *The King's Hall*, 60n2.

106. Almonries schools are discussed in Orme, *English Schools*, 243–45. Roger Bowers is currently engaged in a much-needed study of these institutions.

107. Bowers, "Choral Institutions," 4086; Orme, *English Schools*, 242. At St. Albans statutes were drawn up to regulate the almonry boys' activities (in H. T. Riley, ed., *Registra Quorundam Abbatum Monasterii S. Albani, Qui Sæculo XVmo. Floruere*, Rolls Series 28, pt. 6 [London, 1872–73], 2:305–15).

108. See Roger Bowers, "The Musicians of the Lady Chapel of Winchester Cathedral Priory, 1402–1539," *Journal of Ecclesiastical History* 45 (1994): 215–16; repr. in Bowers, *English Church Polyphony: Singers and Sources from the 14th to the 17th Century* (Aldershot: Ashgate, 1999); and Orme, *English Schools*, 245, for the boys' duty maintaining altars. A mid-thirteenth-century customary from Norwich, however, does contain a few references to *pueri* in the celebration of their services on special occasions such as Palm Sunday and the Feast of All Saints (*The Customary of the Cathedral Priory Church of Norwich*, ed. J. B. L. Tolhurst, Henry Bradshaw Society 82 [London: Henry Bradshaw Society, 1948], 76, 135, 187).

109. On the English preoccupation with the Lady Mass and on Lady Chapel choirs in general (including those that did not maintain boys), see F. Ll. Harrison, *Music in Medieval Britain*, 40–45, 185–94; and Bowers, "Choral Institutions," 4075–4100, 5032–36, 6034.

110. Bowers, "Choral Institutions," also describes boys' choirs in Durham, 1414, (4094–97); Abingdon; 1420, Glastonbury, 1420 (4098); Bridlington Priory, 1447; Peterborough Abbey, 1448; and Christchurch Canterbury, 1439 (5032–45). There are later foundations, since the trend lasted until the Reformation.

111. Moran Cruz's description of the type of language used in wills provides useful examples of these kinds of bequests (*Growth of English Schooling*, 94–95, 227–36).

112. Orme, *Education in the West of England*, 10; Bowers, "The Performing Ensemble for English Church Polyphony, c. 1320–c.1390," in *Studies in the Performance of Late Mediaeval Music*, ed. Stanley Boorman (Cambridge: Cambridge University Press, 1983), 161–92; repr. in Bowers, *English Church Polyphony*.

113. Langley, of course, also served as chancellor but was not holding the position in 1414. My account of the schools of Durham follows those provided by Leach in *The Victoria History of the Counties of England: Durham*, ed. William Page (London: Constable, 1905–28), 1:371–75 and Bowers, "Choral Institutions," 4094–97. Brian Crosby shows that there had been an almonry school in Durham from 1338. See his *Durham Cathedral Choristers and Their Masters* (Durham: Dean and Chapter of Durham, 1980), 4–12, where Crosby gives the subsequent, complicated history of the Durham song school after its foundation.

114. "Capellani in cantaria predicta intitulandi sint, unus in grammatica, alter in cantu, ita sufficienter provecti et instructi, quod unus eorum scolas in grammatica, alter in cantu, in civitate dunelmie sciat regere, juvenesque et alios indoctos in huiusmodi scienciis sufficienter instruere et proinde informare" (quoted by Leach, *The Victoria History of the Counties of England: Durham*, 1:371).

115. It is worth noting that one of the few sources that refer to town "song schools" as distinct "reading schools" before 1450 also comes from Durham Cathedral (London, British Library, MS Cotton Faustina A.vi, fols. 81, 84v, 97v, 108v, 109v; discussed in Moran Cruz, *Growth of English Schooling*, 55, 56, 256, 264; Leach, *Early Yorkshire Schools*, 2:60–74, 84–87). See note 133 below.

116. Orme, *English Schools*, 60.

117. Moran Cruz, *Growth of English Schooling*, 53–62, 39–49.

118. I stress "late medieval practice" because Giles Constable, in a personal communication, pointed out to me that memorization was not valued in this way in

earlier periods. This late medieval ideology of song is discussed more fully in Chapter 2. It is worth noting here, however, that the grammatical understanding of *lectio* also had "musical" associations, particularly since classical *lectio* pertained to poetic verse. Irvine quotes Diomedes' discussion of *accentus*, the first part of *lectio*, in which he provides an etymology: "It is termed 'accent' from *accinendo* (singing), because it is like a certain singing of each syllable" (*Making of Textual Culture*, 70).

119. Thompson, *English Clergy*, 256.

120. New College Statutes, Rubric 1. The text is from *Statutes of the Colleges of Oxford, with Royal Patents of Foundation, Injunctions of Visitors* (Oxford, 1853).

121. *Reg. Grandisson*, 2:828. This kind of competence in reading and singing was explicitly required of adult priests well into the fifteenth century, as in the similarly worded requirement of the chapel staff in the 1443 statutes of King's College, Cambridge, where priests and clerks of the chapel are required to be "in cantu et lectura ... sufficienter instructi" (Heywood and Wright, *Ancient Laws for King's College*, Rubric 1, p. 20).

122. "in lectura et cantu et aliis sufficenter instructi secundum ipsorum gradum ad statuum exigenciam." From "The Statutes of the College of St. Mary and All Saints, Fotheringhay," ed. A. H. Thompson, *Archaeological Journal* 75 (1918): 272–73.

123. "Item, statuimus quod nullus uicarius aut secundarius recipiatur, uel aliquid in ecclesia percipiat, nisi secum portet habitum chori bonum et honestum, et bene sciat legere, et cantare Tonaleque cum differencijs, et Uenitarium; de quibus primo et principaliter in eorum recepcione examinentur. ¶ Idem fiat, quo ad habitum, et legere uel cantare competenter, quo ad pueros recipiendos" (Dalton, *Collegiate Church of Ottery St. Mary*, 134). The secondaries (young men at least eighteen years old) were required to have "scienciam legendi et cantandi" in the following statute. The Tonary and Invitatorium are described in more detail in Andrew Hughes, *Medieval Manuscripts for Mass and Office: A Guide to Their Organization and Terminology* (Toronto: University of Toronto Press, 1982), 112–17.

124. Leach, *Educational Charters*, 234; my translation is based on Leach's (235).

125. See Orme, *Medieval Children*, 242–72, for the fullest account of early reading pedagogy.

126. These minor orders are discussed in William Durandus, *Rationale divinorum officiorum*, ed. A. Davril and T. M. Thibodeau, 3 vols., Corpus Christianorum Continuatio Mediaevalis 140–140B (Turnhout: Brepols, 1995), II.3.1–30, II.5.1–35 (140:148–51). All further citations will refer to this edition.

127. Full terms of the scholarships, which Grandisson carried out on the initiative of his predecessor, Walter Stapledon, are in *Reg. Grandisson*, 2:666–69.

128. Irvine, *Making of Textual Culture*, 70; Alcuin's redefinition of *lectio* as a skill for non-native speakers is discussed on pp. 328–30.

129. Clanchy, *From Memory*, 226–30. See also A. Grundmann, "*Litteratus–illitteratus:* Der Wandel einer Bildungsnorm vom Altertum zum Mittelalter," *Archiv für Kulturgeschichte* 40 (1958): 1–65.

130. Paradoxically, only the grammar scholars are required to be free of bodily defects or anything else that would disqualify them from the priesthood (Kirby,

Annals of Winchester College, 457–58, Rubric 2). The choristers, who were actually performing clerical duties, had no such requirement (Rubric 3).

131. *The Victoria History of the Counties of England: Northamptonshire*, ed. W. Ryland D. Adkins and R. M. Serjeantson (Westminster: Constable, 1902–37), 2:280; *Wykeham's Register*, ed. T. F. Kirby, Hampshire Record Society 12 (London and Winchester, 1896–69), 2:285–89; G. O. Sayles, ed., *Select Cases in the Court of King's Bench*, Selden Society 55, 57, 58, 74, 76, 82, 88 (London: Quaritch, 1936–71), 6:142–43. Evidence of the case of Kingston-on-Thames appears in a dispute over the endowment and duties of the vicar in which it is stated that he is required "scolas quoque puerorum literarum, cantus, et aliorum usque Donatum inclusive tenere seu aliis concedere." Though the document refers to *literarum* rather than *lectura*, *literarum* does fit the pattern of an implied sequence of "reading, song, and Donatus" that appears elsewhere.

132. *Literae Cantuarienses*, 2:126–27. See also the evidence of Kingston-on-Thames in note 131 above.

133. Moran Cruz has found records of "reading schools" mentioned independently of "song schools" (*Growth of English Schooling*, 56), but examples are few and, in fact, mostly come from a single document, a cartulary from Durham Cathedral (London, British Library, MS Cotton Faustina A.vi). Other evidence from before 1450 for "reading schools" in her study has been extrapolated from wills, which do not explicitly identify "schools," though they surely identify educational activity.

134. On the history of Books of Hours, see Roger S. Wieck, "The Book of Hours," in *The Liturgy of the Medieval Church*, ed. Thomas J. Heffernan and E. Ann Matter (Kalamazoo, Mich.: Medieval Institute, 2001), 473–513; and Wieck, *Time Sanctified: The Book of Hours* (New York: Braziller, 1988). On their use as school texts and the possible distinction between Books of Hours and primers, see Orme, *Medieval Children*, 89. The devotional use of such books is discussed more fully in Chapter 4.

135. For examples of "psalter (reading) and song," see evidence from Canterbury St. Martin's, 1321 (*Leach, Educational Charters*, 260–67); and Penrith, 1361 (J. Nicholson and R. Burn, *History and Antiquities of Westmorland and Cumberland* [London, 1777], 2:410–11). For "singing the psalms and reading," see Richard Rolle, The *"Incendium amoris" of Richard Rolle of Hampole*, ed. Margaret Deanesly (Manchester: Manchester University Press, 1915), 189–90.

136. A provision is made in the statutes that choristers may present themselves for examination in "lectura plano cantu et antiquo donato" for admission up to their twelfth year (Kirby, *Annals of Wincester College*, 462, Rubric 3).

137. In an undated document in the Winchester College Archives, the Warden, Fellows, and Scholars of Winchester College ask Wykeham to reimburse them for expenses for "choristarum domini ... de capella sua," among other expenses (Winchester, Winchester College Archives, Doc. 70a).

138. As shown in some accounts from 1400 (A. F. Leach, *History of Winchester College* [New York, 1899], 189–92).

139. John Tyes was indentured in 1402 to teach song to no more than four boys (Winchester Cathedral Dean and Chapter, Priory Reg. I, fols. 15v–16r).

A full account of the Lady Chapel choir can be found in Bowers, "The Musicians of the Lady Chapel."

140. Winchester Cathedral Dean and Chapter, Priory Reg. I, fols. 18v–19r.

141. Oxford, New College Archives, MS 3691, f. 22v.

142. Collocation is often studied in terms of oral "formulae"—as a mode of linguistic constraint rather than creativity (though such constraints are ultimately creative; see Alfred Bates Lord's discussion of the "formula" in *The Singer of Tales*, ed. Stephen Mitchell and Gregory Nagy, 2nd ed. [Cambridge, Mass.: Harvard University Press, 2000], 30–45). My usage is much looser and closer to that used by lexicologists who study all occurrences of words that tend to appear together (see, for example, Dirk Siepmann, "Collocation, Colligation and Encoding Dictionaries, Part I: Lexical Aspects," *International Journal of Lexicology* 18 [2005]: 409–43). For a recent study of Old English poetry that examines the creative stylistic potential of this broader survey of "collocation," see Elizabeth M. Tyler, *Old English Poetics: The Aesthetics of the Familiar in Anglo-Saxon England* (York: York Medieval Press, 2006), 38–100.

Chapter 2

1. See J. Goody and I. Watt, "The Consequences of Literacy," *Comparative Studies in Society and History* 5 (1962–63): 304–45 (repr. in *Literacy in Traditional Societies*, ed. J. Goody [Cambridge: Cambridge University Press, 1968], 27–68); Ong, *The Presence of the Word*, 52; Ong, *Orality*, 104–5; Pierre Bourdieu, *Outline of a Theory of Practice*, trans. Richard Nice (Cambridge: Cambridge University Press, 1977), 186–87.

2. This construction of literacy has much in common with Paolo Freire's "banking concept" of education, which similarly presumes knowledge and education to be fully objectified such that "Education becomes an act of depositing, in which the students are the depositories and the teacher is the depositor" (*Pedagogy of the Oppressed*, trans. Myra Bergman Ramos [New York: Continuum, 1993], 72). Humanist histories of education generally offer narratives of decreasing elitism and increasing "access" to that objectified knowledge, while Freire points out that defining knowledge as an object also allows the witholding or expropriation of that object.

3. Bourdieu, *Outline*, 187.

4. Stock, *Implications of Literacy*, 6–8.

5. See Chapter 1, pp. 30–31.

6. For further discussion of the relations of power enacted by ritual reading, see Zieman, "Playing *Doctor*," 309–13.

7. "Psalmus dissidentes copulat, discordes sociat, offensos reconciliat; quis enim non remittat ei, cum quo unam ad deum vocem emiserit?" Quoted and translated by Holsinger, *Music*, 259n1.

8. For an analysis and critique of music as embodied practice in the Middle Ages, see Holsinger, *Music*, 4–17 passim.

9. The "*cursus* of psalms" involved the distribution of the entire Psalter among the psalms sung in the Office on ferias, or non-feast days, over the course

of a week. For the actual distribution in monastic and secular rites, see Roger E. Reynold's entry, "Divine Office," in *The Dictionary of the Middle Ages*, ed. Joseph R. Strayer (New York: Scribner, 1982–89). On the arrangment of psalters in general and ferial psalters in particular, see Hughes, *Medieval Manuscripts*, 224–37.

10. The "David cycle" of illuminations appears to have its origin in thirteenth-century France; see Adelaide Bennett, "The Transformation of the Gothic Psalter in Thirteenth-Century France," in *The Illuminated Psalter: Studies in the Content, Purpose and Placement of Its Images*, ed. F. O. Büttner (Turnhout: Brepols, 2004), 211–21. The characteristic illuminations are described at length in Karl-Georg Pfändtner, *Die Psalterillustration des 13. und beginnenden 14. Jahrhunderts in Bologna* (Neuried: Ars Una, 1996), 39–49, and more generally in J. J. Tikkannen, *Psalterillustration im Mittelalter* (Helsingfors, 1895–1900; repr. Soest: Davaco, 1975). For tables listing the subjects of illuminations in fourteenth-century English psalters in particular (where the David cycle is clearly dominant), see Lucy Freeman Sandler, *The Peterborough Psalter in Brussels & Other Fenland Manuscripts* (London: Miller, 1974), 98–99 (for English psalters, c. 1300–1340), and Kathleen L. Scott, *Later Gothic Manuscripts, 1390–1490* (London: Miller, 1996), 2:378–79.

11. For an alternative tradition concerning the "new song," see Holsinger, *Music*, 32–46. As it is for Holsinger, the embodied nature of song is important to my understanding of its ideological implications. My account, however, focuses on sociopolitical relations between bodies more than the relation of body to subject. Disembodiment, in my terms, is more a function of institutionalization than any rejection of the body or flesh.

12. Oxford, Bodleian Library, MS Rawlinson G. 185, dated 1350–80. The other initials in this mansuscript are not all representative of those found in the David cycle (which might in part explain its more emphatic portrayal of the "old song"). Psalm 80, for example, depicts the music-making of Christian clerics rather than David (f. 68v).

13. On the Judenhut, see Ruth Mellinkoff, *The Horned Moses in Medieval Art and Thought*, California Studies in the History of Art 14 (Berkeley: University of California Press, 1970).

14. This notion of spiritually informed psalmody was reinforced in practice by the singing of the *Gloria patri* at the end of every psalm.

15. In the traditional examples cited above, the salvation narrative implicit in this progression is then completed, as it were, by Psalm 109—"Dixit Dominus Domino meo sede a dextris meis" ("The Lord said unto my Lord, Sit thou at my right hand")—whose initial usually depicts the Trinity. A few psalters provide a similar, though less disparaging, juxtaposition of the old and new songs by showing David looking at the singing Christian clerics of Psalm 97 (London, Lambeth Palace Library, MS 3285, f. 132 [first half of the fifteenth century], Bod. MS Douce 18, f. 151 [c. 1433]).

16. Irvine, *Making of Textual Culture*, 21.

17. On the use of prayer books, see Duffy, *Stripping of the Altars*, 117–23, and Chapter 4, pp. 129–41.

18. For a discussion of the equation of the two terms, see Clanchy, *From Memory*, 226–30.

19. Leona Gabel, *Benefit of Clergy in England in the Later Middle Ages*, Smith College Studies in History 14 (1929; repr. New York: Octagon, 1969), 63. Although Clanchy quotes more generalized uses of *clericus* from the same period, these pertain to "common parlance" (*From Memory*, 228), whereas Gabel's attention is on the legal eligibility to claim benefit of clergy.

20. Clanchy, *From Memory*, 234.

21. Several of these documents, along with other official instruments of the dispute, also survive in Wykeham's official episcopal register (*Wykeham's Reg.*, 2:28–57).

22. Richard Kaeuper, "Two Early Lists of Literates," *English Historical Review* 99 (1984): 363–69.

23. The history of St. Cross is detailed in *The Victoria History of the Counties of England: Hampshire*, ed. H. A. Doubleday and William Page (Westminster: Constable, 1900–14), 2:193–97, from which I have drawn much of my account.

24. *Clementinarum* III.11.2, in Emil Friedberg, ed., *Corpus iuris canonici* (Leipzig, 1879), 2:1170–71.

25. "Domus ipsa sancte Crucis extra omne naturam et usum zenadochiorum, leprosariorum, et hospitalium, precipue cum eadem domus sancte Crucis principaliter fundata erat et est ad honorem cultus diuini, prout ibidem pro iudicia notaria apparet manifeste. Ipsaque domus sancte Crucis debitis temporibus visitacioni tanquam beneficium perpetuum et non curatum subiacere antiquitus consueuit" (f. 58v).

26. *Wykeham's Reg.*, 1:15–16, 30. The fact that Wykeham approved of these exchanges only lent credence to Cloune's position.

27. Thompson, *History*, 41–42.

28. *The Victoria History of the Counties of England: Yorkshire*, 3:336–44.

29. For the general practice, see Nicholas Orme and Margot Webster, *The English Hospital: 1070–1570* (New Haven, Conn.: Yale University Press, 1995), 64–66. Of course any claims concerning terminological practice can never be fully supported, yet there is a surprisingly strong correlation in surviving documents, where *pauperes clerici* appear in records of St. John's Hospital, Ripon (1341), Holy Trinity Hospital, Fossgate, York (1373), and St. John's Hospital, Exeter (1418) (J. T. Fowler, ed., *Memorials of the Church of SS Peter and Wilfrid, Ripon*, Surtees Society 74, 78, 81, 115 [Durham, 1882], 1:217; Dugdale, *Monasticon Anglicanum*, 6:737; *The Register of Henry Chichele, Archbishop of Canterbury, 1414–1443*, ed. E. F. Jacob, Canterbury and York Society 42, 45–47 [Oxford: Clarendon, 1938–43], 2:156).

30. "Solebant recipi in hospitali predicto per custodem eiusdem vel eius locumtenentem cotidie tresdecim pauperiores scolares scole gramaticalium, ibidem misse per magistrem summe scole gramaticalium Ciuitatis Wyntoniensis" (f. 23r).

31. "Consueuerunt esse in hospitali predicto septem pauperes pueri litterati, qui vixerunt de elimosina aule custodis dicte domus vel eius locumtenentis, et vltra . . . quilibet illorum percipere solebat vnum panem de pastu et pondere panis familie sicut vnus tresdecim clericorum supradictorum percipere consueuit et seruisiam carnes et pisces de fragmento mensarum tocius aule ad sufficienciam victus dictorum pauperum puerorum, qui quidem septem pauperes pueri litterati predicti vocabantur choriste et solebant interesse et ministrare omnibus diuinis officijs ac

horis canonicis in ecclesia hospitalis predicti et illis expletis solebant scolas exercere in dicto hospitali" (f. 23r and passim).

32. Richard de Upton, Wykeham's proxy, is quoted as claiming that the hospital was intended for "pauperibus debilibus et imbecillibus *scolaribus* clericis et presbyteris" (f. 13v). The thirteen clerks who performed divine service are referred to in one person's testimony as "seculares pauperes clericos scolares" (f. 36r). "Seculares," generally abbreviated "sclares," was, of course, easy to confuse with "scolares," but the many categories of *clerici* encouraged such confusion.

33. This list has been published and discussed in Kaeuper, "Two Early Lists," 369. To his list should be added "Adam Jacob, *clericus*, born near the gate of St. Cross," aged eighty (f. 29r, listed later as "Adam Jacob, *litteratus*"). Kaeuper mentions one other such list from 1334, and Clanchy has described a similar categorization of witnesses in secular proceedings in 1297 (*From Memory*, 224–26).

34. Oxford, New College Archives, MS 3691, fols. 26v, 30v, 35v, 47v. The one priest, Walter Edyndon, had served in the hospital as a clerk, then as a priest and sacrist. He was also the uncle of one of the defendants and therefore had close connections to the case.

35. E.g., Richard Winchester, Lord of Otterbourne, *litteratus*, said that "audiuit multociens loqui et referri de cartis fundacionis dicti hospitalis ... set illas nunquam vidit" (f. 34v).

36. Gabel, *Benefit of Clergy*, 77.

37. Clanchy, *From Memory*, 232–34.

38. Gabel, *Benefit of Clergy*, 77–78; Clanchy, *From Memory*, 234.

39. For one example of derision toward the "neck verse," see Chapter 5, pp. 173–74, 178–79.

40. Gabel, *Benefit of Clergy*, 73, provides an actual example much like this.

41. Ibid., 77–78.

42. Ibid., 63–64.

43. London, Public Record Office, JUST 3/145, m. 54d. Discussed in Gabel, *Benefit of Clergy*, 73. This particular case shows that sometimes the secular judge participated in the decision, since it was he who challenged the claimant, but only the ecclesiastical Ordinary had the authority to claim the defendant in the end.

44. "Examinatus fuit et ipse nesciebat legere super librum nec silabicare nisi in quibusdam locis in quibus ipse eruditus fuit et illud ... sciuit extra librum pro vsum."

45. Gabel, *Benefit of Clergy*, 72n44.

46. So much is clear from my initial investigation of the Gaol Delivery Rolls. Some examples from 1391–94 can be found in London, Public Record Office, JUST 3/176, mm. 2, 11d, 18; JUST 3/178, mm. 3, 10d; and JUST 3/179, mm. 11d, 13, 19, 29d. A more thorough examination of the rolls might turn up earlier occurrences of the formula.

47. Again, this assertion awaits full confirmation, but the regularity found thus far supports the claim of a definite pattern.

48. Gabel, *Benefit of Clergy*, 77–81. Gabel does not provide the actual number of such claimants. My own brief survey corroborated her impressions, but confirmation is still pending.

49. For an examination of the musical aspects of song pedagogy, see Holsinger, *Music,* 259–92.

50. Green, *Crisis of Truth,* 47.

51. See Margaret Jennings, C.S.J., "Tutiuillus: The Literary Career of the Recording Demon" *Studies in Philology Texts and Studies* 74, no. 5 (1977).

52. "Hec sunt sillabe et dictiones syncopate et versus psalmodie, que isti clerici in hiis matutinis furati sunt Deo; hec utique ad eorum accusationem diligenter reservo." Quoted from Jacques de Vitry's *Sermones Vulgares* in Jennings, "Tutiuillus," 11.

53. Quoted by Jennings, "Tutiuillus," 15.

54. Jennings, "Tutiuillus," 18–19.

55. Thomas Walsingham, *Gesta Abbatum Monasterii Sancti Albani,* ed. Henry Thomas Riley, Rolls Series 28, pt. 1 (London, 1867), 2:396.

56. *"Piers Plowman": The C Version,* ed. George Kane and George Russell (Berkeley and London: University of California Press/Athlone, 1997), C 17.188. All further citations of the C–Text will refer to this edition and be cited parenthetically by text, Passus, and line number.

57. London, British Library, MS Lansdowne 763, f. 60. This is the famous collection of treatises, partly composed and owned by John Wylde, Precentor of Waltham Abbey (c. 1460), that eventually wound up in the hands of Thomas Tallys. Jennings mentions the Titivillus verses that appear on f. 58v and provides a close analogue from MS Lansdowne 762, f. 99. For more citations of the Titivillus verses, see Jennings, "Tutiuillus," 11–23. Verses on psalmody could appear independently of the Titivillus story, however, as in MS Royal 17 C.xvii, f. 17v (early fifteenth century).

58. See Chapter 3, pp. 92–100.

59. "Nam antea, more fabrorum qui ferrum ignitum feriunt, cantabatur Psalmodia sine requie, sine pausa; quod zelatori sanctae religionis videbatur absurdum" (Walsingham, *Gesta Abbatum,* 2:396). For the fundamental irony of this musical smithy, see Katherine Zieman, "Chaucer's *Voys,*" *Representations* 60 (1997): 70–91.

60. F. Ll. Harrison reports that thirty-eight masses were said daily at Lincoln Cathedral by 1501 (*Music in Medieval Britain,* 56n5). The conflicts that the multiplication of masses could cause will be discussed in the next chapter. Monks in priests' orders could easily be called upon to perform chantry masses in their conventual church. Such chantry masses could also be performed at the conventual churches of nunneries as was the case, for example, at Shaftesbury, where Robert Osgood and his wife, Edith, endowed a chantry in the early fifteenth century (form of ordination is dated 1415 in London, British Library, MS Egerton 3135, f. 100vff.).

61. *"Piers Plowman": The B Version,* ed. George Kane and E. Talbot Donaldson (London: Athlone, 1975), B 15.383. All further citations of the B-Text will refer to this edition and be cited parenthetically by text, Passus, and line number.

62. See Bowers, "Choral Institutions," 2022ff. for a discussion of the admission of vicars choral. See also a document published with the Salisbury Statutes, in which Roger Martival complained that unfit vicars were being admitted "sometimes by reason of partiality, at another because of inordinate affection,

and frequently because of the recompense given to existing or expected services; sometimes also because of the importunity of those who seek office—who, unmeet though they be, and bringing scandal upon the Church by the open discovery of their canvassing and by the solicitations of partialities of extern and secular persons, that show malice the moment a deaf ear is turned to them, procure their own appointment to the place, not only of deceased Vicars, but even of on occasion living ones" (*Statute et Consuetudines Ecclesiae Cathedralis Beatae Mariae Virginis Sarisburiensis*, ed. Christopher Wordsworth and Douglas Macleane [London: Clowes, 1915], 1:210–13).

63. "Quare fremuerunt gentes et populi meditati sunt inania? Adstiterunt reges terrae et principes convenerunt in unum adversus Dominum et adversus christum eius."

64. Salisbury Cathedral Dean and Chapter, Reg. Dunham, f. 43v. The entry was noted by Bowers ("Choral Institutions," 2022).

65. Though listed as two separate gestures, the curses and lapses of knowledge both occurred during matins, when responsories are sung.

66. See in particular Ralph Hanna III, "Pilate's Voice/Shirley's Case," in *Pursuing History: Middle English Manuscripts and Their Texts* (Stanford, Calif.: Stanford University Press, 1996), 267–75; and Anne Middleton, "Acts of Vagrancy: The C–Version 'Autobiography' (C 5.1–108) and the Statute of 1388," in *Written Work: Langland, Labor, Authorship*, ed. Steven Justice and Kathryn Kerby-Fulton (Philadelphia: University of Pennsylvania Press, 1997), 235–44.

67. sc., Tu *trinitatis* vnitas, hymn sung at matins from after Epiphany until Lent (*Breviarium ad Usum Insignis Ecclesiae Sarum*, ed. Francis Procter and Christopher Wordsworth [Cambridge, 1879–86], 2:149), a telling, secularizing slip, which at least shows that the scribe did not know his services either.

68. Bowers, "Musicians of Lincoln Minster."

69. The entry is dated 4 January, i.e., the day after the Octave of St. John the Apostle.

70. Salisbury Cathedral Dean and Chapter, Reg. Coman, pp. 26, 66–67.

71. Bowers, "Choral Institutions," 2016.

72. Some groups of vicars, like those of York Minster, actually did gain license for corporate status. See Frederick Harrison, *Life in a Medieval College: The Story of the Vicars-Choral of York Minster* (London: Murray, 1952), 32, 98.

Chapter 3

1. Oxford, New College Archives, MS 3691, f. 70r.

2. "mandamus quatinus cum legere et non intelligere sit necgligere, nouicijs et alius nimis sufficienter litteratis idoneus decetero deputet magister qui ipsos in primitivis sciencijs instruat diligenter" (Oxford, New College Archives, MS 3691, f. 70r).

3. Irvine, *Making of Textual Culture*, 70. Early print editions of the Salisbury Breviary contain "accentuaries" that could be consulted to determine whether a syllable was long or short. See *Brev.*, 3:(iii)–(xx).

4. *Disticha Catonis*, ed. M. Boas (Amstelodami: North–Holland, 1952), 4 (*Epistula*).

5. On these matters, see Watson, "Censorship," 840–51; Justice, *Writing and Rebellion*, 13–66 passim; Copeland, *Pedagogy*, 99–140 passim. More recent work on contested reading and heretical concerns beyond Lollardy can be found in Kerby-Fulton, *Books Under Suspicion*.

6. On vocatives as pure vocality, see Barbara Johnson, *A World of Difference* (Baltimore: Johns Hopkins University Press, 1987), 187.

7. Jacques Derrida, *Dissemination*, trans. Barbara Johnson (Chicago: University of Chicago Press, 1981), 74–75.

8. Louis Althusser, "Ideology and Ideological State Apparatuses (Notes Towards an Investigation)," in *Lenin and Philosophy and Other Essays*, trans. Ben Brewster (New York: Monthly Review Press, 1971), 170–83.

9. Ibid., 174–75.

10. See in particular ibid., 177–83.

11. Judith Butler, *Excitable Speech: A Politics of the Performative* (London: Routledge, 1997), 31.

12. See ibid., 31–35, for a discussion of the limitations of this model.

13. *Confessionum libri* XIII, ed. Lucas Verheijen, Corpus Christianorum Series Latina 27 (Turnholt: Brepols, 1981), 8:12.

14. Butler, *Excitable Speech*, 31.

15. This experience is discussed in narrative terms as "paroxysmic homology" to other human responses to the divine in Paul Ricoeur, "The Summoned Subject in the School of the Narratives of the Prophetic Vocation," in *Figuring the Sacred: Religion, Narrative, and Imagination*, trans. David Pellauer, ed. Mark I. Wallace (Minneapolis: Fortress Press, 1995), 266.

16. For discussion of these commentaries and their implications, see Zieman, "Playing *Doctor*," 309–13.

17. See Chapter 2, pp. 67–70.

18. On disenchantment, see H. Marshall Leicester's discussion, based on writings of Max Weber, in *The Disenchanted Self: Representing the Subject in "The Canterbury Tales"* (Berkeley: University of California Press, 1990), 26–27 passim.

19. For the text of the Lambeth Councils, see *Councils and Synods, with Other Documents Relating to the English Church, II (1205–1313)*, ed. F. M. Powicke and C. R. Cheney (Oxford: Clarendon, 1964), 2:900–905. See also Leonard E. Boyle, "The *Oculus Sacerdotis* and Some Other Works of William of Pagula," *Transactions of the Royal Historical Society*, 5th ser., 5 (1955): 81–104; and Rubin, *Corpus Christi*, 88ff.

20. For texts and manuscripts, see R. Raymo, "Works of Religious and Philosophical Instruction," in *Manual of Writings in Middle English, 1050–1400*, ed. J. Burke Severs and Albert E. Hartung (New Haven, Conn.: Connecticut Academy of Arts and Science, 1967–93), 7:2348–57, 2555–58.

21. *The Lay Folks' Mass Book, or the Manner of Hearing Mass*, ed. Thomas Frederick Simmons, EETS, o.s., 71 (London, 1879). All further citations will refer to this edition and be cited parenthetically by manuscript siglum and line number.

22. Simmons, *Lay Folks' Mass Book*, lxviii.

23. Watson, "Middle English Mystics," 553.

24. Watson, "Censorship," 837.

25. J. L. Austin distinguishes illocutionary acts that perform an action *in* the saying, for example, "In promising her, I gave my word," and perlocutionary acts that bring about a certain consequence as an effect of saying, for example, "By promising, I placated her" (*How to Do Things with Words*, 2nd ed., ed. J. O. Urmson and Marina Sbisà [Cambridge, Mass.: Harvard University Press, 1975], 101–8). While there are some parts of the Mass that would arguably qualify as illocutions because of the specific actions they perform (*Hoc est corpus meum, Ite missa est*), the Liturgy of the Word involves the performance of texts primarily for the purpose of sacralizing them. In this sense, they are not "performatives" at all. One might say that performatives involve the use of formulaic speech, whereas reading and singing involves the use of textualized language, or "rhetic" and "phatic" acts, respectively, to use Austin's terms (92–93, 95–98). As we shall see, however, these distinctions are not always that easy to maintain (see, in particular, Chapter 4, pp. 142–44). Because the performance of these texts is governed by convention and regulated by institutions (characteristics of illocutions), I do refer to their "illocutionary force" in the same sense that Pierre Bourdieu uses when he describes "that surplus of meaning which gives [ritual language] its 'illocutionary force'" (*Language and Symbolic Power*, ed. John B. Thompson, trans. Gino Raymond and Matthew Adamson [Cambridge, Mass.: Harvard University Press, 1991], 109).

26. See, for example, Durandus, *Rationale divinorum officiorum*, IV.24.334–50 (140: 351); Joseph A. Jungmann, *The Mass of the Roman Rite: Its Origins and Development*, trans. Francis A. Brunner (1951; repr., Westminster, Md.: Christian Classics, 1992), 1:442–55.

27. "A Treatise on the Manner and Mede of the Mass," in *Lay Folks' Mass Book*, pp. 128–47, ll. 428–36. All further quotations will refer to this edition and will be cited parenthetically by line number.

28. Watson, "Middle English Mystics," 551.

29. Raymo, "Works of Religious and Philosophical Instruction," 2345.

30. Thomas Lentes, "Counting Piety in the Late Middle Ages," in *Ordering Society: Perspectives on Intellectual and Practical Modes of Shaping Social Relations*, ed. Bernhard Jussen (Philadelphia: University of Pennsylvania Press, 2001), 69–71.

31. On *commercium sacrum*, see Arnold Angenendt et al., "Counting Piety in the Early and High Middle Ages," in *Ordering Society: Perspectives on Intellectual and Practical Modes of Shaping Social Relations*, ed. Bernhard Jussen (Philadelphia: University of Pennsylvania Press, 2001), 19–20.

32. Bourdieu, *Language*, 109. See note 25, above.

33. On levation prayers in general, see Rossell Hope Robbins, "Levation Prayers in Middle English Verse," *Modern Philology* 40 (1942): 131–46; Rubin, *Corpus Christi*, 155–63; and Duffy, *Stripping of the Altars*, 117–21.

34. Rubin, *Corpus Christi*, 155–56.

35. Robbins, "Levation Prayers," 140–41.

36. Rubin, *Corpus Christi*, 55.

37. For examples, see Robbins, "Levation Prayers," 134–39.

38. Jonathan Culler, *The Pursuit of Signs: Semiotics, Literature, Deconstruction* (Ithaca, N.Y.: Cornell University Press, 1981), 141.

39. See Chapter 2, pp. 67–70.

40. Jennings, "Titiuillus," 24–32.

41. Jürgen Habermas, *The Structural Transformation of the Public Sphere: An Inquiry into a Category of Bourgeois Society*, trans. Thomas Burger (Cambridge, Mass.: MIT Press, 1991), 5–14.

42. Maura Nolan, *John Lydgate and the Making of Public Culture* (Cambridge: Cambridge University Press, 2005), 7.

43. Habermas, *Structural Transformation*, 7.

44. Ibid., 9.

45. One could claim, of course, that the disjunction between public and private speech merely reinforces the exclusive nature of "representative publicness." My purpose is not so much to dispute Habermas's characterization (still less to chart the emergence of a "public sphere") but to reconsider his assessment of Christian liturgy within his model.

46. Bourdieu, *Language*, 109. Bourdieu's point is that it is the social position of the speaker that creates ritual authority rather than the circumstance, but this is not inconsistent with my claim that social position provides knowledge of and access to systems of meaning constructed as lying outside the cleric's control.

47. For examples, see Aberdeen, Aberdeen University Library, MS 271, f. 45v (Hours-Psalter, fifteenth century); Cambridge University Library, MS Ii.6.2, f. 72v (Book of Hours, late fourteenth century); Oxford, Bodleian Library, MS Rawlinson liturg. g.2, f. 18r (Missal, second quarter of the fifteenth century).

48. Rubin, *Corpus Christi*, 155.

49. Justice provides examples of this sort of critique (*Writing and Rebellion*, 143).

50. R. N. Swanson, *Religion and Devotion in Europe, c. 1215–c. 1515* (Cambridge: Cambridge University Press, 1995), 113–16.

51. Habermas, *Structural Transformation*, 8.

52. Jungmann, *Mass of the Roman Rite*, 1:219.

53. Angenendt, "Counting Piety," 32; for an account of prayer fraternities in England in the fourteenth century, see Caroline Barron, "The Parish Fraternities of Medieval London," in *The Church in Pre-Reformation Society: Essays in Honor of F. R. H. DuBoulay*, ed. Caroline Barron and Christopher Harper-Bill (Woodbridge, Boydell, 1985), 13–37.

54. For Maitland, the beginning of contract law in the period rested on the distinction between corporeal and incorporeal things—between possession and ownership, propriety and action (Frederick Pollock and Frederic William Maitland, *The History of English Law Before the Time of Edward I*, 2nd ed. rev. S. F. C. Milsom [Cambridge: Cambridge University Press, 1968], 2:206). See Green, *Crisis of Truth*, 44–50, for a more recent discussion of this distinction. Though Green associates contract law with writing, my label "contractual" is not concerned with the influence of writing or written documents as such, even though liturgical agreements often took the form of dispositive documents; my focus here is simply the distinction between rights *in rem* vs. rights *in personam*.

55. For a discussion of the possibility of a "public sphere" in late medieval England, see David Lawton, "Dullness and the Fifteenth Century," *English Literary History* 54 (1987): 797; and Nolan, *John Lydgate*, 5–10.

56. This distinction (in Marx's writings) is emphasized by Gayatri Chakravorty Spivak, "Can the Subaltern Speak?" in *Marxism and the Interpretation of Culture*, ed. Cary Nelson and Larry Grossberg (Urbana: University of Illinois Press, 1988), 275.

57. Habermas, *Structural Transformation*, 7; Habermas, *Strukturwandel der Öffentlichkeit: Untersuchungen zu einer Kategorie der bürgerlichen Gesellschaft* (Neuwied: Luchterhand, 1962), 19. Though Habermas generally uses the word *Repräsentation* to describe signification, the distinction he draws here, using the word *Vertretung* to describe political representation, is analogous to the distinction between *Darstellung* (signify, or "re-present") and *Vertretung* discussed by Spivak, "Can the Subaltern Speak?" 276–80. *Repräsentation*, however, is capable of covering both senses.

58. Bourdieu makes a related critique of Austin and, by extension, of Habermas, in claiming that "the illocutionary force of expressions cannot be found in the very word, such as 'performatives,' in which that force is *indicated* or, better, *represented*—in both senses of this term" and by pointing to the "*delegated power* of the spokesperson" (*Language*, 107). Austin places enough emphasis on the importance of convention that I am not sure he would necessarily disagree that the power of performatives results from misrecognition (which, at any rate, have "real" effects that can be studied as such). As a critique of Habermas, however, it is extremely useful.

59. Rubin, *Corpus Christi*, 49–82 passim.

60. Ibid., 50; Angenendt, "Counting Piety," 44.

61. Angenendt et al. cite Aquinas's *Summa Theologica*, Suppl. a. 14 ad 2 ("Counting Piety," 44, 44n225).

62. K. L. Wood-Legh, *Perpetual Chantries in Britain* (Cambridge: Cambridge University Press, 1965), 3–4.

63. For examples of the difficulties that beset chantries constituted as benefices, see ibid., 65–78.

64. Pollock and Maitland, *History of English Law*, 1:488n1.

65. Corporate status was usually granted only to chantries funded by benefices, rather than those constituted as "services," in which a trustee would hold title to the land. It was not, therefore, available to priests who were paid by stipend but to those who merely needed the means to maintain the rights to land and income they had been already been granted. Thus while the development of corporations sole did nothing to secure the livelihood of stipendiary priests, it does seem significant that this extreme of advantageous alienation would be needed to protect what was considered the most secure form of income for a chantry chaplaincy (Wood-Legh, *Perpetual Chantries*, 326).

66. James A. Brundage, *Medieval Canon Law* (London and New York: Longman, 1995), 98–100.

67. "Interim eciam, quod nec oraciones secreta dicant in missa, dum cantanda est; nec eciam in eleuacione Domini dum chorus cantat" (Dalton, *Collegiate Church of Ottery St. Mary*, 136).

68. "Inhibentes expresse ipsis omnibus et singulis sub poena infrascripta ne ipsi aut quivis ipsorum matutinas aut horas aliquas per se, vel cum sociis pluribus, aut uno in choro ipsius capelle, dum psallantur in eodem, divina officia supradicta dicant voce submissa vel alias in privato" (Kirby, *Annals of Winchester College*, 507). For New College statutes, see *Statutes of the Colleges of Oxford*, 76.

69. Wykeham's mandate was retained in the statutes for Eton and King's colleges (1440), and other choral foundations, such as Fotheringhay College (1415), made similar provisions (Heywood and Wright, *Ancient Laws for King's College*, 118, 569; Thompson, "Statutes," 293).

70. Wood-Legh, *Perpetual Chantries*, 89.

71. A. T. Bannister, ed., "Visitation Returns of the Diocese of Hereford in 1397," *English Historical Review* 44 (1929): 279–89, 444–53; 45 (1930): 92–101, 444–63. See 44:282, 285; 45:445.

72. Burgess, "'For the Increase of Divine Service.'" Wood–Legh, however, notes that English chantries were generally more "single-minded" than their continental counterparts, concerning themselves with above all with the perpetuation of masses and "seldom permit[ting] anything which might hinder this," such that other parochial or pastoral duties would be subordinated to performance (*Perpetual Chantries*, 183).

73. "et eius pretextu postea incontinenter quidam eorum ad tabernas et commessaciones transiunt insolenter et nimium se ibidem ingurgitant et quidam negociis secularibus se immiscent non curantes ulterius eisdem diebus audire matutinas, altam missam parochialem de die, vesperas, et alia divina officia" (*Registrum Johannis Gilbert, Episcopi Herefordensis*, A.D. *MCCCLXXV–MCCCLXXXIX*, ed. J. H. Parry, Canterbury and York Society 18 [London: Canterbury and York Society, 1915], 90–91).

74. See Chapter 4, pp. 144–47.

75. *Calendar of Patent Rolls 1391–1396*, 386; London, Public Record Office, C 66/339, m. 28 (17 Richard II, part 2). See note 97 below.

76. A. K. McHardy, "Ecclesiastics and Economics: Poor Priests, Prosperous Laymen, and Proud Prelates in the Reign of Richard II," in *The Church and Wealth*, ed. W. J. Shields and Diana Wood (Oxford: Blackwell, 1987), 137.

77. Wood-Legh, *Perpetual Chantries*, 294.

78. Salisbury Cathedral Dean and Chapter, Reg. Corfe, p. 11. The regulation was reiterated in 1387 (Reg. Coman, p. 92).

79. For the effects of the plague on manual laborers, see Christopher Dyer, "Work Ethics in the Fourteenth Century," in *The Problem of Labour in Fourteenth-Century England*, ed. James Bothwell, P. J. P. Goldberg, and W. M. Ormrod (York: York Medieval Press, 2000), 26–41.

80. W. M. Ormrod, *The Reign of Edward III: Crown & Political Society in England, 1327–1377* (New Haven, Conn.: Yale University Press, 1990), 121.

81. Wood-Legh, *Perpetual Chantries*, 93–102.

82. Positions in perpetual chantries were often constituted as benefices and thus were not always the subject of complaints. Modern scholars tend to confuse these positions with those of the unbeneficed mass priests described below (Wood-Legh, *Perpetual Chantries*, 190–91).

83. *The Simonie: A Parallel-Text Edition*, ed. Dan Embree and Elizabeth Urquhart (Heidelberg: Carl Winter, 1991), A.97–102. All further quotations will refer to this edition and be cited parenthetically by line number.

84. *Knighton's Chronicle, 1337–1396*, ed. G. H. Martin (Oxford: Clarendon, 1995), 102.

85. Ormrod, *Reign of Edward III*, 121; Bertha Haven Putnam, "Maximum Wage-Laws for Priests After the Black Death, 1348–1381," *American Historical Review* 21 (1915): 13.

86. "Infra breve confluebant ad ordines maxima multitudo, quorum uxores obierant in pestilencia, de quibus multi illiterati et quasi meri laici, nisi quantenus aliqualiter legere sciebant licet non intellegere" (*Knighton's Chronicle*, 102).

87. This same logic underlies many of the complaints that parishioners were attending chantry masses instead of parish High Mass, like that of Gilbert, quoted above.

88. Wood-Legh, *Perpetual Chantries*, 193–94. Phyllis Pobst even found a significant decrease in the number of resignations from and exchanges of benefices during the years of the plague in the register of William Bateman (*The Register of William Bateman*, ed. Phyllis E. Pobst, Canterbury and York Society 84, 90 [Woodbridge, Suffolk: Boydell, 1996–2000], 1:xxxii).

89. A. K. McHardy, "Careers and Disappointments in the Late-Medieval Church: Some English Evidence," in *The Ministry: Clerical and Lay*, ed. W. J. Shields and Diana Wood (Oxford: Blackwell, 1989), 111–30.

90. Wood-Legh, *Perpetual Chantries*, 193–94; H. F. Westlake, *Parish Guilds of Medieval England* (London: Society for Promoting Christian Knowledge, 1918), 48.

91. Putnam, "Maximum Wage-Laws," 18–27.

92. "nec [sc. sacerdotes] erubescentes quod eorum insatiabilis avaritia ab aliis operariis etiam laicis nequiter et perniciose trahitur in exemplum.... curas animarum gerere negligunt, et onera curatorum charitate mutus supportare; quinimmo eis penitus derelictis, ad celebrand. annualia, et ad alia peculiaria se conferunt obsequia" (David Wilkins, *Concilia Magnae Britanniae et Hiberniae* (1737) [Brussels: Culture et Civilisation, 1964], 3:1).

93. *Knighton's Chronicle*, 102.

94. Bertha Haven Putnam, *The Enforcement of the Statute of Labourers During the First Decade After the Black Death, 1349–1359*, Studies in History, Economics and Public Law 32 (1908; repr., New York: AMS, 1970), 187–89.

95. Text quoted in ibid., appx 432*–433*.

96. See ibid., 188n2, in which a defendant accused of failing to perform duties "in officio balliui" claimed that he had been retained to serve "in officio capellani ad celebrandum missas."

97. Wood-Legh, *Perpetual Chantries*, 278. "Non-binding" or charitable agreements for liturgical services other than chantries also invoked volition: In 1393/4 the vicars choral of York Minster set down an agreement with Richard II by which they would, "ex libere voluntate," celebrate an obit for the king and his wife after their deaths and additionally sing *Inter natos* nightly after compline, in exchange for which Richard granted them corporate status and appropriated to them the

church of St. Sampson "in perpetuam elimosinam" (London, Public Record Office, C 66/339, m. 28. [17 Richard II, part 2]).

98. *The Anonimalle Chronicle, 1333–1381*, ed. V. H. Galbraith (Manchester: University Press, 1929), 147: "null ne deveroit servire ascune home mes a sa volunte de mesme et par covenante taille." See Putnam, *Enforcement*, 190; and Justice, *Writing and Rebellion*, 145–7.

99. From the text of the 1378 *Effrenata* (Wilkins, *Concilia*, 3:135–36), which, according to Putnam, quotes the second (1362) version ("Maximum Wage-Laws," 22).

100. *The Complete Works of John Gower*, ed. G. C. Macaulay (Oxford, 1899), vol. 1, ll. 20497–20502. All further citations of Gower's works will refer to this edition and will be noted parenthetically by text and line number.

101. Translation modified from William Burton Wilson, *John Gower: Mirour de l'Omme (The Mirror of Mankind)*, rev. Nancy Wilson Van Baak (East Lansing, Mich.: Colleagues, 1992), 274. All further translations are largely Wilson's with silent modifications where necessary.

102. Putnam, *Enforcement*, 190. See note 98 above.

103. There is no clearly identifiable source for the phrase itself, which expresses a common Augustinian sentiment. Elsewhere in the *Mirour*, Gower quotes one formulation from *Serm.* xxix. 1: "Clamor ad Dominum qui fit ab orantibus, si sonitu corporalis vocis fiat, non intento in Deum corde, quis dubitet inaniter fieri?" (cf. *MO*, 10381–428, and Macaulay's note).

104. The paradoxical locution "prestre lays" appears to be Gower's own. While it is first invoked in this passage, where "lays" appears to mean "illiterate," he continues to use it to refer to stipendiary clerics in places where the meaning "illiterate" is not clearly evoked by it (e.g., 20575). The "layness" of such priests, then, seems to involve more than their illiteracy and refers to an ethical posture inappropriate to a cleric.

105. Ong, "Orality."

Chapter 4

1. The term "vernacular theology" was first used by A. I. Doyle, "A Survey of the Origins and Circulation of Theological Writings in English in the 14th, 15th, and Early 16th Centuries with Special Consideration of the Part of the Clergy Therein" (Ph.D. diss., Downing College, Cambridge, 1953), 1:5–7, and developed by Bernard McGinn, "Introduction: Meister Eckhart and the Beguines in the Context of Vernacular Theology," in *Meister Eckhart and the Beguine Mystics: Hadewijch of Brabant, Mechthild of Magdeburg, and Marguerite de Porete*, ed. Bernard McGinn (New York: Continuum, 1994), 1–14, and McGinn, *The Flowering of Mysticism: Men and Women in the New Mysticism (1200–1350)* (New York: Crossroads, 1998), 19–24 passim. Watson's use of the term is elaborated in two seminal articles: "Censorship" and "Middle English Mystics." For a more recent overview, see Vincent Gillespie, "Vernacular Theology," in *Oxford Twenty-First Century Approaches to Literature: Middle English*, ed. Paul Strohm (Oxford: Oxford University Press, 2007), 401–20.

2. Watson, "Middle English Mystics," 544.

3. Nicholas Watson, "Cultural Changes," *English Language Notes* 44 (2006): 128; Linda Georgianna, "Vernacular Theologies," *English Language Notes* 44 (2006): 86–88.

4. Watson, "Middle English Mystics," 550; Watson, "Censorship," 858.

5. Watson, "Cultural Changes," 131, Watson echoes a critique made by Sarah Stanbury, though she is less interested in the historical truth value than in the historiographical nostalgia such a championing of the vernacular implies ("Vernacular Nostalgia and *The Cambridge History of Medieval Literature*," *Texas Studies in Literature and Language* 44 [2002]: 95–99).

6. An influential exception to this trend is Duffy, *Stripping of the Altars*, 220–27.

7. See Chapter 1, pp. 1, 5, 213nn1–2.

8. Watson, "Middle English Mystics," 544.

9. Nicholas Watson, "The Politics of Middle English Writing," in *The Idea of the Vernacular: An Anthology of Middle English Literary Theory, 1280–1520*, ed. Jocelyn Wogan-Browne, Nicholas Watson, Andrew Taylor, and Ruth Evans (University Park: Pennsylvania State University Press, 1999), 339.

10. Lee Patterson, "'The Living Witness of Our Redemption': Martyrdom and Imitation in Chaucer's *Prioress's Tale*," *Journal of Medieval and Early Modern Studies* 31 (2001): 514, 518.

11. Watson emphasizes *Pearl's* formalism in relation to its modification of discussions of virginity that replace its central ideal of "heroic suffering" with the mere "concept of physical 'intactness'": "Here, the brides of the lamb are no longer career virgins but children, who are claimed to be superior to everyone precisely because they have *done nothing*, and have therefore retained all the pristine integrity with which they came forth from the baptismal font" (Watson's emphases; "The *Gawain*-Poet as Vernacular Theologian," in *A Companion to the Gawain-Poet*, ed. Derek Brewer and Jonathan Gibson [Woodbridge, Suffolk: Brewer, 1997], 301–2).

12. *The Cloud of Unknowing and The Book of Privy Counselling*, ed. Phyllis Hodgson, EETS, o.s., 218 (London: EETS, 1944), 75/3–4, 74/1–5.

13. Ralph Hanna III, *London Literature, 1300–1380* (Cambridge: Cambridge University Press, 2005), 13–15; see also Vincent Gillespie, "Vernacular Books of Religion," in *Book Production and Publishing in Britain, 1375–1475*, ed. Jeremy Griffiths and Derek Pearsall (Cambridge: Cambridge University Press, 1989), 317–44.

14. Watson, "Censorship," 823–24n4.

15. Malcolm Parkes, "The Literacy of the Laity," in *Literature and Western Civilization*, vol. 2, *The Medieval World*, ed. David Daiches and Anthony Thorlby (London: Aldus, 1973), 555–78. Another extragrammatical literacy might be Margaret Aston's "devotional literacy," described in *Lollards and Reformers: Images and Literacy in Late Medieval England* (London: Hambledon, 1984), 101–33.

16. For an examination of the possibility of extragrammatical literacies beyond vernacular hermeneutics in English, see Katherine Zieman "The Perils of *Canor*: Mystical Authority and the Site of Affect in Rolle, Hilton, and the *Cloud*–author" (forthcoming).

17. Paul Saenger, "Books of Hours and the Reading Habits of the Later Middle Ages," in *The Culture of Print: Power and the Uses of Print in Early Modern Europe*, ed. R. Chartier (Cambridge: Polity, 1989), 141–73. While this mode of literacy has a demonstrable existence, as I will discuss, it is more properly termed "phonemic" than "phonetic." "Phonetics" pertains to describing the sounds of language and articulatory processes in general. "Phonetic" reading, therefore, requires phonetic symbols that attempt to re-create all possible sounds that can be made in the vocal tract. "Phonology," by contrast, pertains to sounds as they are perceived in the mind. "Phonemic" reading requires an understanding of how a particular alphabet represents sounds specific to a particular language (the "phonemes" of that language, which in medieval formal pedagogy were taught in terms of syllables). Phonemic reading is thus a form of linguistic knowledge, not an abstract knowledge of sounds that substitutes for linguistic knowledge. Thus, except when quoting Saenger, I use "phonemic."

18. See Chapter 1, pp. 13–15, 33–36.

19. Nicholas Orme distinguishes between primers and Books of Hours by pointing to the importance of the primer's alphabet as a marker of formal learning (*Medieval Children*, 89); such a distinction implies that Books of Hours were not used for *formal* instruction, but it is surely possible that they were used for *informal* instruction of the type I discuss later in this chapter.

20. The fact that this activity is also sometimes viewed as mindless is, in turn, a reflection of modern attitudes toward fundamentalism.

21. On reading as "skilled information processing," see Geoffrey Underwood and Vivienne Batt, *Reading and Understanding: An Introduction to the Psychology of Reading* (Oxford: Blackwell, 1996), 29–36. To demonstrate that readers use strategies beyond serial recognition of letters and corresponding sounds, cognitive psychologists often create orthographically deviant yet readable sentences etieht by rarenargnnig the ltteers of ivdianuidl wrdos, r*pl*c*ng v*w*ls w*th s*mb*ls, xr rxplxcixg exerx thxrd xetxer xitx an x.

22. The opposition of speech and writing in Western metaphysics is explicated and challenged in Jacques Derrida, *Of Grammatology*, trans. Gayatri Chakravorty Spivak (Baltimore and London: Johns Hopkins University Press, 1976).

23. Orme, *Education and Society*, 192.

24. Moran Cruz, *Growth of English Schooling*, 46.

25. Saenger, "Books of Hours," 142–43.

26. Ibid., 142.

27. On the publication of Thoresby's *Catechism*, see Thomas Frederick Simmons and Henry Edward Nolloth, eds., *The Lay Folks' Catechism, or the English and Latin Versions of Archbishop Thoresby's Instructions for the People*, EETS, o.s., 118 (London: EETS/Oxford University Press, 1901), xv–xx; on Love's *Mirror*, see Michael Sargent's introduction in Nicholas Love, *The Mirror of the Blessed Life of Jesus Christ: A Full Critical Edition*, ed. Michael G. Sargent (Exeter: University of Exeter Press, 2005), intro 36–37.

28. Richard Ullerston's 1401 defense of biblical translation summarizes his opposition's position that "[the laity's] devotion is actually improved by their lack of understanding of the psalms and prayers they say" (as reported by Watson in

"Censorship and Cultural Exchange," 843). This thirdhand account is the only example I have found that actively promotes illiterate devotional recitation.

29. For more on the practices of women religious, see Katherine Zieman, "Reading, Singing, and Understanding: Constructions of the Literacy of Women Religious in Late Medieval England," in *Learning and Literacy in Medieval England and Abroad*, ed. Sarah Rees-Jones (Turnhout: Brepols, 2003), 97–120. The concept of "extragrammatical literacies" expounded in this present study is meant to supersede the less fully developed "liturgical literacy" described in that essay.

30. *The Chastising of God's Children and The Treatise of Perfection of the Sons of God*, ed. Joyce Bazire and Eric Colledge (Oxford: Blackwell, 1957), 221. All further citations will refer to this edition and be noted parenthetically by page and line number.

31. Saenger, "Books of Hours," 148.

32. *The Scale of Perfection*, ed. Thomas H. Bestul (Kalamazoo, Mich.: Medieval Institute, 2000), 65 (1.33).

33. "Quisquis orat vocaliter orationem quam tenetur exsolvere—quia de voluntariis secus est—non oportet repetitionem fieri, si percipit orans quod evagatur nec attendit ad verba vel ad sententiam, si facit hoc ex inadvertentia et displicit sibi dum advertit" (Jean Gerson, *Œuvres complètes*, ed. Mgr. Glorieux [Paris: Desclée, 1961], 2:186; all further quotations will refer to this edition).

34. "Est itaque multiplex attentio sive intentionis cordialis directio: una actualis, alia habitualis, alia quasi media scilicet virtualis. Rursus harum quaelibet dividitur; quoniam alia refertur in solas voces et verba, alia in verborum significationes, alia nec verborum formas nec significationes attendit sed in affectus aliquos circa coelestia et divina transit" (Gerson, *Œuvres complètes*, 2:184).

35. Saenger, "Books of Hours," 148–49.

36. *The Myroure of Oure Ladye*, ed. John Henry Blunt, EETS, e.s., 19 (London, 1873), 49. All further quotations will refer to this edition and be cited parenthetically by page number. For a more extensive analysis of the *Myroure* and its instruction on reading, see Elizabeth Schirmer, "Reading Lessons at Syon Abbey: The *Myroure of Oure Ladye* and the Mandates of Vernacular Theology," in *Voices in Dialogue: New Problems in Reading Women's Cultural History*, ed. Kathryn Kerby-Fulton and Linda Olson (Notre Dame, Ind.: Notre Dame University Press, 2005), 345–76.

37. On scriptural translation, see Watson, "Censorship," 840–51. The emphasis on the accessibility of the spiritual senses may be an attempt to counter the Lollards' elevation of the literal sense. See Copeland, *Pedagogy*, 99–140.

38. See Chapter 3, p. 111.

39. "Nempe et ipsae moniales pro magna parte primitus illiteratae fuerunt, et servitium nullum dixerunt; sed in loco cujuslibet Horae certas Orationes Dominicas et Salutationes Angelicas" (Walsingham, *Gesta Abbatum*, 2:401).

40. Walsingham, *Gesta Abbatum*, 2:402.

41. Hilton, *Scale of Perfection*, 246 (2.42).

42. "Exemplum legimus de quondam qui volens rusticam convicere de cordis instabilitate dum fit oratio, nam ille devotum se simulabat et attentum, pollicitus est se daturum sibi asinum si posset orationem dominicam nihil aliud actualiter cogitans perficere. Qui mox ut ad orationem se divertit securus de asini lucro, coepit

distrahi in hanc cogitationem si sellam habiturus esset cum asino. Qui tandem ad se rediens et se redarguens instabilitatem sui cordis confessus est" (Gerson, *Œuvres complètes*, 2:184–85).

43. David Bevington, ed., *Medieval Drama* (Boston: Houghton Mifflin, 1975), ll. 680–81. All further quotations will refer to this edition and be cited parenthetically by line number.

44. Lawrence Clopper has argued that *Mankind* was written for an "educated" rather than "popular" audience, but his primary evidence for this claim is the amount of untranslated Latin and latinate wit in the play ("*Mankind* and Its Audience," *Comparative Drama* 8 [1975]: 349–50). My purpose is less to establish the audience of the play or to suggest that its wit was universally accessible than to point to the kinds of knowledge that might be intuited even by those without "formal" training.

45. See Chapter 1, p. 34.

46. Transmission of particular texts from person to person arguably continues in the "repertory-based," yet advanced, discipline of "literature," which in modern practice has been separated from the skill-based disciplines of "reading" and "grammar." "Literature" can be defined as texts that are primarily transmitted through institutionally authorized interpreters.

47. On the history of these images, see Pamela Sheingorn, "'The Wise Mother': The Image of St. Anne Teaching the Virgin Mary," *Gesta* 32 (1993): 69–80; Wendy Scase, "St. Anne and the Education of the Virgin: Literary and Artistic Traditions and Their Implications," in *England in the Fourteenth Century: Proceedings of the 1991 Harlaxton Symposium*, ed. N. Rogers (Stamford: Watkins, 1993), 81–96; and Ayers Bagley, "St. Anne Teaching the Virgin, 14th–15th Centuries," *St. Anne Teaching the Virgin to Read*, 12 February 2004, University of Minnesota, http://education.umn.edu/edpa/iconics/St_Anne/St_Anne_Text.htm (accessed 19 May 2006). In discussing these images as realistic depictions, I do not mean to ignore their possible symbolic meanings (see Sheingorn, "'The Wise Mother,'" 71–72). On their relationship to practice, see M. T. Clanchy, "Learning to Read and the Role of Mothers," in *Studies in the History of Reading*, ed. Greg Brooks and A. K. Pugh. ([Reading]: University of Reading, 1984), 33–39.

48. On the "alphabetic principle," see Brian Byrne, *The Foundation of Literacy: The Child's Acquisition of the Alphabetic Principle* (East Sussex: Psychology Press, 1998), 1–4 passim. On "phonemic" or "phonological awareness," see Underwood and Batt, *Reading and Understanding*, 96–104. It is worth noting in this respect that modern illiterates are capable of recognizing particular words if seen in exactly the same form such that they are not required to abstract letter forms but can recognize general shapes. See Victoria Purcell-Gates, *Other People's Words: The Cycle of Low Literacy* (Cambridge: Harvard University Press, 1997), 10–15, 45–65. The consistency of scripts used in liturgical books (as opposed to cursive hands, for example) would facilitate this kind of decoding. To claim that medieval readers had means of word recognition other than phonics is not to claim that readers did not read aloud.

49. Duffy, *Stripping the Altars*, 212–27. To quote just few examples: a rubric in a late fourteenth-century Book of Hours states: "[Q]ui ceste oreison dirra ou

portera nul enemi mortel iames mortel pecche ie murra li greuera ne iames en mortel pecche ne murra" (Oxford, Bodleian Library, MS Rawlinson liturg. G.2, f. 6). A similar promise is made in a Latin rubric in an early fifteenth-century Book of Hours: "Incipit oratio uenerabilis bede presbeteri de qua fertur cotidie et devote flexis genibus eam dicens nec dyaboli nec mali homines ei nocere poterint nec sine confessione morietur" (Oxford, Bodleian Library, MS Laud latin 15, f. 68v).

50. See Chapter 3, pp. 83–84.

51. *The Gast of Gy: Eine englische Dichtung des 14. Jahrhunderts*, ed. Gustav Schleich (Berlin, 1898), l. 1104. This edition contains both a Middle English translation and a Latin recension of the text. Unless specified otherwise, all further citations will refer to this edition and be cited parenthetically by line number (Middle English) or page number (Latin).

52. The text of the Hours of the Cross (as well as other texts found in Books of Hours) can be found in Roger S. Wieck, *Painted Prayers: The Book of Hours in Medieval and Renaissance Art* (New York: Braziller, 1997), 138–43.

53. Carl Horstmann, ed., *The Minor Poems of the Vernon MS, Part I*, EETS, o.s., 98 (London, 1892), 37–43, ll. 50–54. A somewhat closer translation of the hymn appears in some Englished Hours of the Cross found in Oxford, Bodleian Library, MS Liturgical 104 (c. 1340): "At midday was Ihesus Crist ynailed to þe rode./Bitwixe tweye þeues he hongid for houre gode./For þyurst of stronge pine yfuld he was wiþ galle./Þe holi louird so god ywrout ybuȝt houre sinnes alle" (fols. 69r–69v).

54. Alexandra Barratt, "The Prymer and Its Influence on Fifteenth-Century English Passion Lyrics," *Medium Ævum* 44 (1975): 274.

55. J. Kail, ed., *Twenty-Six Political and Other Poems from the Oxford MSS. Digby 102 and Douce 322*, EETS, o.s., 124 (London: Kegan Paul, 1904), 120–49. All further citations will refer to this edition and be cited parenthetically by line number. The liturgical resonances of this poem is also discussed, though in different terms by Holsinger, who claims that its readership "was almost certainly in orders rather than lay" ("Liturgy," 304). The surviving manuscripts, however, do not support the idea of such an exclusive audience. See Susanna Greer Fein, ed., *Moral Love Songs and Laments* (Kalamazoo, Mich.: Medieval Institute, 1998), 311. At any rate my primary interest in the poem is in the nominalizing strategies it employs; these are attested in earlier sources that had a demonstrably broader readership. See, for example, Chapter 5, pp. 157–59.

56. John H. Alford, "A Note on *Piers Plowman* B.xviii.390, 'Til *parce* it hote,'" *Modern Philology* 69 (1972): 324.

57. "Quia humiliasti tamquam vulneratum superbum, et tumore meo separabar abs te" (*Conf.* 7.7); cf. Ps. 88:11: "tu confregisti quasi vulneratum superbum."

58. On code-switching and borrowing, see John J. Gumperz, *Discourse Strategies*, Studies in Interactional Sociolinguistics 1 (Cambridge: Cambridge University Press, 1982), 59-99; Tim William Machan considers Langland's linguistic practice in these terms in "Language Contact in *Piers Plowman*," *Speculum* 69 (1994): 359–98.

59. "Untethering the speech act from the sovereign subject founds an alternative notion of agency and, ultimately, of responsibility, one that more fully acknowledges the way in which the subject is constituted in language, how what

it creates is also what it derives from elsewhere" (Butler, *Excitable Speech*, 15–16). Butler's theorizing linguistic agency in the context of hate speech seems apposite primarily because medieval users of ritual texts had no pretensions to be sovereign subjects. To draw this parallel is not to suggest that these extragrammatical engagements are more politically responsible or liberating but to underscore the persistent legacy of *grammatica*.

60. Ong, *Orality and Literacy*, 45–46.

61. See Durandus, *Rationale divinorum officiorum*, V.9.22–36 (140A:106). Durandus, however, refers to symbolic associations for vespers in general, not solely the Vespers for the Dead. Edward E. Foster's edition of *The Gast of Gy* contains the following lines, omitted from Schleich's copy-text: "Tha fyve Psalmes when thae er mett/For fyve wittes of the saule er sett" (ll. 1115–16, in *Three Purgatory Poems: The Gast of Gy, Sir Owain, The Vision of Tundale* [Kalamazoo, Mich.: Medieval Institute, 2004]).

62. Duffy, *Stripping of the Altars*, 298.

63. Ayers Bagley shrewdly points out that not all of these images necessarily represent the act of teaching ("St. Anne").

64. Scase, "St. Anne," 84.

65. Ibid., 96.

66. One does not need to be so concrete as to imagine that Gabriel's appearance is simultaneous with her reading the passage. The point is merely that the iconography of Anne and the Virgin focuses attention on the Virgin's conscious awareness of the prophecy, which she has gained from her own reading of the text.

67. *Aelred of Rievaulx's "De institutione inclusarum": Two English Versions*, ed. John Ayto and Alexandra Barratt, EETS, o.s., 287 (Oxford: Oxford University Press, 1984), 18/698–700.

68. Sheingorn, "'The Wise Mother,'" 76–77.

69. One image of the Education of the Virgin (complete with fescue) occurs in the early fifteenth-century French Breviary made for John the Fearless (London, British Library, MS Harley 2897, f. 340v), which suggests that men were believed to be edified or inspired by the image as well as women.

70. Habermas, *Structural Transformations*, 9.

71. Rubin, *Corpus Christi*, 5–6; Beckwith, *Signifying God*, 46–47, 63–65 passim; and Aers, *Sanctifying Signs*.

72. Denys Turner, "The Darkness of God and the Light of Christ: Negative Theology and Eucharistic Presence," in *Catholicism and Catholicity: Eucharistic Communities in Historical and Contemporary Perspectives*, ed. Sarah Beckwith (Oxford: Blackwell, 1999), 43. The theological and philosophical difficulty is perhaps enhanced by the sacramental power of the Eucharist, but there are other parts of the Office and Mass that "do what they say" (or, technically, allow God to do what they say), such as the opening of matins: *V. Domine labea mea aperies. R. Et os meum annuntiabit laudem tuam.*

73. Foster, *Three Purgatory Poems*, 15.

74. Schleich, *The Gast of Gy*, 64–65. The manuscripts of *De spiritu Guidonis* vary significantly enough that we cannot presume that the Middle English

version was translated from the version edited by Schleich. Variants, however, suggest that the critical phrase "reficiunt animas" is consistent, while the precise mechanics caused difficulties: cf. "in Placebo sunt .v. psalmi, .v. antiphoni qui cum dicuntur reficiunt animam pro qua dicuntur quoad .x. precepta Dei que aliquando dum fuerat in hac vita compleverat ea saltim quantum ad suum affectum et non quantum ad eorum effectum in omnibus" (Uppsalla, Universitätsbibliothek, C.175, f. 51v, fourteenth century); and "officium istud est magnum misterium, nam quinque psalmi cum quinque antiphoni in Placebo reficiunt animam quoad decem preceptorum complementum" (Cologne, Historical Archive, W.153, f. 197v, fifteenth century). I am indebted to Marie Anne Polo de Beaulieu for providing me with these materials from her forthcoming critical edition of the Latin text.

75. According to Marie Anne Polo de Beaulieu, all fourteenth-century vernacular translations of *De spiritu Guidonis* are English. The many other translations into German, French, and other vernaculars can be dated only to the fifteenth century (private communication).

76. "in placebo & dirige ben [five] psalmus and fyue antempnes: þe wȝuche antempnes whon þei ben seid folfullen þe soule þat hit is iseid fore [as] to þe comaundemens of god, wȝuche comaundemens he folfullede mony a tymes þe wȝiles he was a-lyue aftur his talent, þouȝ he dude not in al þinges to heor beoinge" (Carl Horstmann, ed., *Yorkshire Writers: Richard Rolle of Hampole and His Followers* [London, 1896], 2:315). A second, early fifteenth-century prose version, however, suggests the translator also had trouble with this passage: "as to þe ten comaundementes of god which comaundementes he fulfild noȝt oþer while, þe while he was on lyue" (*The Gast of Gy: A Middle English Religious Prose Tract Preserved in Queen's College, Oxford MS. 383*, ed. R. H. Bowers [Leipzig: Tauchnitz, 1938], 30/447–49).

77. It is not clear that this translator actually imagines lay performers when speaking of the effects of these utterances. He rather describes the benefits accruing to souls when their friends "for þam will *ger* syng or rede" (1587), suggesting that they support the singing and reading (which in this text seems to be a decisively clerical activity) rather than singing and reading themselves. He does, however, presume his lay audience is familiar enough with the text that the details of its *misterium* would be of interest to them.

78. Though Durandus does not discuss the intercessory functions of psalms and antiphons in the Office of the Dead, he does concern himself more generally with the question of whether souls in purgatory are aware that they are being prayed for (*Rationale divinorum officiorum*, VII.35.240–46 [140B:94]).

79. Or, in Austin's terms, *by* reminding the soul of her performance of the Commandments, I comforted her, which is distinguishable from "*in* invoking God's aid, I was helping her" (*How to Do Things with Words*, 122–32).

80. Votive antiphons are described in F. Ll. Harrison, *Music in Medieval Britain*, 81–88, and Bowers, "Choral Institutions," 4059–64. For the later cultivation of the votive antiphon, see pp. 5082–85.

81. One example of votive antiphons deputed to nuns can be found in Henry V's foundation of Syon Abbey, which made provision for the nightly singing of

Salve regina, Regina caeli, and *O mitissime,* according to season (F. Ll. Harrison, *Music in Medieval Britain,* 82).

82. Henry died before the foundation of the college was completed but was reckoned a principal founder at Edward's request. See "Statutes of Fotheringhay," 245.

83. Statute xxxvij. "De antiphonis per socios et choristas cotidie decantandis," "Statutes of Fotheringhay," 292–3.

84. Bowers, "Choral Institutions," 4022.

85. F. Ll. Harrison, *Music in Medieval Britain,* 87; G. H. Cook, *Mediaeval Chantries and Chantry Chapels* (London: Phoenix, 1947), 40–41.

86. Barrie Dobson, "Citizens and Chantries in Late Medieval York," in *Church and City, 1000–1500: Essays in Honour of Christopher Brooke,* ed. David Abulafia, Michael Franklin, and Miri Rubin (Cambridge: Cambridge University Press, 1992), 311–32.

87. Ibid., 321.

88. Ibid.

89. Rubin, *Corpus Christi,* 258.

90. The most extensive study of this kind of civic pageantry is Gordon Kipling, *Enter the King: Theatre, Liturgy, and Ritual in the Medieval Civic Triumph* (Oxford: Clarendon, 1998).

91. Anne Lancashire, *London Civic Theatre: City Drama and Pageantry from Roman Times to 1558* (Cambridge: Cambridge University Press, 2002), 44.

92. Ibid., 44–48.

93. Kipling states that the text is "a processional hymn" for church dedications, "found in most medieval missals" (*Enter the King,* 19, 18). The hymn can be found in the Salisbury Breviary as the hymn sung at first vespers for the Dedication of a Church, but the Salisbury Missal and Processional contain a different text for the procession (*Salve festa die,* in *Sarum Missal,* ed. J Wickham Legg [Oxford: Clarendon, 1969], 202), though one with similar imagery. (Granted, these modern editions do not reflect the variants of particular medieval manuscripts and thus may not be fully representative.) Both the hymn and the processional text are based on Apoc. 21:2–5, which is the Epistle lesson at Mass or simply Apoc. 21:2, which is the chapter used at first vespers. Given the importance of the Apocalypse text to Kipling's analysis, its connection to the Dedication of a Church and its liturgy might bear further consideration.

94. Richard Maidstone, *Concordia (The Reconciliation of Richard II with London),* ed. David R. Carlson, trans. A. G. Rigg (Kalamazoo, Mich.: Medieval Institute, 2003).

95. Kipling, *Enter the King,* 205–9.

96. *Gesta Henrici Quinti: The Deeds of Henry the Fifth,* trans. Frank Taylor and John S. Roskell (Oxford: Clarendon, 1975), 100–13; Kipling, *Enter the King,* 45–47.

97. John Bossy, *Christianity in the West, 1400–1700* (Oxford: Oxford University Press, 1985), 153ff.

98. Justice, *Writing and Rebellion,* 156–76.

Chapter 5

1. For some examples, see Jocelyn Wogan-Browne et al., eds., *The Idea of the Vernacular An Anthology of Middle English Literary Theory, 1280–1520* (University Park: Pennsylvania State University Press, 1999), 20–21, 127–28, 242–43.

2. Translations of the Latin verses can be found in John Gower, *The Latin Verses in the "Confessio amantis": An Annotated Translation*, trans. Siân Echard and Claire Fanger (East Lansing, Mich.: Colleagues, 1991).

3. Gower's claim that he chooses to write in the vernacular "for that fewe men endite/In oure englissh" (*CA*, Prol. 22–23) is most likely an ironic claim to be making in the 1390s, given his circle of associates.

4. Anne Middleton, "The Idea of Public Poetry in the Reign of Richard II," *Speculum* 53 (1978): 94, 95. Middleton's discussion deals primarily with features of Langland's and Gower's work that are "only indirectly and intermittently represented in the works of Chaucer" (94). Here I am redefining the terms of "public" in a way that emphasizes the similarities between Langland and Chaucer more explicitly. On public representation, see also Nolan, *John Lydgate*, 4–5.

5. Matthew Giancarlo also discusses the "public" nature of *Piers Plowman* but from the more secular perspective of Parliament rather than liturgy ("*Piers Plowman*, Parliament, and the Public Voice," *Yearbook of Langland Studies* 17 [2003]: 135–74).

6. Again, however limited they may have imagined its membership to have been. Nolan makes the useful distinction between an audience imagined as a "public" and one made up as "an inchoate group of readers of viewers" (*John Lydgate*, 4). In this definition, it is not the size or even the inclusiveness of the public that matters.

7. Given that the emphasis on voice and song in *The Nun's Priest's Tale* is an important part of its parody of Gower's *Vox clamantis* (see Justice, *Writing and Rebellion*, 213–23), it is fair to say that Chaucer sometimes aligns poetic endeavors (Gower's, at any rate) with the verbal performance of a privately retained priest.

8. The prophetic is invoked by Gower in his *Vox clamantis* (Justice, *Writing and Rebellion*, 207–13) and by Langland, as detailed in Kathryn Kerby-Fulton, *Reformist Apocalypticism and "Piers Plowman"* (Cambridge: Cambridge University Press, 1990), 1–4 passim. For the "advisor to princes," see Richard Firth Green, *Poets and Princepleasers: Literature and the English Court in the Late Middle Ages* (Toronto: University of Toronto Press, 1980); and Judith Ferster, *Fictions of Advice: The Literature and Politics of Counsel in Late Medieval England* (Philadelphia: University of Pennsylvania Press, 1996). David Lawton also mentions the locus of the preacher (*Chaucer's Narrators* [Woodbridge, Suffolk: Brewer, 1985], 12), which differs from that of the *persona ecclesie* in that its function is to convey knowledge about scripture rather than to perform it as such. While it emanates from within the hierarchical structures of parish communities in its idealized mode (*The Parson's Tale*), it too has an "unmoored" counterpart that is perhaps even more ethically fraught than that of the unmoored *persona ecclesie* (as in, for example, *The Pardoner's Tale*).

9. Elizabeth Fowler has argued that this period saw the first development of the "social person" as "models of the person, familiar concepts of social being that attain currency through common use" (*Literary Character: The Human Figure in English Writing* [Ithaca, N.Y.: Cornell University Press, 2003], 2). Because of my focus on the temporary, performative nature of the *persona*, I treat it in this context as a locus of articulation, rather than as a representation of social beings.

10. Bourdieu, *Outline*, 187–88.

11. On "common voice," see Middleton, "Public Poetry;" on "fellowship" as a resource of authority in *The Canterbury Tales*, see David Wallace, *Chaucerian Polity: Absolutist Lineages and Associational Forms in England and Italy* (Stanford, Calif.: Stanford University Press, 1997).

12. The term "double-voicing" is derived from Mikhail Bakhtin's notion of "double-voiced discourse" (*Problems of Dostoevsky's Poetics*, trans. Caryl Emerson [Minneapolis: University of Minnesota Press, 1984], 195; and, Bakhtin, *The Dialogic Imagination: Four Essays*, trans. Caryl Emerson and Michael Holquist [Austin: University of Texas Press, 1981], 324). I prefer "double-voicing" to acknowledge the differences between the literary context of Bakhtin's analysis (i.e., novelistic discourse and the incorporation of "everyday language") and my emphasis (particularly with Langland) on the incorporation of Latin texts and the general centrality of performativity in my understanding of Ricardian poetics.

13. Burt Kimmelman discusses the emergence of the literary persona depending on the acknowledgment of the autonomy of language. His discussion, however, is linked more closely to scholastic thinking on the subject (*The Poetics of Authorship in the Later Middle Ages: The Emergence of the Modern Literary Persona* [New York: Lang, 1996]).

14. Lawton, *Chaucer's Narrators*, 62–75. According to Lawton, the "courtly" persona is both opposed to and derived from the public voice through a process by which the "poetic voice, no longer public, is individualised and addressed to a group of like-minded people" (37). To my mind, this account does not fit well with the traditional chronology of Chaucer's works (*The Book of the Duchess* seems to presume shared knowledge with its audience to a far greater extent than *The Canterbury Tales*), nor with the pattern of imagining increasingly larger and more diverse audiences that one sees in the works of Hilton (Books 1 and 2 of *The Scale*), the *Cloud-author* (From the *Cloud of Unknowing* to *Privy Counselling*), and, arguably, post-1381 Langland (Justice, *Writing and Rebellion*, 231–51). For more on Chaucer's increasingly complex sense of audience, see Paul Strohm, *Social Chaucer* (Cambridge, Mass.: Harvard University Press, 1989), 47–83, esp. 51, 64–71.

15. To call attention to the proximity of these tales to Chaucer's own is not to impute any grand linear or dramatic design to the frame narrative of the sort Derek Pearsall has warned against (*The Canterbury Tales* [London: Routledge, 1985], 24–51). It is simply to acknowledge that Chaucer's is a poetics of juxtaposition and that Fragment Seven has a stable enough textual reality that it is not untoward to draw some conclusions from such juxtapositions.

16. The most extensive treatments of "quotation" have been John H. Alford, "The Role of Quotation in *Piers Plowman*," *Speculum* 52 (1977): 80–99,

along with his useful *"Piers Plowman": A Guide to the Quotations*, Medieval and Renaissance Texts and Studies 77 (Binghamton, N.Y.: Center for Medieval and Renaissance Studies, 1982). More recent treatments include Helen Barr, "The Use of Latin Quotations in *Piers Plowman* with Special Reference to Passus XVIII of the 'B' Text," *Notes & Queries*, n.s., 33 (1986): 440–48; A. V. C. Schmidt, *The Clerkly Maker: Langland's Poetic Art* (Cambridge: Brewer, 1987); Edward Peter Nolan, *Now Through a Glass Darkly: Specular Images of Being and Knowing from Virgil to Chaucer* (Ann Arbor: University of Michigan Press, 1990), 219–38; Dieter Mehl, "Die lateinischen Zitate in *Piers Plowman*: Intertextualität und Traditionalität," in *Traditionswandel und Traditionsverhalten*, ed. Walter Haug and Burghart Wachinger (Tübingen: Niemeyer, 1991), 46–60; Machan, "Language Contact"; Michael P. Kuczynski, *Prophetic Song: The Psalms as Moral Discourse in Late Medieval England* (Philadelphia: University of Pennsylvania Press, 1995), 189–215; Helena Halmari and Robert Adams, "On the Grammar and Rhetoric of Language Mixing in Piers Plowman," *Neuphilologische Mitteilungen* 103 (2002): 33–50; and Fiona Somerset, "Expanding the Langlandian Canon: Radical Latin and the Stylistics of Reform," *Yearbook of Langland Studies* 17 (2003): 73–92. In addition to Latin, Langland also uses French words and phrases in the poem, but these phrases are not on the whole as fully textualized as those derived from Latin *litteratura*: a phrase such as *"chaud* and *plus chaud"* (B 6.311) refers to a manner of speaking rather than to a particular text (see Alford, *Guide*, 12).

17. Andrew Galloway notes the possibility that the final phrase added to the scriptural passage, "or ellis ye don ille," need not be set off by quotation marks, but can be understood as Holy Church's voice merging with the scriptural voice as she explicates it (*The Penn Commentary on "Piers Plowman,"* vol. 1, *C Prologue-Passus 4; B Prologue-Passus 4; A Prologue-Passus 4* [Philadelphia: University of Pennsylvania Press, 2006], 172). These ambiguities and the resulting indeterminacy of voicing is a critical feature of Langland's style. My point here, however, is merely to note an instance in which English words ("þat *Cesari* bifalleþ") are clearly marked as the words of another.

18. In this case *Cesari* has been changed from the Vulgate "Cesaris," declined in the dative, as required by the English verb "bifalleþ."

19. See Chapter 4, pp. 136–37.

20. The passage may stress the power of verbal performance too much by attributing to it salvific agency that properly belongs to Christ. In C, the passage is revised in ways that make clear that Christ is the one to avenge or have pity: "And so of alle wykkede y wol here take veniaunce./A[c] ʒut my kynde [in] my kene ire shal constrayne my will—/*Domine ne in furore tuo Arguas me &c.*" (C 20.434–35α). In the place of *Parce*, Langland has substituted the incipit of the first penitential psalm (Ps. 6), to which, as *The Gast of Gy* also made clear, a similar intercessory function had been attributed.

21. Robert Adams, "Langland and the Liturgy Revisited," *Studies in Philology* 73 (1976): 275–76.

22. In addition to Alford's *Guide*, cited above, see his *"Piers Plowman": A Glossary of Legal Diction* (Cambridge: Brewer, 1988), Judson Boyce Allen, "Langland's Reading and Writing: *Detractor* and the Pardon Passus," *Speculum*

59 (1984): 342–62, is a seminal article on Langland's use of biblical concordances; see also Kerby-Fulton, *Reformist Apocalypticism*; and Emily Steiner, *Documentary Culture and the Making of Medieval English Literature* (Cambridge: Cambridge University Press, 2003), 93–190.

23. For a recent discussion situating Langland's relationship to the alliterative tradition more specifically, see Hanna, *London Literature*, 259–64.

24. The line's alliteration ironically comes at the cost of some "overskipping" itself; cf. James 2:10: "quicumque autem totam legem servaverit offendat autem in uno factus est omnium reus." Langland, of course, may have encountered his version of the phrase in a collection of biblical *sententiae* and merely recognized its serendipitous metrical structure.

25. Alford, *Glossary*, 68.

26. Ibid., 108.

27. Bakhtin, *Dialogic Imagination*, 67. Technically Bakhtin would refer to the triglossic situation of late medieval England as "polyglossia," which invokes differentiation across languages. Throughout this study, however, I have been attempting to call attention to heteroglossia in Latin as a site of conflict and creativity (and to the possibility that such a thing can exist within an "official" language).

28. Anne Middleton, "Narration and the Invention of Experience: Episodic Form in *Piers Plowman*," in *The Wisdom of Poetry: Essays in Honor of Morton W. Bloomfield*, ed. Larry D. Benson and Siegfried Wenzel (Kalamazoo, Mich.: Medieval Institute, 1982), 96–98.

29. Ibid., 97.

30. Raymond St.-Jacques has illuminated the liturgical underpinnings of these Passus in a series of articles: "Langland's Christ-Knight and the Liturgy," *Revue de l'Université d'Ottawa* 37 (1967): 146–58; "The Liturgical Associations of Langland's Samaritan," *Traditio* 25 (1969): 217–30; "Conscience's Final Pilgrimage in *Piers Plowman* and the Cyclical Structure of the Liturgy," *Revue de l'Université d'Ottawa* 40 (1970): 210–23; "Langland's Easter Bells of the Resurrection and the Easter Liturgy," *English Studies in Canada* 3 (1977): 129–35; and "Langland's *Christus Medicus* Image and the Structure of *Piers Plowman*," *Yearbook of Langland Studies* 5 (1991): 111–27. The liturgical references of Visions Six through Eight have now been compendiously documented in Stephen A. Barney, *The Penn Commentary on "Piers Plowman,"* Vol. 5, *C Passus 20–22; B Passus 18–20* (Philadelphia: University of Pennsylvania Press, 2006), 3, which indexes the references discussed in the rest of the volume.

31. *Brev.* 1:ccccclxxxiii–dccvi.

32. St.-Jacques, "Liturgical Associations," 215–23.

33. James Simpson, *"Piers Plowman": An Introduction to the B-Text* (London: Longman, 1990), 165.

34. St.-Jacques, "Langland's Christ-Knight," 146–50 passim.

35. Hanna suggests that this scene may have been based on the singing of *Veni creator* by the clergy at Richard II's coronation (*London Literature*, 250). If such a connection is present it would reinforce a connection between Langland's ideal vision and civic pageantry, which Kipling has connected to coronations in

general (*Enter the King*, 74). In this regard, see also the possible allusion to the pageant that preceded Richard's coronation in B Pro.128; C Pro.152 (Galloway, *Penn Commentary*, 125–26).

36. Robert Adams has called into question the authenticity of these rubrics as later editorial additions ("The Reliability of the Rubrics in the B-Text of *Piers Plowman*," *Medium Ævum* 54 [1985]: 208–31). For a more recent discussion of how the text was labeled, see Hanna, *London Literature*, 246–47.

37. Whether this "stalling" and the apparent gesture of closure I examine here implies the writer's intent that this version of the poem was to be "published" in this state or whether A is merely an "escaped" state of the poem on its way to becoming the longer B Version is beyond the scope of this chapter. See Hanna, *Pursuing History*, 203–43, esp. 236–37.

38. *"Piers Plowman": The A Version*, rev. ed., ed. George Kane (Berkeley and London: University of California Press/Athlone, 1988), 11.250–51. All further quotations of the A Version will refer to this edition and be cited parenthetically by text, Passus, and line number.

39. James Simpson, "The Role of *Scientia* in *Piers Plowman*," in *Medieval English Religious and Ethical Literature: Essays in Honour of G. H. Russell*, ed. Gregory Kratzmann and James Simpson (Woodbridge, Suffolk: Brewer, 1986), 61–65. Simpson, however, does not restrict his discussion of *scientia* to the words of Clergie or to the concept *clergie* and does not fully distinguish between the two. The idea of *clergie* as a central concept of *Piers Plowman* is treated in Fiona Somerset, *Clerical Discourse and Lay Audience in Late Medieval England* (Cambridge: Cambridge University Press, 1998), 22–62, though she is primarily interested the vernacular translation of *clergie*. Because the concept of *clergie*, rather than the character, is central to my understanding of Vision Three, I distinguish them by using lowercase italics for the concept *(clergie)*, capitalized roman type for the character (Clergie) and lowercase modernized spelling to refer to the clerical body as a whole (the clergy).

40. On the distinction between *scientia* and *sapientia*, see James Simpson, "From Reason to Affective Knowledge: Modes of Thought and Poetic Form in *Piers Plowman*," *Medium Ævum* 55 (1986): 1–23.

41. As with the passage from James, above (note 23), the wording does not match that of modern editions of its source, which qualifies the possession of knowledge (*Conf.* 8.8: "Surgunt indocti et caelum rapiunt, et nos cum doctrinis nostris sine corde ecce ubi uolutamur in carne et sanguine!"), yet Alford has found versions similar enough to Langland's to suggest that he may have found this more sentential version in a collection (*Guide*, 70).

42. James Simpson, "The Power of Impropriety: Authorial Naming in *Piers Plowman*," in *William Langland's "Piers Plowman": A Book of Essays*, ed. Kathleen M. Hewett-Smith (London: Routledge, 2001), 159.

43. Middleton, "Narration," 97.

44. The presence of this tradition as it is invoked in *Piers* is documented in Joseph S. Wittig, "*Piers Plowman* B, Passus IX–XII: Elements in the Design of the Inward Journey," *Traditio* 28 (1972): 211–80.

45. Anne Middleton, "William Langland's 'Kynde Name': Authorial Signature and Social Identity in Late Fourteenth-Century England," in *Literary Prac-*

tice and Social Change in Britain, 1380–1530, ed. Lee Patterson (Berkeley: University of California Press, 1990), 47–50.

46. Middleton, "'Kynde Name,'" 50–51.

47. I follow both Kane-Donaldson and Schmidt in assigning this speech to the Dreamer. Given the fluidity of the "I" throughout the poem—a fluidity that, one should note, takes on new force insofar as Langland has now established a locus of articulation ("Dreamer") within the economy of the dream—it is possible to understand these words as spoken "in the voice of the poem," as the entire speech had been in the A Version. Such a decision, however, would have to be based on an a priori association of the use of direct address with this voice. The fact that some manuscripts omit the last three lines does suggest that scribes perceived them as rhetorically dissonant, if not a shift in persona/voice altogether. I am instead calling attention to the analogous rhetorical gestures assigned to the "heiʒe men" to underline the self-conscious performativity I sense in this addition.

48. Kerby-Fulton, *Reformist Apocalypticism*, 76–132 passim.

49. David Lawton describes the persona of *Piers* as an "open" one ("The Subject of *Piers Plowman*," *Yearbook of Langland Studies* 1 [1987]: 11–13), a useful concept that he elaborates more fully in "Skelton's Use of *Persona*," *Essays in Criticism* 30 (1980): 9–28.

50. Wendy Scase, *"Piers Plowman" and the New Anticlericalism* (Cambridge: Cambridge University Press, 1989), 41.

51. The lection "clergie" in B 10.107 is favored by Kane and Donaldson over "clerkes," which appears in their copy-text along with several other MSS. The change is, in my opinion, appropriate, but the different lections do suggest that scribes had difficulty distinguishing between the two concepts.

52. The passage comes from the pseudo-Bernardian text, *Meditationes Piisimae de Cognitione Humanae Conditionis*, discussed by Wittig "*Piers Plowman* B, Passus IX–XII," 212ff., and Simpson, "The Role of *Scientia*," 51–53.

53. This tradition is discussed more fully in my forthcoming "Perils of *Canor*."

54. See Chapter 2, p. 53.

55. While Kane and Donaldson attribute the speech to the poetic "I," A. V. C. Schmidt assigns it to Trajan (*"The Vision of Piers Plowman": A Critical Edition of the B-Text* [New York: Dutton, 1978]). Wittig, following Skeat, assigns it to Lewtee (*"Piers Plowman* B, Passus IX–XII," 255n143).

56. *Piers Plowman: An Edition of the C-Text*, ed. Derek Pearsall (Berkeley: University of California Press, 1978), 238.

57. Ibid., 241.

58. The seeming inappropriateness of the "murye verset" seems to have caused trouble for lexicographers as well. While the compilers of the *MED* place this use of "murye" under their entry "miri(e (adj.)," 4.a., with the definition "spiritually delightful or agreeable," they add to this definition "also, effectual in preserving one's neck [quot.: *PPl.B*]" to accommodate the decidely less spiritual glee Langland implies. An alternative possibility, "mer(e (adj.1)," related to WS *mære*, defined as "good, fine" in relation to prayers, among other things (2.d.), is tempting, but implausible on philological grounds. "Verset (n.)" is usually the vernacular term for a liturgical versicle (a), though here, too, Langland's usage warrants its own

definition (b): "a short verse in one of the Psalms used as a neck-verse"—a definition that in its overspecificity obscures the ironic liturgical resonances of Langland's use.

59. Lawrence M. Clopper, "Need Men and Women Labor? Langland's Wanderer and the Labor Ordinances," in *Chaucer's England: Literature in Historical Context*, ed. Barbara Hanawalt (Minneapolis: University of Minnesota Press, 1992), 117–26.

60. Middleton, "Acts," 216–77.

61. Ibid., 249.

62. Ibid., 277–78.

63. It is worth noting also in this respect that the passage concerning the legitimacy of complaint for *lewid* speakers in particular (discussed above, pp. 170–71) has been replaced by a less confrontationally binary claim licensing "men þat ben trewe," proffered, in this case, by the Dreamer, not Lewtee himself (C 12.28).

64. Middleton, "Acts," 263–64.

65. The ambiguous status of Will's performance is reflected in the manuscripts. Kane and Russell have chosen "synge" over their copy-text's "segge," but the two lections appear with equal frequency. Elsewhere in the poem, however, there is a consistent distinction (both within and across MSS) between the two verbs in that "synge" denotes a liturgical, "public" activity, while "segge" marks a private, devotional act. The penitent Hawkyn in B (Avarice in C) admits that he "neuere penaunce parfournede ne Paternoster *seide*" (B 13.396; C 6.283), but the priestly Sloth, who admits to his singing and reading illiteracy ("Yet kan I neyþer solue ne synge ne seintes lyues rede" [B 5.416; C 7.30]), also states, "I kan noȝt my Paternoster as þe preest it *syngeþ*" (B 5.394; C 7.10). In some cases it is clear that the text performed generates the verb: one "sings" a mass, for example (the usual vernacular expression). The newly converted Saracens similarly "sing" the *Gloria*, as a unison liturgical performance of the Christian community (B 3.328). Yet when Langland changed the text to the *Credo* in C 3.81, several scribes changed "sing" to "say," taking their cue from the text (the *Credo* being one of the most basic devotional texts of the reading and singing repertoire). This regularity, especially striking given that there is no metrical difference between the two verbs, makes the equivocation in C 5 stand out as a particularly "unlocatable" speech act.

66. See Chapter 3, pp. 105–7.

67. The gospel passage makes the textualized and performative nature of the utterance clear: "*Dixit scriptum est* non in pane solo vivet homo sed in omni verbo quod procedit de ore Dei." Given the material overtones with which the passage has been endowed, it is also more than a little ironic to note that Will's choice of text is that in which Christ chose to resist the temptations of Satan in the desert.

68. Middleton, "Acts," 262.

Chapter 6

1. Middleton, "Public Poetry," 96–97, though Middleton refers to a particular "public" instantiation of love that is most explicitly represented in Gower's *Confessio amantis* or Usk's *Testament of Love*.

2. Lynn Staley, *Languages of Power in the Age of Richard II* (University Park: Pennsylvania State University Press, 2005), 2.

3. On Chaucer's complex sense of multiple audiences, see Strohm, *Social Chaucer*, 47–83; for manuscript evidence concerning the dissemination of Chaucer's, and other Ricardian writers', texts, see Kathryn Kerby-Fulton and Steven Justice, "Scribe D and the Marketing of Ricardian Literature," in *The Medieval Professional Reader at Work: Evidence from Manuscripts of Chaucer, Langland, Kempe, and Gower*, ed. Kathryn Kerby-Fulton and Maidie Hilmo (Victoria, B.C.: English Literary Studies, University of Victoria, 2001), 217–37.

4. Glending Olson discusses the distinction between "makere" and "poete," which loosely corresponds to my description of work governed by Love and by *grammatica* ("Making and Poetry in the Age of Chaucer," *Comparative Literature* 31 [1979]: 272–90). See also Lee Patterson, "'What Man Artow?': Authorial Self-Definition in *The Tale of Sir Thopas* and *The Tale of Melibee*," *Studies in the Age of Chaucer* 11 (1989): 118–19.

5. If Langland did share this desire, he was less successful in finding the means (beyond the use of alliterative meter) to calcify his verses, but the Latin tags that ground and at points generate his poetry compensate in a manner that suggests different priorities.

6. Irvine, "Medieval Grammatical Theory and Chaucer's *House of Fame*," *Speculum* 60 (1985): 850–76. For a more detailed discussion of *The House of Fame* as coping with the challenges of a vernacular *ars poetica*, see Zieman, "Chaucer's Voys," 80–85.

7. Ruth Evans, Andrew Taylor, Nicholas Watson, and Jocelyn Wogan-Browne, "Latin and Vernacular Literary Theory," in *The Idea of the Vernacular: An Anthology of Middle English Literary Theory, 1280–1520*, ed. Jocelyn Wogan-Browne, Nicholas Watson, Andrew Taylor, and Ruth Evans (University Park: Pennsylvania State University Press, 1999), 329.

8. Manly and Rickert claim that this assignment is virtually unanimous in the manuscripts (John Matthews Manly and Edith Rickert, *The Text of the "Canterbury Tales,"* [Chicago: University of Chicago Press, 1940], 2:424. For studies examining a potential dialogue, see, for example, Gail Berkeley Sherman, "Saints, Nuns, and Speech in the *Canterbury Tales*," in *Images of Sainthood in Medieval Europe,* ed. Renate Blumenfeld-Kosinki and Timea Szell (Ithaca, N.Y.: Cornell University Press, 1991), 136–60; Lisa Lampert, *Gender and Jewish Difference from Paul to Shakespeare* (Philadelphia: University of Pennsylvania Press, 2004), 80–91; Holsinger, *Music*, 284–85; and Leicester, *The Disenchanted Self*, 198, 205.

9. Beverly Boyd, *Chaucer and the Liturgy* (Philadelphia: Dorrence, 1967), 67–75; for the tale's use of the Little Office of the Virgin, see Sister M. Madeleva, *A Lost Language and Other Essays on Chaucer* (New York: Sheed, 1951), 52–53.

10. Carleton Brown, "The Prologue of Chaucer's 'Lif of Seint Ceceile," *Modern Philology* 9 (1911): 7–8. See Boyd, *Chaucer and the Liturgy*, 26–33, for other examples.

11. G. H. Gerould, "The Second Nun's Prologue and Tale," in *Sources and Analogues of Chaucer's "Canterbury Tales,"* ed. W. F. Bryan and Germaine Dempster (Chicago: University of Chicago Press, 1941), 667–77. For a more detailed

discussion of Chaucer's sources beyond the *Legenda aurea*, see Sherry L. Reames, "The Sources of the 'Second Nun's Tale,'" *Modern Philology* 76 (1978): 111–35; and Reames, "A Recent Discovery Concerning the Sources of Chaucer's 'Second Nun's Tale,'" *Modern Philology* 87 (1990): 337–61. For more on the relationship between liturgical *lectiones* and the *Legenda aurea*, see Alain Boureau, *La légende dorée: Le système narratif de Jacques de Voragine (1298)* (Paris: Cerf, 1984).

12. "*R.* Cantantibus organis Cecilia virgo in corde suo soli Domino decantabat dicens. Fiat cor meum et corpus meum immaculatum ut non confudar. *V.* Biduanis ac triduanis jejuniis orans suam Domino pudicitiam commendabat" (*Brev.* 3:1080).

13. Turner, *Ritual Process*, 95–6.

14. See Chapter 4, pp. 122–27; Schirmer, "Reading Lessons."

15. This similarity has been noted by J. C. Wenk, "On the Sources of the Prioress's Tale," *Mediaeval Studies* 17 (1955): 214–19, and Holsinger, *Music*, 284–85, among others.

16. On *lectiones* as a form of teaching, see Zieman, "Playing *Doctor*," 309–11.

17. Staley, "Chaucer and the Postures of Sanctity," in David Aers and Lynn Staley, *Powers of the Holy: Religion, Politics, and Gender in Late Medieval English Culture* (University Park: Pennsylvania State University Press, 1996), 180.

18. Such "public" moments in general occur in tales with a self-conscious investment in rhetoric—the two other rime royal tales (*The Man of Law's Tale*, *The Clerk's Tale*) as well as *The Knight's Tale*. None of these, however, focuses so emphatically on verbal performance as such as do the *The Prioress's Tale* and *The Second Nun's Tale*.

19. "Domine Dominus noster quam admirabile est nomen tuum in universa terra quoniam elevata est magnificentia tua super caelos: ex ore infantium et lactantium perfecisti laudem propter inimicos tuos ut destruas inimicum et ultorem" (Ps. 8:1–2).

20. As Nicholas Orme points out, medieval theorists considered *infancia* to extend to the age of seven, so there would be nothing unusual about calling the *clergeon* an "infant" ("The Education of the Courtier," in *Education and Society*). Rita Copeland, however, points to the ideological force in defining those with only pre-grammatical knowledge as "infants" (*Pedagogy*, 84).

21. A similar opposition does, however, appear in Richard Rolle's commentary on the English Psalter: "Noght anly thou art loued of perfit men, bot of the mouthe of barnes that spekis noght ȝit" (*The Psalter or Psalms of David and Certain Canticles with a Translation and Exposition in English by Richard Rolle of Hampole*, ed. H. R. Bramley [Oxford, 1884], 28).

22. The *clergeon* also attends "A litel scole of Cristen folk" (7.498)—the word "litel" appears twelve times in a tale that contains only 200 lines.

23. See Chapter 4, p. 129.

24. Lee Patterson, *Chaucer and the Subject of History* (Madison: University of Wisconsin Press, 1991), 349.

25. Ibid., 361. See also Gerhard Joseph, "Chaucer's Coinage: Foreign Exchange and the Puns of the *Shipman's Tale*," *Chaucer Review* 17 (1983): 341–47.

26. Judith Ferster, "'Your Praise Is Performed by Men and Children': Language and Gender in the *Prioress's Prologue* and *Tale*," *Exemplaria* 2 (1990): 153.

27. "Hou þe Iewes, in Despit of Vre Lady, þrewe A Chyld in a Gonge," analogue C. 5 in Carleton Brown, "The Prioress' Tale," in *Sources and Analogues of
Chaucer's "Canterbury Tales,"* ed. W. F. Bryan and Germaine Dempster (Chicago:
University of Chicago Press, 1941), ll. 13–14. For more on the sources of the tale,
see Brown's *Study of the Miracle of Our Lady Told by Chaucer's Prioress*, Publications of the Chaucer Society, ser. 2, no. 45 (London: Kegan Paul, 1910).

28. Lampert, *Gender and Jewish Difference*, 77–78.

29. Louise O. Fradenburg, "Criticism, Anti-Semitism, and *The Prioress' Tale*,"
Exemplaria 1 (1989): 93.

30. The Latin phrase found in foundation statutes is usually *ad divini cultus
augmentum*. See, for example, the papal license for the foundation of Winchester
College (Kirby, *Annals of Winchester College*, 456).

31. Fradenburg, "Criticism," 89.

32. See Chapter 4, pp. 125–26.

33. Hilton, *The Scale*, 248 (2.42).

34. Carolynn Van Dyke, *Chaucer's Agents: Cause and Representation in
Chaucerian Narrative* (Madison: Fairleigh Dickinson University Press, 2005),
167–68.

35. Fradenburg, "Criticism," 100.

36. Ibid., 100-101, 94–95.

37. Patterson, "Living Witnesses"; see also Carolyn P. Collette, "Sense and
Sensibility in the 'Prioress's Tale,'" *Chaucer Review* 15 (1981): 138–50.

38. Rolle's interest in the surfaces of language is the subject of my forthcoming
article, "'The Perils of *Canor*." For the repetition of a single word, see *Cloud*, 75.

39. Fradenburg, "Criticism," 94.

40. Ibid., 97.

41. This unanimity has been remarked upon by Fradenburg, "Criticism," 97;
and Denise L. Despres, "Cultic Anti-Judaism and Chaucer's Litel Clergeon," *Modern Philology* 91 (1994): 423. Lawrence Besserman disagrees with characterizing
the pilgrims' response as one of positive "wonder" ("Ideology, Antisemitism, and
Chaucer's *Prioress's Tale*," *Chaucer Review* 36 [2001]: 66). The character of their
reaction, however, is less important than their uncharacteristic agreement.

42. Indeed, the Abbot's removal of the grain serves less as a reflection of clerical dominance than as an extension of the Prioress's own anxieties that override her
anti-clericalism. Reminiscent of her compulsively fastidious eating habits described
in the *General Prologue* (1.128–31), the grain seems like yet another morsel of food
she worries will end up in the wrong place. This anxiety is in part simply another
manifestation of the Prioress's obsession with intactness—the taking in of food
being an activity that confuses the boundary between inner and outer—as well as a
correlative fear of scattering (or of being scattered) should that boundary fail.

43. In several of the analogues of the "C" group, by contrast, the child begins singing again because of his desire to "correct" the priests who have begun
to sing a requium mass in his honor. In these cases the child begins a new (and
presumably miraculously "learned") song, *Salve sancta parens*, which is the beginning of the Office of the Virgin—a service he finds more suited to his devotion.
See Brown, "The Prioress's Tale," 459, 469–70, 475.

44. See Sherman Hawkins, "Chaucer's Prioress and the Sacrifice of Praise," *Journal of English and Germanic Philology* 63 (1964): 618.

45. For a more extensive analysis of the violence perpetrated on the *clergeon's* body, see Holsinger, *Music*, 272–88.

46. In alternative versions of the tale, the boy speaks without such conjuring; see note 43 above.

47. Van Dyke makes a useful distinction between "primary" and "secondary" agency to distinguish between "the power to execute one's own intentions" and acts of representation, in which one person serves as the "agent" of another (*Chaucer's Agents*, 18–19). It might be useful to consider the difference between the *clergeon's* modes of performance in terms of degrees of primary and secondary agency in each.

48. This passage merely restores the agency to God that was obscured in the Prioress's translation of Psalm 8 in her prologue when she translated the active *perfecisti* ("you perfect praise") with the passive "parfourned is," which emphasizes God's need of human performers (Ferster, "'Your Praise,'" 153).

49. Rosalynn Voaden discusses the importance of this kind of instrumentality to visionary discourse in particular (*God's Words, Women's Voices: The Discernment of Spirits in the Writing of Late-Medieval Women Visionaries* [Woodbridge, Suffolk: York Medieval Press, 1999]).

50. Richard H. Osberg, "A Voice for the Prioress: The Context of English Devotional Prose," *Studies in the Age of Chaucer* 18 (1996): 44–45.

51. "Nisi granum frumenti cadens in terram mortuum fuerit, ipsum solum manet, si autem mortuum fuerit multum fructum adfert. Qui amat animam suam perdet eam et qui odit animam suam in hoc mundo in vitam aeternam custodit eam."

52. *Brev.* 1:ccxlv. See Sister Nicholas Maltman, O.P., "The Divine Granary, or the End of the Prioress's 'Greyn,'" *Chaucer Review* 17 (1976): 164. See also the prosa *Clangat pastor*, which likens martyrdom to "granum purgatum palea/In divina transfertur horrea" (165; *Brev.* 1:ccxlv–vi). These texts are associated with the feast of St. Thomas, which occurs on the day after Holy Innocents (December 27 and 26, respectively). Because major feasts begin with vespers on the evening before ("first vespers"), the first vespers of St. Thomas coincides with the second vespers (celebrated on the day of feast itself) of Holy Innocents. Although in these texts the *granum* refers to the "fruit" alone, the *granum* of the gospel text does seem to refer to the soul and body together, before the body has died.

53. Hilton and his sense of unruly interiors is treated in my forthcoming "Perils of *Canor*."

54. Fradenburg, "Criticism," 100, 102–3, 106.

55. I would contend further that critical anxiety over the tale's anti-Semitism, though clearly an important motivator for modern scholars and clearly related to the notion of language set forth in the tale, is not the sole cause of interest in her motives.

56. If one imagines the prologue as a response to *The Prioress's Prologue*, there is even an implicit insult that the Prioress's exalting of pure repetition is simply a form of laziness. Such an interpretation, however, would require that the

Second Nun's Prologue follow *The Prioress's Prologue* in the ordering of the tales, which it does not in all manuscript traditions. See *The Riverside Chaucer*, 1120–21.

57. See, for example, Brown, *Study*, 6, 19, 21, 23, 25, 33.

58. Robert M. Longsworth, "Privileged Knowledge: St. Cecilia and the Alchemist in the *Canterbury Tales*," *Chaucer Review* 27 (1992): 87.

59. Lee Patterson, "Perpetual Motion: Alchemy and the Technology of the Self," *Studies in the Age of Chaucer* 15 (1993): 39–42.

60. This parallel might be underscored still further if one understands the substantive transformations of *The Canon's Yeoman's Tale* to allude to the Eucharist (see Joseph E. Grennen, "The Canon's Yeoman's Alchemical Mass," *Studies in Philology* 62 [1965]: 550–51; Staley, "Chaucer," 212). The canon's con game, at least, is likened to sacred performance: "Loo, how this theef koude his service beede!" (8.1065).

61. Joseph E. Grennen, "St. Cecilia's 'Chemical Wedding': The Unity of the *Canterbury Tales*, Fragment VIII," *Journal of English and Germanic Philology* 65 (1966): 472–73; Patterson, "Perpetual Motion," 31–33.

62. V. A. Kolve, "Chaucer's Second Nun's Tale and the Iconography of Saint Cecilia," in *New Perspectives on Chaucer Criticism*, ed. D. M. Rose (Norman, Okla.: Pilgrim, 1981), 152.

63. Osberg, "A Voice," 40–41; Fradenburg, "Criticism," 106.

64. Though scholars disagree on the dates of composition, the parallels between the *Second Nun's Tale* and *The House of Fame* are striking. Their diametrically opposed depictions of the vernacular are offset by a similar self-consciousness of the use of the English language and similar spatial imagery (cf. the theory of sound provided by the Eagle), complemented by allusions to Dante in their prologues. If they are not contemporary, it is intriguing to imagine that they are in some sense companion pieces.

65. Patterson, "Perpetual Motion," 31, 33.

66. On Chaucer's subject as the subject, see Patterson, "Perpetual Motion," 31, after Leicester, *The Disenchanted Self*, 15.

67. Patterson, "Perpetual Motion," 32–33; Holsinger, *Music*, 264–65.

68. Russell A. Peck, "The Ideas of 'Entente' and Translation in Chaucer's *Second Nun's Tale*," *Annuale Mediaevale* 8 (1967): 21.

69. Fradenburg, "Criticism," 97.

70. Staley, "Chaucer," 201; Michael Wilks, "Wyclif and the Great Persecution," in *Prophecy and Eschatology*, ed. Michael Wilks, Studies in Church History, Subsidia, vol. 10 (Oxford: Blackwell, 1994), 50–51; Ghosh, *Wycliffite Heresy*.

71. Staley, "Chaucer," 209. Suffice it to say, my brief mention is an oversimplification of her reading of this passage.

72. This is not to suggest that the phrase "yow that reden that I write" is a conscious addition, as opposed to the flaw in adaptive editing it is usually taken to be. It is, however, a suggestive "flaw" when viewed in this oppositional context.

73. On the juxtaposition of orality and literacy in *Thopas* and *Melibee*, see Seth Lerer, "'Now Holde Youre Mouth': The Romance of Orality in the *Thopas-Melibee* Section of the *Canterbury Tales*," in *Oral Poetics in Middle English Poetry*, ed. Mark C. Amodio and Sarah Gray Miller (New York: Garland, 1994), 181–205.

74. See Patterson, "'What Man Artow,'" 152–53, who points to Chaucer's use of the word "sentence" five times in eighteen lines.

75. For more on the similarities between *The Second Nun's Tale* and *Melibee*, see Staley, "Chaucer," 181–82.

76. Ferster places Melibee's performance within the "mirror for princes tradition" (*Fictions of Advice*, 89–107), whereas Wallace situates it within a tradition of civic politics (*Chaucerian Polity*, 216–21) and thus beyond the court.

77. Alan T. Gaylord, "The 'Miracle' of *Sir Thopas*," *Studies in the Age of Chaucer* 6 (1984): 66. See also Helen Cooper, who states that Thopas's "sudden vision-inspired devotion *threatens* to parody the child's vision of a protecting Virgin" (*Oxford Guides to Chaucer: "The Canterbury Tales"* [Oxford: Oxford University Press, 1989], 308, my emphasis).

78. Mary Hamel, "'And Now for Something Completely Different': The Relationship Between the *Prioress's Tale* and the *Rime of Sir Thopas*," *Chaucer Review* 14 (1980): 251–59.

79. Green, *Poets and Princepleasers*, 143; Patterson, "'What Man Artow,'" 122–24. See, however, Wallace's less courtly assessment (*Chaucerian Polity*, 212–46).

80. Staley, "Chaucer," 181.

81. Paul Zumthor records this usage as early as the eleventh-century *Vie de Saint Alexis* ("The Vocalization of the Text: The Medieval 'Poetic Effect,'" trans. Nancy Rose and Peter Haidu, *Viator* 19 [1988]: 275). See also Manfred Günter Scholz, "On Presentation and Reception Guidelines in the German Strophic Epic of the Late Middle Ages," trans. Rebecca Williams Duplantier and Crozet Duplantier, Jr., *New Literary History* 16 (1984): 137–51. For examples among Chaucer's contemporaries, see Gower, *CA*, 5.5272–55, 6.974–85, 6.1224–26; John Clanvowe, *The Two Ways* (in *The Works of Sir John Clanvowe*, ed. V. J. Scattergood [Cambridge: Brewer, 1975], 69; and Thomas Usk, *The Testament of Love*, ed. R. Allen Shoaf (Kalamazoo, Mich.: Medieval Institute, 1998), 148.

82. It is worth noting in this respect that there is a similar connection between public performance of poetry and ecclesiastical loci in the famous frontispiece to the *Troilus* in Corpus Christi College, Cambridge MS 61, which is based on the iconography of preachers (Derek Pearsall, "The *Troilus* Frontispiece and Chaucer's Audience," *Year in English Studies* 7 [1977]: 70–71). Such a connection on the less formal level of reading and singing might give an added dimension to the famous Hoccleve portrait and its relations, in which Chaucer holds a rosary (see Pearsall, *The Life of Geoffrey Chaucer: A Critical Biography* [Oxford: Blackwell, 1992], 285–91). Both portraits might be usefully compared to those of the "courtly" Guillaume de Machaut, who appears throughout the well-known "MS C" with a roll of parchment and a pen (Paris, Bibliothèque nationale de France, Français 1586, fols. 26r, 28v, 45v, 46v, 47v, 56v).

Bibliography

MANUSCRIPT SOURCES

Aberdeen University Library

MS 25
MS 271

Cambridge University Library

Ii.6.2

Cologne, Historical Archive

W.153

London, British Library

Cotton Augustus VI
Cotton Faustina A.vi
Egerton 3135
Harley 2897
Lansdowne 762
Lansdowne 763
Royal 17 B.xvii
Royal 17 C.xvii

London, Lambeth Palace Library

MS 3285

London, Public Record Office

C 66/339
JUST 3/145

JUST 3/176
JUST 3/178
JUST 3/179

Oxford, Bodleian Library

Donation d.85
Douce 18
Laud latin 15
Liturgical 104
Rawlinson G.185
Rawlinson liturg. g.2

Oxford, New College Archives

MS 3691

Paris, Bibliothèque nationale de France

Français 1586

Salisbury Cathedral Dean and Chapter

Reg. Coman
Reg. Corfe
Reg. Dunham

San Marino, Huntington Library

EL 9 H 17

Uppsalla, Universitätsbibliothek

C.175

Winchester Cathedral Dean and Chapter

Priory Reg. I

Winchester College Archives

Doc. 70a

PRINTED SOURCES

Published Documents

Bannister, A. T., ed. "Visitation Returns of the Diocese of Hereford in 1397."
     English Historical Review 44 (1929): 279–89, 444–53; 45 (1930): 92–101,
     444–63.
Calendar of Patent Rolls. London: H. M. Stationery Office, 1891–.
A Calendar of the Register of Henry Wakefield, Bishop of Worcester, 1375–95. Ed. W. P.
     Marett. Worcestershire Historical Society, n.s., 7. Leeds: Maney, 1972.
A Calendar of the Register of Wolstan de Bransford, Bishop of Worcester, 1339–49.
     Ed. R. M. Haines. Worcestershire Historical Society, n.s., 4. London: H. M.
     Stationery Office, 1966.
The Cartulary of the Priory of St. Gregory, Canterbury. Ed. Audrey Woodcock.
     London: Royal Historical Society, 1956.
Corpus iuris canonici. Ed. Emil Friedberg. 2 vols. Leipzig, 1879.
Councils and Synods, with Other Documents Relating to the English Church, vol. 2,
     1205–1313. Ed. F. M. Powicke and C. R. Cheney. Oxford: Clarendon, 1964.
Dalton, John Neale, ed. *The Collegiate Church of Ottery St. Mary.* Cambridge:
     Cambridge University Press, 1917.
Documents Relating to the University and Colleges of Cambridge. 3 vols. London,
     1852.
Dugdale, William. *Monasticon Anglicanum, Enriched with a Large Accession of
     Materials.* Ed. J. Caley. 6 vols in 8. London, 1817–30.
Fowler, J. T., ed. *Memorials of the Church of SS. Peter and Wilfrid, Ripon.* 4 vols.
     Surtees Society 74, 78, 81, 115. Durham, 1882.
Heywood, J., and Thomas Wright, eds. *The Ancient Laws for King's College Cam-
     bridge and Eton College.* London, 1850.
*The Household Book of Queen Isabella of England for the 5th Regnal Year of Edward
     II.* Ed. F. D. Blackley and G. Hermansen. Edmonton: University of Alberta
     Press, 1971.
Leach, A. F., ed. *Early Yorkshire Schools.* 2 vols. Yorkshire Archaeological Society
     Record Series 27, 33. Leeds, 1898–1903.
———, ed. *Educational Charters and Documents, 598 to 1909.* Cambridge, 1911,
     Reprint, New York: AMS, 1971.
*Literae Cantuarienses: The Letter Books of the Monastery of Christ Church, Canter-
     bury.* Ed. J. Brigstocke Sheppard. 3 vols. Rolls Series 85. London, 1887–89.
Monumenta Germaniae Historica. Leges. Sectio II: Capitula Regum Francorum.
     Ed. Alfred Boreti and Victor Krause. 2 vols. Hanover, 1883.

Monumenta Germaniae Historica: Epistolae Merowingici et Karolini aevi. 8 vols. Berlin: Weidmann, 1892–1939.

The Register of Edmond Stafford, Bishop of Exeter, 1395–1419. Ed. F. C. Hingeston-Randolph. London and Exeter, 1886.

The Register of Henry Chichele, Archbishop of Canterbury, 1414–1443. Ed. E. F. Jacob. 4 vols. Canterbury and York Society 42, 45–47. Oxford: Clarendon, 1938–42.

The Register of John Grandisson, Bishop of Exeter, 1327–1369. Ed. F. C. Hingeston-Randolph. 3 vols. London: Bell; Exeter: Eland, 1894–99.

The Register of John Waltham, Bishop of Salisbury, 1388–1395. Ed. T. C. B. Timmons. Canterbury and York Society 80. Suffolk: Canterbury and York Society, 1994.

The Register of Walter Bronescombe, Bishop of Exeter, 1257–1280. Ed. F. C. Hingeston-Randolph. London, 1889.

The Register of William Bateman. Ed. Phyllis E. Pobst. 2 vols. Canterbury and York Society 84, 90. Woodbridge: Boydell, 1996–2000.

The "Registrum antiquissimum" of the Cathedral Church of Lincoln. Ed. C. W. Foster. 10 vols. Lincoln: Lincoln Record Society, 1931.

Registrum Johannis Gilbert, Episcopi Herefordensis, A.D. *MCCCLXXV-MCCCLXXXIX.* Ed. J. H. Parry. Canterbury and York Society 18. London: Canterbury and York Society, 1915.

Registrum Rogeri Maritival. Ed. C. Y. Erlington. Canterbury and York Society 58. London: Canterbury and York Society, 1972.

Reynalds, H. E., ed. *Wells Cathedral: Its Foundation, Constitutional History and Statutes.* Leeds, 1881.

Riley, H. T., ed. *Registra Quorundum Abbatum Monasterii S. Albani, Qui Sæculo XVmo. Floruere.* 2 vols. Rolls Series 28, pt. 6. London, 1872–73.

Sayles, G. O., ed. *Select Cases in the Court of King's Bench.* 7 vols. Selden Society 55, 57, 58, 74, 76, 82, 88. London: Quaritch, 1936–71.

Statute et Consuetudines Ecclesiae Cathedralis Beatae Mariae Virginis Sarisburiensis. Ed. Christopher Wordsworth and Douglas Macleane. London: Clowes, 1915.

Statutes of Lincoln Cathedral. Ed. Henry Bradshaw and Christopher Wordsworth. 3 vols. Cambridge, 1892.

Statutes of the Colleges of Oxford, with Royal Patents of Foundation, Injunctions of Visitors and Catalogues of Documents Relating to the University. 12 vols. Oxford, 1853.

Statutorum et Consuetudinum Ecclesiae Cathedralis Sancti Pauli Londoniensis. Ed. W. Sparrow Simpson. London, 1873.

Thompson, A. H., ed. "The Statutes of the College of St. Mary and All Saints, Fotheringhay." *Archaeological Journal* 75 (1918): 241–309.

Weaver, F. W., ed. *Somerset Medieval Wills, 1383–1500.* 3 vols. Somerset Record Society 16, 19, 21. London, 1901–5.

Wilkins, David. *Concilia Magnae Britanniae et Hiberniae* (1737). 3 vols. in 4. Brussels: Culture et Civilisation, 1964.

Woolgar, C. M., ed. *Household Accounts from Medieval England*. 2 vols. Records of Social and Economic History, n.s., 17–18. Oxford: Oxford University Press, 1992–93.

Wykeham's Register. Ed. T. F. Kirby. 2 vols. Hampshire Record Society 12. London and Winchester, 1896–99.

Literary and Liturgical Texts

Aelred of Rievaulx's "De institutione inclusarum": Two English Versions. Ed. John Ayto and Alexandra Barratt. EETS, o.s., 287. Oxford: Oxford University Press, 1984.

The Anonimalle Chronicle, 1333–1381. Ed. V. H. Galbraith. Manchester: University Press, 1929.

Augustine of Hippo. *Confessionum libri XIII*. Ed. Lucas Verheijen. Corpus Christianorum Series Latina 27. Turnholt: Brepols, 1981.

Babb, Warren, trans. *Hucbald, Guido, and John on Music: Three Medieval Treatises*. Ed. Claude V. Palisca. New Haven, Conn., and London: Yale University Press, 1978.

Bede. *Bede's Ecclesiastical History of the English People*. Ed. Bertram Colgrave and R. A. B. Mynors. Oxford: Clarendon, 1969.

Bevington, David, ed. *Medieval Drama*. Boston: Houghton Mifflin, 1975.

Breviarium ad Usum Insignis Ecclesiae Sarum. Ed. Francis Procter and Christopher Wordsworth. 3 vols. Cambridge, 1879–86.

The Chastising of God's Children and The Treatise of Perfection of the Sons of God. Ed. Joyce Bazire and Eric Colledge. Oxford: Blackwell, 1957.

Chaucer, Geoffrey. *The Riverside Chaucer*. 3rd ed. Ed. Larry Benson. Boston: Houghton Mifflin, 1987.

Clanvowe, John. *The Works of Sir John Clanvowe*. Ed. V. J. Scattergood. Cambridge: Brewer, 1975.

The Cloud of Unknowing and The Book of Privy Counselling. Ed. Phyllis Hodgson. EETS, o.s., 218. London: EETS, 1944.

The Customary of the Cathedral Priory Church of Norwich. Ed. J. B. L. Tolhurst. Henry Bradshaw Society 82. London: Henry Bradshaw Society, 1948.

Disticha Catonis. Ed. M. Boas. Amstelodami: North-Holland, 1952.

Durandus, William. *Guillelmi Duranti Rationale divinorum officiorum*. Ed. A. Davril and T. M. Thibodeau. 3 vols. Corpus Christianorum Continuatio Mediaevalis 140–140B. Turnholt: Brepols, 1995.

Fein, Susanna Greer, ed. *Moral Love Songs and Laments*. Kalamazoo, Mich.: Medieval Institute, 1998.

Foster, Edward E., ed. *Three Purgatory Poems: The Gast of Gy, Sir Owain, The Vision of Tundale*. Kalamazoo, Mich.: Medieval Institute, 2004.

The Gast of Gy: Eine englische Dichtung des 14. Jahrhunderts. Ed. Gustav Schleich. Berlin, 1898.

The Gast of Gy: A Middle English Religious Prose Tract Preserved in Queen's College, Oxford MS. 383. Ed. R. H. Bowers. Leipzig: Tauchnitz, 1938.

Gerson, Jean. *Œuvres complètes.* Ed. Mgr. Glorieux. 2 vols. Paris: Desclée, 1961.

Gesta Henrici Quinti: The Deeds of Henry the Fifth. Trans. Frank Taylor and John S. Roskell. Oxford: Clarendon, 1975.

Gower, John. *The Complete Works of John Gower.* Ed. G. C. Macaulay. 4 vols. Oxford: Clarendon, 1899–1902.

———. *The Latin Verses in the "Confessio amantis": An Annotated Translation.* Trans. Siân Echard and Claire Fanger. East Lansing, Mich.: Colleagues, 1991.

———. *Mirour de l'Omme (The Mirror of Mankind).* Trans. William Burton Wilson. Rev. Nancy Wilson Van Baak. East Lansing, Mich.: Colleagues, 1992.

Guido of Arezzo. *Guidonis Aretini Micrologus.* Ed. Jos. Smits van Waesberghe. Corpus Scriptorum de Musica 4. [Rome]: American Institute of Musicology, 1955.

Hilton, Walter. *The Scale of Perfection.* Ed. Thomas H. Bestul. Kalamazoo, Mich.: Medieval Institute, 2000.

Horstmann, Carl, ed. *The Minor Poems of the Vernon MS, Part I.* EETS, o.s., 98. London, 1892.

———. *Yorkshire Writers: Richard Rolle of Hampole and His Followers.* 2 vols. London, 1896.

Kail, J., ed. *Twenty-Six Political and other Poems from the Oxford MSS. Digby 102 and Douce 322.* EETS, o.s., 124. London: Kegan Paul, 1904.

Knighton, Henry. *Knighton's Chronicle, 1337–1396.* Ed. G. H. Martin. Oxford: Clarendon, 1995.

Langland, William. *"Piers Plowman": An Edition of the C-Text.* Ed. Derek Pearsall. Berkeley: University of California Press, 1978.

———. *"Piers Plowman": The A Version.* Rev. ed. Ed. George Kane. Berkeley and London: University of California Press/Athlone, 1988.

———. *"Piers Plowman": The B Version.* Ed. George Kane and E. Talbot Donaldson. London: Athlone, 1975.

———. *"Piers Plowman": The C Version.* Ed. George Kane and George Russell. Berkeley and London: University of California Press/Athlone, 1997.

———. *"The Vision of Piers Plowman": A Critical Edition of the B-Text.* Ed. A. V. C. Schmidt. New York: Dutton, 1978.

The Lay Folks' Catechism, or the English and Latin Versions of Archbishop Thoresby's Instructions for the People. Ed. Thomas Frederick Simmons and Henry Edward Nolloth. EETS, o.s., 118. London: EETS/Oxford University Press, 1901.

The Lay Folks' Mass Book, or the Manner of Hearing Mass. Ed. Thomas Frederick Simmons. EETS, o.s., 71. London, 1879.

Love, Nicholas. *The Mirror of the Blessed Life of Jesus Christ: A Full Critical Edition.* Ed. Michael G. Sargent. Exeter: University of Exeter Press, 2005.

Maidstone, Richard. *Concordia (The Reconciliation of Richard II with London).* Ed. David R. Carlson. Trans. A. G. Rigg. Kalamazoo, Mich.: Medieval Institute, 2003.

Missale ad Usum Insignis et Praeclarae Ecclesiae Sarum. Ed. Francis Henry Dickinson. Burntisland, 1861–83.

The Myroure of Oure Ladye. Ed. John Henry Blunt. EETS, e.s., 19. London, 1873.

Rolle, Richard. *The "Incendium amoris" of Richard Rolle of Hampole.* Ed. Margaret Deanesly. Manchester: Manchester University Press, 1915.

———. *The Psalter or Psalms of David and Certain Canticles with a Translation and Exposition in English by Richard Rolle of Hampole.* Ed. H. R. Bramley. Oxford, 1884.

Sarum Missal. Ed. J. Wickham Legg. Oxford: Clarendon, 1969.

The Simonie: A Parallel-Text Edition. Ed. Dan Embree and Elizabeth Urquhart. Heidelberg: Carl Winter, 1991.

The Use of Sarum. Ed. W. H. Frere. 2 vols. Cambridge: Cambridge University Press, 1898–1901.

Usk, Thomas. *The Testament of Love.* Ed. R. Allen Shoaf. Kalamazoo, Mich.: Medieval Institute, 1998.

Walsingham, Thomas. *Gesta Abbatum Monasterii Sancti Albani.* Ed. Henry Thomas Riley. 2 vols. Rolls Series 28, pt. 1. London, 1867.

Wogan-Browne, Jocelyn, et al. eds. *The Idea of the Vernacular: An Anthology of Middle English Literary Theory, 1280–1520.* University Park: Pennsylvania State University Press, 1999.

STUDIES

Adams, Robert. "Langland and the Liturgy Revisited." *Studies in Philology* 73 (1976): 266–84.

———. "The Reliability of the Rubrics in the B-Text of *Piers Plowman.*" *Medium Ævum* 54 (1985): 208–31.

Aers, David. "Altars of Power: Reflections on Eamon Duffy's *The Stripping of the Altars: Traditional Religion in England, 1400–1580.*" *Literature and History* 3 (1994): 90–105.

———. *Sanctifying Signs: Making Christian Tradition in Late Medieval England.* Notre Dame, Ind.: University of Notre Dame Press, 2004.

———. "A Whisper in the Ear of Early Modernists; or, Reflections on Literary Critics Writing the 'History of the Subject.'" In *Culture and History, 1350–1600: Essays on English Communities, Identities and Writing,* ed. David Aers. New York: Harvester Wheatsheaf, 1992. 177–202.

Alford, John H. "A Note on *Piers Plowman* B.xviii.390, 'Til *parce* it hote.'" *Modern Philology* 69 (1972): 323–25.

———. *"Piers Plowman": A Glossary of Legal Diction.* Cambridge: Brewer, 1988.

———. *"Piers Plowman": A Guide to the Quotations.* Medieval and Renaissance Texts and Studies 77. Binghamton, N.Y.: Center for Medieval and Early Renaissance Studies, 1982.

———. "The Role of Quotation in *Piers Plowman.*" *Speculum* 52 (1977): 80–99.

Allen, Judson Boyce. "Langland's Reading and Writing: *Detractor* and the Pardon Passus." *Speculum* 59 (1984): 342–62.

Althusser, Louis. "Ideology and Ideological State Apparatuses (Notes Towards an Investigation)." Trans. Ben Brewster. In *Lenin and Philosophy and Other Essays.* New York: Monthly Review Press, 1971. 127–86.

Angenendt, Arnold, et al. "Counting Piety in the Early and High Middle Ages." In *Ordering Society: Perspectives on Intellectual and Practical Modes of Shaping Social Relations,* ed. Bernhard Jussen. Philadelphia: University of Pennsylvania Press, 2001. 15–54.

Aston, Margaret. *Lollards and Reformers: Images and Literacy in Late Medieval Religion.* London: Hambledon, 1984.

———. *Thomas Arundel: A Study of Church Life in the Reign of Richard II.* Oxford: Oxford University Press, 1967.

Austin, J. L. *How to Do Things with Words.* 2nd ed. Ed. J. O. Urmson and Marina Sbisà. Cambridge, Mass.: Harvard University Press, 1975.

Bagley, Ayers. "St. Anne Teaching the Virgin, 14th–15th centuries." *St. Anne Teaching the Virgin to Read.* 12 February 2004. University of Minnesota. http:// education.umn.edu/edpa/iconics/St_Anne/St_Anne_Text.htm (accessed 19 May 2006).

Bakhtin, Mikhail. *The Dialogic Imagination: Four Essays.* Trans. Caryl Emerson and Michael Holquist. Austin: University of Texas Press, 1981.

———. *Problems of Dostoevsky's Poetics.* Trans. Caryl Emerson. Minneapolis: University of Minnesota Press, 1984.

Barney, Stephen A. *The Penn Commentary on "Piers Plowman,"* Vol. 5, *C Passus 20–22; B Passus 18–20.* Philadelphia: University of Pennsylvania Press, 2006.

Barr, Helen. "The Use of Latin Quotations in *Piers Plowman* with Special Reference to Passus XVIII of the 'B' Text." *Notes & Queries,* n.s., 33 (1986): 440–48.

Barratt, Alexandra. "The Prymer and Its Influence on Fifteenth-Century English Passion Lyrics." *Medium Ævum* 44 (1975): 264–79.

Barron, Caroline. "The Parish Fraternities of Medieval London." In *The Church in Pre-Reformation Society: Essays in Honor of F. R. H. DuBoulay,* ed. Caroline Barron and Christopher Harper-Bill. Woodbridge: Boydell, 1985. 13–37.

Bateson, Mary. "The Huntingdon Song School." *English Historical Review* 18 (1903): 710–12.

Beckwith, Sarah. *Signifying God: Social Relation and Symbolic Act in the York Corpus Christi Plays.* Chicago: University of Chicago Press, 2001.

Bell, Catherine. *Ritual Theory, Ritual Practice.* New York and Oxford: Oxford University Press, 1992.

Bennett, Adelaide. "The Transformation of the Gothic Psalter in Thirteenth-Century France." In *The Illuminated Psalter: Studies in the Content, Purpose and Placement of Its Images,* ed. F. O. Büttner. Turnhout: Brepols, 2004. 211–21.

Bent, Ian. "The Early History of the English Chapel Royal, ca. 1066–1327." Ph.D. diss., St. John's College, Cambridge, 1968.

———. "The English Chapel Royal Before 1300." *Proceedings of the Royal Musical Association* 90 (1963/4): 77–95.

Besserman, Lawrence. "Ideology, Antisemitism, and Chaucer's *Prioress's Tale*." *Chaucer Review* 36 (2001): 48–72.

Black, Robert. *Humanism and Education in Medieval and Renaissance Italy: Tradition and Innovation in Latin Schools from the Twelfth to the Fifteenth Century.* Cambridge and New York: Cambridge University Press, 2001.

Bossy, John. *Christianity in the West, 1400–1700.* Oxford: Oxford University Press, 1985.

———. "The Mass as a Social Institution, 1200–1700." *Past and Present* 100 (1983): 29–61.

Bourdieu, Pierre. *Language and Symbolic Power.* Ed. John B. Thompson. Trans. Gino Raymond and Matthew Adamson. Cambridge, Mass.: Harvard University Press, 1991.

———. *Outline of a Theory of Practice.* Trans. Richard Nice. Cambridge: Cambridge University Press, 1977.

Boureau, Alain. *La légende dorée: Le système narratif de Jacques de Voragine (1298).* Paris: Cerf, 1984.

Bowers, Roger. "Choral Institutions Within the English Church: Their Constitution and Development, 1340–1500." Ph.D. diss., University of East Anglia, 1975.

———. *English Church Polyphony: Singers and Sources from the 14th to the 17th Century.* Aldershot: Ashgate, 1999.

———. "Musicians of Lincoln Minster 1090–1642." Typescript, n.d.

Boyd, Beverly. *Chaucer and the Liturgy.* Philadelphia: Dorrence, 1967.

Boyle, Leonard E. "The *Oculus Sacerdotis* and Some Other Works of William of Pagula." *Transactions of the Royal Historical Society*, 5th ser., 5 (1955): 81–104.

Brown, Carleton. "The Prioress's Tale." In *Sources and Analogues of Chaucer's "Canterbury Tales,"* ed. W. F. Bryan and Germaine Dempster. Chicago: University of Chicago Press, 1941. 447–85.

———. "The Prologue of Chaucer's 'Lif of Seint Ceceile,'" *Modern Philology* 9 (1911): 1–16.

———. *A Study of the Miracle of Our Lady Told by Chaucer's Prioress.* Publications of the Chaucer Society, ser. 2, no. 45. London: Kegan Paul, 1910.

Brundage, James A. *Medieval Canon Law.* London and New York: Longman, 1995.

Burgess, Clive. "'For the Increase of Divine Service': Chantries in the Parish in Late Medieval Bristol." *Journal of Ecclesiastical History* 36 (1985): 46–65.

———. "Strategies for Eternity: Perpetual Chantry Foundation in Late Medieval Bristol." In *Religious Belief and Ecclesiastical Careers in Late Medieval England: Proceedings of the Conference Held at Strawberry Hill, Easter, 1989,* ed. Christopher Harper-Bill. Woodbridge, Suffolk: Boydell, 1991. 1–32.

Butler, Judith. *Excitable Speech: A Politics of the Performative.* London: Routledge, 1997.

Byrne, Brian. *The Foundation of Literacy: The Child's Acquisition of the Alphabetic Principle*. East Sussex: Psychology Press, 1998.

Catto, Jeremy. "Religious Change Under Henry V." In *Henry V: The Practice of Kingship*, ed. G. L. Harriss. Oxford: Oxford University Press, 1985. 97–116.

Certeau, Michel de. *The Writing of History*. Trans. Tom Conley. New York: Columbia University Press, 1988.

Clanchy, M. T. *From Memory to Written Record: England, 1066–1307*. 2nd ed. Oxford: Blackwell, 1993.

———. "Learning to Read and the Role of Mothers." In *Studies in the History of Reading*, ed. Greg Brooks and A. K. Pugh. [Reading]: University of Reading, 1984. 33–39.

Clopper, Lawrence M. "*Mankind* and Its Audience." *Comparative Drama* 8 (1975): 347–55.

———. "Need Men and Women Labor? Langland's Wanderer and the Labor Ordinances." In *Chaucer's England: Literature in Historical Context*, ed. Barbara Hanawalt. Minneapolis: University of Minnesota Press, 1992. 110–29.

Cobban, Alan B. *The King's Hall Within the University of Cambridge in the Later Middle Ages*. Cambridge: Cambridge University Press, 1969.

Collette, Carolyn P. "Sense and Sensibility in the 'Prioress's Tale.'" *Chaucer Review* 15 (1981): 138–50.

Cook, G. H. *Mediaeval Chantries and Chantry Chapels*. London: Phoenix, 1947.

Cooper, Helen. *Oxford Guides to Chaucer: The Canterbury Tales*. Oxford: Oxford University Press, 1989.

Copeland, Rita. *Pedagogy, Intellectuals, and Dissent in the Later Middle Ages: Lollardy and Ideas of Learning*. Cambridge: Cambridge University Press, 2001.

———. *Rhetoric, Hermeneutics, and Translation in the Middle Ages: Academic Traditions and Vernacular Texts*. Cambridge: Cambridge University Press, 1991.

Courtenay, William J. *Schools and Scholars in Fourteenth-Century England*. Princeton, N.J.: Princeton University Press, 1987.

Crosby, Brian. *Durham Cathedral Choristers and Their Masters*. Durham: Dean and Chapter of Durham, 1980.

Culler, Jonathan. *The Pursuit of Signs: Semiotics, Literature, Deconstruction*. Ithaca, N.Y.: Cornell University Press, 1981.

Derrida, Jacques. *Dissemination*. Trans. Barbara Johnson. Chicago: University of Chicago Press, 1981.

———. *Of Grammatology*. Trans. Gayatri Chakravorty Spivak. Baltimore and London: Johns Hopkins University Press, 1976.

Despres, Denise L. "Cultic Anti-Judaism and Chaucer's Litel Clergeon." *Modern Philology* 91 (1994): 413–27.

Dobson, Barrie. "Citizens and Chantries in Late Medieval York." In *Church and City, 1000–1500: Essays in Honour of Christopher Brooke*, ed. David Abulafia, Michael Franklin, and Miri Rubin. Cambridge: Cambridge University Press, 1992. 311–32.

Doyle, A. I. "A Survey of the Origins and Circulation of Theological Writings in English in the 14th, 15th, and Early 16th Centuries with Special

Consideration of the Part of the Clergy therein." 2 vols. Ph.D. diss., Downing College, Cambridge, 1953.

Duffy, Eamon. *The Stripping of the Altars: Traditional Religion in England, 1400–1580*. 2nd ed. New Haven, Conn.: Yale University Press, 2005.

Dyer, Christopher. "Work Ethics in the Fourteenth Century." In *The Problem of Labour in Fourteenth-Century England*, ed. James Bothwell, P. J. P. Goldberg, and W. M. Ormrod. York: York Medieval Press, 2000. 21–41.

Dyer, Joseph. "The *Schola cantorum* and Its Roman Milieu in the Early Middle Ages." In *De musica et cantu: Studien zur Geschichte der Kirchenmusik und der Oper. Helmut Hucke zum 60. Geburtstag*, ed. Peter Cahn and Ann-Katrin Heimer. Hildesheim; New York: Olms, 1993. 19–40.

Edwards, Kathleen. *English Secular Cathedrals in the Middle Ages*. 2nd ed. Manchester: Manchester University Press; New York: Barnes and Noble, 1967.

Evans, Ruth. "Historicizing Postcolonial Criticism: Cultural Difference and the Vernacular." In *The Idea of the Vernacular: An Anthology of Middle English Literary Theory, 1280–1520*, ed. Jocelyn Wogan-Browne, Nicholas Watson, Andrew Taylor, and Ruth Evans. University Park: Pennsylvania State University Press, 1999. 366–70.

Evans, Ruth, Andrew Taylor, Nicholas Watson, and Jocelyn Wogan-Browne. "Latin and Vernacular Literary Theory." In *The Idea of the Vernacular: An Anthology of Middle English Literary Theory, 1280–1520*, ed. Jocelyn Wogan-Browne, Nicholas Watson, Andrew Taylor, and Ruth Evans. University Park: Pennsylvania State University Press, 1999. 314–30.

Fassler, Margot. "The Office of the Cantor in Early Western Monastic Rules and Customaries: A Preliminary Investigation." *Early Music History* 5 (1985): 29–51.

Ferster, Judith. *Fictions of Advice: The Literature and Politics of Counsel in Late Medieval England*. Philadelphia: University of Pennsylvania Press, 1996.

———. "'Your Praise Is Performed by Men and Children': Language and Gender in the *Prioress's Prologue* and *Tale*." *Exemplaria* 2 (1990): 149–68.

Fowler, Elizabeth. *Literary Character: The Human Figure in English Writing*. Ithaca, N.Y.: Cornell University Press, 2003.

Fradenburg, Louise. "Criticism, Anti-Semitism, and the *Prioress's Tale*." *Exemplaria* 1 (1989): 69–115.

Freire, Paolo. *Pedagogy of the Oppressed*. Trans. Myra Bergman Ramos. New York: Continuum, 1993.

Gabel, Leona. *Benefit of Clergy in England in the Later Middle Ages*. Smith College Studies in History 14. 1929, Reprint, New York: Octagon, 1969.

Galloway, Andrew. *The Penn Commentary on "Piers Plowman,"* Vol. 1, *C Prologue-Passus 4; B Prologue-Passus 4; A Prologue-Passus 4*. Philadelphia: University of Pennsylvania Press, 2006.

Gambassi, Osvaldo. *"Pueri Cantores" nelle Cattedrali d'Italia Tra Medioevo e Età Moderna: Le Scuole Eugenianes: Schole de Canto Annesse alle Cappelle Musicali*. Historiae Musicae Biblioteca 80. Florence: Olschiki, 1997.

Gaylord, Alan T. "The 'Miracle' of *Sir Thopas*." *Studies in the Age of Chaucer* 6 (1984): 65–84.

Gehl, Paul F. *A Moral Art: Grammar, Society, and Culture in Trecento Florence.* Ithaca, N.Y.: Cornell University Press, 1993.

Georgianna, Linda. "Vernacular Theologies." *English Language Notes* 44 (2006): 87–94.

Gerould, G. H. "The Second Nun's Prologue and Tale." In *Sources and Analogues of Chaucer's "Canterbury Tales,"* ed. W. F. Bryan and Germaine Dempster. Chicago: University of Chicago Press, 1941. 664–84.

Ghosh, Kantik. *The Wycliffite Heresy: Authority and the Interpretation of Texts.* Cambridge: Cambridge University Press, 2002.

Giancarlo, Matthew. "*Piers Plowman*, Parliament, and the Public Voice." *Yearbook of Langland Studies* 17 (2003): 135–74.

Gillespie, Vincent. "Vernacular Books of Religion." In *Book Production and Publishing in Britain, 1375–1475*, ed. Jeremy Griffiths and Derek Pearsall. Cambridge: Cambridge University Press, 1989. 317–44.

———. "Vernacular Theology." In *Oxford Twenty-First Century Approaches to Literature: Middle English*, ed. Paul Strohm. Oxford: Oxford University Press, 2007. 401–20.

Goody, J., and I. Watt. "The Consequences of Literacy." In *Literacy in Traditional Societies*, ed. J. Goody. Cambridge: Cambridge University Press, 1968. 27–68.

Green, Richard Firth. *A Crisis of Truth: Literature and Law in Ricardian England.* Philadelphia: University of Pennsylvania Press, 1999.

———. *Poets and Princepleasers: Literature and the English Court in the Late Middle Ages.* Toronto: University of Toronto Press, 1980.

Grennen, Joseph E. "The Canon's Yeoman's Alchemical Mass." *Studies in Philology* 62 (1965): 546–60.

———. "St. Cecilia's 'Chemical Wedding': The Unity of the *Canterbury Tales*, Fragment VIII." *Journal of English and Germanic Philology* 65 (1966): 466–81.

Grundmann, A. "*Litteratus-illitteratus*: Der Wandel einer Bildungsnorm vom Altertum zum Mittelalter." *Archiv für Kulturgeschichte* 40 (1958): 1–65.

Gumperz, John J. *Discourse Strategies.* Studies in Interactional Sociolinguistics 1. Cambridge: Cambridge University Press, 1982.

Habermas, Jürgen. *The Structural Transformation of the Public Sphere: An Inquiry into a Category of Bourgeois Society.* Trans. Thomas Burger. Cambridge: MIT Press, 1991.

———. *Strukturwandel der Öffentlichkeit: Untersuchungen zu einer Kategorie der bürgerlichen Gesellschaft.* Neuwied: Luchterhand, 1962.

Halmari, Helena, and Robert Adams. "On the Grammar and Rhetoric of Language Mixing in *Piers Plowman*." *Neuphilologische Mitteilungen* 103 (2002): 33–50.

Hamel, Mary. "'And Now for Something Completely Different': The Relationship between the *Prioress's Tale* and the *Rime of Sir Thopas*." *Chaucer Review* 14 (1980): 251–59.

Hanna, Ralph, III. *London Literature, 1300–1380.* Cambridge: Cambridge University Press, 2005.

————. *Pursuing History: Middle English Manuscripts and Their Texts.* Stanford, Calif.: Stanford University Press, 1996.

Harrison, Frank Ll. *Music in Medieval Britain.* 2nd ed. London: Routledge, 1968.

Harrison, Frederick. *Life in a Medieval College: The Story of the Vicars-Choral of York Minster.* London: Murray, 1952.

Hawkins, Sherman. "Chaucer's Prioress and the Sacrifice of Praise." *Journal of English and Germanic Philology* 63 (1964): 599–624.

Holsinger, Bruce. "Liturgy." In *Twenty-First Century Approaches to Literature: Middle English*, ed. Paul Strohm. Oxford: Oxford University Press, 2007. 295–314.

————. *Music, Body, and Desire in Medieval Culture: Hildegard of Bingen to Chaucer.* Stanford, Calif.: Stanford University Press, 2001.

Hudson, Anne. "A Lollard Mass." In *Lollards and Their Books.* London: Hambledon, 1985. 111–23.

Hughes, Andrew. "Charlemagne's Chant or The Great Vocal Shift." *Speculum* 77 (2002): 1069–1106.

————. *Medieval Manuscripts for Mass and Office: A Guide to Their Organization and Terminology.* Toronto: University of Toronto Press, 1982.

Irvine, Martin. *The Making of Textual Culture: 'Grammatica' and Literary Theory, 350–1100.* Cambridge: Cambridge University Press, 1994.

————. "Medieval Grammatical Theory and Chaucer's *House of Fame*." *Speculum* 60 (1985): 850–76.

Jaeger, C. Stephen. *The Envy of Angels: Cathedral Schools and Social Ideas in Medieval Europe, 950–1200.* Philadelphia: University of Pennsylvania Press, 1993.

Jennings, Margaret, C.S.J. "Tutiuillus: The Literary Career of the Recording Demon." *Studies in Philology Texts and Studies* 74, no. 5 (1977).

Johnson, Barbara. *A World of Difference.* Baltimore: Johns Hopkins University Press, 1987.

Jonsson, Ritva, and Leo Treitler. "Medieval Music and Language: A Reconsideration of the Relationship." *Studies in the History of Music* 1 (1983): 1–23.

Joseph, Gerhard. "Chaucer's Coinage: Foreign Exchange and the Puns of the *Shipman's Tale*." *Chaucer Review* 17 (1983): 341–47.

Jungmann, Joseph A. *The Mass of the Roman Rite: Its Origins and Development.* 2 vols. Trans. Francis A. Brunner. 1951, Reprint Westminster, Md.: Christian Classics, 1992.

Justice, Steven. *Writing and Rebellion: England in 1381.* Berkeley: University of California Press, 1994.

Kaeuper, Richard. "Two Early Lists of Literates." *English Historical Review* 99 (1984): 363–69.

Kerby-Fulton, Kathryn. *Books Under Suspicion: Censorship and Tolerance of Revelatory Writing in Late Medieval England.* Notre Dame, Ind.: University of Notre Dame Press, 2006.

————. *Reformist Apocalypticism and "Piers Plowman."* Cambridge: Cambridge University Press, 1990.

Kerby-Fulton, Kathryn, and Steven Justice. "Scribe D and the Marketing of Ricardian Literature." In *The Medieval Professional Reader at Work: Evidence from Manuscripts of Chaucer, Langland, Kempe, and Gower*, ed. Kathryn Kerby-Fulton and Maidie Hilmo. Victoria, B.C.: English Literary Studies, University of Victoria, 2001. 217–37.

Kimmelman, Burt. *The Poetics of Authorship in the Later Middle Ages: The Emergence of the Modern Literary Persona*. New York: Lang, 1996.

Kintzinger, Martin. "*Varietas puerorum*: Unterricht und Gesang in Stifts- und Stadtschulen des späten Mittelalters." In *Schule und Schüler im Mittelalter: Beiträge zur europäischen Bildungsgeschichte des 9. bis 15. Jahrhunderts*, ed. Martin Kintzinger, Sönke Lorenz, and Michael Walter. Cologne: Böhlau, 1996. 299–326.

Kipling, Gordon. *Enter the King: Theatre, Liturgy, and Ritual in the Medieval Civic Triumph*. Oxford: Clarendon, 1998.

Kirby, T. F. *Annals of Winchester College from Its Foundation in the Year 1382 to the Present Time*. London, 1892.

Knowles, David, and R. Neville Hadcock. *Medieval Religious Houses*. New York: St. Martin's, 1971.

Kolve, V. A. "Chaucer's Second Nun's Tale and the Iconography of Saint Cecilia." In *New Perspectives on Chaucer Criticism*, ed. D. M. Rose. Norman, Okla.: Pilgrim, 1981. 137–76.

Kuczynski, Michael P. *Prophetic Song: The Psalms as Moral Discourse in Late Medieval England*. Philadelphia: University of Pennsylvania Press, 1995.

Lampert, Lisa. *Gender and Jewish Difference from Paul to Shakespeare*. Philadelphia: University of Pennsylvania Press, 2004.

Lancashire, Anne. *London Civic Theatre: City Drama and Pageantry from Roman Times to 1558*. Cambridge: Cambridge University Press, 2002.

Lawson, John and Harold Silver. *A Social History of Education in England*. London: Methuen, 1973.

Lawton, David. *Chaucer's Narrators*. Woodbridge, Suffolk: Brewer, 1985.

———. "Dullness and the Fifteenth Century." *English Literary History* 54 (1987): 761–99.

———. "Skelton's Use of *Persona*." *Essays in Criticism* 30 (1980): 9–28.

———. "The Subject of *Piers Plowman*." *Yearbook of Langland Studies* 1 (1987): 1–30.

Leach, A. F. *History of Warwick School*. London, 1906.

———. *History of Winchester College*. New York, 1899.

———. *The Schools of Medieval England*. 1915, Reprint, New York and London: Barnes and Noble and Methuen, 1969.

———. "St. Paul's School Before Colet." *Archaeologia* 62, pt. 1 (1910): 191–238.

Leclercq, Jean. *The Love of Learning and the Desire for God: A Study of Monastic Culture*. 3rd ed. Trans. Catharine Misrahi. New York: Fordham, 1982.

Leicester, H. Marshall, Jr. *The Disenchanted Self: Representing the Subject in the "Canterbury Tales."* Berkeley: University of California Press, 1990.

Lentes, Thomas. "Counting Piety in the Late Middle Ages." In *Ordering Society: Perspectives on Intellectual and Practical Modes of Shaping Social Relations*, ed. Bernhard Jussen. Philadelphia: University of Pennsylvania Press, 2001. 55–91.

Lerer, Seth. "'Now Holde Youre Mouth': The Romance of Orality in the *Thopas-Melibee* Section of the *Canterbury Tales*." In *Oral Poetics in Middle English Poetry*, ed. Mark C. Amodio and Sarah Gray Miller. New York: Garland, 1994. 181–205.

Longsworth, Robert M. "Privileged Knowledge: St. Cecilia and the Alchemist in the *Canterbury Tales*." *Chaucer Review* 27 (1992): 87–96.

Lord, Alfred Bates. *The Singer of Tales*. Ed. Stephen Mitchell and Gregory Nagy. 2nd ed. Cambridge, Mass.: Harvard University Press, 2000.

Machan, Tim William. "Language Contact in *Piers Plowman*." *Speculum* 69 (1994): 359–98.

Madeleva, Sister M. *A Lost Language and Other Essays on Chaucer*. New York: Sheed, 1951.

Maltman, Sister Nicholas, O.P. "The Divine Granary, or the End of the Prioress's 'Greyn.'" *Chaucer Review* 17 (1976): 163–70.

Manly, John Matthews, and Edith Rickert. *The Text of the "Canterbury Tales."* 8 vols. Chicago: University of Chicago Press, 1940.

McGinn, Bernard. *The Flowering of Mysticism: Men and Women in the New Mysticism, 1200–1350*. New York: Crossroads, 1998.

———. "Introduction: Meister Eckhart and the Beguines in the Context of Vernacular Theology." In *Meister Eckhart and the Beguine Mystics: Hadewijch of Brabant, Mechthild of Magdeburg, and Marguerite de Porete*, ed. Bernard McGinn. New York: Continuum, 1994. 1–14.

McHardy, A. K. "Careers and Disappointments in the Late-Medieval Church: Some English Evidence." In *The Ministry: Clerical and Lay*, ed. W. J. Shields and Diana Wood. Oxford: Blackwell, 1989. 111–30.

———. "Ecclesiastics and Economics: Poor Priests, Prosperous Laymen, and Proud Prelates in the Reign of Richard II." In *The Church and Wealth*, ed. W. J. Shields and Diana Wood. Oxford: Blackwell, 1987. 129–37.

McKinnon, James. "*Gregorius presul composuit hunc libellum musicae artis*." In *The Liturgy of the Medieval Church*, ed. Thomas J. Heffernan and E. Ann Matter. Kalamazoo, Mich.: Medieval Institute, 2001. 673–94.

Mehl, Dieter. "Die lateinischen Zitate in *Piers Plowman*: Intertextualität und Traditionalität." In *Traditionswandel und Traditionsverhalten*, ed. Walter Haug and Burghart Wachinger. Tübingen: Niemeyer, 1991. 46–60.

Mellinkoff, Ruth. *The Horned Moses in Medieval Art and Thought*. California Studies in the History of Art 14. Berkeley: University of California Press, 1970.

Middleton, Anne. "Acts of Vagrancy: The C Version 'Autobiography' (C 5.1–108) and the Statute of 1388." In *Written Work: Langland, Labor, Authorship*, ed. Steven Justice and Kathryn Kerby-Fulton. Philadelphia: University of Pennsylvania Press, 1997. 208–317.

———. "The Idea of Public Poetry in the Reign of Richard II." *Speculum* 53 (1978): 94–114.

———. "Narration and the Invention of Experience: Episodic Form in *Piers Plowman*." In *The Wisdom of Poetry: Essays in Honor of Morton W. Bloomfield*, ed. Larry D. Benson and Siegrfried Wenzel. Kalamazoo, Mich.: Medieval Institute, 1982. 92–122.

———. "William Langland's 'Kynde Name': Authorial Signature and Social Identity in Late Fourteenth-Century England." In *Literary Practice and Social Change in Britain, 1380–1530*, ed. Lee Patterson. Berkeley: University of California Press, 1990. 15–82.

Minnis, Alastair. *Medieval Theory of Authorship: Scholastic Literary Attitudes in the Later Middle Ages*. 2nd ed. Philadelphia: University of Pennsylvania Press, 1988.

Moran Cruz, Jo Ann H. *The Growth of English Schooling, 1340–1548: Learning, Literacy, and Laicization in Pre-Reformation York Diocese*. Princeton: Princeton University Press, 1985.

Nicholson, J., and R. Burn. *History and Antiquities of Westmorland and Cumberland*. 2 vols. London, 1777.

Nissé, Ruth. *Defining Acts: Drama and the Politics of Interpretation in Late Medieval England*. Notre Dame, Ind.: University of Notre Dame Press, 2005.

Nolan, Edward Peter. *Now Through a Glass Darkly: Specular Images of Being and Knowing from Virgil to Chaucer*. Ann Arbor: University of Michigan Press, 1990.

Nolan, Maura. *John Lydgate and the Making of Public Culture*. Cambridge: Cambridge University Press, 2005.

Olson, Glending. "Making and Poetry in the Age of Chaucer." *Comparative Literature* 31 (1979): 272–90.

Ong, Walter J. *Orality and Literacy: The Technologizing of the Word*. London and New York: Routledge, 1982.

———. "Orality, Literacy, and Medieval Textualization." *New Literary History* 16 (1984): 1–12.

———. *The Presence of the Word: Some Prolegomena for Cultural and Religious History*. New Haven, Conn.: Yale University Press, 1967.

Orme, Nicholas. *Education and Society in Medieval and Renaissance England*. London: Hambledon, 1989.

———. *Education in the West of England, 1066–1548: Cornwall, Devon, Dorset, Gloucestershire, Somerset, Wiltshire*. Exeter, University of Exeter Press, 1976.

———. *English Schools in the Middle Ages*. London: Methuen, 1973.

———. *From Childhood to Chivalry: The Education of the English Kings and Aristocracy, 1066–1530*. London: Methuen, 1984.

———. *Medieval Children*. New Haven, Conn.: Yale University Press, 2001.

———. *Medieval Schools*. New Haven, Conn.: Yale University Press, 2006.

Orme, Nicholas and Margot Webster. *The English Hospital: 1070–1570*. New Haven, Conn.: Yale University Press, 1995.

Ormrod, W. M. *The Reign of Edward III: Crown & Political Society in England, 1327–1377*. New Haven, Conn.: Yale University Press, 1990.

Osberg, Richard H. "A Voice for the Prioress: The Context of English Devotional Prose." *Studies in the Age of Chaucer* 18 (1996): 25–54.

Parkes, Malcolm B. "The Literacy of the Laity." In *Literature and Western Civilization*, Vol. 2, *The Medieval World*, ed. David Daiches and Anthony Thorlby. London: Aldus, 1973. 555–78.

Patterson, Lee. *Chaucer and the Subject of History.* Madison: University of Wisconsin Press, 1991.

———. "'The Living Witnesses of Our Redemption': Martyrdom and Imitation in Chaucer's *Prioress's Tale.*" *Journal of Medieval and Early Modern Studies* 31 (2001): 507–60.

———. "Perpetual Motion: Alchemy and the Technology of the Self." *Studies in the Age of Chaucer* 15 (1993): 25–57.

———. "'What Man Artow?': Authorial Self-Definition in *The Tale of Sir Thopas* and *The Tale of Melibee.*" *Studies in the Age of Chaucer* 11 (1989): 117–76.

Pearsall, Derek. *The Canterbury Tales.* London: Routledge, 1985.

———. *The Life of Geoffrey Chaucer: A Critical Biography.* Oxford: Blackwell, 1992.

———. "The *Troilus* Frontispiece and Chaucer's Audience." *Year in English Studies* 7 (1977): 68–84.

Peck, Russell A. "The Ideas of 'Entente' and Translation in Chaucer's *Second Nun's Tale.*" *Annuale Mediaevale* 8 (1967): 17–37.

Peter, T. C. *History of Glasney Collegiate Church, Cornwall.* Camborne, Cornwall: Camborne Printing, 1903.

Pfändtner, Karl-Georg. *Die Psalterillustration des 13. und beginnenden 14. Jahrhunderts in Bologna.* Neuried: Ars Una, 1996.

Pollock, Frederick, and Frederic William Maitland. *The History of English Law Before the Time of Edward I.* 2nd ed. Rev. S. F. C. Milsom. 2 vols. Cambridge: Cambridge University Press, 1968.

Purcell-Gates, Victoria. *Other People's Words: The Cycle of Low Literacy.* Cambridge, Mass.: Harvard University Press, 1997.

Putnam, Bertha Haven. *The Enforcement of the Statute of Labourers During the First Decade After the Black Death, 1349–1359.* Studies in History, Economics and Public Law 32. 1908, Reprint, New York: AMS, 1970.

———. "Maximum Wage-Laws for Priests After the Black Death, 1348–1381." *American Historical Review* 21 (1915): 12–32.

Raine, Angelo. *History of St. Peter's School, York, A.D. 627 to the Present Day.* London: Bell, 1926.

Rankin, Susan. "Carolingian Music." In *Carolingian Culture: Emulation and Innovation*, ed. Rosamund McKitterick. Cambridge: Cambridge University Press, 1994. 275–79.

Raymo, R. "Works of Religious and Philosophical Instruction." In *Manual of Writings in Middle English, 1050–1400*, ed. J. Burke Severs and Albert E. Hartung. 11 vols. New Haven: Connecticut Academy of Arts and Science, 1967–93. Vol. 7: 2255–378, 2467–582.

Reames, Sherry L. "A Recent Discovery Concerning the Sources of Chaucer's 'Second Nun's Tale.'" *Modern Philology* 87 (1990): 337–61.

———. "The Sources of the 'Second Nun's Tale.'" *Modern Philology* 76 (1978): 111–35.

Reynold, Roger E. "Divine Office." In *The Dictionary of the Middle Ages*, ed. Joseph R. Strayer. 13 vols. New York: Scribner, 1982–89.

Reynolds, Suzanne. *Medieval Reading: Grammar, Rhetoric, and the Classical Text.* Cambridge: Cambridge University Press, 1996.

Riché, Pierre. *Écoles et enseignement dans le Haut Moyen Age: Fin du Ve siècle–milieu du XIe siècle.* 2nd ed. Paris: Picard, 1989.

Ricoeur, Paul. "The Summoned Subject in the School of the Narratives of the Prophetic Vocation." In *Figuring the Sacred: Religion, Narrative, and Imagination*, trans. David Pellauer, ed. Mark I. Wallace. Minneapolis: Fortress Press, 1995. 262–75.

Robbins, Rossell Hope. "Levation Prayers in Middle English Verse." *Modern Philology* 40 (1942): 131–46.

Rubin, Miri. *Corpus Christi: The Eucharist in Late Medieval Culture.* Cambridge: Cambridge University Press, 1991.

Saenger, Paul. "Books of Hours and the Reading Habits of the Later Middle Ages." In *The Culture of Print: Power and the Uses of Print in Early Modern Europe*, ed. R. Chartier. Cambridge: Polity, 1989. 141–73.

St.-Jacques, Raymond. "Conscience's Final Pilgrimage in *Piers Plowman* and the Cyclical Structure of the Liturgy." *Revue de l'Université d'Ottawa* 40 (1970): 210–23.

———. "Langland's Christ-Knight and the Liturgy." *Revue de l'Université d'Ottawa* 37 (1967): 146–58.

———. "Langland's *Christus Medicus* Image and the Structure of *Piers Plowman.*" *Yearbook of Langland Studies* 5 (1991): 111–27.

———. "Langland's Easter Bells of the Resurrection and the Easter Liturgy." *English Studies in Canada* 3 (1977): 129–35.

———. "The Liturgical Associations of Langland's Samaritan." *Traditio* 25 (1969): 217–30.

Sandler, Lucy Freeman. *The Peterborough Psalter in Brussels & Other Fenland Manuscripts.* London: Miller, 1974.

Scase, Wendy. *"Piers Plowman" and the New Anticlericalism.* Cambridge: Cambridge University Press, 1989.

———. "St. Anne and the Education of the Virgin: Literary and Artistic Traditions and Their Implications." In *England in the Fourteenth Century: Proceedings of the 1991 Harlaxton Symposium*, ed. N. Rogers. Stamford: Watkins, 1993. 81–96.

Schirmer, Elizabeth. "Reading Lessons at Syon Abbey: The *Myroure of Oure Ladye* and the Mandates of Vernacular Theology." In *Voices in Dialogue: New Problems in Reading Women's Cultural History*, ed. Kathryn Kerby-Fulton and Linda Olson. Notre Dame, Ind.: Notre Dame University Press, 2005. 345–76.

Schmidt, A. V. C. *The Clerkly Maker: Langland's Poetic Art.* Cambridge: Brewer, 1987.

Scholz, Manfred Günter. "On Presentation and Reception Guidelines in the German Strophic Epic of the Late Middle Ages." Trans. Rebecca Williams Duplantier and Crozet Duplantier, Jr. *New Literary History* 16 (1984): 137–51.

Scott, Kathleen L. *Later Gothic Manuscripts, 1390–1490.* 2 vols. London: Miller, 1996.

Sheingorn, Pamela. "'The Wise Mother': The Image of St. Anne Teaching the Virgin Mary." *Gesta* 32 (1993): 69–80.

Sherman, Gail Berkeley. "Saints, Nuns, and Speech in the *Canterbury Tales.*" In *Images of Sainthood in Medieval Europe,* ed. Renate Blumenfeld-Kosinki and Timea Szell. Ithaca, N.Y.: Cornell University Press, 1991. 136–60.

Siepmann, Dirk. "Collocation, Colligation and Encoding Dictionaries, Part I: Lexical Aspects." *International Journal of Lexicology* 18 (2005): 409–43.

Simon, Joan. *The Social Origins of English Education.* London: Routledge, 1970.

Simpson, James. "From Reason to Affective Knowledge: Modes of Thought and Poetic Form in *Piers Plowman.*" *Medium Ævum* 55 (1986): 1–23.

———. *The Oxford English Literary History.* Vol. 2, *1350–1547: Reform and Cultural Revolution.* Oxford: Oxford University Press, 2002.

———. *"Piers Plowman": An Introduction to the B-Text.* London: Longman, 1990.

———. "The Power of Impropriety: Authorial Naming in *Piers Plowman.*" In *William Langland's "Piers Plowman": A Book of Essays,* ed. Kathleen M. Hewett-Smith. London: Routledge, 2001. 145–65.

———. "The Role of *Scientia* in *Piers Plowman.*" In *Medieval English Religious and Ethical Literature: Essays in Honour of G. H. Russell,* ed. Gregory Kratzmann and James Simpson. Woodbridge: Brewer, 1986. 49–65.

Smits van Waesberghe, Joseph. *Musikerziehung: Lehre und Theorie der Musik im Mittelalter.* Musikgeschichte im Bildern, vol. 3. Ed. Heinrich Besseler and Werner Bachmann. Leipzig: Deutscher Verlag für Musik, 1969.

Somerset, Fiona. *Clerical Discourse and Lay Audience in Late Medieval England.* Cambridge: Cambridge University Press, 1998.

———. "Expanding the Langlandian Canon: Radical Latin and the Stylistics of Reform." *Yearbook of Langland Studies* 17 (2003): 73–92.

Spiegel, Gabrielle M. "Memory and History: Liturgical Time and Historical Time." *History and Theory* 41 (2002): 149–62.

Spivak, Gayatri Chakravorty. "Can the Subaltern Speak?" In *Marxism and the Interpretation of Culture,* ed. Cary Nelson and Larry Grossberg. Urbana: University of Illinois Press, 1988. 271–313.

Staley, Lynn. "Chaucer and the Postures of Sanctity." In *Powers of the Holy: Religion, Politics, and Gender in Late Medieval English Culture,* by David Aers and Lynn Staley. University Park: Pennsylvania State University Press, 1996. 179–259.

———. *Languages of Power in the Age of Richard II.* University Park: Pennsylvania State University Press, 2005.

Stanbury, Sarah. "Vernacular Nostalgia and *The Cambridge History of Medieval Literature.*" *Texas Studies in Literature and Language* 44 (2002): 92–107.

Steiner, Emily. *Documentary Culture and the Making of Medieval English Literature*. Cambridge: Cambridge University Press, 2003.

Stock, Brian. *The Implications of Literacy: Written Language and Models of Interpretation in the Eleventh and Twelfth Centuries*. Princeton, N.J.: Princeton University Press, 1983.

———. *Listening for the Text: On the Uses of the Past*. Baltimore and London: Johns Hopkins University Press, 1990.

Strohm, Paul. *Social Chaucer*. Cambridge, Mass.: Harvard University Press, 1989.

Swanson, R. N. *Religion and Devotion in Europe, c. 1215–c. 1515*. Cambridge: Cambridge University Press, 1995.

Symes, Carol. "The Appearance of Early Vernacular Plays: Forms, Functions, and the Future of Medieval Theater." *Speculum* 77 (2002): 778–831.

Thompson, A. H. *The English Clergy and Their Organization in the Later Middle Ages*. Oxford: Clarendon, 1947.

———. *The History of the Hospital and the New College of the Annunciation of St. Mary in the Newarke, Leicester*. Leicester: Leicester Archeology Society/ Backus, 1937.

———. "Notes on Colleges of Secular Canons in England (Appendix: The Statutes of the New Collegiate Church of St. Mary, Leicester, 1355–6 and 1490–1)." *Archaeological Journal* 74 (1917): 200–240.

———. *Song-Schools in the Middle Ages*. Church-Music Society Occasional Papers 14. London: Society for Promoting Christian Knowledge and Humphrey Milford, 1942.

Tikkannen, J. J. *Psalterillustration im Mittelalter*. Helsingfors, 1895–1900, Reprint, Soest: Davaco, 1975.

Treitler, Leo. "Homer and Gregory: The Transmission of Epic Poetry and Plainchant." *Musical Quarterly* 60 (1974): 333–72.

———. "Reading and Singing: On the Genesis of Occidental Music-Writing." *Early Music History* 4 (1984): 135–208.

Trowell, Brian. "Music Under the Late Plantagenets." Ph.D. diss., Cambridge University, 1960.

Turner, Denys. "The Darkness of God and the Light of Christ: Negative Theology and Eucharistic Presence." In *Catholicism and Catholicity: Eucharistic Communities in Historical and Contemporary Perspectives*, ed. Sarah Beckwith. Oxford: Blackwell, 1999. 31–46.

Turner, Victor. *The Ritual Process: Structure and Anti-Structure*. Ithaca, N.Y.: Cornell University Press, 1969.

Tyler, Elizabeth M. *Old English Poetics: The Aesthetics of the Familiar in Anglo-Saxon England*. York: York Medieval Press, 2006.

The Victoria History of the Counties of England: Berkshire. Ed. P. H. Ditchfield and William Page. 5 vols. London: Constable, 1906–27.

The Victoria History of the Counties of England: Durham. Ed. William Page. 3 vols. London: Constable, 1905–28.

The Victoria History of the Counties of England: Hampshire. Ed. H. A. Doubleday and William Page. 6 vols. Westminster: Constable, 1900–1914.

The Victoria History of the Counties of England: Lincolnshire. Vol. 2. Ed. William Page. London: Constable, 1906.

The Victoria History of the Counties of England: Northamptonshire. Ed. W. Ryland D. Adkins and R. M. Serjeantson. 4 vols. Westminster: Constable, 1902–37.

The Victoria History of the Counties of England: Suffolk. Ed. William Page. 2 vols. London: Constable, 1907–11.

The Victoria History of the Counties of England: Yorkshire. Ed. William Page. 3 vols. London: Constable, 1907–13.

Underwood, Geoffrey, and Vivienne Batt. *Reading and Understanding: An Introduction to the Psychology of Reading*. Oxford: Blackwell, 1996.

Van Dyke, Carolynn. *Chaucer's Agents: Cause and Representation in Chaucerian Narrative*. Madison, N.J.: Fairleigh Dickinson University Press, 2005.

Voaden, Rosalynn. *God's Words, Women's Voices: The Discernment of Spirits in the Writing of Late-Medieval Women Visionaries*. Woodbridge, Suffolk: York Medieval Press, 1999.

Wallace, David. *Chaucerian Polity: Absolutist Lineages and Associational Forms in England and Italy*. Stanford, Calif.: Stanford University Press, 1997.

Wathey, Andrew. *Music in the Royal and Noble Households in Late Medieval England: Studies of Sources and Patronage*. London and New York: Garland, 1989.

Watson, Nicholas. "Censorship and Cultural Exchange in Late-Medieval England: Vernacular Theology, the Oxford Translation Debate, and Arundel's Constitutions of 1409." *Speculum* 70 (1995): 822–64.

———. "Cultural Changes." *English Language Notes* 44 (2006): 127–36.

———. "The *Gawain*-Poet as Vernacular Theologian." In *A Companion to the Gawain-Poet*, ed. Derek Brewer and Jonathan Gibson. Woodbridge, Suffolk: Brewer, 1997. 293–313.

———. "The Middle English Mystics." In *The Cambridge History of Medieval English Literature*, ed. David Wallace. Cambridge: Cambridge University Press, 1999. 539–65.

———. "The Politics of Middle English Writing." In *The Idea of the Vernacular: An Anthology of Middle English Literary Theory, 1280–1520*. Ed. Jocelyn Wogan-Browne, Nicholas Watson, Andrew Taylor, and Ruth Evans. University Park: Pennsylvania State University Press, 1999. 331–352.

Wenk, J. C. "On the Sources of the Prioress's Tale." *Mediaeval Studies* 17 (1955): 214–19.

Westlake, H. F. *Parish Guilds of Medieval England*. London: Society for Promoting Christian Knowledge, 1918.

Wieck, Roger S. "The Book of Hours." In *The Liturgy of the Medieval Church*, ed. Thomas J. Heffernan and E. Ann Matter. Kalamazoo, Mich.: Medieval Institute, 2001. 473–513.

———. *Painted Prayers: The Book of Hours in Medieval and Renaissance Art*. New York: Braziller, 1997.

———. *Time Sanctified: The Book of Hours*. New York: Braziller, 1988.

Wilks, Michael. "Wyclif and the Great Persecution." In *Prophecy and Eschatology*, ed. Michael Wilks. Studies in Church History. Subsidia, vol. 10. Oxford: Blackwell, 1994. 39–63.

Williams, Raymond. *Marxism and Literature*. New York and Oxford: Oxford University Press, 1977.

Wittig, Joseph S. "*Piers Plowman* B, Passus IX–XII: Elements in the Design of the Inward Journey." *Traditio* 28 (1972): 211–80.

Wood-Legh, K. L. *Perpetual Chantries in Britain*. Cambridge: Cambridge University Press, 1965.

Woodruff, C. E. and H. J. Cape. *Schola Regia Cantuariensis: A History of Canterbury School*. London: Mitchell, 1908.

Zahnd, Urs Martin. "Chordienst und Schule in eidgenössischen Städten des Spätmittelalters: Eine Untersuchung auf Grund der Verhältnisse in Bern, Freiburg, Luzern, und Solothurn." In *Schule und Schüler im Mittelalter: Beiträge zur europäischen Bildungsgeschichte des 9. bis 15. Jahrhunderts*, ed. Martin Kintzinger, Sönke Lorenz, and Michael Walter. Cologne: Böhlau, 1996. 259–98.

Zieman, Katherine. "Chaucer's *Voys*." *Representations* 60 (1997): 70–91.

———. "Playing *Doctor*: St. Birgitta, Ritual Reading, and Ecclesiastical Authority." In *Voices in Dialogue: New Problems in Reading Women's Cultural History*, ed. Kathryn Kerby-Fulton and Linda Olson. Notre Dame, Ind.: University of Notre Dame Press, 2005. 307–34.

———. "Reading, Singing, and Understanding: Constructions of the Literacy of Women Religious in Late Medieval England." In *Learning and Literacy in Medieval England and Abroad*, ed. Sarah Rees-Jones. Turnhout: Brepols, 2003. 97–120.

Zumthor, Paul. "The Vocalization of the Text: The Medieval 'Poetic Effect.'" Trans. Nancy Rose and Peter Haidu. *Viator* 19 (1988): 273–82.

Index